For Hani and Euis

In memory of Sam Wright who loved words

Contents

Acknowledgements   xi
About the Author   xiii
Glossary/Abbreviations   xv
Age Bandings   xviii

Introduction   1

1   'Pen-to-Paper' Stories   **29**
       Idea 1.1 Shaped Stories   36
       Idea 1.2 Sized Stories   37
       Idea 1.3 Colour Stories   38
       Idea 1.4 Tactile Stories   39
       Idea 1.5 Body Stories   40
       Idea 1.6 Bedroom Stories   41
       Idea 1.7 Bathroom Stories   42
       Idea 1.8 Kitchen Stories   43
       Idea 1.9 Living Room Stories   44
       Idea 1.10 Garden Stories   45

2   'Design and Make' Stories   **46**
       Idea 2.1 Design Stories   54
       Idea 2.2 Booked Stories   55
       Idea 2.3 Box Stories   56

Idea 2.4 Story Books   57
Idea 2.5 Gamed Stories   58
Idea 2.6 Un-Folded Stories   59
Idea 2.7 Twist Stories   60
Idea 2.8 Moving Stories   61
Idea 2.9 Construction Stories   62
Idea 2.10 Recycled Stories   63

3   **'Being' Stories**   **64**
Idea 3.1 Baby Stories   72
Idea 3.2 Sibling Stories   73
Idea 3.3 Mum Stories   74
Idea 3.4 Dad Stories   75
Idea 3.5 Pet Stories   76
Idea 3.6 Friend Stories   77
Idea 3.7 Teacher Stories   78
Idea 3.8 Neighbour Stories   79
Idea 3.9 Character Stories   80
Idea 3.10 Celebrity Stories   81

4   **'Craft' Stories**   **82**
Idea 4.1 Crafty Stories   89
Idea 4.2 Water Stories   90
Idea 4.3 Paint Stories   91
Idea 4.4 Penned Stories   92
Idea 4.5 Papered Stories   93
Idea 4.6 Tall Stories   94
Idea 4.7 Decorated Stories   95
Idea 4.8 TV Stories   96
Idea 4.9 Sweet Stories   97
Idea 4.10 Fabric Stories   98

5   **'Engaging' Stories**   **99**
Idea 5.1 Party Stories   106
Idea 5.2 Parcel Stories   107
Idea 5.3 Competition Stories   108
Idea 5.4 Toy Stories   109
Idea 5.5 Clothing Stories   110

Idea 5.6 Crazy Stories 111
Idea 5.7 Soft Stories 112
Idea 5.8 Scroll Stories 113
Idea 5.9 DIY Stories 114
Idea 5.10 Either–Or Stories 115

6   'Technology' Stories   **116**

Idea 6.1 Technological Stories 124
Idea 6.2 ICT Stories 125
Idea 6.3 CD/DVD Stories 126
Idea 6.4 Internet Stories 127
Idea 6.5 Networking Stories 128
Idea 6.6 Track Stories 129
Idea 6.7 Calendar Stories 130
Idea 6.8 Extended Stories 131
Idea 6.9 Upside-down Stories 132
Idea 6.10 Slapstick Stories 133

7   'Location' Stories   **134**

Idea 7.1 Carpet Stories 142
Idea 7.2 Table-top Stories 143
Idea 7.3 Playground Stories 144
Idea 7.4 Assembly Stories 145
Idea 7.5 Lunchtime Stories 146
Idea 7.6 Library Stories 147
Idea 7.7 Toilet Stories 148
Idea 7.8 Weathered Stories 149
Idea 7.9 Environmental Stories 150
Idea 7.10 Local Area Stories 151

8   'Boys" Stories   **152**

Idea 8.1 Me Stories 160
Idea 8.2 Superhero Stories 161
Idea 8.3 Adventure Stories 162
Idea 8.4 Chase Stories 163
Idea 8.5 Sports Stories 164
Idea 8.6 Funny Stories 165
Idea 8.7 Frightful Stories 166

Idea 8.8 Fairy Stories   167
Idea 8.9 Free Stories   168
Idea 8.10 Futures Stories   169

9   'Creative' Stories   170
Idea 9.1 Flip-flap Stories   177
Idea 9.2 Flash Stories   178
Idea 9.3 Patchwork Stories   179
Idea 9.4 Jigsaw Stories   180
Idea 9.5 Window Stories   181
Idea 9.6 Junk Stories   182
Idea 9.7 Stationery Stories   183
Idea 9.8 Hat Stories   184
Idea 9.9 Framed Stories   185
Idea 9.10 Chain Stories   186

10 'Random' Stories   187
Idea 10.1 Slice of Life Stories   195
Idea 10.2 Punctuation Stories   196
Idea 10.3 Silly Stories   197
Idea 10.4 Collaborative Stories   198
Idea 10.5 Bedtime Stories   199
Idea 10.6 Border Stories   200
Idea 10.7 Picture Prompt Stories   201
Idea 10.8 Speech Stories   202
Idea 10.9 Squigglehop Stories   203
Idea 10.10 Threaded Stories   204

Appendices   205

References   243
Index   282

Acknowledgements

It is with the most heartfelt thanks that the following people are recognised:

- Mark Woodfield, my best bud, for being the principal editor of this book before it went to the publishers. Thank you for the TinyURL.com suggestion and your brutal honesty! However, after long deliberation, I decided against your suggested editorial foreword on the front cover: *You should've seen it before I got it!*

- Jude Bowen and Miriam Davey at Sage Publications for their support and encouragement in the writing of this book. Thank you for putting me in print again!

- Karen Fisher for the initial proposal thought showering session and 'Smelly' (Kelly) Fisher for her critical comments and additional ideas by the poolside!

- My numerous friends who willingly took Ideas from this book and tried them out in their respective classrooms/schools – Emily Nocita, Andy Gotheridge, Curtis Jordan, Malcolm Hetherington, Vanessa Platts and Lydia Sellek.

- Dave Orwin for his useful and very speedy 'pens and paper' information.

- Stacey Woolley and Lauren Bull for their diligent 'proofing' and contributions to some of the Ideas.

- Bethany Hanson for her 'words of wisdom' about story writing at Val Rose in France.

- My Mom, Pop, Sugarfluff, Andy, Wilf, my wonderful friends, my fantastic colleagues at University of Cambridge, and the brilliant staff and students I had the great fortune to work with at the University of Derby.

Thank you all *very* much indeed.

SPB

About the Author

Dr Simon Brownhill is a Senior Teaching Associate at the University of Cambridge. He was previously a Senior Lecturer in the Faculty of Education, Health and Sciences at the University of Derby where he taught on the BA (*Hons*) Child and Youth Studies, FdA Children's and Young People's Services (*Pathway*), and MA Education programmes. He also worked on the Initial Teacher Training programmes (BEd Primary; PGCE 3–7 and 5–11) and the BA Education Studies programme. Prior to being employed in Higher Education Simon worked as a qualified class teacher, gaining experience of teaching across the full 3–11 age range in a variety of contexts. He was also an Assistant Headteacher for the Early Years (3–6) in a large, culturally diverse, inner-city primary school. His research interests include creative learning and teaching in the classroom, cultural diversity, children's physical development, supporting adult learners, and the male role model in the early years (the focus of his doctoral thesis). He has presented his research at local, national and international conferences including Limerick, Barcelona, Gothenburg, Quebec and Indonesia. His infinite fascination with children's behaviour has led him to write several single authored and co-authored books on this topic. During the writing of this book Simon has discovered that his 'writing flow' is best when he works in his new bed!

Glossary/Abbreviations

The following terms/abbreviations are used throughout this book:

ALS	Additional Literacy Support (for Years 3 and 4 – 7–9-year-olds)
APA	American Psychological Association
APP	Assessing Pupils' Progress
ASC	Australian Sports Commission
ATL	Association of Teachers and Lecturers
BA	Bachelor of Arts
BBC	British Broadcasting Corporation
BEd	Bachelor of Education – an undergraduate academic degree which qualifies the graduate as a teacher in schools
BFI	British Film Institute
CCEA	Council for the Curriculum, Examinations and Assessment
CD	Compact Disc
Chronology	The sequence in which events occur
Classroom	Any location (indoors/outdoors) where writing activity can take place
CLLD	Communication, Language and Literacy Development (DCSF, 2008b), now known as Communication and Language (C&L) – a Prime Area – and Literacy (a Specific Area) (DfE, 2012a)
CV	Curriculum Vitae

DCSF	Department for Children, Schools and Families
DfE	Department for Education
DfEE	Department for Education and Employment
DfES	Department for Education and Skills
DNA	Deoxyribonucleic acid – the hereditary material in humans and almost all other organisms
DVD	Digital Versatile Disc
EAL	English as an Additional Language
ECaT	Every Child a Talker
ECaW	Every Child a Writer
ELS	Early Literacy Support (for Years 1 and 2 – 5–7-year olds)
EYFS	Early Years Foundation Stage (for children aged 0–5+ years)
FLS	Further Literacy Support (for Years 5 and 6 – 9–11-year-olds)
GTP	Graduate Teacher Programme. Now the School Direct Training Programme (SDTP)
ICT	Information and Communication Technology
KS	Key Stage
KSUA	Knowledge, Skills, Understanding and Attitudes
LSCWC	The 'Look, Say, Cover, Write, Check' approach to spelling
Mark-making	Marks made by children aged 3–5 that have meaning
MIF	Mission Impossible Force
NACCCE	National Advisory Committee for Creative and Cultural Education
NC	National Curriculum
n.d.	No date of publication indicated
NICHD	National Institute of Child Health and Human Development
NLT	National Literacy Trust
NWP	National Writing Project (American based)
OFSTED	Office for Standards in Education – now known as The Office for Standards in Education, Children's Services and Skills
ORT	Oxford Reading Tree
OT	Occupational Therapist
PFA	Parents and Friends Association
PoS	Programme of Study

PNS	Primary National Strategy
Practitioner	Any person working or training in the early years (3–5). Other references include Key Worker; see *Teacher*
PSHE	Personal, Social and Health Education
PTA	Planning, Teaching and Assessment
QCA	Qualifications and Curriculum Authority
School	Any educational setting for children aged 3–11
SEAL	Social and Emotional Aspects of Learning
SEF	School Evaluation Form
SEND	Special Educational Needs and Disabilities
SIP	School Improvement Plan, also known as a School Development Plan (SDP)
SMART	Specific, Measurable, Achievable, Realistic, Time-related
SMT	Senior Management Team, also known as a Senior Leadership Team (SLT)
SNS	Social Networking Sites
Story	An account of imaginary or real people and events told to inform, educate and entertain; synonyms include *narrative, tale, yarn, fable, fiction*
Teach	To show or explain to someone how to do something
Teacher	Any individual who is training or is working (voluntary/ paid) with children aged 3–11 in an educational setting
VLE	Virtual Learning Environment
UK	United Kingdom
USA	United States of America
Weekend Work	Homework
Writing	The representation of language in a textual medium through the use of a set of signs or symbols that have meaning for the writer

Age bandings

The following age bandings are used in this book to indicate particular age groups of children that different Ideas are pertinent to:

3–5: The Early Years (36 months – 60 months+) – part of the *EYFS*	**7–9**: Lower Key Stage Two – Primary – '*Lower Juniors*'
5–7: Key Stage One – Primary – '*Infants*'	**9–11**: Upper Key Stage Two – Primary – '*Upper Juniors*'

Introduction

Consider this . . .

The children immediately noticed the *Mission Impossible* theme tune playing on the CD player as they came into class from morning play. Miss Henley, their class teacher, was sitting on the chair by the book area so the children quickly assembled together on the carpet in front of her. As the final exclamations of the theme tune died away there was a rapid *knock-knock-knock* on the classroom door and in walked the Head teacher, carrying a large puffy brown envelope.

'This has just arrived for your class, Miss Henley!' said the Head. 'It was sent Special Delivery! I was instructed to bring it *straight* to your classroom.'

'Oh – thank you,' said Miss Henley, puzzled, as the Head teacher turned and quickly walked out of the room. Looking up from the envelope, Miss Henley saw all of her Year 4 class (8–9-year-olds) staring at her, silent and intrigued. She slowly turned the envelope over in her hands; across the front in big letters were the words **OPEN ME**.

'Go on, Miss!' said one of the children. 'Open it!'

Miss Henley paused for a moment before tearing the top of the envelope off, tipping its contents into her lap. The children all strained to see what was inside it – out fell a silver dictaphone, a large white addressed envelope, and a note. The note read **PLAY ME**. Miss Henley did as the note instructed and pressed 'play' on the dictaphone.

'Good morning, child authors. My name is Jackson Rindley. Parkview Publishers have made contact with MIF – they *urgently* need your help. International sales of published story books for children are falling rapidly. There are just no new story ideas out there – it seems as if they have all been used up by popular children's authors. Our undercover contact, Miss Henley, claims that you are the 'authors of the future' – we need you to write some stories that are going to get parents and carers buying story books again and, more importantly, children reading them.

Your mission, should you choose to accept it, is to write an exciting story about a world where there are no stories. As always, you should actively use the writing skills you have developed in your literacy lessons to assist you. Time is rather short so you have only five working days to plan, draft and produce a final version of your story. These should be posted, in the envelope provided, to Parkview Publishers who will identify the most stimulating stories for publication in an online class anthology. This tape will self-destruct in five seconds. Good luck.'

Miss Henley quickly passed the dictaphone to her teaching assistant, who ran out of the classroom with it.

'So . . . who's up for some story writing?' Miss Henley inquired.

Thirty-two arms shot up into the air.

It may come as a bit of a disappointment to learn that the description of practice above is a work of fiction. A made-up tale. A 'little white story', if you will. Imagine, however, if it was realised practice. Children *could* experience this kind of story writing activity if those reading this book willingly embrace the different Ideas that are offered to them and creatively make them come *alive* in the classroom. Miss Henley's practice is clearly designed to *engage* her class – it 'hooks them in' by using the 'wow' factor (Beauchamp and Parkinson, 2005: 97) – and succeeds in motivating the children to *want* to put pen to paper/finger to keyboard. It is strongly believed that it is our job as teachers to put fire in the 'writing bellies' of the children that we have the good fortune of teaching. When one reflects on the 'current climate' it is apparent that teachers do not really have a choice in the matter – we have to act with a sense of urgency to positively address the numerous concerns that are associated with children's writing and English as a whole at this present time.

Considering the 'Current Climate'

Glance through any mainstream newspaper, look at any OFSTED report, or read any educational-based publication, and headlines/statements similar to those offered below are likely to be found in them:

- OFSTED: English standards in primary schools 'too low' (Paton, 2012).
- Speech problems 'hamper children's reading [and writing] ability' (Richardson, 2011).
- Since 2008, there has been no overall improvement in primary pupils' [English] learning (OFSTED, 2012b).
- Children's grasp of the 3Rs at its worst in a decade: One in five struggling to spell at age seven (Daily Mail, 2010).
- 4m [million] children in UK do not own a single book, study finds (Bloxham, 2011).
- On average, girls outperform boys in digital reading (Vayssettes, 2012).
- Boys' negative attitudes towards writing in the primary classroom (Gingell, 2011).

For further headlines, see All-Party Parliamentary Group for Education (2011: 2).

The headlines/statements above do not make pleasant reading. They reinforce McGaw's view that '[l]iteracy education is frequently discussed in the context of a crisis' (cited in Freebody, 2007: iii). Problematic issues relating to boys' adverse attitudes towards literacy based activity (writing in particular), children's poor attention spans, limited parental support in children's literacy development, and the damage seemingly being caused by the surge of children's active engagement with digital literacy (e.g. 'text-speak' appearing in children's writing) all contribute to the 'concerning' standards of literacy attainment across the early years and primary school sectors (see Hill, 2012). As a result, reading and writing are ever present as priority targets in the School Improvement Plans (SIPs) of virtually all schools in the country in an effort to meet/exceed government 'floor targets' and create a more literate generation.

This book deliberately locates itself in the heart of 'the turbulent times of literacy' by offering professional support for teachers to effectively engage children aged 3–11 in stimulating story writing activity. Its contribution is purposefully designed to maximise children's achievements in story writing and encourage them to reach their full learning potential.

Note!

The use of the word *stimulating* in the previous paragraph is deliberate: *stimulating* in the sense of helping teachers to motivate children into *wanting* to write stories thought their input and support, and *stimulating* in the sense of the engaging stories that children *can* and *should* write. Teachers are encouraged to evaluate the impact of this book on their provision and practice in the classroom and the children's written output by critically reflecting on the word *stimulating*:

- How did this book *stimulate* my teaching in the classroom?
- How did this book *stimulate* children in my class into wanting to write stories?
- How did this book impact on the quality and quantity of the *stimulating* story writing produced by children in my class?

Considering Who This Book is Written For

An important question that all writers should ask themselves, ideally before they put pen to paper/finger to keyboard, is: *Who am I writing for?* It is in the author's best interest to have an awareness of their intended audience as this can support them to effectively communicate with their readers by ensuring that the written text/content is 'pitched' appropriately – the academic professor who writes a picture book for babies about educational theory using hypherluted language is *clearly* unaware of the needs of these young infants!

Ask children who they write for and they are likely to say 'My teacher!'. This is supported by Tamburrini et al. (1984: 195), whose research into 10–11-year-olds' sense of audience in writing found that 'the vast output of writing in schools was written almost entirely for teachers'. Clearly this is a consideration which needs be addressed; children should be encouraged to write stories for a *wide range* of readers including themselves, their peers, visitors, 'parents, friends, local community leaders, or sports heroes' (Strange, 1988).

By becoming more aware of and writing for different audiences, Butt (1993) claims that 'audience-centred' teaching helps children to produce written work that is more personal and involving, and can improve the quality of the writing eventually produced (also see Butt, 1998; http://tinyurl.com/6su8eum). But the discussion offered above relates to *children* and *their* audiences for writing (see http://tinyurl.com/cggcpmq for further information about this). This book has not been penned for the reading eyes of 3–11-year-olds!

Getting Children Writing has been written for those who work/wish to work with children aged 3–11 in the education sector. In an effort to challenge the perception that professional education-based texts are just for class teachers, Table 0.1 is presented by way of acknowledging the wide range of readers this book aims to serve.

Table 0.1   Readership that *Getting Children Writing* is designed for

Those who are training in the education sector	Those who are in the infancy of their career	Those who are established in their working role
Initial Teacher Training – B.Ed. (Primary, Secondary), Post Graduate Certificate in Education (PGCC Early Years, Primary, Secondary), Graduate Teaching Programme (GTP), now SDTP	Newly Qualified Teachers (NQTs) – Early Years, Primary, Secondary	Class teachers – Early Years, Primary, Secondary
	Any persons listed in the adjacent column – *'Those who are established in their working role'* – who are new to their post	Teachers of pupils with SEND
Undergraduates on Foundation Degrees and BA programmes including Child and Youth Studies, Early Childhood Studies and Education Studies		Teaching Assistants/Learning Support Assistants/Learning Mentors
		Supply teachers
		Early Years Practitioners – Key Workers
Students studying for Level 3 practice-based qualifications – CACHE, BTEC, NVQ		Co-ordinators – English, Literacy, SEND, Key Stage
		Senior Management Team – Head teachers, Deputy Head teachers, Assistant Head teachers
		School governors
		Practitioners working at children's centres, playgroups, and hospital schools
		Lecturers – college, university

This book has been written to support this extensive readership in three areas, as proposed by Flower (2000):

- the reader's knowledge about the topic;
- his or her attitude toward it; and
- his or her personal or professional needs.

This book will support those who are training in the education sector by developing their knowledge and understanding of story writing, and of quality practice that is associated with it in the classroom (think *initial* professional development). For those who are in the infancy of their career, this book will positively respond to their personal and professional needs by offering them a wealth of Ideas, strategies, tips, and activities to build classroom confidence and help them to 'survive' the first few years (think *developing* professional practice)! For those who are established in their working role, this book strives to rejuvenate positive attitudes towards learning and teaching and story writing in the classroom by presenting interesting theory and innovative practice to refine their craft and re-energise provision with the children they work with (think *continuing* professional development).

Points to Note!

1. Readers will note that even though this book is specific for those working with the 3–11 age range, secondary school teachers are included in the intended readership of this book, particularly those who support the transition of children between primary and secondary school, those who educate children in their first year of secondary education, and those who work with children aged 11+ who are of lower ability or have special educational needs or disabilities (SEND). Staff can support these children by using practice advocated in this book to positively respond to considerations linked to young people's confidence levels, writing abilities and individual needs.

2. Parents and carers (or the special people who look after/care for us) do not appear in the intended readership table on p. 5 but they *are* considered to be key to improved student achievement (Hara and Burke, 1998). The notion of parents and carers as a partner or 'integral ingredient' in their child's education is one that is positively embraced in this book (see http://tinyurl.com/6uwoo2b). Efforts to encourage parents and carers to engage their child in story writing activities at home are presented via the voluntary/Weekend Work (homework) suggestions offered throughout this book for teachers to advocate. Using these adults as characters for children's stories, an authentic writing audience and a source of story stimuli all make parents and carers an essential 'component' in getting children story writing and improving their subsequent attainment.

Considering the *Does* and *Does Nots* of This Book

As with most professional books, it is deemed necessary to 'set out one's stall' in the sense of clarifying what this book aims to do (*does*) and not do (*does not*). As this book has been written to an agreed word count, readers are reminded that no book of this nature is 'complete'. With this in mind, clarification of the *does nots* are initially presented for awareness purposes.

This book *does not* consider ways of getting children writing poetry or non-fiction in the classroom – its focus is solely on fiction. This book *does not* aim to convince the reader of the value of story in children's education – stories have long been an important aspect of human culture, and continue to be used as an effective way of helping children to learn about language and life. This book *does not* intend to assure the reader of the place and purpose of story writing in the curriculum – this is considered to be 'a given' based on the reader's active decision to pick this book up off the shelf/purchase it/download it. This book *does not* serve to justify why children should write stories – Tompkins (1982) offers seven pertinent reasons to warrant this (see http://tinyurl.com/cweszpw). This book *does not* advocate a 'cookie-cutter' approach to engage children in story writing activity where one method of learning and teaching matches the story writing needs and abilities of every child in the classroom. This book also *does not* 'push' certain strategies or ways of engaging children in writing activity onto the reader (e.g. *Big Writing* by Ros Wilson, 2012).

Take a Look!

For those readers who *do* wish to acquire/refresh their knowledge and understanding of select *does not* points offered above, consider engaging with the following recommended readings:

- **Academic article:** The value of story in children's education – see *Stories and their Importance in Language Teaching* by Wright (2000).

- **Professional briefing paper:** How story helps children learn about language and life – see *Storytelling: The Heart and Soul of Education* by Koki (1998).

- **Academic essay:** The place and purpose of story writing in the classroom – see '*In defense of creative-writing classes*' by Hugo (1992).

Also see Romei (n.d.) (3–5) and http://tinyurl.com/6np9qe (5–11) for some real-life reasons to write.

What this book *does* aspire to do is 'arm' teachers with an exciting array of Ideas to stimulate story writing composition in the 3–11 classroom. This book offers readers a wealth of creative Ideas (both established and new), innovative teaching strategies, top tips, refreshing activities, practical suggestions, quality advice and 'tested' resources that can be used to 'reinvigorate writing practice' (OFSTED, 2009: 48) and increase the engagement levels of children they work with. Many children 'do not see the point' with regard to writing stories – after all, the kind of writing they will mostly likely engage with in their adult life is linked to non-fiction (e.g. writing lists and filling in forms). This book is written to support teachers in helping all children to 'see the point' of story writing by 'providing more effective purposes and audiences for writing' (OFSTED, 2009: 48), 'opportunities to writ[e] for enjoyment' (2009: 50) and 'engage and motivate pupils through practical, creative and purposeful activities' (2009: 53).

This book also presents noteworthy theoretical perspectives, thought-provoking research findings, personal/professional reflections, and links to fascinating professional literature/websites (see http://tinyurl.com/cmxclxu, for example) to inform, educate and deepen the knowledge, skills, understanding and attitudes (KSUA) of teachers so that readers appreciate '*why* they are doing *what* they doing' as they adopt and adapt Ideas for their writing room (classroom). In doing so it is hoped that the reader will recognise the benefits, both personally and professionally, of putting the 'theory into practice' and the 'practice into theory'.

As the reader reflects on the ambitious claims made above, it is recognised that story writing does not happen in a vacuum; there are many considerations which shape provision and practice in 3–11 classrooms, and it is to a number of these considerations that this Introduction will turn its attention.

Considering the Current Constraints

Teachers work within particular constraints, these being at an individual institution level (the school itself), a local level (Local Authority guidance) or a national level (government policy). Whilst it is not possible to acknowledge the specifics of individual Local Authority constraints (e.g. the advocated use of particular schemes of work for speaking and listening for children with English as an additional language (EAL); the intricacies of the intervention programmes used to support children with additional literacy needs), or those constraints at an individual institution level (e.g. hearing every child in class read each day; weekly monitoring of writing books by the SMT for 4–11-year-olds), consideration is given to those constraints that all teachers are bound by at a national level through statutory frameworks (see Table 0.2).

Table 0.2 National statutory teaching frameworks for the early years (0–5) and primary (5–11) sectors

Statutory framework	Details
The Early Years Foundation Stage (EYFS) (3–5+)	During the writing of this book a revised EYFS Framework was issued by the Government in 2012 based on the recommendations of the Tickell Review (2011). Its implementation from 1 September 2012 replaces existing arrangements of the EYFS (DCSF, 2008b) – see http://tinyurl.com/3zv96ao.
The National Curriculum (NC) for Key Stages 1 and 2 (5–11)	During the writing of this book the Government launched a review of the National Curriculum in England for children in Key Stages 1–4 (5–16). Proposed changes were informed, in part, by the report of the Expert Panel (DfE, 2011a). Draft Programmes of Study for English, Mathematics and Science at KS1 and KS2 were published in 2012 to initiate 'a debate on the content of the primary curriculum with key stakeholders, including learned societies, subject associations and teacher unions' (see http://tinyurl.com/bvmtb9d). Until the new National Curriculum has been finalised/published schools are to still work to the existing National Curriculum statutory framework (DfEE/QCA, 1999).

Many schools continue to use materials – both paper-based and online (archived) – linked to the Primary National Strategy (PNS) (DfES, 2006) to support their teaching of communication, language and literacy development (CLLD) (DCSF, 2008b) – now C&L/Literacy (DfE, 2012a) – and literacy in Key Stage 1 and 2 (KS1, KS2). Due to the change in government in 2010 it is important to recognise that whilst there is a value to these materials their content does not necessarily reflect current government policy – readers are encouraged to make reference to the Department for Education (DfE) website for updates (see http://tinyurl.com/28gyxba). This book, however, makes no apologies in signposting readers to quality pre-2010 materials in an effort to develop teachers' subject knowledge and enrich their classroom practice with different ideas, for example:

- For those working with children aged 3–5, visit http://tinyurl. com/br6ceha for some valuable 'Gateway to Writing' materials linked to the role of Early Years practitioners in supporting and developing children's skills, enthusiasm and enjoyment in writing.
- For those working with children aged 5–11, visit http://tinyurl. com/clb3tto for some valuable 'Support for Writing' materials in relation to 'Progression and text-type support in Narrative'.

In an effort to maximise the level of currency in this book, links to the Early Years Foundation Stage (EYFS) (DfE, 2012a) and the draft National Curriculum (NC) for English KS1 and KS2 (DfE, 2012b) are offered in Appendices 31 and 32 (see p. 238; 239–242 respectively) to aid teachers in recognising how the Ideas and features of this book support children in relation to the Developmental Statements (EYFS) and Programme of Study statements (NC) *for writing only.* Whilst statutory frameworks offer educators a national structure to work to, many teachers at an individual institution level seek the support of professional materials to aid them in bringing these curriculums to life in the classroom. It is to these professional materials this Introduction now turns its attention.

Considering the PTA of English

Whilst schools work hard to meet the learning requirements of the EYFS (DfE, 2012a) and the NC (DfEE/QCA, 1999; DfE, 2012b), it is recognised that many schools make use of schemes of work developed by their Local Authority or invest in commercially published programmes to support teachers in the **p**lanning (long/ medium/short term), classroom delivery (**t**eaching) and **a**ssessment of the many Areas of Learning and Development (EYFS)/subjects (NC) they teach. Within the context of Literacy there are numerous schemes available for purchase, both online and in printed form, that offer secure structures and 'ready-made resources' for teachers to use in the classroom. Select examples of these are listed in Table

0.3. However, it is worthy of note that this list does not include literacy intervention programmes such as *Every Child a Writer (ECaW)*, *ELS/ALS/FLS*, and *Reading Recovery*. For useful guidance on interventions for literacy see http://tinyurl.com/c2g24aj.

Table 0.3 Examples of commercially published schemes related to the teaching of English

Type of scheme	Examples
Reading	*Oxford Reading Tree, Collins Big Cat, Rigby Star, Ladybird.*
Phonics	*Jolly Phonics, Phonics Bug, Thrass, Sounds-Write, Read Write Inc.*
Reading and writing	*Quest, Rapid Writing, Focus on (Writing Composition), Literacy Evolve.*
Handwriting	*Nelson Thornes, PenPals, Morrells Handwriting, Letter-join.*

Whilst it is not deemed appropriate to offer a critique of the merits/shortcomings of published schemes, it is considered important to acknowledge the thinking of Wyse and Jones (2008: 224) who warn that '[t]oo often even commercially successful published schemes contain poor activities and generally their use, without adaptation, is not regarded as "good practice"'. To guard against an over-reliance on unmodified schemes teachers are actively encouraged to use purchased materials 'as a starting point for teaching' (OFSTED, 2012a: 23), supplementing and extending these with other resources – this is where *Getting Children Writing* comes in! Select suggestions to ensure that teachers do not 'follow the book to the letter' include:

- 3–7: Use well-known characters such as Peppa Pig/Biff, Chip and Floppy (ORT) as the 'stars' (lead characters) of the stories that young children talk about and write, examples of which include *Un-folded stories* (p. 59) and *Free stories* (p. 168).
- 5–11: Combine opportunities for children to practice their handwriting whilst composing a new *Penned story* (p. 92).

- 7–11: Use the 'powerful short films' offered by Literacy Evolve (see http://tinyurl.com/czqwctx) as stimuli for an *Extended story* (p. 131); for example, what happens to the characters *after* the credits roll on the film? Also see *Look Again!* (BFI, 2003).

Whilst published schemes strive to offer teachers 'the answer', personal experience of these schemes highlight that it is not possible for them to know the children in *your* class and the specific needs that individuals/groups have, which is why the adaptation of these materials is so important. Because children 'develop at their own rates, and in their own ways' (DfE, 2012a: 6) it is important for teachers to recognise how children 'grow' with regard to their writing development.

Considering Children's Writing Development

An important consideration in children's writing is the way in which their writing capabilities develop. It is suggested that children progress through a number of sequential writing stages (see Hill, 2006). Researchers and academics refer to these stages using different labels/terms; there is also variation in the number of stages that children seemingly progress through. For example, Juel (1991) suggests that children move through three stages as they learn to write: *emergent, beginning* and *fluent*; Gentry (n.d.), Schickedanz and Casbergue (2005) and Sulzby and Teale (1985) all propose more than three stages, as is demonstrated in Table 0.4.

Table 0.4   Stages of writing development: a comparison

Gentry (n.d.)	Schickedanz and Casbergue (2005)	Sulzby and Teale (1985)
Scribbling	Making a mark Marks have a meaning	Drawings Wavy scribbles
Letter-like symbols	Marks begin to resemble letters	Letter-like scribbles
Strings of letters	Writing more closely resembles standard letters Writing includes 'mock words'	Random letters in a line

Beginning sounds emerge	Phonemic or invented spelling	Patterned letters/ strings
Consonants represent words		Conventional writing
Initial, middle, and final sounds		
Transitional phases		
Standard spelling		
For details see http://tinyurl. com/cak739y	For details see http://tinyurl. com/cv848eh	For details see Sulzby and Teale (1985)

This book serves to support different stages of these developmental models by offering pertinent Ideas and exploratory discussions at the beginning of select chapters (through the chapter introductions). Whilst these links are not made explicit, teachers will recognise how particular Ideas and discussions relate to particular writing stages (see Table 0.5).

Table 0.5   Stages of writing development and associated Chapter introductions and Ideas in *Getting Children Writing*

Writing stage	Chapter introduction	Idea (example)
Drawings	Chapter 4 (p. 82)	*Window stories* (p. 181)
Making a mark Marks have a meaning	Chapter 3 (p. 64)	*Free stories* (p. 168)
Conventional writing	Chapter 8 (p. 152)	*Recycled stories* (p. 63)

Like all aspects of children's development it is important to stress that the different writing stages proposed overlap and that children progress and reach writing stages at different ages, at different rates and with different skills. In support of this, non-statutory guidance materials in the EYFS (DfE 2012a: 30) offer the following statement:

The development statements and their order should not be taken as necessary steps for individual children. They should not be used as checklists. The age/stage bands overlap because these are not fixed age boundaries but suggest a typical range of development.

Similar support is evident in the draft NC for KS1 and KS2 (DfE, 2012b: 4) where 'maintained schools . . . have the flexibility to introduce content earlier or later than set out in the Programme of Study [PoS]'. There is, however, acknowledgement that children engage in a 'rapid pace of development' between the ages of 5 and 7, and this is reflected in the PoS (see DfE, 2012b: 5–14). It is anticipated that teachers will take the above into consideration when matching writing provision advocated in this book (via the 'Suggested age group' feature) to children's actual capabilities.

Take a Look!

In an effort to support those who wish to develop their knowledge and understanding of children's writing development, readers are encouraged to refer to the following:

- **Downloadable document:** Pages 3–4 of *Developmental Stages of Writing* – available at http://tinyurl.com/7u8gpqe.
- **PowerPoint presentation:** *Developmental Writing* – available at http://tinyurl.com/7zt9ope.
- **Website:** The six stages of writing development (Levine, 1998) – see http://tinyurl.com/6lr46cz.

Not only is it advocated that teachers should have an appreciation of how children's writing develops, they also need to recognise the importance of speaking and listening as an integral tool to support and enhance children's story writing.

Considering Speaking and Listening and Children's Writing

In the Interim Report of *The Independent Review of the Teaching of Early Reading* Rose (2005: 15) stated that 'listening and speaking are the roots of reading and writing'. As a fundamental feature that supports children's learning and development, the term 'oracy', as coined by Wilkinson in the 1960s (cited in MacLure et al., 1988), serves to emphasise the importance of children being able to communicate competently through verbal means and also to listen attentively. Observations of young children highlight that their ability to talk naturally comes before their ability to write; babies babble, coo and gurgle long before they begin to mark-make. By 'targeting talk' (Jones, 2007: 31) as a vehicle for children's communication and learning and thinking, teachers are able to help children to build up their vocabulary, develop social skills and relationships with others, learn how language works and is constructed, and hone comprehension skills, all of which contribute over time to support children in producing 'strong writing' (see Ciccone, 2001).

This book recognises the emphasis that is placed on language development and oral skills in early years classrooms (3–5), particularly as this is considered to be 'a common feature of the most successful schools' (OFSTED, 2011: 19) in terms of 'removing barriers to literacy' (2011: 1). Programmes such as *Every Child a Talker* (DCSF, 2008c, 2009) and the presence of *Communication and Language* as a Prime Area of the EYFS (DfE, 2012a) highlight the value of speaking and listening in a child's infancy and the positive impact it can have on improving standards in children's mark-making/writing (see DCSF, 2008a: 41). It is anticipated that the ideas in this book will be embraced within language-rich contexts where story, role play, visual stimuli (e.g. pictures, objects, finger puppets) and game play are used to support children's (3–5) mark-marking/writing efforts. For example, children can work-in-role to dramatise what happens to them when they consume the new confectionary they have invented (see *Sweet stories*, p. 97), possibilities of which include the ability to jump really high, run like a cheetah, turn into a giant or develop super strength. Following this, children can then commit their story ideas to paper using drawings, marks, letters, words or simple sentences.

There is concern, however, that the emphasis on speaking and listening in the EYFS is not a sustained feature in primary classrooms (5–11) as children get older. Efforts to positively address this are evident through publications such as *Speaking, Listening, Learning: Working with Children in Key Stages 1 and 2* (DfES, 2003) and *Talk for Writing* (DCSF, 2008d: 3) which is described as a 'developmental exploration, through talk, of the thinking and creative processes involved in being a writer' (see http://tinyurl.com/c9csg4g). In an effort to embrace Ros Wilson's 'If a child can say it they can write it' principle, this book offers a range of opportunities to promote purposeful speaking and listening for 5–11-year-olds to support them *prior to*, *during* and *post* their writing, 'fuelling' discussions to stimulate ideas and thinking so that oracy is used as an *integral* as opposed to a 'neglected part of the writing process' (Reid, 1983: 2). For example, in *Weathered stories* (p. 149) children are encouraged to talk about their own experiences of different weather types, considering ways they have dealt with the problems the weather posed (5–7) and how different weathers make people/characters feel (7–9).

Take a Look!

In an effort to support those who wish to develop their knowledge and understanding of speaking and listening to aid children's writing, readers are encouraged to refer to the following:

- **Downloadable PDF:** *Teaching Speaking, Listening and Writing* by Wallace et al. (2004).
- **Case study:** *Building a Bridge Between Speaking and Listening and Children's Writing* by Core (n.d.).
- **Report:** *Talk to Text: Using Talk to Support Writing* by Fisher et al. (2006).

Whilst Richards (2008a: 1) acknowledges the 'prominent place' of speaking and listening in supporting children's writing, Donovan (2007) claims that 'reading is the single most important activity that leads to better writing'. Does this mean that if we want children to write stimulating stories we should simply get them to read more?

Considering Reading and Children's Writing

The American-based National Writing Project (NWP) (2012) claims that '[b]etter writers tend to be better readers, and better readers produce better writing'.

Reflect!

Take a moment to identify those children you work with who you consider to be 'better readers' – are they the children who also 'produce better writing'? Why do you think that this is the case?

It is argued that reading not only helps to give children ideas for their stories but it also provides prior knowledge, helps to improve spelling, and increases vocabulary acquisition by introducing them to new words. More importantly, children learn how to write by looking at how authors 'put it down on the page' (see http://tinyurl. com/bs2x35g). Indeed, Calkins (1980) observed that children learn about punctuation from their reading, and that exposure to written language may help them learn about print and language structures, which may in turn influence writing.

Langer et al. (2000) argue that reading and writing are interrelated; it is suggested that you cannot have one without the other. It is strongly believed that in order for children to be able to write they need to have read; after all, how can they be expected to commit a sentence to the page if they have never seen/read one 'in print'? Interestingly, this is challenged by the Steiner philosophy where children are taught to write words and read their own writing before working with printed literature (see Carnie, 2003). Nevertheless, Poersch (2007: 107) claims that '[p]rescriptive or formal instruction is not sufficient for conveying everything writers need to know'. Smith (1983) supports this, proposing that a good number of writing conventions enter into our memory without awareness of the learning that is taking place. This occurs when children actively engage with reading material, not just story books but also signs, newspapers, leaflets, magazines, posters, CD inserts and letters.

This book advocates the principle of 'read more to write better' by encouraging teachers to expose children to a wealth of high-quality stories that not only emulate 'familiar themes, rhythms, structures and linguistic patterns [which] can be identified and explored' (Bower, 2011: 4) but also can be used to stimulate children's story writing. By using these as powerful story models it is personally felt that children will write quality stories as they will be mirroring the literature they have come into contact with – 'what children write reflects the nature and quality of their reading' (Barrs and

Cork, 2001: 35). In relation to *Getting Children Writing*, *Carpet stories* (p. 142) encourage children (3–11) to 'recycle' carpet-based stories written by bestselling authors such as E. Nesbit, David Lucas and Terry Pratchett by using text structures and language from these well-written tales that they can then transfer to their own writing (also see *Recycled stories*, p. 63). *Fairy stories* (p. 167) offer children (5–11) the opportunity to *extend* 'rich' stories following the 'happy-ever-after', using a traditional style of storytelling. For young children (3–7), *Flip-flap stories* (p. 177) highlight popular flip-flap authors such as Rod Campbell who children can learn from in terms of 'how it is done' (see http://tinyurl.com/d2hre4k).

Take a Look!

In an effort to support those who wish to develop their knowledge and understanding of the importance of reading on children's writing, readers are encouraged to refer to the following:

- **Online video:** *How Reading Impacts* [on] *Children's Writing* by Pie Corbett – available at http://tinyurl.com/c7jsqdo.

- **Research:** *Developing Reading–Writing Connections: The Impact of Explicit Instruction of Literary Devices on the Quality of Children's Narrative Writing* by Corden (2007).

- **Webpage:** *Want to Improve Writing Standards? Let Them Read Books!* by Shoo (2011) – available at http://tinyurl.com/cbngcl2.

Whilst Brummitt-Yale (2011) advocates the 'major role' that reading plays in writing, she is quick to suggest that 'practice in writing [also] helps children build their reading skills':

> This is especially true for younger children who are working to develop phonemic awareness and phonics skills. Phonemic awareness . . . develops as children read and write new words. Similarly, phonics skills or the ability to link sounds together to construct words are reinforced when children read and write the same words.

It is to the phonics 'pillar of reading' that this Introduction now turns its attention.

Considering Phonics and Children's Writing

In an effort to help children to be able to write, and indeed read (Rose, 2005), great emphasis has been placed on the essential role that phonics plays in supporting children to become literate. Roberts and Meiring (2006: 690) state that '[t]here is abundant evidence that phonics instruction is crucial in developing beginning literacy competence'; this is strongly advocated in the EYFS (DfE, 2012a: 29) and the draft NC for KS1 and KS2 (DfE, 2012b: 3), which both stress the importance of high-quality, regular, rigorous and systematic synthetic phonics input so that emergent readers and writers (from the age of 5, and those who are struggling to decode in KS2) can gain a 'functional command' of the English language (see OFSTED, 2010 and http://tinyurl.com/bppbks9). But what is meant by the term 'phonics' and how can this be used to support children's story writing, particularly in relation to this book?

The DfES (2007a: 18) suggests that '[p]honics consists of knowledge of the skills of segmenting and blending, knowledge of the alphabetic code and an understanding of the principles underpinning the way the code is used in reading and spelling'. Torgerson et al. (2006: 13) offer a more succinct definition, proposing phonics to be 'approaches which focus on the relationships between letters and sounds'. This notion of 'letters and sounds' has been used as the title of a national 'time-limited' programme of phonic work (DfES, 2007a: 3) which offers 'a powerful phonics teaching tool to ensure that young children are well-placed to read and spell words with fluency and confidence by the time they reach the end of Key Stage 1' (2007a: 1). With an integral emphasis on developing children's speaking and listening skills, the teaching of phonics, particularly synthetic phonics, is regarded as the best proven way to teach early reading in UK schools (see Camilli et al., 2003).

As children progressively learn about phonemes (the smallest unit of spoken sound in a word, e.g. **b/a/t**) and graphemes (the written symbol (letter/s) of the phoneme, e.g. **b-a-t**), it is advocated that they can then *apply* this phonic knowledge not only to their reading, but also to their writing. For example, the child who can orally blend and segment/recognise/write the letters **s a t p i n** should be able to, in time, read and write simple words/captions/ sentences with support and encouragement (e.g. *tap*; *Sit*(!); *Pat sat in a tin*). Johnston and Watson (2005: 69) 'conclude that a synthetic phonics programme, as a part of the reading curriculum, has a major and long lasting effect on children's reading and spelling attainment'. This is considered to be of real benefit to children's ability to *write with ease*, as is highlighted by the thinking of the DfE (2012b: 3):

> Writing down ideas fluently depends on effective transcription, that is, on spelling quickly and accurately through knowing the relationship between sounds and letters (phonics) and understanding the morphological (word structure) and orthographic (spelling structure) patterns of words.

This book mirrors sentiments shared by the DfES (2007a: 16) who suggest that '[t]he relevance of phonics to reading and spelling is implicit in these materials'. The application of children's phonic knowledge is an *integral* feature to making the Ideas in this book 'come alive' – children should be actively encouraged to use the practical skills they have been explicitly taught though their discrete daily phonics input to help them encode (spell/write) the words they want to use to tell their story with, whilst also decoding (reading) to check that what they have written 'reads' the way they want it to (i.e. makes sense). This can also be emphasised through whole-class shared writing, guided group writing and individual independent writing opportunities. For example, children can use their developing phonic knowledge to write interesting *Toy stories* (p. 109) (see Figure 0.1).

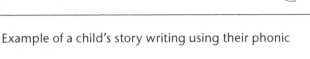

Wen I went to skool teddi had sum red jelli and pop in bed.

He dided a big burp. He was a slep wen I got bak hom.

Max, 5¾ years old. Independent writing.

Figure 0.1   Example of a child's story writing using their phonic knowledge

> **Take a Look!**
> In an effort to support those who wish to develop their knowledge
> and understanding of phonics, readers are encouraged to refer to the
> following:
>
> - **Professional publication:** *Teaching Systematic Synthetic Phonics in
>   the Primary Classroom* by Jolliffe et al. (2012).
> - **Academic paper:** *Teaching Phonics in Whole Language Classrooms* by
>   Wilson (2006) – available at http://tinyurl.com/che3qn2.
> - **Academic website:** *Phonics Instruction* by NICHD (2010) – available at
>   http://tinyurl.com/7b2gfuy.

By using a 'rigorous [and] sequential approach to developing
speaking and listening and teaching reading, writing and spelling
through systematic phonics' (OFSTED, 2011: 5) it is argued that
this will lead to 'measurable improvements' in the attainment of
learners in literacy. However, it is important for children to be able
to *apply* the knowledge, skills and understanding linked to the above
within the context of their story writing. But how do children learn
about the 'how' of story writing?

Considering the Approach to (Story) Writing

For children to be able to effectively write stimulating stories
teachers must make the 'implicit *explicit*' by teaching children *how*
to write a story; after all, a child cannot normally be expected to
produce a 'complete' story in a single attempt. Badger and White
(2000) suggest there are three approaches to the teaching of
writing: *product, process* and *genre*. These are summarised in Table
0.6, along with an indication as to how these approaches 'see'
writing development.

Table 0.6   Three approaches to teaching story writing (Badger and White, 2000)

Product	Process	Genre
'Product-based approaches see writing as mainly concerned with knowledge about the structure of language, and writing development as mainly the result of the imitation of input, in the form of texts provided by the teacher' (2000: 154).	'Process approaches see writing primarily as the exercise of linguistic skills, and writing development as an unconscious process which happens when teachers facilitate the exercise of writing skills' (2000: 155).	'Genre-based approaches see writing as essentially concerned with knowledge of language, and as being tied closely to a social purpose, while the development of writing is largely viewed as the analysis and imitation of input in the form of texts provided by the teacher' (2000: 156).

Whilst there are pros and cons linked to each approach, Hairston (1982, cited in McKensie and Tomkins, 1984: 201) suggests that 'the teaching of composition has been revolutionised by a shift in emphasis from product to process'. Thirty years on and researchers continue to 'investigate the efficiency of the writing process approach in improving written expression (composition) skills of . . . students in primary education' (see Cavkaytar and Yasar, 2010). Instead of focussing on the 'rote repetition and technical instruction' of writing, for example spelling, grammar and diction (Kamehameha Schools, 2007: 2), it is advocated that teachers should teach children (4–11) about the *process* of writing, particularly as Zemelman et al. (2005: 87) argue that '[m]any children never see skilful writers at work and are unaware that writing is a staged, craft like process that competent authors typically break into manageable steps'.

Spivey (2006: 1) states that '[l]earning to write is like learning to read. Both follow a sequential process'. It is suggested that effective educators teach writing through a series of logical steps that 'guide children [5-11] from the beginning of writing to creating a finished piece' (2006: 1). These steps are summarised in Table 0.7.

Table 0.7 Logical steps for teaching writing (adapted from Spivey, 2006: 1–2)

Step no.	Step	Details
1	*Prewriting*	Children *thought shower* to generate ideas for writing through verbal and written means.
2	*Rough draft*	Children put their ideas on paper.
3	*Peer editing*	Classmates share their rough drafts and make suggestions to each other for improvement.
4	*Revising*	The children use the suggestions from classmates to make additions or clarify details.
5	*Editing*	Children work with the teacher and/or peers to correct all mistakes in grammar and spelling.
6	*Final draft*	Children produce a copy of their writing with all corrections made from the editing stage.
7	*Publishing*	Children publish their writing by making a copy in their neatest handwriting or using a word processor.

Peha (2003b) largely supports the steps identified in Table 0.7 but refers to the writing process as a series of *stages*, identifying these using different labels, the last of which is called 'Assessing' during which the author reflects on their published work, reviews the comments from others and thinks about their next piece of writing (see 2003b: 10c–14b). It is interesting to note that different authors claim there to be a varying number of *steps* or *stages* in the writing process; these range between two ('drafting and revising') and nine (see Milwaukee Public Schools, n.d.: 18)! Most descriptions of the writing process, however, average five or six stages: *prewriting, drafting, revising, editing* and *publishing*.

Note!

Whilst it is recognised that there is a number of writing stages it is important to guard against thinking that the writing process is *formulaic*; for example a 'neat, linear, step-by-step procedure' (Jones-Shoeman, 2010). Flower and Hayes (1981) and Bereiter and Scardamalia (1982) argue that the writing stages, like the stages of writing development, are fluid and overlapping, implying that the writing process is *recursive* and somewhat messy, depending on what is being written. To develop their proficiency in story writing children, particularly those aged 7–11, should be actively encouraged to skip and revisit different stages in an effort to improve their story writing output.

Teachers are positively encouraged to teach children about the writing process as this is seen as an authentic and effective way of helping them to 'get into' story writing; Tompkins (2008) suggests that the more students learn how to use this process efficiently, the more they can express themselves efficiently. Clearly it is important for teachers to *adapt* the way in which they present and use the writing process with children from different age phases; practical suggestions are offered in Table 0.8.

Table 0.8   Practical ways to adapt and present the writing process to children aged 3–11

3–5	• Verbalise the writing process during focused carpet input sessions/adult-led writing activities, guiding children through select stages of the process; e.g. prewriting, drafting and editing. • Model an 'early years friendly' version of the process when indoors/outdoors; e.g. *Think and Talk about it! Write about it! Tell others about it!*
5–7	• Over time introduce and explain the stages of the writing process to the children. • Model strategies, approaches and techniques linked to each stage through shared and guided writing opportunities (Daniel, 2001). • Actively encourage children to apply their *process* learning to their independent story writing tasks.
7–11	• Use visual prompts to remind children of the writing process; e.g. flow diagrams and posters – see http://tinyurl.com/d8uzchv (7–9) and http://tinyurl.com/dxmrzzv (9–11). • Allow children to gain confidence in using the process when writing other genres; e.g. poetry and non-fiction. • Critically explore each stage in more depth, particularly the revision stage (see Lehr, 1995).

Take a Look!

Readers are encouraged to refer to the following sources of information in an effort to support those who wish to develop their knowledge and understanding of the writing process further:

- **Academic article:** *All Children Can Write* by Graves (1985) – available at http://tinyurl.com/7r69q3o.

- **Professional booklet:** *Writer's Workshop Handbook: Elementary – Grades K-5* by Joplin School District (2011) – available at http://tinyurl.com/d7av7ps.

- **Academic website:** *Writing: Writing Process* by Nortz (n.d.) – available at http://tinyurl.com/7qdutow.

Considering How the Book Works

Unlike a story book which is usually read from cover to cover, this book has been written to serve different kinds of readers. Some may wish to 'jump right in', flicking through the pages for some planning inspiration. Other may decide to go right to the back of the book and start using the photocopiable resources found in the Appendices. Some readers may prefer to look at the Recommended Readings which are offered at the end of each chapter introduction to support their writing of their coursework. Other readers may choose to read the book from 'cover to cover'. All of the above are personally considered to be effective ways of engaging with this book.

Getting Children Writing is organised into ten chapters, each consisting of ten story Ideas. Each chapter has a central focus which all of the ten Ideas are based around. The introduction to each chapter presents the central focus and then briefly describes each of the Ideas. The Ideas are organised into two halves: the first five Ideas are linked to a theme associated with the central focus, with the remaining five Ideas being linked to another theme – see Table 0.9 for an outline example.

Table 0.9 An example of the chapter organisation used throughout *Getting Children Writing*

Chapter/focus	Theme	Ideas
Chapter 5 *'Engaging' stories*	Parties	Party stories
		Parcel stories
		Competition stories
		Toy stories
		Clothing stories
	Building	Crazy stories
		Soft stories
		Scroll stories
		DIY stories
		Either–Or stories

Each chapter introduction then focuses its attention on exploring a particular story writing *consideration*. These are linked to a point of discussion from one of the Ideas offered in the chapter. These *considerations* are explored under the heading 'Taking a closer look at . . .'. An overview of the ten considerations is offered in Table 0.10.

Table 0.10 The ten writing considerations: an overview

Chapter	Chapter title	'Taking a closer look at' focus
1	*'Pen-to-Paper' Stories*	'Blank minds' – exploring writer's block
2	*'Design and Make' Stories*	'The problems they face' – considering types of conflict in stories
3	*'Being' Stories*	'Suggested age group' – adapting *'Being' stories* for 3–5-year-olds
4	*'Craft' Stories*	'Developing an effective control over pencils and pens' – writing stories and handwriting
5	*'Engaging' Stories*	'Varying the plot' – exploring the differences between 'story' and 'plot'
6	*'Technology' Stories*	'Stimulating story ideas' – examining ways of generating story ideas
7	*'Location' Stories*	'The characters they create' – creating memorable story characters
8	*'Boys'' Stories*	'Relaxing expectations with regard to accurate spellings' – story writing and spelling
9	*'Creative' Stories*	'Conflict resolution' – writing the resolution of a story
10	*'Random' Stories*	'Story endings' – addressing the all-important 'good' story ending

All introductions offer a selection of recommended readings associated with the central focus of the chapter; these include academic and professional books, book chapters and research journal articles/papers, reports, online documents and resources, and websites. A brief description of each reading is presented along with a point for reflective consideration for those readers who choose to actively engage with the reading and the Ideas being presented.

Points to Note!

- Many of the readings offered are written by authors from a national and international perspective. This is purposeful so that readers can reflect on the thinking, research and provision associated with story writing that is offered to children in different countries, considering its implications (if any) on their own practice in the classroom.

- Readings in this book have been selected from a wealth of literature on the subject that has been published in the last 40 years; readers are encouraged to actively reflect on the theory/practice being discussed, taking into account its applicability (possible/actual) in today's classroom.

The Ideas in this book largely follow a varied presentation. Two features that remain consistent in all of the Ideas are the *Suggested age group* and the *Explanation*. Each Idea is linked to a suggested age group; these may be broad in age range (3–11), specific to a Key Stage (5–7) or are written for particular year groups (9–11). Readers are kindly reminded that the suggested age group is *merely a suggestion*; Ideas presented may be too difficult or 'lacking in challenge' for the children that particular teachers work with. Should this be the case, teachers are encouraged to embrace the basic premise of the Idea being offered, adapting it to suit the abilities and diverse needs of their 'young authors' by using appropriate differentiation strategies (see http://tinyurl.com/cy3lu6o for ideas). The *Explanation* feature discusses the main Idea, supporting the reader in gaining an overview of the kind of story being advocated and the reasoning for this. The remainder of the page is dedicated to an abundance of practical suggestions, ideas and information to support teachers in bringing the main Idea 'alive' in their classroom. Again, teachers are asked to select the most appropriate Ideas for the children they work with, matching these to children's needs based on their continued assessment of pupil attainment (through the use of

Assessing Pupils' Progress (APP) materials for example, see http://tinyurl.com/cxfacqm; http://tinyurl.com/35w9zqk).

It is hoped that this book will both stimulate provision and practice in the classroom and stimulate the stories that children produce in class and at home. Some children will respond more positively to certain Ideas than others; the beauty of this book is that if a particular Idea has limited success, there are *plenty* of others which can be used!

Whilst most professionals in education consider one of their key roles to be teaching, it is firmly believed that when it comes to story writing our key role is to *sell* it to children so that they *buy* into the brilliance that is writing stories.

So go forth . . . and *sell well*!

Note!

At the time of writing all of the tinyurl.com links offered in this book were active. As information on the web is regularly changed, updated or removed, it is anticipated that some links may not work for the reader. The author apologises for this, but it is hoped that readers will recognise that this is out of the author's control.

1

'Pen-to-Paper' stories

The focus of this initial chapter centres on the notion of getting children across the early years (3–5) and primary age phases (5–11) to actually put 'pen to paper'. Whilst many teachers use different strategies to stimulate potential stories in children's minds (e.g. video footage, role play, speaking and listening opportunities, pictures and images, and music – see Wijaya and Tedjaatmadja, n.d.), it is important for children to be able to turn this 'story potential' into reality by making a record of their story, evidence of which is typically presented in written form but can also include drawings/illustrations and audio recordings.

This chapter presents a variety of Ideas to effectively motivate children into *wanting* to record their story in written form by focusing on two key considerations: *what* should children physically write their stories on, and *where* should they write? Children in classrooms today are faced too often with the same kinds of writing paper which they are expected to fill with a story – white A4 or lined paper in exercise books. The first half of this chapter suggests Ideas that make adjustments to the shape (*Shaped stories*), size (*Sized stories*), colour (*Colour stories*) and 'feel' of the paper that children work on (*Tactile stories*) in an effort to 'hook children in' and stimulate the stories that they write in the classroom. Innovative story writing is promoted by getting children to write stories which use their whole body (*Body stories*), not only as story stimuli but also as a human display board for the shameless self-promotion of their writing efforts!

The second half of this chapter focuses its attention on taking story writing outside of the classroom and promoting its under-taking in the familiar setting of the home or place of residence, highlighting different 'spaces' where children can create, develop and present stories to family members or those close to the child (see *Bedroom stories*, *Bathroom stories*, *Kitchen stories*, *Living room stories* and *Garden stories*). The chapter offers teachers unusual, exciting and effective strategies and ideas which can be shared with parents and carers to promote story writing in different locations in the home/place of residence; do refer to Graham-Clay (2005), who offers a critical exploration of practical communication strategies which teachers can use to effectively share these writing strategies and ideas with parents and carers as stimulating Weekend Work (homework) for children.

Taking a Closer Look at 'Blank Minds'

One of the initial points made in *Shaped stories* (p. 36) emphasises the fact that when they are asked to write a story 'some children['s] creative minds can be a little like [a] piece of paper: *blank!*'. This is commonly referred to as 'writer's block', which Rose (1984: 3) defines as 'an inability to begin or continue writing for reasons other than a lack of basic skill or commitment'. This highlights two important considerations for teachers when thinking about children's story writing:

1. Teachers are reminded that children's writing output is influenced by their age, their stage of writing development (see Introduction, p. 12), and whether they have any SEND which may contribute in some way to 'a lack of basic skill' noted in their written work (e.g. limited language proficiency or a physical disability). Teachers should ensure that they have *high* writing expectations of their children but that these should be *realistic* in relation to the children's *actual* capabilities. These expectations can be monitored through the use of regular assessment and 'next steps' targets (APP – see http://tinyurl.com/d7vx65r).

2. There are children in our classrooms who lack writing commitment; many teachers would suggest that this typically relates to boys in their class (Safford et al., 2004), particularly

in light of the results of national testing (see DfE, 2012c). Writing commitment is important for all writers, irrespective of their gender or age. There are numerous reasons why children may lack dedication to their writing; these include:

- having other curriculum strengths/interests;
- finding that they do not have enough time to actually write in class; or
- having too many distractions around them (e.g. their friends).

One of the key roles of a teacher is to promote and model practical strategies to help improve children's commitment levels to writing in the classroom. These include:

- Set writing targets that are specific, measurable, achievable, realistic and time-related (SMART) for children to work towards and achieve (see http://tinyurl.com/75uzh94 for information about the meaning and setting of SMART targets).

- Ensure that sufficient time is offered on the timetable for quality writing activity each day.

- Offer children a choice about their writing – what they are going to write *about*, what they are going to write *on* (paper, computers, acetates) and *where* they are going to write (inside, outside, on the floor, next to friends).

- Offer frequent and purposeful praise for both children's written *output* and their *efforts*.

- Use rewards to acknowledge children's increasing levels of writing commitment (see Cremin et al., 2006 and Nolen, 2007 for further ideas).

Smith (1982, cited in Cowie and Hanrott, 1984: 200) suggests that there are three main types of writer's block:

1. 'Procedural blocks [that] arise when the writer's mind has gone blank and it is not clear what should be written next';
2. Psychological blocks that occur when 'the writing task appears too difficult, or the audience is perceived as a threatening one'; and

3. Physical blocks that refer to 'the sheer physical demands of the writing process [which] can inhibit the young writer from completing the task'.

An awareness of these different writing blocks can help teachers to select appropriate strategies to positively address these in the classroom. Select practical 'encouragement' suggestions are summarised in Table 1.1 to initially support teachers' practice across the 3–11 age phase.

Table 1.1 Practical 'encouragement' suggestions to help children combat different types of writer's block

	3–5 age phase	**5–7 age phase**	**7–11 age phase**
Procedural blocks	Encourage children to repeatedly verbalise what they want to write down.	Encourage children to make use of writing prompts/ questions.	Encourage children to create a story plan before they initiate their writing.
Psychological blocks	Encourage children to mark-make as part of their play based activities, both indoors and outdoors.	Encourage children to work towards targets that are appropriate to their stage of writing development (see p. 12).	Encourage children to seek constructive criticism in both verbal and written form from different audiences to help alleviate the threat posed by them.
Physical blocks	Encourage children to engage in activities which develop both their fine motor and gross motor skills.	Encourage children to 'use a writing style which is easier for them e.g. print vs. cursive' (Sansosti et al., 2010: 96).	Encourage children to work on their stories over several sessions, 'breaking up' the writing into manageable 'chunks'.

Other strategies are available to help children cope with and overcome writer's block; these include:

- Where possible/appropriate, encourage children to 'step away' from the writing, doing some physical exercise or a different activity and then coming back to the writing later on (3–7).

- Reduce the amount of distractions around the child so that they can devote their attention to the writing of their story (3–11).

- Suggest that children read something, as it may offer them some story inspiration. Do ensure that this is not used as an opportunity for children to plagiarise others' work! (5–11).

- Encourage children to adopt some self-belief by telling themselves that they *can* write and that they *can* write well (3–7).

- Advocate that children just get something (*anything!*) down on paper, irrespective of whether it is good or 'not so good'. Robertson (cited in Tanner, 2011) calls this the 'Dump Version': 'It's sort of diarrh[o]ea on the page – get it all out in concrete words, ignoring order and mechanics and cohesion. Literally dump it on the page.' If children 'dump' their words on whiteboards using dry wipe pens it is easy for them to revise and edit their story with the simple wipe of a dry wipe board rubber.

To further support teachers, quality readings and websites that advocate a wealth of additional strategies to help children overcome writer's block are offered below:

- **Website:** *Writers Block in Elementary-Aged Children from an OTs Perspective* by Schulken (2008) – available at http://tinyurl.com/chq3za4. A smashing collection of ideas across the primary age phase from an American occupational therapist's perspective.

- **Book:** Bowkett, S. (2013) *Get Them Thinking Like Writers!* London: Continuum. See section 1.

- **Website:** *Writer's Block* – available at http://tinyurl.com/c6v4gjp – useful for parents and carers.

Table 1.2   Recommended readings associated with *'Pen-to-paper' stories*

Books	National Writing Project and Nagin, C. (2003) *Because Writing Matters: Improving Student Writing in Our Schools*. San Francisco, CA: Jossey-Bass.
	This stimulating book 'examines the myths and realities surrounding the teaching of writing in schools' in the USA. It 'reveals how kids learn to write, what schools need to do to teach writing effectively' and 'shows that effective writing teachers address more than content and skills' (quotes taken from inside dust cover). Consider how subject knowledge from this book can be used to inform your practice and enrich children's *'Pen-to-paper'* stories.
	Cleaver, P. (2006) *Ideas for Children's Writers*. Oxford: How To Books.
	This book, whilst being written for adults wishing to write for children, is a 'comprehensive resource book of plots, themes, genres, lists, what's hot & what's not' (book's subtitle) *in the world of children's story writing. The book is full of brilliant lists, ranging from* Colours *(and variations) of the Rainbow to* Ranks in the Armed Forces *which can be used by teachers to help children enrich their* 'Pen-to-paper' stories.
Research journal articles	Bearne, E. (2007) *Writing*. ITE English: Readings for Discussion. [Online]. Available at: http://tinyurl.com/chbw5em (Accessed: 7 April 2012).
	This fascinating paper explores, amongst other things, young writers' perceptions of writing, writing as both a process and product, and the range of purposes and readers for writing. Consider how the findings from this paper compare to the views of children in your class (where appropriate) in relation to the aspects identified above.
	Giles, R. M. and Wellhousen Tunks, K. (2009) Putting the power in action: Teaching young children 'how to' write. *Texas Child Care*. Fall. [Online]. Available at: http://tinyurl.com/d7ayw6c (Accessed: 14 April 2012).
	This interesting article advocates an 'I do, we do, you do' model to introduce children to writing by providing strong support initially and gradually encouraging more independence as they gain the basic skills. Consider adopting this approach when engaging children with *'Pen-to-paper'* stories.

Websites

Anonymous (2012) *Ideas for Developing Writing in Your Setting.* [Online]. Available at: http://tinyurl.com/bqdcaho (Accessed: 14 April 2012).

This website has a valuable PDF that offers a wealth of practical ideas linked to resources and practice to promote writing in the classroom and in other 'spaces' in the early years setting (3–5). Consider integrating ideas from this PDF into your learning and teaching as children engage in select *'Pen-to-paper'* stories.

Parents in Touch (n.d.) *Help Your Children 'Have fun with writing' . . . using imagination and creativity!* [Online]. Available at: http://tinyurl.com/cbfglmp (Accessed: 14 April 2012).

This website offers a comprehensive 'parent friendly' handout to help their children overcome spelling issues, difficulties with handwriting, and having a lack of imagination and creativity. Further ideas are also offered via active web links. Consider integrating ideas from these web links into your learning and teaching as children engage in select *'Pen-to-paper'* stories.

Idea 1.1: Shaped stories	**Suggested age group:** 3-year-olds to 11-year-olds

Explanation:

Many children are regularly faced with a blank piece of white rectangular paper which teachers ask them to 'fill' with a story. For some children their creative minds can be a little like the piece of paper: *blank**! *Shaped stories* not only help to kick-start children's imaginations, they are also very effective in helping to motivate children to *want* to put pen to paper. This Idea offers children paper which is cut into a variety of stimulating and interesting shapes, e.g. *crowns, dinosaur feet, dolls, IPods* and *cricket bats*. Children can either write on lines drawn *across* the shape or *in parallel to each side*; this encourages children, particularly those aged 5+, to think about the sentences they are writing, i.e. *will my sentence fit on one line or will I need to carry it on to the start of the next line?*

The cross-curricular benefits of shaped paper:

Jeppson and Myers-Walls (2010) suggest that working on shaped paper helps to build on children's skills and learning acquired from early play-based activities with shapes. Use *Shaped stories* to thus use and strengthen the mathematical knowledge in those children you teach.

Shaped story **suggestions:**

- Stories about *sports* (circular shaped paper to represent footballs, tennis balls and baseballs).
- Stories about a *warning*, e.g. a storm, traffic, people, or a haunted house (triangular paper to represent a warning road sign).
- The *rainy* day (cloud/raindrop shaped paper. An alternative could be an umbrella).
- *'Being a Star for a Day'* (star shaped paper).

Varying the shape:

- Offer regular 2-D shaped paper for children to write on, e.g. *crosses* (a 'bad day' story), *octagons* and *hearts* (a love story).
- Suggest irregular 2-D shapes for children to create themselves, e.g. *'splats'*, *foot/paw prints* and *puddles*.
- See Appendix 1 (p. 207) for some interested shaped ideas.

Shaped stories **– practical recommendations:**

- Encourage children to shape the paper themselves with hand-drawn lines, rulers and snips/scissors (as appropriate) to develop and hone their fine motor/manipulative skills (3–11).
- Provide writing guidelines if you do not want children to draw their own lines on their shaped paper (3–7).
- Offer larger line-spacing on *Shaped story* papers for children aged 3–5 to mark-make on.
- Save *Shaped story* paper offcuts and use as 'jotter' paper for children's story ideas, attempts at difficult spellings and bookmarks (7–11).

Useful 'shaped' websites:

1. For some useful 'time-saving' shaped pages, visit http://tinyurl.com/d7rpax8
2. *To help children aged 5–11 overcome 'writer's block', offer them writing prompts that are available from http://tinyurl.com/crfjp5j, e.g. '[w]rite a story about something that has been recycled, like a can . . . or plastic bag, and its adventures along the way', shaping the paper as appropriate.

Idea 1.2: Sized stories	Suggested age group: 3-year-olds to 11-year-olds

Explanation:

As has been previously highlighted in *Shaped stories* (p. 36), children are often presented with A4 pieces of plain paper on which they are to record their stories. *Sized stories* adapt the Idea of *Shaped stories* by altering the *size* of the paper that children are asked to write on. Both teachers and children can be creative with the dimensions of the paper – *from the long and narrow to the short and broad*! In fact, by combining *Shaped stories* with *Sized stories*, teachers have access to a potential wealth of story possibilities to help children unlock their writing creativity!

Types *of Sized story*:

- *Long stories* – involving characters with long parts of their body (think *Mr. Tickle* by Hargreaves, 1971), e.g. legs/arms (3–7); stories of a substantial length over several chapters (7–11).
- *Thin stories* – stories involving one small story plot (5–7); short stories that compel children to write sentences which are formed over a number of lines (7–11).
- *Big stories* – stories with an ensemble of characters that are located in different settings and are involved in a number of different storylines (7–11).
- *Wide stories* – written on wide pieces of paper which encourage a number of sentences to appear on one line (5–7); stories with titles that have a 'wide' range of ways that the story could develop and progress, e.g. *Freddy's Magical House Move*; *The Silent Singing Competition* (7–11).
- *Broad stories* – mark-making on large sheets of thick paper/card with 'broad' (thick) felt-tip pens (3–5); stories involving strong, muscular or 'bulky' characters – think *The Hulk* (5–11).
- *Tiny stories* – simple, short stories (e.g. *My Pets*) for the younger reader written by the younger writer (3–7).
- *Slim stories* – stories written on narrow pieces of paper with fine (thin) pencils/pens (7–11).

Capturing the *process* and *product* of children's story writing:

Children aged 5–11 are likely to be encouraged to plan out story ideas, produce story drafts, test out spellings and then produce a 'final version' of their story using different writing books, jotters or separate pieces of paper. Consider offering children a large A2/A3 sheet of paper that they can use to work on their *Large story*; this will allow them to capture both the *process* and the *product* in one informative document, which can be useful for assessment purposes (both formative and summative).

Stimulating *Sized story* titles:

Fagerlie (1975) claims that brand names help to stimulate children's story writing. Consider integrating these into *Sized story* titles to inspire young writers, for example:

1. Long John Silver's enormous rocket ride adventure to the planet *Nike*!
2. Tiddly Tom's gone and lost his tiny *Disney* voice!
3. Wendy's wide *McDonald* mouth!
4. Captain Sam's skiing holiday on the huge slopes of *Ugg*!
5. Harry the hamster's new *Mattel* activity wheel!

Idea 1.3: Colour stories	**Suggested age group:** 5-year-olds to 11-year-olds

Explanation:

Personal observations of writing practice in primary schools highlight that most children are used to writing stories on white paper. *Colour stories* make one small yet significant change to this paper provision by giving children the opportunity to record their stories on paper of different colours. Not only is this considered to be 'visually stimulating' for both the writer *and* the reader, but the choice of colour can influence the *type* of story the children write (see table below) and *what* they actually write*.

*Colours, what they symbolise and associated story genres/age bandings:

Colour	What the colour symbolises	Associated story genres	Age
Red	Action, confidence, courage	Adventure, suspense, fantasy	7–11
Pink	Love and beauty	Fairy tale, fantasy, romance	5–11
Brown	Earth, order and convention	Stories from other cultures	5–11
Orange	Vitality and endurance	Classic, inspirational, nature, drama	7–11
Yellow	Wisdom, joy and happiness	Traditional, humour	5–11
Green	Life, nature and well-being	Historical, western, truth, country life	7–11
Blue	Youth, truth and peace	Myths, personal, realistic	7–11
Purple	Royalty, magic and mystery	Fantasy, mystery, science fiction	7–11

(Information adapted from Emily Gems, n.d.)

Using colour to stimulate stories:

- Possible *Colour stories* children could write include 'The day the world turned blue'; 'My big red balloon'; 'An orange envelope for me?'; 'Sam and his multi-coloured rabbit' (5–7).
- For children aged 7–11 *Colour story* possibilities include extended stories about events in characters' lives over the four 'colourful' seasons, stories where characters decide to inject some 'colour' (excitement/adventure) into their lives, or stories which include 'colourful' idioms, for example *see red* and *tickled pink* (see Townend, 2012).
- Encourage children (7–11) to think about colours when describing characters, e.g. the colour of their eyes (*piercing blue*), their teeth (*yellowing*), their hair (*bright orange*), their clothes (*jet black*) – how do these colour choices shape the way readers perceive them as characters?
- Bolton (in Bolton et al. 2006) advocates getting children to '[w]rite a blue, purple or yellow thought' with coloured paper and pens as a writing warm-up activity. Encourage children (9–11) to use these as the thoughts of different characters in their *Colour stories*.

Colour stories considerations:

1. *Colour stories* may pose some difficulties for children who have dyslexia, e.g. issues with paper glare and the 'dazzling' effect of certain colours. The use of pastel colours not only supports these children, but they are also seemingly of benefit for *all* children as they are considered to be 'less distracting to the mental concentration of each stage of [children's] development' (Steiner, cited in Atkinson, 2004).
2. Think about children who are colour-blind or who have other eyesight difficulties such as Meares-Irlen syndrome/scotopic sensitivity (visual stress). Consult with parents/carers and the children themselves to identify appropriate coloured resources to support their writing, e.g. coloured overlays and glass lenses. See http://tinyurl.com/cu522w7 for further information.

Idea 1.4: Tactile stories	Suggested age group: 3-year-olds to 9-year-olds

Explanation:

Teachers, particularly those working with 3–5-year-olds, would agree that children learn through activities that involve 'touch'. Popular children's story books by Carle (1969; 1984), Campbell (1984; 2009) and Emberley (1992) are attractive to young children because they have sensory features. *Tactile stories* aim to offer children the opportunity to write 'sensory stimulating' stories in an effort to maintain young writers' motivation levels and engage their readers, particularly those who are reluctant readers or those who are visually impaired.

Writing *Tactile stories* (3–5):

Young children will feel empowered as writers if they are able to adapt stories that have a strong structure. Stories such as *Are You My Mother?* (Eastman, 2006) and *'I Don't Care!' said the Bear* (West, 1997) have predictable repetitive content and use recurring words to make the text memorable and easy to comprehend. Help young children to identify these functional carrier phrases in simple stories, e.g. 'I see a _____ looking at me' (*Brown Bear, Brown Bear, What Do You See?* Martin, Jnr. 1995), using these as a frame for their own writing e.g. *I see a* **hen** *looking at me.*

Tactile stories and 'tangible' vocabulary (5–9):

The writing of *Tactile stories* offers children the opportunity to extend their vocabulary and vary their starter sentences. Sensory boxes, feely games and handling textured objects/materials will help children to develop an understanding of tactile adjectives which they can use, e.g. 'Harry's dad has a *fuzzy* chin'; 'Doggy put his *wet* nose on Bethany's foot' (5–7). Tactile adverbs can also be used to begin sentences, e.g. '*Roughly*, David dried himself'; '*Softly*, Gemma crept down the stairs' as opposed to children's sentences typically starting with the names of people, things or places (7–9).

Tactile stories and the importance of illustrations:

For a *Tactile story* to be effective they need to 'feature illustrations that can be explored and perceived . . . through touch. Tactile elements [should] allow . . . children to feel, stroke, pull, lift, shake, rattle and squeak their way through a story' (Clearvision, 2006). Practical ways to achieve this include:

- Layering materials to emphasise thickness.
- Using real life objects.
- Offering raised outlines using pipe cleaners or wool.
- Cutting out textured silhouette shapes.
- Filling an outline with a 'dotted' surface using small paper balls or holes poked through the back of card.

Top tip! Visit http://tinyurl.com/6v36t5a for a wealth of downloadable 'tactile' ideas.

Making *Tactile story* text tactile:

Not only are there ways to make story illustrations tactile but also the story text that children write. Practical ways this can be achieved include:

- Very thick paint.
- Words made out of yarn.
- Felt-tip pen lines on sponge paper.
- Glitter mixed into thick glue.
- Sandpaper letters (derived from the Montessori Method – see http://tinyurl.com/7zcnrcn).

Read it! See http://tinyurl.com/7ajdwct for a wonderful PDF on making tactile books.

Idea 1.5: Body stories	Suggested age group: 5-year-olds to 7-year-olds

Explanation:

Many of the stories that children write are unfortunately 'locked away' in their literary books. This means that opportunities for their work to be read and reviewed by others is limited to when teachers mark their work, parents/carers scan their books at Parents' Evening, or when children flick through their book to start work on a 'clean page'. *Body stories* not only use the body as 'story stimuli' (Buttery and Reitzammer, 1987), but also use different body parts as a living 'display board' on which children's written stories can be worn. This not only promotes the purposeful exposure of children's story writing but offers opportunities for others to read and comment on what they have read to the author in an effort to raise writers' motivation* levels!

*The importance of motivation for young writers – *key findings from academic research*:

Reilly and Reilly (2005: xvi) suggest that 'the best way of motivating children to write is to . . . encourage them to share their writing with others'. *Body stories* actively promote this sharing of children's writing by using the author as the promoter[†]!

Pudewa (2008: 1) argues a reader's reaction to a piece of writing has a direct impact on the writer: 'a positive response . . . will motivate the writer to continue presenting his words . . . to his audience'. It is therefore suggested that children who receive encouraging feedback from others about their story writing are more likely to want to write *more* stories. Consider the value of using *Body stories* in an effort to keep young children writing.

[†]Promoting *Body stories* – 'display board' possibilities:

There are various items children can make and wear to display their *Body stories*; these include *sashes, hats, wristbands, belts, ankle bracelets, headbands* and *necklaces* (discuss with children appropriate materials to make these out of). Allow children to see how much physical space they have to write their *Body story* on so that they can think about the length of story they can write, as this will influence the number of characters they can have in their story and the complexity of the plot.

Body stories and real life experiences:

Children experience life through their bodies, e.g. *feeling poorly, taking part in running races, breaking bones, dancing at a disco, picking up heavy boxes, swimming 25 metres, grazing one's elbows/knees*. Through speaking and listening opportunities invite children to contribute to whole class/group discussions about favourite body parts or *what makes my body special* in an effort to stimulate *Body story* thinking.

Various story titles to stimulate *Body stories*:

1. Bethany's bulging biceps save the day!
2. Little Rabbit Foo Foo's talking foot!
3. King Rollo's mighty BTM (*bottom*)!
4. Kalvin and his wibbly wobbly tummy!
5. Abdulmalik's *huge* headband!
6. Cinderella's amazing knees!
7. The Money Monster's purse nose!
8. Helen's hollow legs on Halloween!

| **Idea 1.6: Bedroom stories** | **Suggested age group:** 3-year-olds to 11-year-olds |

Explanation:

A child's bedroom is *the* place where many 'authors of the future' are exposed to a wealth of different stories in written, verbal and pictorial form; Heath (1982: 51) supports this, describing bedtime stories as 'a major literacy event' in children's lives. *Bedroom stories* are designed to emulate a similar level of importance in relation to getting children writing. *Bedroom stories* not only offer children a productive space at home for them to think and write in, they also offer a wealth of story possibilities for writing activities in the classroom!

Bedrooms as *the* writing space for authors:

Smedley (2011) argues that 'you write best where you're most comfortable':

1. Former Children's Laureate Michael Morpurgo (*Private Peaceful*) states that he writes his 'scribbly script' in a 'writing bed' in his 'storyteller's house' (see http://tinyurl.com/6ddzfqs for more information).
2. During his early years, Robert Louis Stevenson (*Treasure Island*) spent much of his time in bed as a result of tuberculosis, and there composed stories *before* he had learned to read.

Try it! Offer children blankets, pillows and teddy bears during literacy activities/sessions to nurture/improve stories written in the classroom and in the outdoor play area/playground (3–7).

Story stimulation in the bedroom:

A child's bedroom offers some cracking stimuli for fuelling story writing:

- *The bed* – who's underneath it? What's hidden under the mattress/pillow? What's inside that dusty old box/chest at the bottom of it? Who sleeps in it during the daytime? Why?
- *The wardrobe* – who lives in it? What's stored in it? What's behind it? Who do people see when they look in the mirror attached to the wardrobe (think *Snow White*)? Where does it lead to if you stepped into the wardrobe (think *The Lion, the Witch & the Wardrobe*)?
- *Teddy bears* – which of them can talk? Who is the friendliest/meanest (think *Toy Story*)?
- *Clothing* – which pieces give you special powers when you put them on? Do you have any magical footwear like Dorothy's ruby slippers (from *The Wizard of Oz*)?

Addressing the issue of reluctant writers:

Many teachers work with children across the 3–11 age range who write the bare minimum or will only write their *Bedroom story* (as an example) when a teacher/parent/carer is next to them. Graham (2010: 206) claims that there are two reasons why young writers behave like this: 'anxiety about getting it wrong and a shortage of ideas'. Ways to positively address this include:

- Encourage children to just 'HAG it' – *Have A Go*.
- Use computers/tablets as a writing incentive.
- Set small 'challenges', e.g. *write two sentences in three minutes . . . GO!*
- Encourage children to talk about what they are going to write *before* they put pen to paper.
- Maintain high writing expectations.
- Encourage peer reviewing of children's writing.
- Offer literacy aids, e.g. spelling books, scribble pads, alphabet strips or key word cards for support.

Idea 1.7: Bathroom stories	**Suggested age group:** 3-year-olds to 11-year-olds

Explanation:

Children get so used to mark-making/writing stories at school they sometimes think that this is the *only* place where they can/should write stories. Many authors, however, write at home; novelist Julia Green, for example, admits to moving her laptop around her house and 'writ[ing] in different rooms' (Cyprus Well, 2010). *Bathroom stories* embrace this practice by offering children a stimulating opportunity to use the bathroom as an unusual yet interesting place to write their stories in and present them for other family members to read!

Creative story writing opportunities in the bathroom:

There are a number of ways children can become creative story writers in their bathroom at home:

1. Writing on steamed-up mirrors using their fingers as their writing tool (ensuring that the mirror is positioned low and poses no threat to the child's safety) to continue rhyming strings, e.g. **wet** – *get* – *let* – *set* – *pet* – *met* – *bet* – *jet* – *net* (3–7).
2. Pasting moist paper with stories written on them onto the bathroom tiles with water (5–7).
3. Taping written stories to the inside toilet lid so that male family members have something to read. For the ladies in the house stories can be taped to the back of the bathroom door (7–11).
4. Laminating stories for different family members to read whilst they have a bath (5–11).
5. Using foam/sponge letters to create simple words/sentences on the inside of the bath (3–5).
6. Hanging small self-made story books off bathroom hooks/rails so that bathroom users have something to read as they wash themselves (5–11).
7. Mark-making/writing stories on old shower curtains* (3–11).

> It is acknowledged that there are a number of health and safety considerations linked to the ideas presented above which need to be effectively managed to ensure that children do not come to any harm. Do make parents/carers aware of these when proposing *Bathroom stories* as Weekend Work (home tasks/homework) for children.

Useful online 'bathroom-linked' stories to stimulate *Bathroom story* discussions (7–11):

- 7–9: *Nasty bathrooms* by Josie – available at http://tinyurl.com/78ptofw.
- 9–11: *Fancy Nancy and the Bathroom Plant* by R. Craft – available at http://tinyurl.com/87mhbpz.

Stimulating *Bathroom story* titles to spark children's imaginations:

- 'Duncan's fallen down the plughole, Mum!'
- Suzie and the talking toilet!
- The Super Seven's battle of the baths!
- My *hundreds and thousands* shower!
- Monica's mirror-less reflection!
- The secret sink ride to the South Pole!

Top Tips!

- Encourage children to think carefully about the best time to use the bathroom for their writing ventures – first thing in the morning and last thing at night are usually busy times!
- *'Be sure to test . . . dry-erase marker[s] on any new surface you intend to mark with [as] some surfaces don't erase very well' (Wax, 2011).

Idea 1.8: Kitchen stories	Suggested age group: 3-year-olds to 11-year-olds

Explanation:

The role of the kitchen in modern households today is very different to that of kitchens 20 or 30 years ago; in years gone by kitchens were the 'hub' of activity, and stories were shared freely with family members/carers and friends in verbal form during meal times. This Idea strives to support children in appreciating the wealth of stimulating possibilities that the kitchen can offer their story writing when in class and at home.

Developing the Idea of *Kitchen stories* for children aged 3–5:

- Encourage children to physically write stories through 'marks that have meaning' (Hallissy, 2010: 3), e.g. marks made by fingers in salt (Marquess, 2011), flour or seeds which are sprinkled over the kitchen table at home. Alternatives to using the kitchen table include a food tray, a place mat or a marked area of the floor.
- Suggest children use their kitchen table at home as their 'special' story writing space.
- Ask children to tell stories through pictures/marks that can be presented on paper placemats for parents/carers to read/discuss at mealtimes where possible/appropriate.

Ways of 'promoting' *Kitchen stories* at home for children aged 5–7:

1. Encourage children to display their written stories on the fridge with magnets for parents/carers and other family members to read and comment on.
2. Suggest that children glue/paste their story writing efforts on the side of cereal boxes and soap-powder packets for heightened exposure.
3. Don't forget the kitchen memo board for a quick five-minute story!

'What if . . .' *Kitchen stories* and inspiring appliances for children aged 7–11:

There are many kitchens appliances which offer valuable plot stimulation for children's (7–11) story writing:

- *Microwave* – what if the microwave is a time machine? What if it could talk/sing?
- *Cooker* – what if the cooker is a porthole to the Ribbon Dimension? What if the cooker is a house for a 'googly' alien? What if the cooker is a secret Transformer?
- *Washing machine* – what if the washing machine could turn soap powder into sweets?
- *Kettle* – what if the kettle had legs? What if it had hidden rockets which propelled it into the air when someone wanted to make a cup of tea? What if it uses steam to write words in the air with (think of the Hookah-Smoking Caterpillar in *Alice In Wonderland*)?
- *Ironing board* – what if it can 'morph' into a surfboard? What if it could shrink and fit in a child's pocket? What if it behaved like a scared cat? What if it could play the piano?

Wonderful *Kitchen story* website:

Visit *The Story Kitchen* by Van Patter (available at http://tinyurl.com/ccvpsnn) – children aged 5–11 can virtually 'cook' together a hero, a place and a villain to generate the opening to a story. But they do not get the complete story – ***they*** have to write the ending!

Idea 1.9: Living room stories	**Suggested age group:** 7-year-olds to 11-year-olds

Explanation:

Many children use their living room/communal area at home as a place to 'chill'; a place where they can listen to music, read or watch TV. Some living rooms, however, have become excessively 'active' with the introduction of *Wiis*, dance mats and other gaming consoles (Sall and Grinter, 2007). *Living room stories* introduce children to the idea of using their living room as both a place to write *about* and to write *in*. *Living room stories* promote the switching off of radios, CD players and computers, and encourage children to use the living room environment, both real and imagined*, as stimuli to fuel their story writing.

*Different types of living room environments:

There are many different types of living rooms which can offer stimulation for children's story writing (9–11). Examples include:

- *Modern* – what makes it modern? Who lives in it? Are they young? What do they do in it?
- *Cluttered* – what different things are 'hoarded' by the character whose living room it is?
- *Old fashioned* – why/how is it old fashioned? How old is the person/people living in it?
- *Small* – is *everything* small in the living room? Is this a problem for the main character?
- *Art nouveau* – what design is on the stained glass windows? Which flowers are on the walls?

A rather 'novel' idea:

Many teachers and children (7–11) are aware of Reading Groups or Book Clubs – groups of people who get together to talk about a book they have all read (O'Donnell-Allen, 2006). The *Story Club* is an adaptation of these gatherings where family members/carers can get together in their living room or communal space and talk about the stories that children have written.

Stimulating story titles for *Living room stories*:

- A snowman came for morning coffee!
- The attack of the killer armchairs!
- The Sunday dinner mash-up!
- 'Henry's lost the TV remote!'
- The 'living' room coffee table!
- The vocal living room carpet!

'*Getting started*!' Using story spinners:

Overcoming the initial writing hurdle of 'getting started' can be difficult for children when they are asked to write a story such as a *Living room story*. Story spinners are an active and quick way to offer children some initial ideas to work with. The spinners are simply pieces of hexagonal shaped card with a pencil or piece of dowel pushed through the centre*. On each spinner is written a collection of different ideas related to a key element of a story, e.g. 'main characters, setting[s], problem[s] . . . [and] ending[s]' (Baumann and Bergeron, 1993: 413). See Appendices 2 and 3 (p. 208 and 209) for examples of different spinners for children aged 5–7 – the spinners should be laminated for durability. A blank template is also offered Appendix 4 (p. 210) for children/teachers to photocopy to create their own.

*Top Tip! As an alternative, spin a paperclip (acting as a 'pointer') around a pencil/piece of dowel which is positioned over the centre of the story spinner.

Idea 1.10: Garden stories	Suggested age group: 3-year-olds to 11-year-olds

Explanation:

An interesting place for children to write and get inspiration for their story writing is the garden (Babauta, 2012); according to James (2010), Roald Dahl wrote his stories in a shed at the bottom of his garden! *Garden stories* offer children plenty of exciting choices to make about their story, e.g. shall I set my story *in* or *under* a garden? What kind of characters will be in my *Garden story – humans? Animals? Plants? Personified garden tools?* What is the theme of my *Garden story* to be – *growth? Beauty? Circle of life? Man against nature?* Opportunities for children to 'sit and ponder' in their garden* will help them to get 'closer to nature' (London, 2004: 41) and give them time to make these choices!

*Key consideration for *Garden stories*:

It is acknowledged that some children may not have a garden where they live. This certainly does not preclude them from having access to 'garden-like' environments – visits to the local park, woods or nature park offer valuable alternatives. Small-world garden play, story books set in gardens (e.g. the BBC's *In the Night Garden*) and garden role-play areas can be found/used in classrooms for 3–7-year-olds; window boxes, school allotments and access to non-fiction books and images from the Internet offer alternatives for children aged 7–11.

'Planting the seeds' – questions to stimulate *Garden stories*:

*   *Flowers* – what if the flowers can talk? What language would they speak? Do they have names?
*   *Shed* – what if the shed was a *Shardis* (a combination of a **sh**ed and Doctor Who's **T**ardis) – where might it take the travellers?
*   *Soil* – is there anything buried under the soil? Who lives *in* the soil? What's lurking deep *within* the soil?
*   *Pond* – why are there no fish in the pond? What's hiding at the bottom of the pond?

Useful online/paperback *garden*-related stories (5–11):

For the 5–7 age range	For the 7–11 age range
The Butterfly Garden by Margaret Mahy – available at http://tinyurl.com/7lt52jy	*Millie's Garden* by Pam Zollman – available at http://tinyurl.com/773rqew
The Tale of Peter Rabbit by Potter (1991)	*The Secret Garden* by Burnett (1994)

'Steps in the garden' – the Story Stepper planner:

The Story Stepper is a personal adaptation of Corbett's (2003) story mountain. A Story Stepper is a visual planning aid which helps teachers and children (5–11) to consider the 'goings-on' in their stories (their *Garden story* being a prime example). On each step children can write a word, a phrase, a sentence, a short paragraph or a drawing/sketch to help them work out the sequence of events in their story. Alternatively, Post-it® notes can be used to temporarily fix ideas to the planner. See Appendix 5 (p. 211) for an example of a *Garden story* based Story Stepper (5–7 and 7–11); Appendix 6 (p. 212) offers a blank template for teachers and children to photocopy and use.

Suggestion! Encourage children to create their own Story Steppers using freehand or ICT software.

2

'Design and Make' stories

The notion of *Design and Make*, the former EYFS aspect of learning (DCSF, 2008a), and *Design and Technology*, its NC equivalent (DfEE/QCA, 1999; DfE, 2011a), are used as the overarching theme for the Ideas presented in this second chapter. It will highlight ways in which Design and Technology can be used to facilitate stimulating story writing opportunities for children across the 3–11 age phase.

The first half of the chapter aims to energise children's story writing by linking initial Ideas to books, a key product that is heavily associated with both stories and Design and Technology-based activity (see *Booked stories* and *Story books*). *Design stories* encourage children to use 'a taxonomy of . . . problem solving strategies' (Roden, 1997: 14) by writing stories which involve characters designing and making in response to problems they encounter. *Box stories* and *Gamed stories* serve to support children at the 'prep' stage of their story writing, offering an innovative approach to story planning (*Box stories*) and an assortment of storymaking games (*Gamed stories*) which can be used to help children 'design' (plan) their story through exciting idea generation.

The second half of the chapter recognises select knowledge, skills and understanding that children acquire through Design and Technology activities, embracing and integrating these into story writing provision. *Un-folded stories*, *Twist stories* and *Construction stories* use various resources to help children literally 'build' their narratives, whilst *Moving stories* serve to maintain both the reader's and writer's interest by bringing story plot, character development and speech to life with interactive physical features. The final Idea of this chapter (*Recycled stories*) considers ways in which the notion of recycling can be used to make a physical record of written stories, and helps children to generate new stories from those already known and the story characters established within them.

Taking a closer look at 'the problems they face'

In *Design stories* (p. 54) the point is made that good stories have a problem that a character must solve. Bensko (2010) suggests that this is particularly evident in traditional fiction where plots are based upon 'a problem and solution'. It is useful to be aware of this, as this is principally the kind of fiction that children are going to encounter in the classroom – through the stories that are verbally told to them, the story books that children read, and the stories that they are encouraged to write.

Problems are important because they ensure that something actually happens in a story; they help to 'fuel' the story plot with drama, tension and humour (depending on what the problem is), giving the story substance, momentum and direction to its conclusion where the problem is solved, addressed or resolved. This is clearly evident in examples of well-known children's stories:

- 3–5: Neligan's pig, who gets hotter and hotter in the sunshine, suddenly jumps in the pond to cool down (*The Pig in the Pond* by Waddell, 2006).
- 5–7: Pinkerton has to 'care' for the sand witch before he realises that first is not always best (*Me First* by Lester, 1992).
- 7–11: Jim Hawkins has to elude the pirates and bring home the gold from *Treasure Island* (Stevenson, 2005).

This is not to say that all problems in stories have to be resolved at the end (although it can be frustrating for the reader if this does not happen) – characters can come up against another problem (known as a *subsidiary* or *secondary* problem) which they have to address *first* before they can address the *main/primary* problem, e.g. a man gets a phone call to say his wife has gone into labour (the main problem being he cannot get to the hospital because he has broken his leg) when he suddenly finds water leaking through the bathroom floor (the subsidiary problem – although quite a major one at that)! Dunbar (2012) refers to problems as 'story fodder', arguing that they come in two forms: 'big action packed ones' and 'little problems'. See Table 2.1 for examples.

Table 2.1   Examples of the two forms of 'story fodder' (Dunbar, 2012)

Big action-packed problems	Little problems
Finding oneself lost in the desert	Not being able to button one's coat up
Trying to escape from the jaws of an evil dragon	Trying to find one's lost bedtime bear
Finding someone has stolen all of your money	Forgetting to take one's muddy shoes off before entering the house
Losing one's superpowers	Accidentally knocking over a glass of milk
Finding one's house full of giant lizards	Waking up the baby by playing computer games too loudly

Teachers and children are likely to come across different words and terms that are used to refer to the 'problem' in stories, examples of which include *conflicts, troubles, dilemmas, difficulties, issues, predicaments, quandaries* and *crises*. The pluralisation of the words/terms offered above is deliberate because in short stories (3–7) there is usually only one problem that characters encounter whereas in more substantial stories (extended stories and novels – 7–11) there are many problems. An effort to 'Embrace the *Conflict*', as recommended by Fields (2008b), will be evident in the remainder of this chapter introduction.

An important point to remember is that conflict in stories does not always mean physical/verbal combat (although it could do – think *Harry Potter* or *Lord of the Rings*) but refers more to the idea of a character's struggle, be it something of either an *external* or *internal* nature (see Table 2.2).

Table 2.2 Examples of external and internal conflict (adapted from Baudet, 2011)

Type of struggle	Definition	Examples
External	A struggle against an outside force	The character against . . . • other people; e.g. *parent, sibling, teacher, friend* • animals; e.g. *wild animal, spider, dinosaur, next door's cat* • illness; e.g. *of a parent, friend or self* • weather; e.g. *blizzards, thunderstorms, droughts* • nature; e.g. *an earthquake, an avalanche, rapids* • the surrounding environment; e.g. *wars, revolution, demonstrations or riots, the desert, the jungle.*
Internal	A struggle within the character's mind	The character's . . . • guilt and struggle with their conscience – *should I have stolen that bread from that old lady?* • fear and lack of confidence – *I'm scared! I'm not going to pass my gymnastics exam!* • indecision – *should I go to Sammy's party or Paula's?* • temptation – *I know I've already had seven cream cakes but I want another one!* • depression – *I've got no friends to play with!* • divided loyalties – *Jack does not want me to talk to Greg but Greg is my best buddy!*

The information in Table 2.2 serves as a valuable summary and can be used to support learning and teaching opportunities where teachers highlight different types/examples of conflict in the stories that are read and written in the classroom. Litvin (1975: 1) emphasises the importance of conflict in story writing by arguing that '[c]onflict is the basis of all stories and thus should appear in some form in the first sentence'; in response to this, a range of practical strategies are offered below to help teachers raise children's awareness, understanding and application of conflict in the stories that they discuss, read and write:

- 3–7: Get children to talk about things that happen to them during their day/weekend – *what problems did they encounter and what did they do about them?* Keep a visual/written record of these where possible.

- 5–11: Play *Jack's Problem Chain*, which involves the teacher starting off a verbal story about a boy who *always* has some kind of problem (e.g. he has lost his keys; he gets stuck in the toilet bowl; his football is flat). Invite children to problem solve (e.g. what could Jack do to address the problem he has encountered?). Ideas that children offer should be countered by the teacher or other children with *another* problem; how long can the 'chain of problems' continue before the children/teacher run out of contributing 'links'?

- 5–11: McDougal (n.d.) suggests offering authors the beginning of a story and letting them continue it by 'stirring in' a specified example of external or internal conflict (see box below).

Rashid sighed. So far it had been a perfect day for a picnic. Everyone in his family had been having a great time. But suddenly . . .

External conflict with nature: _____

_____

_____

_____

- 5–11: Provide children with a selection of picture story books (5–7) or extracts from stories (7–11), challenging them to read and sort them into different types of conflict being used to drive the story plot (external/internal).

- 7–11: Use Weekend Work opportunities to get children to log the number of times certain types/examples of conflict appear in the TV programmes/videos they watch.

- 5–11: Macon et al. (1991) suggest that teachers should model the use of a *'Somebody . . . Wanted . . . But . . . So . . .'* chart to help children map out the conflict in the stories they read/write (see Table 2.3).

Table 2.3 Example of a *Somebody . . . Wanted . . . But . . . So . . .* chart

	Somebody . . .	Wanted . . .	But . . .	So . . .
Explanation	The character's name	What the character wanted	The conflict that prevented the character from getting what he or she wanted	What the character did about this
Example	*Harry . . .*	*wanted some yummy chocolate . . .*	*but his mum told him that it was late and he needed to go to bed . . .*	*so Harry went to bed, stuck his hand inside his pillow case and pulled out a bar of yummy chocolate Grandma had told him to keep hidden from Harry's mum!*

To further support teachers, select readings and websites are offered below to develop teachers' understanding of conflict in stories and provide practical strategies to help children effectively use conflict in their written stories:

- **Article:** 'Don't Get Slighted' by Fields (2008a) – available at http://tinyurl.com/c8x5ry5 – an interesting article that highlights the importance of conflict in stories.

- **Research:** 'Children's Construction of fantasy stories: Gender differences in conflict resolution strategies' by Peirce and Edwards (1988) – available at http://tinyurl.com/d9c4r8h – an interesting research article about gender differences in conflict resolution in children's writing of fantasy stories.

- **Professional resource:** *Using Picture Books to Teach Plot Conflict* by ReadWriteThink (2004) – available at http://tinyurl.com/c9yogk8 – a useful 'step-by-step guide' for teaching children about different types of conflict.

Note! Stories do not usually end until the conflict faced by the story characters has been resolved (Sheppard, 2011). It is therefore important to support children in understanding about conflict resolution and help them to apply this to their story writing. This is explored in the introduction to *'Creative' stories* (Chapter 9, p. 171).

Table 2.4   Recommended readings associated with *'Design and Make' stories*

Books	Johnson, P. (2008) *Get Writing! Creative Book-making Projects for Children, Ages 7–12*. London: A&C Black.
	This book practically shows how children can combine words, images and paper engineering to make books as stimulating as those that they enjoy reading and engaging with. Consider the value of this book in supporting your *'Design and make'* story provision in your writing classroom.
	Diehn, G. (2006) *Making Books*. Asheville, NC: Lark Books.
	This book contains a wonderful collection of ideas for children (and teachers) to make books that fly, fold, wrap, hide, pop up, twist and turn! Consider the value of this book in supporting your *'Design and make'* story provision in your writing classroom.

Research journal articles

Elbow, P. (1993) The war between reading and writing – and how to end it. *Rhetoric Review*, 12 (1), 5-24. [Online]. Available at: http://tinyurl.com/4y6jh3p (Accessed: 22 April 2012).

This fascinating paper argues for a better balance and relationship between reading and writing by giving more emphasis to writing in our teaching and using writing in more imaginative ways. Consider its application in today's classrooms in relation to the Ideas offered within this second chapter.

Flutter, J. (2000) *Words Matter – Thinking and Talking about Writing in the Classroom*. [Online]. Available at: http://tinyurl.com/cg55c35 (Accessed: 22 April 2012).

This interesting article highlights the importance of presenting story writing tasks to primary school children in exciting and imaginative ways (through *'Design and make' stories,* for example); *evidence suggests that this sparks children's interests and 'motivate[s] them to put in extra effort' (p. 5).* Consider its application in today's classrooms in relation to the ideas offered within this second chapter.

Websites/web links

Walton, R. (2002) *Coming Up With Story Ideas*. [Online]. Available at: http://tinyurl.com/bwwpku4 (Accessed: 22 April 2012).

This website offers a wealth of different starting points for teachers to use with children to generate story ideas, examples of which include 'Start with a quest or problem' (*see* Taking a closer look: 'the problems they face' – p. 47), 'Start with a thing' and 'Start with a phrase'. Consider integrating the ideas on this website into your *'Design and make'* story provision.

Baum, L. (2011) *Idea Generation*. [Online]. Available at: http://tinyurl.com/cmyxmfz (Accessed: 22 April 2012).

This web link offers an interesting PDF about how to promote idea generation in the classroom (see Gamed stories, p. 58). Activities are offered to help thinkers generate a multitude of unique and novel ideas. Consider using these ideas to support the *'Design and make'* stories children write in your classroom.

Idea 2.1: Design stories	Suggested age group: 5-year-olds to 11-year-olds

Explanation:

This Idea embraces the definition offered by Hoff (1997), who suggests that *Design stories* 'are relatively short stories explaining a design or idea people . . . found useful in solving a problem'. As all good stories have a problem which is resolved during the tale (see Warren, 2007), *Design stories* can be used to support those children whose stories lack the 'problematic' element. Children who write *Design stories* must ensure that the difficulty characters encounter[†] has to be overcome by them designing and making something[*]. The story should explain how characters came up with their ideas, what materials, tools and processes they used, and how they evaluated/modified their design.

[†]The problems characters could encounter:

Problems in stories are usually referred to as 'conflict' – see http://tinyurl.com/6u2nt4c for an engaging explanation of conflict suitable for children aged 7–11. There are different types of conflict that children should be progressively made aware of:

Conflict type	Detail
Interpersonal (5–7)	Conflict based on arguments and fights with those close to the character e.g. siblings, friends, and with more distant enemies (e.g. cyber bullies, bosses).
Intrapersonal (7–11)	Conflict based on a character's personal fears and internal battles, e.g. fear of spiders, heights or depression.
Authority (5–11)	Conflict with different 'authorities' such as school staff, family, the police and the government.
Criminal (7–11)	Conflict with those who break the law, e.g. crime fighters (think *Batman* and *Wonder Woman*) who solve crimes and defeat the baddies.
Nature (5–11)	Conflict with the forces of nature, whereby characters fight against storms, tornadoes, freezing cold and scorching heat. Physical battles can take place on high mountains or in deep caves.
Machines (5–11)	Conflict with machines that characters have invented/built, e.g. cars, computers, gadgets and robots.
Supernatural (7–11)	Conflict with ghosts, aliens, vampires, monsters and witches.

Adapted from ChangingMinds (2011)

[*] *What* to design? *What* to make?:

An interesting *Design story* will see characters designing/making something that relates to the type of conflict that they encounter. Stimulate speaking and listening opportunities by getting children to establish the kind of characters who would design and make the following:

- *Interpersonal* – ear muffs to block out others' nagging; a child-proof safe to keep personal diaries away from 'prying eyes'.
- *Authority* – a 'Head teacher tracker' to let dozing boys know when the Head is coming into their classroom; a dodgem-style car to evade the police during a bumpy getaway.
- *Criminal* – a rainbow beam scanner that detects crimes being committed; a mindreading pair of glasses which 'bore' into the thoughts of wrong-doers.
- *Nature* – a water-filled suit which cools the body and offers a refreshing drink for those when hot; tornado boots that keep you rooted to the ground in very high winds.
- *Machines* – disablement chips and remotes; 'brainy' computers; 'dog bark' controlled cars.
- *Supernatural* – spirit traps; groovy graveyards for ghosts; monster vacuums (think *Ghostbusters*).

Idea 2.2: Booked stories	**Suggested age group:** 5-year-olds to 11-year-olds

Explanation:

The making of books is an established feature of Design and Technology and English provision across the 5–11 age range (see *Story Books*, p. 57; Johnson, 2000). Morpurgo (2003) suggests that 'stories [which can be recorded in these 'made' books] can change a life'. In an effort to support this claim, *Booked stories* allow children to think about books as an integral feature of the stories they write, considering how books affect the lives of the story characters they write about.

Making books an 'integral feature' of a story:

There are many ways that children across the 5–11 age phase can use books to influence the lives of characters they write about:

- *Knowledge* – characters who seek to learn something can make reference to non-fiction books, e.g. how to fly a plane, ways to cure an illness, or ideas on how to make a hat.
- *Entertain* (Campsall, 2009) – bored characters can choose an exciting book to 'get lost in', e.g. during a power cut Sammy chooses to read an exciting pirate story with a torch in a tent made out of his bed sheets.
- *Escapism* – characters who want a distraction from the stresses of their life can 'escape' into a story e.g. after a hard day's work the *Grinch* (Seuss, 2010) sits and reads a marvellous story about driving a huge steam train across Cuba.
- *Imagination* – characters who need creative inspiration can read story books, e.g. Emily wants to enter her school's story writing competition but needs some ideas. She reads *The Ghost of Gringe Hall* by (*enter child author's name here*) to get her creative juices flowing!

Further 'uses' of books in *Booked stories*:

Support children in recognising additional uses of books to stimulate their story writing. Examples include books being:

1. A *companion* (a magic talking book).
2. A *fortress* (built out of lots of hard backed books).
3. A *portal* (open the book and characters are sucked into the pages and are then 'spat out' into another world!).
4. A *step* (on which characters stand to reach something special/heavy/scary/dusty).
5. A *shelter* (for a small child/animal).

Booked story 'accessories':

There is a number of book 'accessories' which children can design and make. These can be used as interesting alternatives to the normal writing paper children write their stories on. Examples include:

5–7 age range		7–11 age range	
Accessory	*Purpose*	*Accessory*	*Purpose*
Bookmarks	For *very* short stories!	Book stands	To display book covers and story titles
Book bags (exterior)	For longer stories	Book flyers	To promote stories children have written for parents, carers and peers
Book jackets	To display story extracts or story blurbs	Book boxes	To store the stories children have written during the year

Idea 2.3: Box stories	Suggested age group: 3-year-olds to 11-year-olds

Explanation:

Writing stories is considered to be 'complex' (National Writing Project and Nagin, 2003: 9) and can be particularly difficult for young writers, especially when they are unsure of how long it will take for them to complete their story, both in terms of time and length. *Box stories* alleviate some of this concern by allowing children to write their story in linked boxes which are spread over the page (see Appendix 7, p. 213). This Idea promotes story mark-making (3–5) and the construction of simple and compound sentences whose length is dictated by the space available in each box. *Box stories* are particularly appealing for readers as they have to 'work' for their story by moving their eyes around the page as opposed to following typical conventions of reading left to right and top to bottom.

Box stories Q & A:

Q: What size of paper should children use for a *Box story*?	A: This is dependent on the age and abilities of your story writers. Ask *them* what size of paper they would like to work on.
Q: What if there are not enough boxes on the page for the children?	A: Attach another *Box story* template to the side of the one the children have been writing on and draw a linking line from the final box to the first box on the new page.
Q: How can I differentiate *Box stories* for the children I work with?	A: Differentiation strategies include: – the *number* of boxes the children have to write in; – the *size* of the boxes the children are to write in; – what children offer as evidence of their story writing e.g. *marks, pictures, sounds represented by letters, words, simple sentences, compound sentences*; – the *simplicity/complexity* of the story plot; – the number of *characters* in the story.

Young writers' response to Box stories – findings from the 'shop floor':

- The boxes help to 'break up' the page and the story that the children are writing on.
- The boxes encourage children to think carefully about story sequencing/structure (Morrow, 1984), e.g. *what does the reader need to know* first? *What must they be told* next? *What comes* after that?
- The *Box story* template can be used as a *planning tool* to sketch out their preliminary ideas (7–11), e.g. one box for *characters*, with others for *settings, plot ideas, conflict* etc.

Creative interpretations of Box stories:

Alternative ways of interpreting the Idea of *Box stories* include:

- 3–5: Save large cardboard boxes (washing machine, TV, fridge) and offer them to children as a physical 'space' for them to mark-make in – provide cushions and blankets for comfort!
- 5–7: Visit http://tinyurl.com/7jqjhqq to find out how to make a story box to stimulate children's storytelling and thus their story writing – see Campbell and Hlusek (2009) for research into the positive impact that storytelling can have on children's writing.

Idea 2.4: Story books	Suggested age group: 3-year-olds to 11-year-olds

Explanation:

A writer really *feels* like a bona fide author when they finally see their written work in print (a view based on personal experience!). For most children, few of them will get their work published in their lifetime so how can they really feel like an author? *Story books* is an established yet effective Idea that addresses this issue – instead of children having to wait for a publisher to print their work, they can self-publish *as they write*! Not only do *Story books* use children's design and make skills, hone fine motor skills and develop creative thinking, they also motivate children right across the 3–5 and 5–11 age phases to write stories (see http://tinyurl.com/c3jq6g8)!

Different types of *Story books*:

There are many different types of *Story books* which teachers and children can make. Simple *Story books* involve securing pieces of paper together using different fasteners, e.g. paper clips threaded through punched holes, paper fasteners or treasury tags (3–5). These can be shaped into *star* books, *rainbow* books or *heart* books, as long as children – and teachers – do not cut the fasteners off (5–7)! More intricate/complex *Story books* can also be made by children aged 7–11 (see Johnson, 2008).

Story book websites:

The selection of websites below offers some effective instructions on how to make simple yet effective *Story books* across the 3–11 age range:

- Making a simple 8-pagebook   http://tinyurl.com/crazwup
- Simple origami book   http://tinyurl.com/27lhn3
- How to make a book for kids   http://tinyurl.com/dxlmkwe
- Impromptu bookmaking   http://tinyurl.com/cht7ku7

Addressing the issue of weak story endings:

When teachers read children's stories in their *Story books* it is likely that they will encounter the following endings: *'And then he woke up!'*; *'They then went home for tea!'*; *'It was all a dream!'* and *'So that was the end of that!* Edwards (2004: 67) argues that story endings 'should be satisfying to the reader' and make us wish that the story did not have to end. Support children (5–11) at the planning stage of their story by using one of Edwards' 'natural and plausible' ending types (2004: 67):

1. *Reflective*, e.g. Sally wondered whether she should jump back into the golden pond again.

2. *Return to the beginning*, e.g. The vortex spun aggressively and then – WHOOSH! – shrivelled back into the blue stone which Sammy had accidently kicked on his way to school.

3. *Twist ending*, e.g. The bell did not sound again as a sign that the evil hamster would not return. But then, on a cold winter's morning, there was a slight *ting* heard in the air followed by the scurrying patter of tiny and *very* angry feet . . . !

4. *Final*, e.g. Amy and Greg had finally beaten the Paper Plane Monster and both agreed *never* to paper-fold again!

For further information about story endings, see the introduction to Chapter 10 (p. 188).

Idea 2.5: Gamed stories	**Suggested age group:** 5-year-olds to 11-year-olds

Explanation:

Denning (2009) suggests that '[n]arrative thrives on the disruptions from the ordinary, the unexpected, the conflicts, the deviations, the surprises, the unusual'. Whilst this certainly helps to fuel interesting stories it can be difficult sometimes for children to think of ideas that stray from the norm. This is where *Gamed stories* come in! *Gamed stories* are tales that are generated by children playing storymaking games; the ideas that emulate from these games can be captured on paper, a dictaphone or on video and used as a basis for children's story writing.

Storymaking for 5–7-year-olds:

Stimulating stories can be generated by children aged 5–7 playing storymaking games:

- *Unfortunately, Fortunately!* Add one sentence at a time that starts with either *Unfortunately* or *Fortunately* to tell a tale, e.g. Unfortunately *the car's engine failed.* Fortunately *the driver had a mobile phone.* Unfortunately *the phone had no battery . . .*
- *Maggie's cat!* Get children to take it in turns to describe Maggie's cat using an adjective that starts with a different letter of the alphabet, e.g. '*Maggie's cat is an* **a***ngry cat*'; '*Maggie's cat is a* **b***eautiful cat*' . . .
- *Muddy puddle moves!* Encourage children to physically imitate how they think different characters would move through a muddy puddle, e.g. an astronaut, a model, a farmer, a dancer, a drunk, a soldier, a singer. Consider why these different characters would be going through the muddy puddle!

Build your own bank of storymaking games to play with children by selecting and adapting ideas from the following website links: http://tinyurl.com/7mgvcsa and http://tinyurl.com/75dkdt7.

The *Class of Corbett* – storymaking games from the expert:

Corbett (2009) offers a wealth of practical games to stimulate children's (7–11) storymaking. Here are a selection of personal favourites:

- Improvise an oral telling of a story about '[t]hree young people [who] are sent out into the world to seek their fortune by an ageing parent. They return at the end' (2009: 43).
- Tell a short story in less than a minute around a story problem, e.g. the main character '. . . has a secret'; '. . . a dream that starts to come true'; '. . . is picked on' (2009: 80).
- Build descriptions of story settings by visualising additional features to those proposed by others, e.g. '*In the city of Rome is a park bench*'; '*In the city of Rome is a park bench* [under which] *is a sleeping dog*' (2009: 45).

Top Tip! Visit http://tinyurl.com/cm9qwyk for a useful PDF on creating a storymaking climate in school and the classroom based on the work of Pie Corbett.

Can you *Spot the difference story?!*:

Spot the difference is a great picture-based game for children to play as it helps children improve their pattern recognition skills and attention spans. But what if these pictures were replaced with words?! Get children (7–11) to write a story and then *rewrite it*, subtly 'tweaking' the text in terms of adding, removing or changing verbs, prepositions, names, adjectives, conjunctions and/or adverbs. Offer the two versions to one of their peers – *how many differences can they find*?

Idea 2.6: Un-folded stories	Suggested age group: 3-year-olds to 11-year-olds

Explanation:

In 2011 a new world record for folding a piece of paper in half was set – the paper (13,000 feet long) was folded an amazing 13 times! *Un-folded stories* offer children the opportunity to not only see how close they can get to beating this record, but it also provides them with a 'shifting' amount of writing space to record their story on. This Idea basically uses the writing area offered by the paper as it is opened to 'unfold' the plot of the story being written.

Un-folded stories – how they work:

Children will find that they are only able to fold a piece of paper in half about seven times. The point at which the children *cannot* fold the paper in half anymore is the point at which they can *start* mark-making/writing their story. On the first small 'face' of the folded paper package created children can offer the title* of their story. By opening up the package children will now have *double* the space available for them to write the first sentence or two of their story. The amount of space to write in is doubled again when they unfold the package for the third time where more of their stimulating story narrative can be revealed.

Un-folded stories and children aged 3–5:

Unfolded stories offer young children (3–4) opportunities to control the marks they make, be they large or small, depending on the writing space available to them. Use the paper packages to get children (4–5) practicing forming individual graphemes of different sizes, e.g. ₚₚ p p p

*Story titles to stimulate *Un-folded stories*:

Floyd (2006) suggests that good story titles 'should not be dull'. Allow children to select/adapt from the following unusual story titles for their *Un-folded stories*:

- Mr. French's funny fish
- The unicorn and the rainbow ribbon
- Hettie the Hippo and the mud sandwich
- The day Dad swallowed a whisk

Rusty Rabbit and the Black Burrow of Light
'My brother's got a foot up his nose!'
Cee Saw's crazy kangaroo ride
The sail on the whale in the gale

Variations on a theme of *folding* and *stories*:

The notion of folding is associated with other kinds of activities involving stories:

1. *Origami:* The Japanese art of folding paper into various forms can be combined with the telling of interesting stories to promote learning and enjoyment in the classroom. Visit http://tinyurl.com/7644g8v for some stimulating ideas to promote speaking and listening and story writing opportunities.

2. *Fold-over stories:* This is an old favourite that children aged 5–7 can engage with. Visit http://tinyurl.com/ctkhoor for instructions on how to create these funny stories.

3. *Folding stories:* An adaptation of *Fold-over stories* involves children collaborating together by adding a sentence to a story that has been started but which they can only see the *previous sentence*. The story is passed between different children but the top of the paper is continuously folded down, hiding all but the preceding line. Try it with children aged 7–11.

Idea 2.7: Twist stories	Suggested age group: 7-year-olds to 11-year-olds

Explanation:

There are many products which have been designed based around the notion of a twist: *'twist wrap'* chocolates, *twist drill bits*, *twist ties*, and *puff pastry twists* to name but a few. The Idea of *Twist stories* has been adapted from a paper sculpture calendar developed by a former colleague. *Twist stories* encourage children to write individual sentences of their stories on strips of coloured paper that are then 'twisted'* into different shapes and attached by the paper ends onto black card so that the strips stand off the card, making the story being told a stimulating '3-D read'!

*Twisting the paper – *the how*:

Children should be encouraged to experiment, exploring how to make the paper strips stand up off the card. *Twisting*, *scrunching*, *creasing*, *folding*, *plaiting*, *bending*, *pleating*, *winding* and *weaving* techniques offer a wealth of 'shaping strategies' for children to use. An awareness of these techniques also helps to extend children's vocabularies, which they may wish to incorporate into their *Twist tale* about a hairdressing salon or a gift-wrapping shop, for example.

A twist in the tale – story twists:

Hopcott (2008) suggests that a 'twist in the tale is one of the best ways of making [stories] satisfying for the reader.' Story twists change the direction of a story plot or the outcome of a tale by surprising readers with a revelation. There are different literary devices children should be taught/encouraged to use to create twists in their stories:

Device	Explanation	Examples for children to use
Discovery (7–9)	A character's true identity or nature is revealed.	• The lead character turns out to be a vampire/ghost/alien/rodent. • A dog that can talk/sing/dance.
Peripeteia (9–11)	The sudden reversal of a character's fortune, whether for good or ill, that emerges naturally from the character's circumstances.	• The king who loses his throne by lying about his illness to his kingdom. • The sailor who thinks she has failed to sail around the world but finds out her watch is an hour slow.
A cliff-hanger (7–9)	An abrupt ending that leaves the main characters in a precarious or difficult situation, creating a strong feeling of suspense that provokes the reader to ask, 'What will happen next?'	• The gang reach the end of the woods only to be faced with the glaring, fiery eyes of the giant killer robot. • The car carrying the rich family hits the barrier and dangles dangerously over the edge of the 90-foot cliff.
Poetic justice (9–11)	Virtue is ultimately rewarded or vice punished in such a way that the reward or punishment has a logical connection to the deed.	• The rabbit catcher gets caught up in his own giant rabbit trap. • A good-hearted woman meets the man of her dreams after helping her friends to find husbands and wives.

For further information see http://tinyurl.com/7oqvb23

Top Tip! When children are reading stories, encourage them to establish which of these literary devices is being used by the author/s to maintain their interest in the story.

| Idea 2.8: Moving stories | Suggested age group: 5-year-olds to 11-year-olds |

Explanation:

When reading a story Rubin (2005) argues that 'the use of wheels, flaps, turn-ups, pull-tabs, and pop-ups grabs the reader's attention and ensures active participation . . . the use of movable paper devices demands the reader interact with the book's content and makes the experience more memorable.' In an effort to make the stories that children write unforgettable, *Moving stories* promote the use of moving parts as a key feature of the story. Whilst this demands thoughtful planning and skill to make objects pop up, disappear, spin, turn and swing across the page, these moveable parts can be used to emphasise stimulating aspects of story plot, character development and speech*.

*Emphasising aspects of stories with moving parts:

There are a number of ways children can emphasise aspects of the stories they write using moving features:

- *Plot* – if characters are travelling from one location to another (e.g. on a plane, on a magic carpet, on a broom, from a cannon or in a train) 'travelling objects' (drawn and cut out of card) could be threaded onto a piece of string so that readers can physically move them across the page to emphasise the journey from one setting to another.

- *Character development* – if a character eats something (e.g. a sweet or a pill – think *Alice in Wonderland*), is injected with something, or is bitten by an animal (think *Spiderman*), children could fasten a cut-out of the character to the page with a split pin, allowing the character to physically 'spin' around, just like their mind and body would as they undergo their transformation into a monster/fairy/superhero/penguin/jester.

- *Speech* – if a character suddenly bellows something out loud (e.g. a cry for help or a frustrated rant), children could present these words in big letters, attaching them to card that physically springs up off the page when readers turn over the page, e.g.

See Appendix 8 (p. 214) for a range of 'moving' ideas for children to use in their *Moving story*.

Alternative interpretations of *Moving stories* for the 7–11 age range:

1. *Moving on* – children can write stories about growing up, e.g. a character who one day decides to leave his friends and family to go and work in India as a cricket coach.

2. *Moving up* – children can write stories about characters who gain a promotion and how this changes them, e.g. the scary caretaker who becomes head teacher of the school for the day.

3. *Moving out* – children can write stories about characters who decide to move out of their family home into a shared house or flat with friends/strangers.

4. *'Moving' stories* – children can write stories which describe emotional scenes (e.g. the death of a pet, friends falling out) or deal with emotional issues (e.g. a loved one has an accident, parental divorce).

Idea 2.9: Construction stories	**Suggested age group:** 3-year-olds to 7-year-olds

Explanation:

In early years settings (3–5) and infant classrooms (5–7) there can be found a selection of different construction kits, ranging from LEGO® and DUPLO® to K'NEX® and Meccano®. *Construction stories* are designed to embrace the engaging learning experience construction kits offer young children by getting them to use these sets either as a practical story resource, a visual writing template (see Appendix 9, p. 215) to 'build' a story, a 3-D illustration, or a physical way of 'constructing' written stories for others to read, look at and enjoy.

Construction kits and story writing (3–5):

Construction kits are a useful resource to support young children's story writing. Ways in which they can be used include:

- Allow young children to physically construct 'static structural creations' (Resnick and Silverman, 2005: 1), e.g. castles, houses and mazes. Encourage children to verbalise a story which involves their model. Display children's models alongside their mark-making efforts as a written record of their verbalised story.

- Support young children in taking digital images of models made out of different construction kits. Download these images onto simple word processing documents under which children can 'type' stories that incorporate their model using child-friendly keyboards.

Construction kits and story writing (5–7):

For children aged 5–7, construction kits offer different ways of stimulating/supporting story writing:

- On different coloured/sized pieces of large 'block style' construction kits (e.g. DUPLO or LEGO), write examples of different kinds of words, for example:

Red pieces – *nouns*	**Long** pieces – *verbs*	**Green** pieces – *adjectives*	**Short** pieces – *characters' names*

Offer children these pieces to construct a 'story wall' which they build, creating sentences out of the different pieces.

Suggestions! Words can be written *directly* onto the blocks using dry wipe pens or can be written on small Post-it® notes/white sticky labels which are then attached to the blocks. Blank blocks should be made available so that children can write on them if they are unable to locate words they wish to use. Permanent markers may be used if these blocks are to be a standard resource to support story writing in your classroom. Use these blocks to help children break the flow of speech into individual words.

- Children can display completed stories or 'stories in progress' on book stands/rests/supports made out of construction kits or construction materials, e.g. straws, woods, paper or card.

Coining characters' 'physical construction':

Bowkett (2001) suggests the physical features of story characters in children's stories can be constructed through the outcome of tossing a coin, e.g. heads = *a boy*, tails = *a girl*; heads = *tall*, tails = *short*; heads = *curly hair*, tails = *straight hair*. Encourage children to closely examine character illustrations in story books to identify/describe their physical features, recording these in both written and pictorial form on a *Physical Features* grid (see Appendix 10, p. 216). Use this as a whole class/group activity to aid the creation of new characters for their *Construction stories*.

Idea 2.10: Recycled stories	Suggested age group: 5-year-olds to 11-year-olds

Explanation:

Sleestak (2007) argues that 'one of the common practices of creators in any medium . . . is to recycle their own work into the same or other media.' This means that stories can be *recycled* or *reused*. Feathers (2004: 150–51) describes *Recycled stories* as 'combining the techniques involved in retelling stories and writing patterned stories'. *Recycled stories* thus encourage children to use a simple story that they already know but which they can rework/adapt by either replicating the structure of the text or altering one or more of the story elements, e.g. the main character, the setting or the plot*.

Engaging children with *Recycled stories*:

Feathers (2004: 152) claims that '[a]ll you need to engage [children] in writing recycled stories is books with clear structures.' Predictable patterned books (e.g. *We're Going on a Bear Hunt*), alphabet books (e.g. '*A is for . . . B is for . . .*') and number books (e.g. '*1 Dog and One Bone; 2 Girls and Two Phones . . .*') offer a useful model for children to use to generate a new text.

Recycled stories can be used across the creative curriculum to help children demonstrate their understanding of subject knowledge in other areas, e.g. life-cycles in Science (5–7) – *Swaying grass, swaying grass, what can you see? I see a white rabbit coming to eat me! White rabbit, white rabbit what do you see?* and World War II in History (7–11) – *A is for* Anne *Frank who hid from the German Nazis; B is for the* bravery *she and her family showed during the war* etc.

'True' *Recycled stories*:

To truly embrace all aspects of the notion of 'recycling' children could write their *Recycled stories* on scrap paper or recycled paper. Plastic containers could be used to 'mount' their *Recycled stories*, and unwanted fabrics could be used as a story border/backdrop. Stories could also be put in unwanted plastic bottles, thus 'recycling' the classic 'Message in a bottle' and turning it into '*Recycled story* in a bottle!'

*Teaching story elements to children through song:

- For children aged 5–7 consider showing them *Parts of a Story Song* (available at http://tinyurl.com/7hs76et). Use speaking and listening opportunities to work with children to extend the song with other story elements.
- For children aged 7–11 consider showing them 'Flocabulary – Five things (Elements of a short story)', which is available at http://tinyurl.com/85pln4m.

Stimulating *Recycled story* titles:

The titles offered below 'recycle' known characters from books, TV programmes, cartoons, fairy stories and films in an effort to stimulate children's story writing:

- Mr Happy's rather sad day
- Harry Potter and the Ghost of Gransaw
- Cinderella's purple panic!
- Pink Panther's search for Scruffy the dog
- Charlie Brown and the mystery muesli!
- Wonder Woman's holiday hat
- Captain Jack Sparrow's hunt for Harry Hippo
- The day it rained orange popcorn on Mr. Benn!

3

'Being' stories

This third chapter focuses its attention on important *beings* in the lives of children who can stimulate their story writing in a variety of exciting ways. These beings are principally humans who play an important role in the care, development and education of the young; animals, in the form of pets, are also included in this chapter due their presence in the homes of many children (see Craighill, 2010).

The first half of this chapter centres on the immediate family, recognising the closest relatives in the family unit. *Baby stories* and *Sibling stories* consider the importance of brothers and sisters as specific audiences for children's story writing, encouraging authors to be mindful of babies' limited 'attention spans' and 'life experiences' (Peres, n.d.), and recognising how different types of relationships between siblings can be used to portray harmony or feuds in their lives. *Mum stories* and *Dad stories* encourage children to think about suitable story themes to engage female readers, whilst getting reluctant male readers 'into stories' (see Telegraph, 2009a) by writing tales either *about* or *for* Dads by putting them in surprise places for them to be found and read! Whilst there are numerous benefits for children writing short stories (see http://tinyurl.com/73o3p26), *Pet stories* acknowledge the benefits of story writing for domesticated animals that experience 'boredom, loneliness or separation anxiety during the day when their owners are either at school/work' (p. 76). By writing these stories children will develop an appreciation of 'writing audience' (see Tabor, 1988).

> **Knowing Your Class**
> It is recognised that parents and siblings may not be part of the home life that all children are familiar with – think of those children in looked-after provision, for example. Teachers are encouraged to carefully consider the individual circumstances of children in their class, adapting the Ideas above to include carers, 'special people we know' or 'individuals who care for us' in an effort to be sensitive and inclusive of all children.

The second half of the chapter considers individuals who have regular contact with children, be it due to their physical location or through media sources. *Friend stories* and *Teacher stories* highlight key people in children's lives during their 'working week', exploring the impact of different kinds of friendships on story dialogue and plot whilst allowing children to take their teachers out of the classroom environment, putting them into exciting and unusual contexts to excite and energise their story writing. *Neighbour stories* serve to foster a sense of community with children using stories as a vehicle for developing meaningful relationships with those who live around them. *Character stories* and *Celebrity stories*, which conclude this chapter, recognise the value of well-known story characters and those in the celebrity spotlight by integrating them (or at least *aspects* of them) into the stories written by children.

Taking a Closer Look At 'Suggested Age Group'

A review of the Ideas contained within this chapter will highlight the fact than none of them offer provision that is considered suitable for children in the early years (3–5 years). As previously discussed in the Introduction to this book (see p. 27), the *Suggested age group* feature of each Idea is just that – merely a suggestion; teachers are actively encouraged to adapt the main Idea and those associated with it to suit the needs, interests and capabilities of those with whom they work. In an effort to promote a healthy range of provision across the full 3–11 age phase, the remainder of this introduction will present a variety of practical activities and suggestions which embrace the main Ideas in this chapter in a manner that is appropriate for our young writers.

Early Years Foundation Stage: Literacy – Writing
(DfE, 2012a: 31)

30–50 months

Sometimes gives meaning to marks as they draw and paint.

- Provide opportunities for children to paint pictures of their parents/siblings by way of subtly introducing them to different story elements, e.g. their physical appearance (*character*), places where they go (*settings*), and funny things they say/do (*dialogue/plot*).

- Offer writing materials in the outdoor play area for children to make a visual record of the pets that they own, making marks and forming shapes/letters to replicate the sounds/'shapes' that they make, e.g. snake – **SSSSSSSSS**; fish – **oooooooo** (mouth shape).

- In the home role-play area suggest that when 'baby' is sleeping children could write down the simple verbal stories they told 'baby' to get him/her off to sleep, e.g. *The Three Little Pigs*.

Ascribes meanings to marks that they see in different places.

- Model the writing of a collaborative short story about one of the practitioners in the classroom on the large whiteboard/ interactive whiteboard, encouraging children to 'read' the writing on the board to others during the session, adding their own marks/writing if they wish.

- Suggest that parents/carers make a written record of stories children tell about different family members (real or made up) as part of suggested Weekend Work so that children see writing taking place in the home.

40–60+ months

Gives meaning to marks they make as they draw, write and paint.

- Ask children to make a written contribution to a class storybook about the day Mrs Tredwell (the class teacher – *replace with your own name*) forgot to go to school!

- Offer children green and red highlighter pens/felt-tips to indicate where their story writing about their Grandma/ Grandpa starts (*green*) and finishes (*red*) to support the reader.

Begins to break the flow of speech into words.

- Encourage children to verbalise simple stories about their best friend, repeating them with a slower telling (by turning the imaginary *Verbaliser Speed Dial* on their forehead down) so. . . that. . . . they. . . . . . can. . . . . hear. . . . . the. . . . . individual. . . . . words . . . . they . . . . say!

Continues a rhyming string.

- Use different 'beings' to initiate rhyming strings, e.g. **dad** – *lad – had – mad – bad – pad;* **mum** – *bum – tum – hum – yum – sum;* **pet** – *wet – jet – get – set – bet – let – net.*

Hears and says the initial sound in words.

- Challenge children to hear/say the initial sound in the names of people in children's lives, e.g. **M**ummy; **D**addy; **B**aby **T**oby; **K**im (*friend*); **P**eter (*brother*).

Can segment the sounds in simple words and blend them together.

- Model the segmentation and blending of sounds using simple names and labels for 'beings', e.g. *M/u/m; D/a/d; B/o/b* (the) *d/o/g; S/a/m* (the) *f/i/sh.*

Links sounds to letters, naming and sounding the letters of the alphabet.

- Encourage children to articulate identified phonemes and letter names in characters' names from popular children's story books, e.g. **B**erna**rd** (*Not Now, Bernard*); **D**ai**s**y (*Come on, Daisy!*).

Uses some clearly identifiable letters to communicate meaning, representing some sounds correctly and in sequence.

- Work with children to use their phoneme–grapheme knowledge to write down their story ideas, e.g. mi dd fel dan a hl ('My daddy fell down a hole' – Amy, 4.8 years).

Writes own name and other things such as labels, captions.

- Encourage children to independently label their story illustrations of their immediate family/those who care for the child, ensuring that their own name is at the top of the page.

Attempts to write short sentences in meaningful contexts.

- At the Book Publishers role-play centre, model and promote the writing of sentences linked to the pictures/images/ illustrations offered to the children (see Figure 3.1).

JLS rnbow went ban g anb kuls went up in thu e.

JLS' (*a popular current UK boy band*) rainbow went bang and colours went up in the air. *Freddie, 4.10 years*

Figure 3.1   Example of a young child's short story in response to a piece of visual stimuli

Encourage the child to talk about his/her writing about a character in their favourite story and read it to an adult.

- See *Character stories* (p. 80).

Early Learning Goal: *Children use their phonic knowledge to write words in ways which match their spoken sounds. They also write some irregular common words. They write simple sentences which can be read by themselves and others. Some words are spelt correctly and others are phonetically plausible.*

- Have an Imaginary Friend Day, encouraging children to bring their imaginary friend with them to school. Get children to write simple stories about the adventures they get up to together. See Malkin (2009) about the benefits of imaginary friends for young children and their story writing.
- Support children in writing simple stories about different ways of getting to school over the week, for example:

On mun day I cam to skol on a star	(On Monday I came to school on a star)
On chuz day I cam to skol on a plan	(On Tuesday I came to school on a plane)
	Bernadette, 4.11 years

- Use well-known stories as the basis for children's story writing, e.g. *Mog and the Vee Eee Tee*; *The Little Red Hen*; *Billy's Bucket*. Encourage children to adapt these stories, integrating themselves into the tale as best friends with the main character.

- Offer portable mark-making boxes (shoe boxes, trays with carrying handles) so that children can write stories for their neighbour/auntie/uncle in different places in the classroom/ outdoor play area.

To further support teachers, select readings and websites are offered below to develop and enrich subject knowledge and the provision of *'Being' story* writing in the early years (3–5):

- **Practical resource pack:** *Storytelling with Children in the Early Years* by Ferguson (2007) – available at http://tinyurl. com/7q4njpu – a wonderful collection of 'rhymes, stories and ideas' to engage young children in storytelling, from which *'Being' story* mark-making and writing opportunities can be developed.

- **Research paper:** *The Effect of Emergent Writing on a Kindergartner's Growth in the Areas of Phonemic Awareness, Sight Word Recognition, and Self-Confidence* by McGuire (n.d.) – available at http://tinyurl.com/cwzyotz – an interesting research study with a useful literature review about what emergent literacy is, phonemic awareness, environmental print, and high-frequency sight words. Consider how knowledge from this can support provision and practice linked to *'Being' stories*.

- **Conference pack:** Pie Corbett, *From Storytelling to Story Writing – A Conference for Reception and Year 1 Teachers* (2008) – available at http://tinyurl.com/bo5kery (click on the *Pie Corbett Ideas Reception and Year 1* link to download the document) – an incredible Word document that is bursting with practical ideas, strategies and approaches for teachers of children aged 4–6 years. Consider how practice from this can support the *'Being' stories* children write. For teachers working with Years 3 and 4, click on the *Pie Corbett Ideas Year 3 and 4* link.

Table 3.1 Recommended readings associated with *'Being' stories*

Books	**KS1:** Corbett, P. (2003) *How to Teach Story Writing at Key Stage 1* [5–7]. London: David Fulton.
	KS2: Corbett, P. (2001) *How to Teach Fiction Writing at Key Stage 2* [7–11]. London: David Fulton.
	These books act as a series of practical manuals to support teachers in the primary classroom. Numerous creative story writing workshops support the reader in helping them to teach story writing to children in a dynamic, creative and imaginative way. Consider how practice from these can support the *'Being' stories* children write.
	Palmer, S. and Corbett, P. (2003) *Literacy: What Works?* London: Nelson Thornes.
	This book helps to identify '[t]he golden rules of primary literacy . . . and how you can use them in your classroom' (book blurb). *It offers readers the most successful ideas for their classroom including resources, practical advice and quality teaching methods.* Consider how advocated provision and practice can support the *'Being' stories* children write.

Book chapter – online/research journal article

Elbow, P. (1981) *Writing Without Teachers*. London: Oxford University Press. [Online]. Available at: http://tinyurl.com/bn9k5ao (Accessed: 28 April 2012).

Chapter Two of Elbow's book (The Process of Writing – Growing) *is a stimulating read which offers a critique of the writing process, arguing that writing should be thought of as 'an organic, developmental process . . . [through which] your words gradually . . . change and grow'.* Consider how what is advocated in the chapter can be used to support children's early approaches to writing *'Being' stories*.

Trepanier-Street, M., Romatowski, J. and McNair, S. (1990) Development of story characters in gender-stereotypic and non-stereotypic occupational roles. *Journal of Early Adolescence*, 10 (4), 496–510. [Online]. Available at: http://tinyurl.com/c6h7ly6 (Accessed: 28 April 2012).

This interesting article 'examined the creative responses of third- and sixth-grade boy and girl writers [8–9 and 11–12-year-olds] *to story characters cast in either stereotypic . . . or non-stereotypic occupational roles' (p. 496). Findings confirm that there remains a 'persistence of gender-stereotypic thinking in school-age subjects' (p. 509).* Consider the implications of this on the roles of different 'beings' in children's *'Being' stories*.

Websites

Lewis, B. L. (n.d.) *Part III, Developing Characters*. [Online]. Available at: http://tinyurl.com/ctahqw8 (Accessed: 28 April 2012).

This website helps teachers and children to explore different characteristics of characters in terms of their personality and their physical features; consideration is also given to how characters can change as stories progress. Consider how practice from this can support the *'Being' stories* children write in your classroom.

Trehearne, M. P. (2006) *Developing Oral Language and Comprehension in Preschool-Grade 2: Practical Strategies That Work!* [Online]. Available at: http://tinyurl.com/c7k46mv (Accessed: 28 April 2012).

This website offers a useful PDF that gives 'many practical, engaging, do-able and developmentally appropriate strategies and activities to assess and develop both vocabulary and comprehension' (p. 2) which can be used to support children's early writing efforts linked to 'Being' stories.

| **Idea 3.1: Baby stories** | **Suggested age group:** 3-year-olds to 7-year-olds |

Explanation:

Writing for a purpose (i.e. for a particular audience) is considered to be 'key' in motivating young children to engage in story writing activities (Cremin, 2010 in Goodwin, 2010). One such audience for children's story writing should be babies and toddlers. *Baby stories* allow young children to write simple stories that parents/carers may wish to read to their babies and toddlers as their tiny offspring enjoy looking at the story text and illustrations. The purpose for children writing for this specific age range is to heighten their awareness of the many challenges of writing tales for the very young*.

*The challenges of writing for babies and toddlers:

There are a number of considerations that children need to be aware of when writing stories for babies and toddlers:

- Babies and toddlers enjoy looking at pictures and listening to stories – *they are not yet able to read the text on the page!*
- Babies and toddlers have short attention spans – *they will lose interest with a long story!*
- Babies and toddlers prefer simple tales with straightforward plots – *the more complicated the story the less likely they are to enjoy, or indeed understand it!*
- Babies and toddlers like stories which revolve around the 'familiar' e.g. the home, the family, friends and pets – *these are the kind of stories babies and toddlers can relate to!*

Adapted from CreativeJuicesBooks.com (2011)

Top Tips! Use speaking and listening opportunities to discuss these considerations with children by reflecting on their knowledge/experiences of young siblings. Invite a parent/carer to bring in a baby/toddler into school for the children to observe as some children may have little experience of babies.

Baby stories for children (5–7) to write:

Offer children opportunities to write different kinds of stories for babies and toddlers:

- Stories about everyday incidents, e.g. going for a walk to the shops, having a picnic in the park, buying new booties, being invited to a birthday party, bedtime routines, or playing with parents/carers, siblings or friends.
- Stories about children who are just like them – *babies and toddlers!*
- Stories about animals, their friends and the adventures they get up to together.
- Stories set in familiar locations, e.g. farms, houses, parks, shops, bedrooms and gardens.

Supporting learning and teaching:

- Ensure that children clearly develop an understanding of the relationship between the text and the illustrations in existing baby books (3–5).
- Provide children with examples of baby and toddler story books so that they can 'get a feel' for the kind of language used and the amount of text on each page (5–7).

Producing Baby stories:

- Present *Baby stories* on thick, laminated card (remember that babies dribble and like to 'mouth' books).
- Produce *Baby stories* on 'shaped' card (this helps to stimulate their interest).
- Create *Baby stories* using sensory fabrics (babies clearly like things that 'feel' – see *fabric stories*, p. 98).

Idea 3.2: Sibling stories	Suggested age group: 7-year-olds to 11-year-olds

Explanation:

Many children have siblings, be they brothers, sisters or both! In modern society it is becoming increasingly common for children to have half/step siblings. Thompson et al. (2011: 1) suggest that this 'add[s] . . . more complexity to family life'. From a story writing perspective this offers wonderful story 'fuel' that children can *ignite* as they write stimulating stories which revolve around characters, their relationships with their siblings*, and how this affects what happens to them as their adventures together progress.

* Sibling relationships – developing subject knowledge:

Gold (1989, cited in Cicirelli, 1995: 59) describes five types of sibling relationships based on their involvement with each other. They include:

1. *Intimate siblings* – these are especially close and extremely devoted. They value their relationship above all others.
2. *Congenial siblings* – these are friends. They are close and caring but place a higher value on their marriage and parent–child relationships.
3. *Loyal siblings* – these base their relationship on their common family history. They maintain regular, periodic contact, participate in family gatherings, and support each other during times of crisis.
4. *Apathetic siblings* – these feel indifferent toward each other. They rarely are in contact.
5. *Hostile siblings* – these have relationships are based on anger, resentment, and very negative feelings (adapted from Shriner, 1999).

Work with children to consider the effect these relationships can have on different situations as they occur in their stories – *might* hostile *siblings become* intimate *siblings if one of them becomes very poorly? Might the friendship of* congenial *siblings be 'tested' if one of them wins the talent contest? Might* loyal *siblings become* hostile *siblings if one 'borrows' (steals) money from the other?*

Sibling rivalry – one of humanity's oldest problems:

Sibling rivalry is used as a common theme in various literary sources, e.g. *King Lear* by Shakespeare and the story of *Cain and Abel* in the Bible. Through speaking and listening opportunities challenge children to identify 'child friendly' ways in which siblings might be in competition with each other, e.g. *getting the best grades at school, being the fastest runner, having the most friends, being the one who loves their mum/carer the most*. Record and display these ideas in thought showers, lists and grids. Get children to reflect how they could use this rivalry in their stories to create conflict.

Sibling story sentence starters:

Help children to 'get started' by allowing them to consider 'where the story could go' from the following *Sibling story* sentence starters:

1. James looked coldly into Jack's eyes.
2. Suzie did not know whether to laugh or cry at Vanessa.
3. The day Phillip came out of hospital was the day Jimmy had to change his hair colour.
4. 'What do you want?' said Poppy to her sister on the phone, smiling.

For more sentence starters see the wonderful book by Dettenrieder and Hlawati (2008).

Idea 3.3: Mum stories	Suggested age group: 3-year-olds to 11-year-olds

Explanation:

Mums/primary female caregivers are extremely busy people who always seem to be working in some way, shape or form – from lovingly supporting their family and friends to being successful at their job and maintaining a wonderful home. All 'manic mums' (Barker, 2010: 413) deserve/*need* a five-minute breather; this is where *Mum stories* come in! This Idea encourages children to draw pictures/make marks/write stories for their mum/caregiver so that they have something to read whilst they enjoy a well-earned cup of tea/coffee!

Selecting suitable themes for *Mum stories* (7–11):

Because children are 'writing for a gender specific audience' (Marsh, 1998: 10) it is important to 'give the reader what they want'. Whilst the suggestions below are by no means written to exacerbate preconceived gender stereotypes, there are prominent themes found in fiction for women which include *love/romance, friendships/relationships, food, security/comfort, warmth, attention* and *shelter*. Work with children to consider ways to use these themes to promote story ideas, e.g. *Mum falls in love with Dad all over again; Mum gets some very unusual food cravings* (might she be pregnant?)*; Mum looks after the homeless; Mum learns how to fly a hot-air balloon.*

Top Tip! Encourage children to speak to their mothers/caregivers at home about the kind of stories they enjoy reading so that they can identify particular themes that can be used to fuel their *Mum story*.

Stimulating *Mum story* titles (5–11):

Support children in generating story titles that really make mums *want* to read the stories they write. Stimulating examples include:

- Mega Mum saves the King of the Seas
- The day that Mum ruled the world
- Mighty Mum and the milk chocolate dragon
- Sunshine, smiles and Mum's tiny secret!
- Mum's weird weekend with her special friends
- The Three Little Pigs and the sweet, kind Mum

Top Tip! Use the word 'Mum' as the starting point for a rhyming string (3–5).

Key learning and teaching:

When writing their *Mum story*, children need to carefully think about their *main characters*. They need to know that there are often two types of characters in a story:

5–7 year olds	7–11 year olds	Possible examples in *Mum stories*
Hero	Protagonist	Mum, Step mum, Grandma, Foster mum, Auntie
Villain	Antagonist	Her boss, her own mum, the next door neighbour, siblings (brother/sister), best friend, school bully

Visit http://tinyurl.com/7fxqtgv for an informative and interactive exploration of this key element of a story to support children's and teachers' knowledge and understanding.

Published 'Mum' stories to stimulate *Mum stories*:

3–7 year olds	7–11 year olds
• *My Mum* (Browne, 2009)	• *The Mum Detective* (Rees, 2005)
• *My Mum is Fantastic* (Butterworth, 2008b)	• *The Illustrated Mum* (Wilson, 2007)

Idea 3.4: Dad stories

Suggested age group: 3-year-olds to 11-year-olds

Explanation:

Most fathers are likely to read non-fiction texts, e.g. reference books, manuals and guides, as opposed to narrative texts. This assumption is supported by Harvey (2002: 12), who suggests that '[n]onfiction is the genre most likely to spur . . . [male] passion and wonder for learning'. This Idea is designed to readdress the balance a little so that Dads have the opportunity to read stimulating stories, particularly those which have been written *by* their children. By writing stories either *about* or *for* their father*, children can engage in meaningful story writing with the purpose of getting more Dads interested in stories.

*Key consideration for *Dad stories*:

Whilst all children have a biological father, a growing number of them do not live with, have any contact with, or even know who their father is (see Ricketts, n.d.). It is important to be sensitive to current family circumstances so that individual pupils do not become distressed by not being able to write a story about or for their father. Writing about step fathers, special uncles, older brothers, or males who are close to the child are useful alternatives for *Dad stories*.

Research into gender influences on literacy behaviours:

Ashley (2002) highlights 'commonsense' assumptions about the power of role models, particularly those who are male, and the effect these can have on boys' engagement in literacy based activities: 'if boys see men reading books [story books about Dads perhaps? See Browne (2003); Gurney (2008); Butterworth (2008a)] and doing lots of neat writing [writing up their own *Dad story* perhaps?], then boys will avidly read books and produce volumes of neat writing'.

Try it! Test this out in your classroom: *if boys in your class mark-make/write stories which are read by their fathers/male caregivers, are the boys motivated to write more stories? If so, does this mean the same thing will happen with mothers/female caregivers and daughters?*

'Getting your flow on' – distractions and the writing process:

Talbot (2010: 25) reflects on the experience of working in a calm working environment and a space free from distractions and interference to aid the writing process: 'As I wrote, I noticed that I maintained a rhythm and constant flow of ideas that I pour[ed] on the page . . . I call this . . . *flow writing*.' Where possible encourage Dads/male caregivers, particularly those who are homemakers, to limit the number of 'outside distractions' at home (e.g. mobile phones, Facebook, music, other people, TV) so that children can maximise the 'time and ideas' (2010: 26) available to them to work on their *Dad story* when/if writing at home, linking sounds to letters to secure learning (3–7).

Surprising places for fathers to find *Dad stories*:

- In Dad's lunchbox – *wrapped around his sandwiches*!
- Fastened to the outside of Dad's shed door!
- Under the windscreen wiper of Dad's car!
- On top of Dad's pillow!
- Inside Dad's sports bag!
- Inserted inside Dad's newspaper!
- By Dad's toothbrush in the bathroom!

Idea 3.5: Pet stories	Suggested age group: 3-year-olds to 7-year-olds

Explanation:

Just like human beings, pets can get lonely too (Carpenter, 2011a), a fact which many children may have never considered before. The Idea behind *Pet stories* is to try to alleviate the boredom, loneliness or separation anxiety that pets may experience during the day when their owners are at school/work. The purpose of children writing *Pet stories* is to keep their pets stimulated until they return home. *Pet stories* could involve children's pets as the lead character of the story, or they could simply be a story for their pets – *it is up to the individual writer*!

Opportunities for learning and teaching:

Pet stories offer valuable opportunities to introduce/revisit aspects of learning and teaching:

- Generate ideas through thought showering *before* children put 'pen to paper' (5–7), e.g. *what different things do pets like to do?* Use these ideas to enable children to believe that pets can relate to the simple story being told. See http://tinyurl.com/823ckoy for a wonderful collection of different talking and listening strategies for the story writing classroom, including thought showers.

- The use of onomatopoeia – if children want to include anthropomorphized characters in their story (pets that can talk) what would they say and how would they say it? Would they need to translate it for other readers, e.g. 'Woof!' barked Barney. 'Who do you think stole the golden stone?'

Pet stories and those 'already known':

Children grow up being told/reading many stories which involve animal characters (Foster, 2006). Reminding children of this will support them in considering known plot ideas they could replicate/ adapt whilst identifying potential animal characters (see below) for their own story:

- 3–5: Traditional stories, e.g. *The Three Little Pigs*, *The Three Billy Goats Gruff*, *Puss in Boots*.
- 5–7: Characters in children's reading schemes, e.g. *Floppy the Dog* (Oxford Reading Tree).
- 3–5: Popular children's characters, e.g. *Disney characters* (Mickey Mouse, Donald Duck), *Peppa Pig*, *Garfield* the cat and *Miffy* the rabbit.
- 5–7: Computer game characters, e.g. *Sonic the Hedgehog*, *Yoshi the Dinosaur* (Super Mario Bros).

'Exposing' animals to Pet stories:

Children need to creatively think of ways to 'get their stories out there' for pets to read and enjoy. Recommended strategies include:

- Weaving the story between the bars of the animal's cage.
- Lining the animal's cage or basket with the story.
- Pasting the story to the outside of the animal's bag/box of food.
- Tacking the story to the wall by the animal's food bowl.
- Taping the story to the side of the animal's tank, text facing inwards.

Opportunities for speaking and listening can be facilitated through children talking about their drawing/mark-making or reading their stories out loud to their pets at home.

Idea 3.6: Friend stories	Suggested age group: 5-year-olds to 11-year-olds

Explanation:

There is much evidence to suggest that friends are essential in supporting the healthy development of children (Bergen, 1993). Research indicates that children who have no friends can suffer from mental and emotional difficulties later on in their life. Claims that there has been a decline in the reported number of close friendships in the past 20 years (see Wang and Wellman, 2010) fuel the Idea behind *Friend stories*; instead of giving each other bracelets as a symbol of their friendship (Ahde, 2007), children are encouraged to write a special story just for their friend(s).

Friend stories and oracy:

One of the benefits of *Friend stories* is that they offer children (and teachers) valuable opportunities to use and develop speaking and listening skills. During circle time and PSHE and Citizenship activities, explore with children the notion of friends and friendships as a topic for discussion, considering *what makes a good friend, how we know we have friends, why friends are important* and *how we can make friends with others*. With older children (9–11), consider why some friendships last longer than others and why we have only a few close friends. Use the points raised in these discussions to fuel the 'goings-on' in their *Friend stories*.

Types of friendships – *developing subject knowledge*:

Adams (2011) reports on the research work of Spencer and Pahl who identify eight different kinds of friendships:

Associates	Useful contacts	Favour friends	Fun friends
Helpmates	Comforters	Confidants	Soul mates

There are some similarities between this list and those presented by Ghosh (2008):

Professional friends	Social friends	Deep/emotional friends	
Intellectual friends	Self-actualised friends	Buddy friends	School friends

Make children aware of these different types of friends when reading story books, helping children to appreciate what it means to be a particular type of friend through discussion opportunities. Support children in considering how these different friendships can influence aspects of their story writing, e.g. dialogue (the way friends talk to each other), relationships between characters (tense? harmonious?), and plot*.

*Possible *Friend story* plots:

- Falling out with friends and then making up.
- Going on adventures together with friends.
- Helping friends out, e.g. doing chores.
- Making friends in a new place/location.
- Being there (emotionally) for friends in need, e.g. loss of a pet, being bullied.
- Sharing friends' interests, e.g. cycling.

Friendship quotations:

Friendship quotations are a wonderful way of stimulating children's story writing. Show children different examples of 'friendship quotations' via *Google Images* – use these to initiate discussions into what these quotations mean and how these could be used to form the basis of a great *Friend story*.

Children's online story books:

Visit http://tinyurl.com/dxh29sk for some splendid online stories to stimulate children's minds and thinking, many of which are about friends and friendship.

Idea 3.7: Teacher stories	Suggested age group: 7-year-olds to 11-year-olds

Explanation:

Most children are fond of their teachers and many of them will be remembered long after the children (and the teachers themselves) have left the school. Whilst many young children (3–5) think that their teachers live in the role-play area (!), *Teacher stories* offer older children (7–11) the opportunity to take teachers out of their normal 'classroom context' and put them into a new and stimulating setting/ situation for younger children/their teacher to read/enjoy!

Interesting locations for *Teacher stories*:

- Inside a hot washing machine!
- A visit to a cold foreign country!
- In a giant hamster cage!
- At a dog racing track!
- At a disco for dinosaurs!
- On an edible rainbow!

Potential titles for *Teacher Stories*:

- Mr. McMillan and the Fire of Flacon.
- Miss Edwards' unicorn umbrella.
- Mrs. Hodgkiss' sunny September.
- Mr. Holder and the Star from Heaven.
- Mrs. Walsh and the peculiar underpants in Pannington Crescent!

The 'fundamental' nature of narrative:

Cameron and Besser (2004: 33) describe narrative as 'one of the basic ways in which we understand our lives as humans'. Teachers can help children to understand different aspects of human life, e.g. *relationships, friendship, love, honour, commitment, support, collaboration* and *enjoyment* by suggesting children use one (or more) of these aspects to drive the storytelling in their *Teacher story*, e.g. *their teacher enjoying windsurfing; their teacher showing commitment by marking her children's book whilst on holiday;* or *their teacher honouring her side of a scary bet with the class!*

Integrating the characteristics of well-known fictional teachers into *Teacher stories*:

Challenge children to identify as many teachers in stories they have read about in two minutes . . . *GO!* Examples are likely to include:

- *The Demon Headmaster*
- Miss Honey from *Matilda*
- The various professors at Hogwarts (*Harry Potter*)
- Mr. Tom (who acts like a teacher to William) in *Goodnight Mister Tom*
- Yoda (*Star Wars*)

Encourage children to think about the temperament of these teachers, e.g. *passionate, restless, angry, anxious, sensitive, courageous* and *moody*. Reflect on how this affects their behaviour towards their pupils and how this translates in the way they move, speak, and their mannerisms, e.g. *floating effortlessly down the corridor; barking at children; twitching when challenged.* Use this knowledge to enrich the characterisation of teachers in children's *Teacher stories*.

Ways of offering *Teacher stories* to children:

Teachers can offer children *Teacher stories* in a variety of exciting ways: as a homework activity; as a 'wet play' activity; as a writing competition (see p. 108); as a piece of extended writing; as a free choice activity; as a Christmas task; as a collaborative activity (children paired up from different classes working on one story); or as a final day piece of work for teachers to remember their children by. Alternatively, it could be a focused piece of assessed writing which is undertaken as part of a unit of literacy work.

Idea 3.8: Neighbour stories	Suggested age group: 9-year-olds to 11-year-olds

Explanation:

There is much concern that the notion of *community* seems to be a thing of the past, particularly as changes in work patterns, developments in ICT-based communication networks, and fast changing populations affect people's sense of 'belonging to their neighbourhood' (Owen, 2008). This Idea aims to respond positively to a need for community re-building by getting children to write stimulating stories for or about their neighbours, either those living directly next door to them or those in the immediate area to the local school.

Stories and the community – *linkage to current thinking*:

Gray et al. (1999) suggest that 'the stories we tell and how we tell them have a huge impact on the life of our community. How we learn and tell about triumphs and disasters, problems and solutions, barriers and breakthroughs affects how we feel about our community.' Children thus need to be supported in thinking about the best way to tell their story through their writing by carefully considering their story theme[†] and their story tone[*].

[†]Recommended story themes for *Neighbour stories*:

Encourage children to base their *Neighbour story* around one of the following neighbour-friendly themes: *home, friendship, quest of discovery, birth, collaboration, love, journey, communication, family, fulfilment, society, pride, union* and *wisdom*.

[*]The meaning of story tone:

Story tone refers to the 'voice' of the writing – see http://tinyurl.com/7odmond for valuable information about this. Some stories have a humorous tone whilst others may be joyful, serious, mysterious, optimistic or anxious. Story tone is expressed through a number of 'tonal aspects':

- The use of imagery.
- How sentences are structured.
- The choice of adjectives/adverbs.
- The diction of characters' speech.
- The level of formality in the writing.
- The point of view from which the story is told.

Help children to analyse the work of children's authors such as Gillian Cross, Phillip Pullman, Anne Fine and Philip Ardagh to establish how they use the aspects identified above to effectively convey a tone appropriate to the story being told. Consider the importance of story tone when children write their *Neighbour stories*. For further information visit http://tinyurl.com/7gzdp49.

Neighbour story considerations:

Prior to putting 'pen-to-paper', children need to take the following into consideration to assure their *Neighbour story* is suitable for their audience:

- Gender – *are they writing for a* male *neighbour, a* female *neighbour or both?*
- Role – *are they writing for a* 'parent' *or* 'child' *neighbour?*
- Age – *what is the age bracket of the neighbour they are going to write their story for? 40–65?*
- Interests – *do the children know what their neighbours are interested in, e.g.* gardening, cars, cooking, sports, clothes, exercise? *How can/will they integrate this into their story?*

Idea 3.9: Character stories	Suggested age group: 5-year-olds to 11-year-olds

Explanation:

All children have a favourite story character, be they from the world of books, comics, TV or films. These characters can be a powerful influence on children's behaviour (Potts et al., 1996) in terms of shaping their attitudes towards learning and other people. *Character stories* aim to use this 'influence' to stimulate story writing by giving children a choice – to write a story that *involves* or is *for* their favourite character. As children already have a clearly established character to work with, they can focus their attention on the development of other story elements in their tale such as an interesting story plot*.

*The importance of character and plot in children's books – *research findings*:

In 2009, Booktrust asked over 1,300 children between the ages of 5 and 12 to identify their favourite literary character (see Flood, 2009). The list of top 20 characters was described by Flood as 'an eclectic mix of classic titles, TV spin-offs, modern favourites and fairy stories', yet (unsurprisingly) identified Harry Potter as Number 1. It was found that the most powerful ingredient for attracting children to a particular book was *character*[†], with 51% citing this as their reason for reading a title, ahead of *plot* at 43%. For the top 20 characters, visit http://tinyurl.com/6kjtbmc.

Stimulating *Character story titles* for children to write:

- Postman Pat's deep sea dive to the Sunken Ship! *Who will Pat meet on this adventure?*
- Harry Potter and the Voyage to Venkontoo. *What is hiding in the depths of Venkontoo?*
- Tracy Beaker's brilliant invention! *What can this brilliant invention do?*
- Doctor Who's quest to the Sea with no Water. *Why does the sea have no water?*
- Cinderella's sparking shopping spree! *What is the occasion Cinderella is going to?*
- Thomas's (the Tank Engine) trip to the sandy seaside. *Which of Thomas' friends go with him?*

Innovative *Character story* ideas:

- When it is World Book Day (see http://tinyurl.com/y8h82g9), encourage both children and staff to dress up as their favourite literary characters. Involve parents and carers by inviting them into school to talk about their favourite literary characters to the children.
- Consider having a school *Mark-making Day* (3–5)/*Writing Day* (5–11) to emphasise the importance of story writing in children's lives, encouraging them to write wonderful stories about interesting yet believable characters[†]. See http://tinyurl.com/7zb7gr8, adapting the materials for personal/professional usage with the children you work with.

[†]What makes a good character?:

Memorable literary characters are both interesting and believable so that they capture the reader's imagination. Help children to build vivid story characters like those in the top 20 (see above*) by considering aspects such as their *appearance*, their *personality*, their *goals* and *ambitions*, their *likes* and *dislikes*, and their *strengths* and *weaknesses* (Stowell et al., 2011). Encourage children to draw pictures of characters they create so that they have a visual image they can refer to when describing their character using written words.

Idea 3.10: Celebrity stories	Suggested age group: 7-year-olds to 11-year-olds

Explanation:

Open any magazine or newspaper, watch any TV programme, or look at any billboard, and you are likely to come across the faces/names of popular celebrities in the form of footballers, pop stars and actors. Whilst teachers' leaders claim that '[c]hildren's educational aspirations risk being damaged by the cult of celebrity*' (ATL, cited in BBC, 2008), *Celebrity stories* strive to help children to aspire to be the best story writer they can be by using celebrities as a 'vehicle' for some stimulating story writing.

*Promoting diverse occupations of new celebrities:

Teachers claim that some children want to be famous 'for the sake of being famous' (ATL, cited in BBC, 2008). Encourage children to write stories about celebrities who have an occupation that gives them a reason for being famous, e.g. *chef, astronaut, ventriloquist, builder, train driver, fashion designer, banker, doctor, music therapist, writer* (!). For an interesting list of 'occupational possibilities', visit http://tinyurl.com/7ozar5y to energise children's story writing.

The dangers of celebrity gossip:

Celebrity-based media sources, including websites and blogs, are accused of frequently speculating and spreading rumours in an attempt to entertain, sell products or boost ratings. An important 'lesson for life' that children should learn at school is about the dangers of gossiping about others. Encourage children to write stories about celebrities and the ridiculous rumours that are said about them which unfortunately have negative repercussions for the celebrity, for example:

Ridiculous rumours	Negative repercussions
Celebrity is the son/daughter of a leprechaun.	Celebrity's morale/self-esteem is damaged.
Celebrity cannot play computer games because they cannot afford the console.	People on the street avoid/jeer at celebrity.
Celebrity lives in a tree house to relive their childhood.	Celebrity goes into hiding.
Celebrity has a real voice which sounds like a little duck.	Celebrity does not get any job offers.
Celebrity has geniophobia (a fear of chins).	Celebrity spends days crying in bed.

Cameron and Besser (2004: 34) suggest that 'the interest of a story for a reader is in how the characters . . . tackle the problems that they encounter'. Talk with children about how their celebrity can overcome these negative repercussions and come out 'on top'. Use Appendix 11 (p. 217) to generate ridiculous 'spoken' rumours and the thoughts of those who hear them.

Celebrity ghost writing:

In recent years there has been a surge of celebrities writing bestselling novels (e.g. Katie Price, Naomi Campbell, Kerry Katona) and children's stories (e.g. Coleen McLoughlin, Madonna, David Walliams) (see Merritt, 2008). It is claimed that much of this fiction is actually written by ghost writers – these are real authors who 'collaborate' with the celebrity but whose name may not be acknowledged in the book. Suggest that children become ghost writers for popular celebrities, writing stories for the likes of David Beckham, Kate Middleton, Beyoncé or the most popular boy band of the day.

'Craft' stories

This chapter explores a range of craft-based Ideas that can be used to stimulate children's story writing. The Ideas presented emphasise the value of *Art and Design* (NC) and *Exploring and Using Media and Materials* (EYFS equivalent) to enrich story writing provision in the classroom. This chapter positively embraces the cross-curricular application of knowledge and skills associated with artistic practices and applies them within a story writing context to engage young authors aged 3–11.

The first half of the chapter acknowledges resources which are common to artistic endeavours, considering how these stimulate story writing. *Craft stories* highlight a wealth of materials which can be used by children to record their stories on and items they can record their stories with. *Water stories* recognise the creative potential of incorporating water and entities associated with it into children's stories, whilst *Paint stories* replace 'traditional' writing implements (think pens and pencils) with paint brushes and rollers, *unleashing* stories from well-known paintings with a little bit of creative imagination! *Penned stories* and *Papered stories* revisit the premise of Chapter 1 by considering the use of writing tools for certain kinds of stories (*Penned stories*), whilst different paper types are acknowledged and explored in terms of fuelling potential stories in *Papered stories*.

The second half of the chapter offers the reader Ideas linked to select aspects of Art and Design. *Tall stories* heighten the fictitious element of stories by using artistic display strategies to promote outlandish tales; *Decorated stories*, on the other hand, capitalise on the therapeutic effects of artistic decoration to effectively manage the intensity of the writing process for children. The notion of *TV stories* see the artistic presentation of children's stories using 'the small screen' as a vehicle for story writing exposure being considered. *Sweet stories* and *Fabric stories,* which close this chapter, both recognise the importance of artistic invention and different materials on which stories are written: *Sweet stories* actively promote 2-D and 3-D story work across the Key Stages whilst *Fabric stories* embrace how different pieces of fabric can be used for a multitude of story purposes.

Taking a closer look at 'developing an effective control over pencils and pens'

In *Crafty stories* (p. 89) a number of practical activities are offered to help young children build strength and control over their manipulation of writing implements. Being able to effectively hold and use a pen/pencil is a key aspect that can either aid or inhibit children's writing development.

Consider this!

With reference to the children you work with, are there any who demonstrate the following:

- Have limited writing endurance?
- Try to avoid writing tasks?
- Are unable to write smoothly and neatly?
- Complain that writing makes their hands/arms ache?
- Make holes in their writing paper?
- Produce writing with limited legibility?
- Take a long time to write a short piece of writing?
- Offer inconsistencies in the size, shape or slant of the letters used in their writing?

If you have answered 'Yes' to any of the above, then it is likely that these children are experiencing handwriting difficulties.

Observing children as they write (the *process*) and looking at their completed work (the *product*) are useful indicators of children's handwriting difficulties, particularly when comparisons are made with other children in class. Davies (2009) suggests that 'approximately 10% of children in each classroom in the UK have a handwriting difficulty' and that these children 'frequently grow up to be adults with writing difficulties [that a]ffect their home and work life'. It is thus important to consider what causes these difficulties and what we as teachers can do to ensure that this does not negatively impact on their writing output.

It is claimed that there are seven different causes behind dysgraphia (the problems with handwriting). The information in Table 4.1 is adapted from Pilgrim (2009). For more information about these causes of handwriting problems, see Davis (2003).

Table 4.1   The seven causes of handwriting problems (adapted from Pilgrim, 2009)

No.	Cause	Details
1	Brain damage	Occurrence due to the brain being starved of oxygen at birth or through near drowning, sustained high temperature, head injury or a stroke.
2	Physical illness or deformity	Could also be due to a birth defect, an illness or an accident.
3	Intentionally poor penmanship	Children with poor spelling, punctuation or grammar may intentionally use poor handwriting in an effort to hide these facts. Those with dyslexia are likely to demonstrate this in their writing.
4	No or inadequate instruction	A child may never have been given any instruction or *quality* instruction in penmanship.
5	Disorientation	Negative emotions based on previous experiences can cause children to alter their focus which creates distortions of perception when creating and copying symbols, such as letters or words.
6	Multiple mental images	Problems arise if teachers offer a visual model (a formed letter/word) to those children who are a 'picture thinker' (a child who has a different mental image in their mind of what the letter/word should look like).
7	Inadequate natural orientation	This is referred to as 'dyspraxia': children with inadequate natural orientation produce writing where the lines they form will not be straight and there will be no symmetry in any of the letters written.

Many of the causes listed in Table 4.1 require proper diagnosis and specialised support from the likes of educational psychologists, paediatricians, neuropsychologists and occupational therapists. English/Literacy co-ordinators and SEND co-ordinators in school, along with Local Authority personnel, serve as valuable sources of information, guidance and advice to support you and children with specific handwriting needs in your class. For those children who intentionally demonstrate poor penmanship, disorientation or have received no or inadequate instruction, teachers need to carefully select, deploy and evaluate the impact of practical strategies to address these issues as part of the handwriting provision in the classroom. The select suggestions offered below are organised into those suited for children aged 3–5, 5–7 and 7–11; recommended readings for *'Craft'* stories are offered under these age headings by way of emphasising how the different *'Craft'* stories children write can be developed with improved handwriting capabilities.

Early Years (3–5)

- Familiarise yourself with the stages of grip development in children from the age of 12 months to 6 years so that you appreciate the different ways young children will hold writing implements – see http://tinyurl.com/bp7kzvm for a visual outline of the progression from the Palmar-Supinate Grasp to the Dynamic Tripod posture.

- Promote sky writing – writing letters in the air. Be creative by getting children to write with their fist, their wrist, their elbow, their 'pinkie' (little finger), their wet (licked) index finger, or with a 'five-finger rainbow' (their hand with fingers and thumb outstretched).

- Remember that 'children [in the early years] should not be asked to copy lines of individual letters or words' (CCEA, n.d.: 10).

- Offer young children a range of practical activities which develop both their gross motor *and* fine motor skills, examples of which are shown in Table 4.2 (p. 86). For teachers wishing to develop the gross/fine motor activities of children aged 6–12, years see Callender (2007).

- Encourage children to write on magnetic gel boards, tissue paper, corrugated cardboard and tin foil to develop appropriate levels of pressure when writing on different surfaces.

Table 4.2 Practical activities for developing gross and fine motor skills in young children

Gross motor activities	Fine motor activities
• Swirl ribbons around on sticks • Wash bikes, trikes and windows • Climb up ladders and nets • Engage in parachute play • Swing from monkey bars • Safely lift, carry and lower boxes	• Play with and manipulate small-world resources • Make music with instruments • Practice cutting with snips and scissors • Pop bubble-wrap ('*Pop!*') • Feed coins into a piggy bank slot

Recommended readings – professional materials:

1. Visit http://tinyurl.com/cvrex2g, which offers a range of practical strategies linked to handwriting in the Early Years (Birth–5) within the context of the South Australian curriculum.

2. Visit http://tinyurl.com/77x52sl for nationally archived materials 'which will support [teachers] about teaching writing to Early Years children and also address the specific needs of boys' (DfE, n.d.) – pay particular attention to the materials under the subheading *Developing Handwriting*.

3. A recommended download is Baird et al.'s (2003) *Pre-K* [Early Years] *and Kindergarten Handwriting Resource*, available at http://tinyurl.com/cpb5we3.

Key Stage One (5–7)

- Encourage children to engage in activities that improve the strength and stability of their shoulder girdle muscles. Visit http://tinyurl.com/7p9rngr for stimulating activities such as *Leopard Crawl*, *Crab Walk* and *The Big Push!*

- Make pencil grips available for children so that they can be added to writing implements to aid control, support and hand positioning (see http://tinyurl.com/d5ojz5t).

- Offer children opportunities to trace and copy shapes, patterns, pictures, images, letters and words.

- Ask children to 'identify or circle their best formed letter or letters' in written work they have produced (Graham, 2009: 27) – *how do they know it is well formed?*

- Challenge children to write in response to a visual cardboard *Write-o-meter* (A4/A3 size – see Figure 4.1). When the arrow is pointing at the yellow part of the *Write-o-meter*, children should form their letters at a controlled pace; when the arrow points to the red part, children need to increase the speed of their letter formation. Letters should be formed with slow, careful movements when the arrow points to the green part of the *Write-o-meter*. Children should progressively work to ensure that letters appear the same in terms of size, shape, formation and legibility, irrespective of the speed they are writing at.

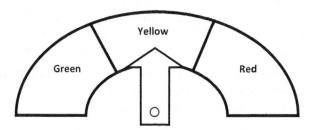

Figure 4.1   The Write-o-meter

- As adults write with pencils that are in proportion to their hand size, allow children to use small pencils (think of those used by golfers to record their scores).

Recommended readings – academic papers:

1. Visit http://tinyurl.com/c2yqd4n which offers an interesting research paper by Marr et al. (2001) about the prerequisite skills needed for 'Handwriting Readiness' in children aged 5–6 years within an American context.

2. Visit http://tinyurl.com/cuv3q3t for a powerful study by Medwell et al. (2007: 1) which 'suggests that handwriting is an important factor in the composition of young children [Year 2]' and that low levels of handwriting automaticity (the ability to writing alphabet letters quickly from memory) can interfere with children's compositions.

3. A useful download is *Common Handwriting Problems and Solutions* (Word document), available at http://tinyurl.com/6u9x65e.

Key Stage Two (7–11)

- *Accommodate, modify* or *remediate* expectations of children and their writing – see Jones (1998) for valuable ideas on practically applying this interesting approach to their handwriting so that children can reach their 'best potential'.

- Offer children opportunities to practise their handwriting *across the curriculum* in a variety of contexts, for example, writing a police report as part of a murder scene (*Drama*); writing a tear-stained letter to a loved one as a child evacuee in World War II (*History*).

- Encourage children to visualise, verbalise and demonstrate to others how to form letters and join them together – see the handwriting sections for Years 1–6 under *Writing: Transcription* in the draft NC for KS1 and KS2: English (DfE, 2012b).

- Ensure that the learning environment is 'handwriting rich', e.g. display labels are written in cursive script; writing on the whiteboard is modelled appropriately.

- Challenge children to write 'better' than you (the teacher) in terms of handwriting fluency, legibility and formation. Take digital images of children's writing and compare standards at the end of each week.

Recommended readings – academic papers:

- Visit http://tinyurl.com/cesujs3 for a stimulating academic paper by Medwell and Wray (2008) that asks whether handwriting is a forgotten language skill, reflecting on international research findings across primary age phase equivalents in relation to handwriting standards and practices.

- Visit http://tinyurl.com/7ozrzrd for an interesting research paper by Medwell et al. (2009) that highlights the importance of handwriting in supporting composition processes used by Year 6 children.

- A recommended book is: Bennett, J. (2007) *The Handwriting Pocketbook*. Alresford: Teachers' Pocketbooks.

Idea 4.1: Crafty stories	Suggested age group: 3-year-olds to 5-year-olds

Explanation:

Young children enjoy opportunities to be creative with different materials, media, surfaces and tools that allow them to explore, experiment and express themselves in a variety of ways (DfE, 2012a). *Crafty stories* encourage teachers to embrace the idea that writing is not just about 'pens and paper' but involves a wide range of *arts and craft* equipment, resources and implements which help young children to make meaningful marks associated with the stories they wish to tell.

Stimulating *Crafty story* suggestions:

Support children (4–5) in creating a *Crafty story* by offering them 'crafty' suggestions as they work:

- *The crafty fox!* Why is the fox crafty? Who does the fox meet on his way to the pigeon coop? Does the fox get to eat one of the pigeons or does the pigeon owner scare the fox away?
- *Invent a craft!* Think Aircraft, Hovercraft, Spacecraft. If children were an inventor for the day what new kind of 'craft' could they create – a Doggie*craft?* A Hat*craft?* A Cycle*craft?* A Book*craft?* What can these different things do? What happens when the 'inventor'/others use them?

Super surfaces to stimulate mark-making:

An effective way of engaging young children in mark-making activities is to keep the surfaces that they mark-make on interesting. Examples include: *newspapers with big thick marker pens; large fallen leaves and 'runny' glue; plastic sheeting and 'splatter paint'; plywood and felt-tip pens; slate and chalk; bed sheets and ball bearings covered in paint; tarpaulin and ink stamps.* Use planning sheets in the setting/ school to ensure that a 'suite' of varied writing surfaces are on offer for children as part of the child initiated/adult-led provision in the classroom/outdoor play area.

Changing stories in the early years:

Clarke and Featherstone (2008: 58) argue that 'children often talk as they work, describing what they are doing, the colours they are using and even the story they are drawing or painting. A story often grows and changes as the child talks and draws or paints, and if you listen and watch the creation change you will hear the story, rather than waiting for an end result.' Have a dictaphone or a digital camera to hand to capture audio/visual evidence of young children's *Crafty stories*, both the process of writing it and the finished product.

Encouraging and strengthening a pincer grip:

To ensure that young children work towards developing an efficient control over pencils and pens when writing their *Crafty story*, they need to acquire a grip (known as the 'pincer grip') that is 'relaxed' and 'facilitates flowing movement' (DCSF, 2008a). Activities that help to encourage and strengthen this grip include:

- Pushing and pulling matchsticks in and out of Play-Doh.
- Playing tiddlywinks and flicking paper balls into a 'goal'.
- Sprinkling sequins on the table and, then picking them up with plastic tweezers.
- Shaping clay, Moon Dough or Plasticine with tiny pinch-like movements.

See Selin (2003) for further ideas.

Idea 4.2: Water stories	Suggested age group: 5-year-olds to 11-year-olds

Explanation:

Ask children to name one of the most important 'necessities' for living things and you are likely to get some or all of the following responses: *'Air!'*, *'Heat!'*, *'X-Box!'*, *'Sun!'*, *'Mobile phone!'*, *'Food!'* and *'Water!'*. The notion of water is very powerful for stimulating story writing, both as a story resource and as a story theme. *Water stories* attempt to emphasise the key role that water plays in the lives of living things by offering children a wealth of creative potential when incorporating water and entities associated with it into their stories.

Exploring the notion of 'water':

There are a number of ways in which water can be explored in children's stories:

- 5–7: Watery weather, e.g. sleet, snow, rain, hail, mist and drizzle. *How does this affect the characters in the story? Is there a change in weather in the tale? Does this signify a change in time (e.g. autumn to winter)?*
- 7–11: Different states of water, e.g. frozen, melting, vapour, running and still. *Where/why is the water like this? How does this affect the behaviour/movements of characters?*
- 5–9: Bodies of water, e.g. fjords, lakes, streams, seas, oceans, ponds and puddles. *Who lives in them/ by them? Why do they live there?*
- 7–11: Dangerous water, e.g. frozen ponds, black ice patches and avalanches. *What problems do these cause different characters in the story?*

Well-known 'watery' characters:

There are many familiar characters in children's stories and films which are associated with water, e.g. *Captain Pugwash*, *Nemo* (the clown fish), *Ariel* (*The Little Mermaid*), *Captain Jack Sparrow* (*Pirates of the Caribbean*), *Rainbow Fish* and *Captain Hook* (*Peter Pan*). Work with children to establish what makes these characters so distinctive and well known, paying particular attention to their physical appearance, the way they move, how they react to others, their speech and their mannerisms. Encourage children to consider how they can use this knowledge to create memorable characters of their own in their *Water stories*.

Water in stories:

There are many ways in which children can incorporate water into their stories:

- Exercise – *swimming, drinking water.*
- Irrigation – *watering plants and crops.*
- Cleaning – *washing up, having showers and baths, cleaning clothes.*
- Growth – *flowers, plants, trees and animals.*
- Power sources – *mills.*
- Healing – *cleaning wounds, rehydration.*

Boys and water-based stimulation:

One of the benefits of integrating water into children's stories is that it can be used to entice boys into writing. Various water-based vehicles can be used to excite and energise boys' stories, e.g. *boats, submarines, yachts, rowing boats, jet skis, ships, dinghies* and *speedboats* – these can bring speed, adventure, races and action into the 'story fold' (Millard, 1997). Underwater lairs, dark ocean depths and secret islands offer boys possibilities in terms of setting their story in interesting locations, along with bringing unusual characters into their stimulating stories, e.g. *monsters, mer-creatures, pirates,* and *talking seaweed men.*

Idea 4.3: Paint stories	**Suggested age group:** 3-year-olds to 7-year-olds

Explanation:

Smith (2006) claims that '[a]ll children love to draw or paint'. This assertion has been the inspiration for *Paint stories*; by replacing pens and pencils with paint brushes and rollers, *Paint stories* serve to encourage young children to *love* writing by not only mark-making/writing stories in paint but also illustrating the stories they create with wonderful painted images.

'Fuelling' young children's story writing with paint:

There are a number of ways in which paint can be used to stimulate young children's story writing:

1. *The magic painting!* An artist paints a picture and overnight the object he/she has painted comes to life – *what did the artist paint? Does the artist meet the object he/she painted? What happens to them both? Does the object stay alive or does it return to the painting?* Alternatively, the artist can be given a magic paint brush – whatever is painted comes alive!

2. *Brown Bear, Brown Bear, What Do You See?* Extend Martin Jr.'s (1995) classic picture book by encouraging children to create additional animals, e.g. a *pink rabbit; a cream zebra; a lilac rat.*

3. *'Refresher' stories!* Encourage children to paint scenes from well-known stories using pastel colours similar to those used to colour Refreshers, the classic sherbety fizzy sweet. 'Refresh' readers' minds with an oral retelling of the story (3–5) or with simple written sentences (5–7).

The importance of painting pictures for early writers:

Crick Software Inc. (2011) argues that there are a number of reasons for young writers (4–7) to paint pictures, particularly if they use interactive ICT computer programmes such as *Clicker Paint*:

- '[They may] paint a picture to show the main idea, helping them to think about what they want to write.

- They may paint pictures to illustrate anecdotal writing or paint several pictures in sequence, helping them to organize their ideas, and to develop an understanding of beginning, middle, and end in story writing.

- [T]hey may simply want to paint a picture to illustrate their story and really enhance their finished work.'

Top Tip! Encourage children to engage with desktop publishing programs, internet-based word processors with voice annotation facilities, and multimedia authoring programs to support young children's story writing. See http://tinyurl.com/757l3vz for a wealth of examples; also see *ICT stories* (p. 125).

'Trapped in a painting' – unleashing stories:

Ng (n.d.) suggests that '[a] writer . . . is an artist whose words paint the picture. And every "painting" drawn or written tells a story.' Show children images of famous paintings such as da Vinci's *Mona Lisa*, Van Gogh's *Sunflowers* or Rousseau's *Surprised! Storm in the Forest*, getting them to think about an interesting story linked to the painting, e.g. *Mona Lisa goes shopping for clown shoes; the Sunflowers become a pop singing sensation; Tiger makes a new 'fishy' friend*. Alternative images for inspiration could be in the form of pictures, photographs or sketches.

Idea 4.4: Penned stories	Suggested age group: 5-year-olds to 11-year-olds

Explanation:

In times gone by writers had a limited range of materials with which they could produce their work e.g. chalk and slate/quill and parchment. With the surge of technological advances over the last 30 years or so, many writers have moved away from scribbling in little notebooks to recording their work through electronic means (Baron, 2009). Whilst schools work hard to embrace these developments through their ICT provision, there is much concern that the 'email and text generation are unable to write properly by hand' (Garner, 2008). *Penned stories* actively strive to address current standards in children's handwriting by promoting the use of different writing tools for children to select from and write their stories with (see the introduction for Chapter 4, p. 83).

The importance of handwriting – *research findings*:

1. Research by Dunsmuir and Blatchford (2004, cited in O'Brien and Neal, 2007: 5) suggests that there is a strong link between handwriting and later achievement in writing.
2. Bowan (2003, cited in O'Brien and Neal, 2007: 5) argues that handwriting is the key to literacy. For boys in particular, problems with handwriting can severely affect their performance in literacy based work.

Penned stories are thus aptly designed to improve children's writing performance and achievements!

Top Tip! To help address various issues related to children's handwriting, consider accessing the following informative and strategy laden web links: http://tinyurl.com/7w7dp44, http://tinyurl.com/7842wrc and http://tinyurl.com/7ybcu8n.

Writing tools and their usage:

Use the grid below to select/offer children appropriate writing tools for the stories/writing activities they are to engage with:

Writing tool	Usage
Unusual pens, e.g. quill pens, reed pens	For stories about olden times, e.g. Ancient Greece
Felt-tip pens/markers	For stories set in a fanciful, colourful wonderland
Fountain pens/free ink rollers	For historical stories, myths, legends or fables
Ball-point pens, e.g. biros	For story planning, e.g. jotting down ideas and thoughts
Highlighter pens – various thicknesses	For emphasising speech and onomatopoeic words
Whiteboard/wipe board markers	For story planning and drafting activities
Gel pens – scented, coloured	For special 'Friday'/'end of term' story writing activities
Fine-line pens – various makes	For writing up 'best' versions of written stories

For those children with SEND, natural materials could be used as *alternative* writing tools to draw/write/plan parts of their story, e.g. sticks and twig in mud.

Stimulating 'penned' potential:

Pens and pencils can offer a wealth of potential for children's story writing, especially when they are identified as being a particular *kind* of pen/pencil. Work with children to consider what could happen in stories that involve *magic pencils, musical pens, fairy pencils, bad-tempered pens, sickly pencils, pens for use in space, fancy dress pencils, dinosaur-loving pens, fast-writing pencils* or *telepathic pens.*

| Idea 4.5: Papered stories | Suggested age group: 3-year-olds to 11-year-olds |

Explanation:

When children are asked to write a story it is standard practice for them to record this either in their literacy books or on separate sheets of writing paper (lined or plain). *Papered stories* aim to offer variety in the material that is offered for children to mark-make/write their stories on. This not only serves to respond to the type and focus of the story being written[†], it also acts as an interesting display strategy that provides children with an incentive to read their peers' stories.

Recording social stories – *links to provision and practice*:

When writing social stories (for information visit http://tinyurl.com/6gf3s7c), myaspergerschild.com (2011) suggests that these 'can be written in book format, bound or placed in a notebook. However, they can also be written on poster board, cardboard, laminated paper, or on a chalk-board'. *Papered stories* embrace this idea by suggesting a wealth of paper types listed in the box below* which can be used to vary the kind of 'page' children use to record their story on.

*Paper types:

There are many different paper types which children should have experience of mark-making/writing on; these include:

Parchment	Construction/craft	Wrapping	Music manuscript	Blotting	Fluorescent
Cotton	Mummy	Filter	Toilet	Art	Wax
Waterproof	Rice	Greaseproof	Graph/grid	Sand/glass	Laid
Sugar	Tissue	Marble	Drawing	Banana	Wall

[†]Link the type of paper being used to different stimulating story ideas, for example:

- Wrapping – *what surprise present is being wrapped up? Who is it for? Do they like it when they open it?* (5–7)
- Waterproof – *what do characters creatively make out of this paper to protect themselves from bad weather?* (7–9)
- Drawing – *what do characters draw that become real entities during the night of the magic storm?* (9–11)

The effects of different 'approaches' to story writing (5–11):

Ellis (2003, cited in Bammens, 2009: 48) argues that largely *unscripted* approaches to story writing (in essence letting children *just get on with it*) encourage pupils to 'use strategic decisions to engage intellectually with the writing process and through this create new ideas and meanings'. Alternatively, strongly *scripted* tasks (those writing activities that are teacher led/adult directed/structured) serve more as a grammatical exercise which does not draw on the child's creativity or trigger any cognitive demands: 'When tasks orchestrate the content and structure of writing, pupils can come to believe that the writing process should be easy and unproblematic' (2009: 48).

Reflect! Consider the implications of the above on your provision for story writing – do you offer a balance of approaches, or is there more of a *scripted* approach used in your classroom? Why so? What effects do you think this might be having on children's story writing in your class? How could you facilitate more of a balance when children are asked to write a *Papered story*?

Idea 4.6: Tall stories	Suggested age group: 7-year-olds to 11-year-olds

Explanation:

Kaye and Jacobson (1999: 2) suggest that stories can be 'true tales or tall tales'. Tall tales refer to stories that are considered to be unbelievable or untrue; Martin (2011) calls them 'pieces of verbal exaggeration or boastfulness which may be intended to deceive or may be openly bogus and merely intended to amuse'. *Tall stories* allow children to deliberately exaggerate, creatively embellishing story events and characters so that they appear 'over the top' and rather 'inflated' to both the writer and the reader.

How and what to exaggerate:

Children need to appreciate that in *Tall stories* everything needs to be '-er'[†]: *bigger, bolder, stronger, taller, thicker, sweeter, faster, lighter, darker, smellier* and *happier*. For stories to be 'tall' they need to include a) imaginary events which seem a little outrageous, and b) 'larger than life' characters:

'Exaggerated' events	Examples of 'larger than life' characters taken from children's literature
Building a paper house during a tornado	*Young James Bond* (007)
Trekking through blizzards at the North Pole in swimming trunks	Willy Wonka (from *Charlie and the Chocolate Factory*)
Lifting a car with one finger to fix a burst tyre	*The Demon Headmaster*
Catching the biggest pike from the lake with one's bare hands	The Queen of Hearts (from *Alice in Wonderland*)*

*It is interesting to note that McCabe et al.'s (2011) study of children's books found 57% of them had males as central characters, with only 31% having female central characters. Use *Tall stories* as an opportunity for children to write stories about 'larger than life' female characters (think Miss Trunchbull in Roald Dahl's *Matilda*) in an attempt to strike a gender balance in character leads.

Accentuating 'tallness' through art:

There are a couple of ways children can use their artistic talents to effectively present and display the *Tall stories* they write:

- *Tall strips* – present *Tall stories* on long, thin colourful strips of paper which can be hung from the classroom ceiling (7–9).
- *Tall tubes* – get children to tape sheets of newspaper together and roll them up into a tube. By pulling the paper from the centre of the roll, children can create a tall paper tube on which they can paste their *Tall story* (9–11).

[†]Adjective Alphabet Logs:

Children can stimulate and intensify descriptions of characters and settings by 'amplifying' the adjectives used in their *Tall story*. Adjective Alphabet Logs encourage children to keep a record of different descriptive words against each letter of the alphabet (see Appendix 12, p. 218). Children can add new words they find to individual, group or whole-class logs, recording these in different colours to indicate their applicability to different genders, if they so wish. This idea can be extended to alternative kinds of logs, for example noun, verb, adverb and setting alphabet logs (see Appendix 13, p. 219), which could be displayed around the classroom for reference. Consider how they can be used to enrich *Tall stories* children write.

Idea 4.7: Decorated stories	Suggested age group: 3-year-olds to 11-year-olds

Explanation:

It is well known that readers should never judge a book by its cover. This Idea challenges this English idiom by actively promoting not only the decoration of title pages, but also the *entirety* of children's stories *as* they are being written, as opposed to once they have been completed. *Decorated stories* aim to combine the skills of writing with the skills of artistic decoration by offering children 'little arty breaks' throughout the writing process, thus allowing them to include appropriate decorative* features and illustrations to their written story in an attempt to stimulate and maintain engagement and concentration levels.

The thinking behind *Decoration stories*:

Story writing demands a lot of the writer (Flower and Hayes, cited in Gregg and Steinberg, 1980), concentration-level wise. In any class there will be children whose minds are prone to wandering; they become restless and rapidly lose interest in the writing activity set because of their limited attention span. *Decorated stories* offer a 'little and often' writing strategy to sustain children's attention levels and raise written productivity. Children may be encouraged to work on their decorations for just 2–3 minutes at a time, but this serves as a useful 'brain breather' for children (see http://tinyurl.com/7gbuxvv). Other brain breathers can be facilitated through the following:

- Children get out of their chairs and have an all over *body wriggle* (3–5).
- Children go outside for a two minute *run-a-round* in the playground (5–7).
- Children perform a simple dance routine to music or a series of stretches prior to returning to their work (7–11).

*The meaning of 'decorate':

Decorating, in the context of story writing, can mean different things:

1. Decorating the border of the paper on which the story is written.
2. Decorating the actual written text.
3. Replacing words with decorative signs and symbols *within* the text.
4. Presenting illustrations which 'decorate' the page.

Various strategies for decorating stories:

- Offering an illustration that relates to a key part of the story using crayons, pencils or paints. Ensure children check that the illustration links to the text (see http://tinyurl.com/7kfnk9x).
- Making the paper the story is written on more visually attractive, e.g. writing on rainbow coloured paper, or adding symbols, shapes, objects and/or numbers *around* the story to reflect its theme, e.g. stars to indicate a story about bedtime or space†.

†Additional strategies for decorating stories:

- Cutting the paper into a specific shape, e.g. a witch's hat.
- Adding transfer stickers to the paper.
- Using inked stamps in and around the outside of the text.
- Creating a 3-D border around the story using tissue paper, glitter, pipe cleaners and glue.
- Creating a border around the story using 'shaped' hole punches.
- Mounting the story on backing paper/fabric for display purposes.

Idea 4.8: TV stories	Suggested age group: 7-year-olds to 11-year-olds

Explanation:

There is a wealth of evidence to suggest that children today watch too much TV (Hersey and Jordan, 2007). However, many of us forget how many of the programmes and films children view are a great way of learning about stories and the art of storytelling through speech, visual images and acting. *TV stories* aim to promote high-quality story writing by getting the very best stories that children write up on TV screens* for their friends and family members/carers to view!

*Types of 'TV screens':

Whilst there are few opportunities available for children to get the stories they write actually broadcast on the TV, the following suggestions are offered as 'TV alternatives':

- Writing stories on a paper TV set template (plasma, portable, old style – see Appendix 14, p. 220).
- Writing on 'screen shaped' paper which can be temporarily fastened to the TV screen at home.
- Making a TV out of a cardboard box (*large* – washing machine box; *small* – cereal box) and pasting the written story on the 'inside wall' of the set.

Top Tip! Visit http://tinyurl.com/bmb725c for an innovative 'TV time display device'!

Developing the Idea:

- Encourage children to identify programmes that family members/carers like to watch – could they integrate different characters, settings and events from these shows into their written story to sustain 'viewers'' interests? (7–9)
- Viewers frequently like to switch channels – could children write an *alternative* story or a *series* of stories just in case someone decides to 'turn over'? (9–11)
- If family members/carers want to get involved in writing a *TV story* together for a *new* channel (e.g. *Who 4*; *r-I-t*), direct them to http://tinyurl.com/7o842f2 to offer them some great story ideas – *an engaging weekend/holiday homework task perhaps?* (7–11)

Approaches to stimulating children's writing – *research findings*:

Ings' (2009) report into the success of the *Writing is Primary* Project (2007–8) highlighted how '. . . stimulating [children's] emotions and imagination gave pupils a reason to write, motivating them to plan, plot and sequence, work on and improve a piece of writing through several drafts' (2009: 41). *TV stories* effectively give children a reason to write as their story is to be presented for others to read and comment on. This will hopefully motivate them through the excitement of presenting their stories for others to read and enjoy in an innovative and interesting way.

Stimulating *TV story* title suggestions:

1. *Peppa Pig*, *Rapunzel* and the terrible tremor!
2. *Hannah Montana* visits the set of *Glee* for the day!
3. The day the *MTV* presenters broke out of the TV set!
4. The cast of *Eastenders* and *Coronation Street* together at the fun fairground!
5. *Wayne Rooney* and *Kate Middleton* dig their way down to the centre of the Earth!

Idea 4.9: Sweet stories	**Suggested age group:** 3-year-olds to 11-year-olds

Explanation:

The inspiration for *Sweet stories* came from a recent reading of *Charlie and the Chocolate Factory* (Dahl, 2001). The incredible array of sweets, treats and chocolates that Willy Wonka invented is clearly something which will impress all children, particularly as research has shown that children are biologically hard-wired to have stronger cravings for sweets than adults (see Stein, 2009). *Sweet stories* encourage children to get their creative juices flowing by inventing new confectionary that has an interesting *effect** on those that eat them!

*The *'sweet effect'* – exploring possibilities:

It is argued that for a story to be interesting something has to happen. *Sweet stories* facilitate this by getting children to think about what happens to characters when they eat their new confectionary. Stimulating suggestions include:

- Characters swell to the size of a hot air balloon!
- Characters change colour (skin, hair, eyes and/or teeth)!
- Characters begin to speak in an unknown language!
- Characters develop super powers!
- Characters start to grow backwards, e.g. an 11-year-old regresses back to being a toddler!
- Characters develop excessive levels of self-confidence!
- Characters turn into an excitable animal!
- Characters suddenly learn everything to know about everything!
- Characters learn to love themselves and others.

Promote active discussions about the effects of eating children's new confectionary by getting them to create 3-D models made out of salt/Play-Dough (3–5), drawings/paintings of their new sweets (5–7), or written descriptions/'fact files' of their new product (7–11), sharing these with teachers and peers to generate 'effect' ideas.

Questions, questions, questions!:

An effective strategy to support children's *Sweet story* writing is by asking questions (Wiltshire LA Literacy Team, 2008). Posing various verbal/written questions to children *prior*, *during* and *post* the writing of their story will help them to organise and order their stories appropriately. Questions stems (*Who . . . ? What . . . ? Where . . . ? How . . . ? Why . . . ? When . . . ?*) actively promote thinking and encourage children to monitor their story and its content (also see http://tinyurl.com/7bwqhej). Story questions e.g. *What happens at the start? What is going to happen next? And then? What about after that? How will it all end?* serve as an example of 'prompts' to inspire young writers.

Download! Visit http://tinyurl.com/7yer623 for some valuable downloadable writing resources for use in the classroom and at home.

Sweet! 'Sweet' stories:

An alternative interpretation of *Sweet stories* is 'Sweet' stories – stories which make readers smile, go 'Aww!' or make them feel good inside. 'Sweet' stories encourage children to mark-make/write heart-warming stories about characters who say and do nice things such as caring for sick people or animals, saying 'I love you', surprising someone with a bunch of flowers or a card, or saying something that shows their naivety or innocence, e.g. *the moon is just the sun out at night.*

Idea 4.10: Fabric stories	Suggested age group: 3-year-olds to 7-year-olds

Explanation:

Erez (2010) claims that Chalayan, a leading name in contemporary art and fashion, 'weaves stories in fabric' – it was this little statement which sparked the Idea for *Fabric stories*. *Fabric stories* are designed to allow young children to use pieces of fabric for a multitude of story purposes: as an alternative 'writing canvas'*, a presentation feature of the story†, as flaps to 'hide and reveal' pictures and text (see *Flip-flap stories*, p. 177), or as a surface onto which written stories can be mounted/presented on.

*An alternative 'writing canvas' – fabrics and children's stories:

Children are so used to writing on paper that in an effort to generate new interest in story writing teachers are encouraged to offer different pieces of fabric for children to mark-make/write on, examples of which include *corduroy, velvet, denim, flannel, bagging* and *satin*. Allow children to mark-make/ write sentences on fabric which is suitably stretched and taped to the table to prevent snagging. Offer a range of fabric markers, ink pens, paint brushes, or thick felt-tip pens for children to experiment/ write with (remembering to put paper underneath the fabric to save the ink staining the table!). Use chequered fabric pieces to help children break the flow of speech into individual words, one word being presented in each square.

Fabrics and 'textured' vocabulary:

When children (5–7) describe what their characters are wearing in their stories there is a tendency for them to give mention to just the colour, e.g. a *red* coat; a *blue* T-shirt. Having access to different fabric offcuts offers a 'sensory learning experience' (Dorrell, 2008) for children to gain knowledge and understanding about different textures, e.g. *soft, hard, silky, wet, rough, smooth, sticky, grainy, woody, raised, scaly, shiny, wavy, bumpy* and *stringy*. Support children to understand how these words can also be associated with other features of a character, e.g. a *silky smooth* face, *wet* hair, *shiny* boots, *soft* ears and *raised* eyebrows.

†Presenting stories on fabric:

There are a number of ways children can present their written stories on fabric:

- *Gluing* – Younger children (3–5) could glue their mark-making efforts on paper directly onto fabric. Alternatives include *stapling* or *pinning* the paper to fabric.
- *Sewing* – Older children (5–7) could write simple sentences onto pieces of fabric and then emphasise significant words/phrases, e.g. **YES!** with a plastic/metal needle and thick cotton.
- *Stamping* – Younger children (3–5) can use letter stamps and ink pads to print their words/ sentences directly onto fabric pieces.
- *Stencilling* – Older children (5–7) could stencil individual letters directly onto fabric with suitable fabric markers to build up words and sentences.

Stimulating story ideas for *Fabric stories*:

1. 3–5: *A blanket made of . . . ?* Get children to identify unusual fabrics to make a blanket out of, considering how it would feel to be wrapped up inside it and who it would be for.
2. 5–7: *A Fabric World!* Imagine that children in your class wake up one morning to find the natural world has been turned into a world made out of fabric – *what are different things made out of? How do they feel? How does this change the way children live their lives?*

5

'Engaging' stories

This chapter focuses its attention on stories which are purposefully designed to 'engage' children, both at a motivational and active level. As OFSTED (2003: 19) favourably acknowledge the 'intense . . . engage[ment]' of children at 'all levels of attainment' in observed writing activities, this chapter serves to offer a range of story Ideas whose principal aim is to absorb, engross and captivate children across the 3–11 age range.

The first half of the chapter uses 'parties' as the engaging theme to link the first five Ideas together. As most children like parties, *Party stories* are offered by way of including story writing into the 'party mix' by making the stories that children write an integral feature of the party provisions! For example, a popular game played during children's parties is 'Pass the parcel' – *Parcel stories*, the second Idea in this chapter, use the basic premise of this game for some innovative story writing/reading opportunities! Healthy competition can be used as a motivating tactic to get children at parties involved in dancing contests, team games and playing 'musical bumps/chairs' – *Competition stories* work to embrace this element of competitiveness as a 'challenge ploy' by engaging children in stimulating story writing competitions in an effort to enhance engagement and attainment levels. The winner of a party game/competition typically receives some kind of prize; for young children this is likely to be a stuffed toy. *Toy stories* consider how children could use these toys as 'story fuel', reflecting on suitable toys that should come alive, be they 3-D or 2-D. Going to a party gives children the opportunity to wear clothes that are distinctively different from their 'working attire' (i.e. their school uniform) – *Clothing stories* encourage children to use some of their old clothing as a fabric canvas for them to literally wear the stimulating stories that they write.

The second half of the chapter aims to engage children through a selection of memorable story writing activities linked to the engaging theme of 'building'. *Crazy stories* embrace the zany world of Dr. Seuss by encouraging children to effectively 'build' crazy story characters and crazy story settings for their stories. *Soft stories* promote 'gentle' story writing, allowing children to write *light stories* which are 'built' around 'informal or light-hearted events, using real-life characters and familiar themes' (p. 112). *Scroll stories* offer children the exciting opportunity to 'build' rolled-up books with long pieces of paper and dowel on which they can unwind/wind their creative stories. *DIY stories* and *Either–Or stories*, which close this chapter, embrace the idea of readers taking ownership of the stories that they read by either 'building' stories through gap-filling (*DIY stories*) or making decisions about the direction in which the story they read should go (*Either–Or stories*).

Taking a closer look at 'varying the plot'

In *Soft stories* (p. 112) it is highlighted that there are a number of basic plots found in literature. Plot is a significant element of a story which children need to develop an appreciation and understanding of; if you were to metaphorically bake a story, the plot would probably be the most important ingredient. But what is meant by the term 'plot'?

Activity!

Read the following definitions of 'plot' and consider the one that mirrors, or is somewhat similar to, your personal understanding of the term:

- The series of events that give a story its meaning and effect (Bedford St. Martin's).
- The pattern of events or main story in a narrative or drama (Thefreedictionary.com).

- The series of events in the story, chronological or not, which serve to move the story from its beginning through its climax or turning point and to a resolution of its conflicts (Frank Schaefer).
- The plan, scheme, or main story of a literary or dramatic work, as a play, novel, or short story. Also called storyline (Dictionary.com).
- The organization of the main events of a work of fiction (Ginny Wiehardt).

What is important to recognise is that plot is *different* from story. This is likely to come as a surprise to many children (and teachers), particularly as it is believed that '"plot" and "story" [are] just two different ways of saying the same thing' (Anders, 2009). This view is challenged by Wyatt (2012b), who claims that '[a] plot is not a story, nor does every story have a strong plot'. In an effort to distinguish between the two terms, Forster (1927) defines *story* as the chronological sequence of events and *plot* as the causal and logical structure which connects events (1927: 93). To illustrate the difference Forster offers the following:

1. *The king died and then the queen died.*
2. *The king died and then the queen died of grief.*

Reflect!

Based on Forster's definitions, which of the above would you say is a *story* – 1 or 2? Why? Which would you say is a *plot* – 1 or 2? Why?

Both of Forster's examples offer the reader *incidences*: the king and queen dying, in the first example the incidents are organised *subsequently* (one after another), whereas in the second example the incidents are linked *consequently* by cause and effect (i.e. the queen died of grief *as a result* of the king dying). By referring back to Forster's definitions the first example is one of a *story*, with the second being an example of *plot*. Chhabria (2011) offers another example, which has been personally adapted:

1. *A girl meets a boy, the boy saves the girl, the girl is charmed by his bravery and falls in love with him.*
2. *A girl and a boy meet and fall in love.*

It is anticipated that the reader is able to recognise that the *first* example is a *plot* – 'there is a series of events, one leading to another in a logical way. This is what a plot is all about' (Chhabria, 2011). The plot presents the events in such a way to show their causality, how one gives rise to another (rather than simply happening prior to it) (Forster, 1927, cited in Chhabria, 2011). The *second* example is a *story*, as it merely consists of the events as they happened in chronological order. In an effort to summarise the above a simple table for reference is offered in Table 5.1.

Table 5.1 The difference between 'story' and 'plot'

Question	Definition	Example
What is story?	A story is a series of events with a beginning, middle and an end. *In essence story is what happens.*	Sammy and Hassan went to the park and played on the swings. It got cold and they ran home.
What is plot?	A plot is a series of events which link together and show cause and effect. *In essence plot is how events are presented – the structure of what happens.*	Sammy and Hassan wanted to play on the swings so they went to the park. Whilst they were there is became dark and cold, and because they did not have their coats with them, they had to run home.
What is the difference between story and plot?	See the examples above – the example of a story merely offers a simple series of events; the example of a plot points out the *cause and effect*; e.g. Sammy and Hassan wanted to play on the swings *so* they went to the park. *Because* they did not have their coats with them, they had to run home *due* to it becoming dark and cold.	

Efforts to help children learn effectively about plot in stories can be supported by teachers selecting from and adapting the following teaching strategies and information in response to the needs of the children they work with:

- Teach children the second verse of *Five Things*, a hip-hop style song that 'covers the five main elements of a story: setting, *plot*, characters, conflict and theme' (see Flocabulary, 2012) (7–11).

- Encourage children initially to write their *story* by getting the events down on paper so that the reader finds out who the characters are and what they do. Any redrafting should be used to 'craft the *plot*', making who the characters are and what they do structurally right and balanced correctly (Klein, 2006) (6–11).

- Use the PowerPoint presentation available at http://tinyurl. com/bn2ph62 to support children's 'visual' understanding of the different plot elements: *exposition, rising action, climax, falling action* and *resolution*. Also see http://tinyurl.com/ dxek38s for a useful PDF (7–11).

- Create a list of five writing tips from the information offered by the Institute of Children's Literature linked to story plot (visit http://tinyurl.com/bwjsegu). Share these as direct teaching points or display them on a *Plots R Uz* class notice board as a visual reminder to support children when writing their stories (5–11).

- Make children aware of different basic plot structures when reading/looking at/talking about picture books (both wordless and with words). See Crum (2006) for a brilliant article about 'story skeletons'; alternatively, download the excellent *Seven Story Plot Patterns* by Moore (2000) (5–11).

- Help children to link story ideas together by using their knowledge of chronology from their work in History (NC)/ Understanding the world: People and communities (EYFS). Use known stories (verbal/written) as a model, for example, *what happens at the start of Little Red Riding Hood? During her walk through the forest who does she meet? Then what happens?* (3–7).

- Model the use of graphic organisers (story maps, for example) to help children visually appreciate how stories are structured and how they can use these to structure the stories that they write. Visit http://tinyurl.com/nlwdg for examples (3–11).

- 'Listening to stories and acting out [working-in-role] the sequence of actions through creative drama, drawing and illustrating plot diagrams . . . and writing stories motivated by wordless books are all ways to help younger students understand plot structures' (Norton, 1992: 254) (4–7).

- Visit http://tinyurl.com/c7hgmmh to develop your personal understanding of plot, identifying key points which you could use when directly teaching the children in your classroom about plot (4–11).

- Encourage children to plot the significant events of their story on individual Post-it® notes/pieces of paper. Shuffle them up and pass them to one of their peers to see if they can sequence the story, justifying their decisions in relation to their understanding of cause and effect (6–11).

Table 5.2   Recommended readings associated with 'Engaging' stories

Books	**5–7:** Grainger, T., Goouch, K. and Lambrinth, A. (2004a) *Creative Activities for Plot, Character and Setting: Ages 5–7*. Warwickshire: Scholastic. **7–9:** Grainger, T., Goouch, K. and Lambrinth, A. (2004b) *Creative Activities for Plot, Character and Setting: Ages 7–9*. Warwickshire: Scholastic. **9–11:** Grainger, T., Goouch, K. and Lambrinth, A. (2004c) *Creative Activities for Plot, Character and Setting: Ages 9–11*. Warwickshire: Scholastic. *Each of these books has a valuable initial chapter that offers a range of practical approaches for teachers to use with children to 'examine . . . discuss . . . experience . . . and compose' story structure in the classroom (2004b: 7). Personal favourites include 'Three seeds of a story' (5–7), 'Story plates' (7–9) and 'Parallel plots' (9–11). Consider their use as part of your direct teaching and as strategies for children to use when creating a structure for their 'Engaging' stories.*

Research papers	Alexander, J. and Griffith, J. (n.d.) *Exploring Flow Charts as a Tool for Thinking*. [Online]. Available at: http://tinyurl.com/7k27ahn (Accessed: 18 May 2012). *This informative research paper describes how teachers in a small American elementary school used different flow diagrams to 'enable students* [aged 6–8] *to see sequences and the relationships between cause and effect* [plot]*' (p. 1) in the stories they read and wrote.* Consider the use of flowcharts in supporting children in your class to clearly identify events that influence plot development in the *'Engaging' stories* that they write. Maclusky, J. and Cox, R. (2011a) *Is There a Way Forward for Creative Writing Pedagogy in the Primary School Curriculum? An International Study*. [Online]. Available at: http://tinyurl.com/7wukcop (Accessed: 18 May 2012). *This interesting paper 'theorises the primary classroom as a "creative space" aligned to the notion of "creative industries"' (p. 1). The researchers reflect on the use of a series of trialled creative writing exercises in both England and Australia which adopt a workshop style pedagogy in the primary classroom.* Consider the impact of the researchers' conclusions (p. 10) on your role in the classroom when children are working on their *'Engaging' stories*.
Website	Teaching Ideas (2011) *Writing Fiction*. [Online]. Available at: http://tinyurl.com/85a3up9 (Accessed: 18 May 2012). *This website offers teachers a wealth of practical ideas and resources linked to story planning, story settings, story characters, and writing ideas to engage children across the primary age phase (5–11) in stimulating story writing opportunities.* Consider the use of these ideas and resources to support your teaching and children's engagement with their *'Engaging' stories*.

Idea 5.1: Party stories	Suggested age group: 3-year-olds to 11-year-olds

Explanation:

Parties are a great time for children to have fun and play games. *Party stories* use this time of socialising and enjoyment by creatively integrating story writing into the 'party mix'. *Party stories* encourage children to mark-make/write stories which become an integral feature of the party provisions – from the invitations and decorations to the cards and party ware! Children are to use these different party resources* as their 'writing paper', either recording their story directly onto the item or attaching it to it in some way. Those children invited to the party can read these *Party stories* as they wait to play party games, whilst they eat their party food, or on their way home from the event (seeing as a *Party story* has been included in their party bag!).

Sensational openings for *Party stories* (7–11):

If there is to be any chance that party goers are going to read the *Party stories* offered to them they need a narrative opening that immediately 'hooks' the reader into the tale. *Once upon a time . . .* and *Long, long ago . . .* are considered to be standard 'traditional' openers (see http://tinyurl.com/96mr2h6 for some interesting alternatives); Peat (2002: 50–55) suggests that children use the following instead:

Story opener	Meaning	*Party story* example
'In medias res'†	Starting the story †'in the middle of things'	*The party music started up again and everyone leapt to their feet, all apart from Mark . . .*
Contradictions	Offering a contradiction in the opening sentence	*I love birthday parties but I knew I was going to hate Gary's as soon as I walked into the scout hut.*
Surreal openings	Offering something 'unexpected'	*We were all sitting under the table eating dry birthday cake when the headless monster burst into the room.*
Asking questions	Presenting a question for the reader to answer	*Do you think it's awful I told Ann's mum that her party was the worst I had ever been to?*
Dialogue	Starting the story with speech	*'**I want a dinosaur-themed party!**' bellowed Jake at the top of his voice.*

Stimulating *Party story* titles:

- 'Thirty three for party tea§'!
- Emily's Christmas crisis!
- The stolen street party prize!
- **BOO!** Halloween at Harry's house!
- The birthday boy's *smelly surprise!*
- The day the Queen came to *par-tay!*
- *James* Lightyear and the Scouts' fancy dress party.

* *Party story* resources (3–11):

Allow children to select from the following resources to mark-make/record their *Party stories* on: *plates* and *place mats, banners* and *flag bunting, hats* and *other headwear, cups* and *glasses (plastic), balloons* and *streamers, cards* and *invitations, napkins* and *table cloths* and *in the party bag.*

§Different kinds of parties children can write *Party stories* about:

Select from the following: *Wedding, Christmas, Tea, Costume/Fancy dress, Fundraising, Halloween, Mardi Gras, Surprise, Easter, Anniversary, Christening, Street, Dinner, Graduation* and *Pet*(!). Also consider celebrations which children may engage with as part of their faith.

Idea 5.2: Parcel stories	Suggested age group: 5-year-olds to 11-year-olds

Explanation:

One of the classic games played during children's parties is 'pass the parcel' (see Kubler and Baker, 2004), which this Idea uses as a basis for some exciting story writing. Just like in pass the parcel, where the removal of each layer of paper gets closer to the prize (see Asquith and McEwen, 2005), a *Parcel story* gets closer to the end of the story! Each layer of paper has written on it part of a child's story; as each layer is removed from the parcel the next layer reveals more of the story until the prize is finally revealed – the last sentence/paragraph of the story!

Learning and teaching opportunities about story writing:

Parcel stories emphasise a number of key learning and teaching opportunities about story writing for teachers to share with their children:

- The narrative formula (Peat, 2002) – *what happens at the* beginning *of the Parcel story? What about in the* middle? How will the story end?
- Ways of planning *Parcel stories* – strategies include *thought-showers, notes, diagrams, grids, lists, sticky labels* and *story maps* (see http://tinyurl.com/7wv8wvl for further ideas).
- The passing of time to structure a sequence of events – *After that . . . Suddenly . . . Next . . . .*
- The length of a *Parcel story* – this *dependent on the number of layers of paper in the parcel!*

Strategies for *Parcel story* differentiation:

5–7:
1. Encourage children to write *at least* one sentence on sheet of paper.
2. Limit the number of layers of paper which make up their *Parcel story* – between six and seven layers, for example, depending on their ability.

7–11:
1. Support children in writing a small paragraph on each sheet of paper.
2. Extend the number of layers of paper to between 8–12, depending on the length and complexity of the story being written.

Stimulating *Parcel story* suggestions:

- *In the dark, dark house there was a dark, dark . . . ?* – What's in the dark, dark box? (5–7)
- *'Is it . . . ?' 'No! It's too . . .'!* – Offer 'spoken' questions and answers on each paper layer to determine what the hidden object is, e.g. *'Is it a book?', 'No! It's too big to be a book!'; 'Is it a TV remote?, No! It's too light!'* (7–9)
- *Seven days before Archie's birthday!* – Each paper layer instructs the birthday boy to do something silly/helpful/fun/weird/brave each day before he finally gets his present! (9–11)

Enriching *Parcel stories*:

- 5–7: Encourage children to 'test' out their *Parcel story* with scrap paper and junk materials *before* creating their final version.
- 7–11: Replace parcel forfeits between each paper layer with 'story writing challenges', e.g. *write a Parcel story about a pet pineapple without using any words with the letter 'M'*!
- 5–11: Save the *Parcel stories* children write, giving one to each child when it is their actual birthday! Children could also write simple *Parcel stories* for young children in the school (3–5) in an effort to learn about audience awareness (see Strange, 1988).

Idea 5.3: Competition stories	Suggested age group: 5-year-olds to 11-year-olds

Explanation:

If you were to say to your class 'We're going to write a story today!' you are likely to get a general murmuring of approval; say to your class 'We're going to have a story writing competition§ today!' and the response is likely to be very different! *Competition stories* are designed to excite, engage and motivate all children in purposeful, active† and healthy* competitive story writing activities which are designed to challenge and drive children to try what is personally referred to as their 'writing best'.

The benefits of competition – *story writing and research findings*:

§Johnson (1993) suggests that competition can 'encourage growth and push a child to excel'. Competitions can therefore help children in your class to practice and refine their story writing skills.

†Nobel and Bradford, (2000) firmly believe that boys in particular like competition as it allows them to 'do something [with their] learning – demonstrate it or transform it'. Boys, therefore, are likely to be more positively engaged in story writing activities through the use of competition in your class.

*Rimm (2008) argues that the 'the ability to function in competition is central to school and . . . achievement'. Offering story writing competitions in your class have the potential to enhance children's attainment and inspire them to *want* to write more stories!

Types of story writing competitions:

There are many different kinds of stimulating story writing competitions that teachers could propose – these are entirely dependent on what you want your children to focus on in terms of their story writing. Suggestions include:

5–7 year olds	7–11 year olds
Stories with the most clearly defined *characters*.	Stories which use the most vivid *descriptions*.
Stories which include clearly demarked '*speech*'.	Stories which effectively build *tension* as the plot develops.
Stories which use *less than 200 words*.	Stories which make readers *giggle* out loud.
Stories which *excite* readers to the point of not wanting the story to end!	Stories which use the most comprehensive *complex sentences*.

Top Tip! Consider linking story writing competitions to class writing objectives and individual/group writing targets – see those proposed by Murton Community Primary School (n.d.) via their downloadable (PDF) writing cards for the Early Years and Levels 1–5.

Competition prizes – *what could be won?*:

- Cash or vouchers (*from PFA funds*).
- Trophy (*personally made or school purchased*).
- Stationary/writing set.
- Story books (*child/teacher selected*).
- Treat from the 'Treasure Chest'.
- Writing 'Star' of the Week.
- Children's own choice of prize.
- Paul's 'Special Day' in school.

Getting into story writing competitions:

- Consider who should be the 'judge/s' for the story writing competition – *you? The child's peers? The Head teacher? Parents and carers? Governors?*
- Undertake a web search for 'children's story writing competitions' held by publishing companies, literary festivals and local/national radio stations for children – *why not submit stories written by your class for consideration?*

Idea 5.4: Toy stories	Suggested age group: 3-year-olds to 11-year-olds

Explanation:

Most children have seen Pixar's *Toy Story* trilogy starring Woody and Buzz Lightyear (see http://tinyurl.com/7mo6x6t). The success of these films can be attributed to great characters, interesting plots, marvellous dialogue and exciting adventures which captivate the viewer. The Idea of *Toy stories* adopts the basic premise of the films – toys that are 'living' – by allowing children to think about the toys that they win at a party or play with at home, considering what happens to them when they [the children] are at school during the day*.

*Possibility thinking for a *Toy Story*:

Carpenter (2011b) states that '[i]n Toy Story 3, the plot revolves around using toys imaginatively . . . it is a movie about kids playing with toys imaginatively.' But what imaginative things could toys get up to when their owners [children in your class] are at school? Use small world play (3–5) and discussion opportunities (5–7) to generate interesting ideas, examples of which include:

- Watch foreign TV channels.
- Bake green food.
- Draw/paint themselves.
- Turn the bedroom into a Toy gym.
- Write nonsense poetry.

- Decorate the house orange.
- Surf the Internet for cool clothes.
- Play silly card games.
- Compose song music/lyrics.

Making the *right* toys come alive:

Most children are fortunate enough to have a range of toys at home, many of which will be electronically based (Evans Schmidt et al., 2005). Children, particularly those aged 7–11, need to think about the toys they intend to bring to life in their *Toy story* as Wiis, Nintendo DS's and Xboxes are rather *limiting* when establishing character and plot. Toys with real story potential include:

- Toys with moveable parts so that they can physically move about, e.g. baby dolls and action figures such as Transformers.

- Toys with mouths or speaking facilities so that they can communicate with other toys, e.g. talking toy dogs, 'beeping' robots and models of animals with painted mouths.

- Toys which emulate the human or animal form, e.g. Action Man, Barbie®, and My Little Pony.

2-D or 3-D toys? Research into using toy stimuli for children's story writing:

1. Buttery et al. (1987) analysed the creative writing of second graders (7–8-year-olds) that was elicited from stuffed animals and wind-up toys. Whilst teachers may be tempted to suggest children bring in toys from home to stimulate their *Toy stories*, the writing process can be hindered if a) children start comparing who has the best/most expensive toy, b) if toys are obsessively handled by their owners, or c) are damaged/broken by others.

2. Bailey et al. (1995) used computer clip art and graphical presentation software with second graders (7–8-year-olds) and found that this *enhanced* the length and quality of written compositions and increased student self-esteem.

Reflect! Consider the most appropriate approach to stimulate *Toy stories* with the children you work with: 2-D images or the 3-D 'real thing'?

Idea 5.5: Clothing stories	Suggested age group: 3-year-olds to 11-year-olds

Explanation:

When it is a child's birthday party or it is Mufti Day (non-uniform day) at school, children have the opportunity to wear clothes that *they* want to wear. Many of the T-shirts and tops worn are likely to be covered in images, words, phrases, slogans or designer label name tags. *Clothing stories* take the Idea of text being displayed on clothing and adapts this as a stimulating story writing opportunity for children: to write creative stories on items of clothing which can then be worn for others to read and enjoy!

Clothing stories considerations and suggestions:

• As opposed to writing on their 'best' clothes, children should be encouraged to bring in from home old clothing or items which they do not wear anymore.
• For those parents and carers who are reluctant for their child to write on their clothing, fabric pieces from the school's art cupboard can be shaped into different clothing items. Alternatively, pieces of paper can be prepared to look like shorts, T-shirts and hats.
• Packs of plain T-shirts can be purchased quite cheaply from a range of shopping outlets.

Clothing items and Clothing story titles:

• T-shirt – *The T-shirt Chronicles*!
• Shorts – *Sam's secret short-shorts*!
• Shirt – *The Year 5 [9–10] wacky Hawaiian shirt design competition*!
• Jumper – *Jumping Jack Flash's jolly jumper*!
• Trousers – *Amanda's talented trousers*!

Additional clothing items and Clothing story titles:

• Vest – *Verity's singing violet vest*!
• Pants – *Peter's rather peculiar pants*!
• Skirt – *The flying skirt from Fentacee*!
• Socks – *'Seventeen socks and not one pair'*!
• Waistcoat – *The tiny heirloom in the pocket*!

Making marks on clothing (3–7):

Adults will know that it is fairly easy to 'mark' clothing – children aged 3–7 seem to be quite capable of doing it in their day-to-day play! To mark-make/write on clothing *with meaning*, fabric pens are recommended as they are designed specifically for this task. Alternatives include highlighter pens, water soluble pencils/pens and oil pastels (see Campbell and Featherstone, 2002). Items of clothing should be stretched out to avoid snagging – this can be achieved by fastening the fabric to a surface with tape or stretching the item around a thick cardboard template which will pull the 'canvas' tight.

Novel ideas for Clothing stories:

• 3–5: Display young children's *Clothing story* mark-making/writing using indoor/outdoor washing lines and pegs. Allow children to hang up their own *Clothing story* to develop fine motor skills.
• 3–7: Using a T-shirt or a template, divide the T-shirt up into squared sections (a chequered pattern – think *Elmer the Elephant*), using each square to write a word (to break down the flow of speech), a sentence or a paragraph to progressively build up a simple story.
• 7–11: Encourage children to write a story which is presented inside an outline of their full-sized body on a large rolled out piece of paper – each section/chapter of the story is to be contained within a different piece of clothing that is drawn/fastened onto the outline.

Top Tip! Visit http://tinyurl.com/8xwms5v for some valuable clothing related activities and downloadable teaching resources.

Idea 5.6: Crazy stories	Suggested age group: 3-year-olds to 7-year-olds

Explanation:

The story books written by Dr. Seuss are loved by children the world over, largely because of the crazy characters that fill them, e.g. *Fiffer-feffer-feff*, *Juggling Jott* and *Humpf-Humpf-a-Dumpfer* (see http://tinyurl.com/747nbgu for a wonderful list of Dr. Seuss characters)! *Crazy stories* embrace the eccentric 'goings-on' portrayed in these books by encouraging young children to become *Dr. _____* (*insert child's first name or surname here*), writing crazy stories about crazy characters in crazy settings where crazy things happen!

Crazy characters (3–5):

Young children can initiate work on their *Crazy story* by developing crazy characters. This can be achieved through their own drawings or cutting out parts of animals or people from magazines/cards and pasting them together to create a new crazy character. Talk with children about the kinds of crazy things their crazy character could get up to, for example:

• Speak words backwards.
• Sleep upside down on swings.
• Shuffle on their bottom all the way to school.
• Bury themselves in a plant pot in the hope to grow quicker.
• Eat trees to grow more arms.
• Sing to the sandpit.

Offer children the opportunity to create stimulating crazy characters using art-based computer packages and/or images from the internet.

Crazy settings (5–7):

Crazy stories allow children aged 5–7 to take established settings such as castles, parks, fairgrounds, the back garden, and the seaside and make them a little 'crazy'! *But how?* Well . . .

• What if the castle was *multi-coloured*?
• What if the park had all the grass, flowers, plants and trees *growing upside down*?
• What if the fairground made *no noise*?
• What if the back garden was *see-through*?
• What if the seaside had *still water* and *sand that moved in waves like the sea*?

Sternberg (2003) suggests that supporting children to think in a creative way like this 'improves school performance'. Evaluate the impact of this on children's writing by comparing pieces of writing over a short period of time to ascertain areas where progress has been made.

***How it looks* or *what it says*? The influence of parents and carers in creating 'great writers':**

Wallace et al. (2004: 16) suggest that to become 'great writers' children need 'supportive parents'. Sometimes there is a tendency for parents/carers to focus more on the *appearance* of writing (its neatness) as opposed to the intended meaning of the marks young children make to 'tell' their story (Lance, 2005). Support parents/carers to actively encourage, guide and express interest in their child's *Crazy story* writing by 'responding to the ideas they [children] are trying to express' (Lance, 2005) through Parents' Evenings, writing workshops, newsletters and writing 'demo days'.

Idea 5.7: Soft stories	Suggested age group: 7-year-olds to 11-year-olds

Explanation:

The news we are exposed to every day is made up of two different types: *hard* and *soft* news (Prior, 2003). Hard news refers to those events which are reported immediately and are presented in a factual and formal tone (e.g. wars, crimes and politics); soft news, on the other hand, relates to stories which advise or are of human interest (e.g. arts, lifestyles and entertainment). *Soft stories* embrace the sensational/personality-centred elements of soft news by getting children to write stories about informal or light-hearted events, using real-life characters and familiar themes in a creative way.

Soft news – *stimulating personal subject knowledge*:

Download a copy of Patterson's (2000) *Doing Well and Doing Good* (http://tingurl.com/664xpd3), which offers some valuable information to develop teachers' knowledge and understanding about soft news and its impact on news coverage. Consider how this information could be used to enrich learning and teaching opportunities when discussing the concept of soft news with your class (relating this, of course, to their writing of *Soft stories*!).

Creative thinking – getting to a *Soft story* imaginary world (7–9):

Fisher (2005) argues that creative thinking skills are essential for success in both learning and life. Creative thinking is evident when children generate ideas and show imagination and originality – this can be promoted through a questioning classroom. A stimulating question to encourage creative thinking is to ask children to think about *how* they can get to a *Soft story* imaginary world:

- Via a singing submarine?
- Through a hole in the ground?
- Crawling into the radiator?
- Stepping into a drawer?
- Drinking liquidised conkers?
- Being wrapped up in a ribbon?
- Peering into a hairdryer?
- Blowing into a flute?
- Jumping into jam?
- Singing a song backwards?
- Diving into a laundry basket?
- Wearing pants inside out?

Soft story possibilities (9–11):

Children can write *Soft stories* about an array of different things, e.g. *animals, health, fitness, fashion, music, food, relationships, home décor, shopping* or *sports*. It is useful for children to see how journalists write hard and soft news stories – allow children to compare and contrast hard and soft news reports (both paper and web-based) to appreciate the differences in style, tone and language. Consider how children might be able to use this knowledge in their own *Soft stories*, titles of which might include:

My wish book!	Happy clothes!	A great hair day!	Sports days!
Splendid sweets!	Snuggle blankets!	Soft comforts!	Hot hats!

Varying the plot – basic story plots for *Soft stories*:

There is much debate about the number of basic plots found in literature; it is suggested that the total is between 1 and 36! Visit http://tinyurl.com/2avp7, identifying appropriate plot types to promote in your learning and teaching to help children vary the plot lines in the *Soft stories* that they write.

Idea 5.8: Scroll stories	**Suggested age group:** 3-year-olds to 11-year-olds

Explanation:

It is suggested that inspiration comes from the most unlikely of places – the Idea of *Scroll stories* was inspired by seeing a rolled up magazine being pushed through a letterbox! A scroll can be considered like a book that is made up of one long page which has to be unwound for it to be read. Scrolls were once the primary source of storing information until the bound book was developed. *Scroll stories* aim to reintroduce rolled-up books as an interesting resource which children can mark-make/write and illustrate their creative stories in.

Putting scrolls 'in context':

The Torah Scroll (see http://tinyurl.com/73annbl) and the Dead Sea Scrolls (see Allon and Zehavi, 2004) are both significant examples of scrolls which are rooted within a religious context. They both contain stories, with the latter offering previously unknown stories about biblical figures such as Enoch, Abraham and Noah (see http://tinyurl.com/m4gnb). Talk sensitively to children about these scrolls, emphasising their importance to the Jewish and Christian faith. Stress to children that their *Scroll stories* are *not* in any way an attempt to replicate these sacred texts.

Scroll stories and story dictation (3–5):

One of the key ways young children can become interested in story writing is through story dictation. This involves practitioners helping children tell stories by recording their words on paper exactly as they are spoken. Gadzikowski (2007) suggests that this is a significant aid in helping children to become literate and express themselves with confidence, whilst also being a valuable tool for assessment purposes. For some interesting information, research and practical strategies/materials linked to story dictation take a look at Daitsman (2011), Pontecorvo and Zucchermaglio (1989) and Chen and McNamee (2007: 120–28). See Appendix 15 (p. 221) for an alternative mark-making scroll for 3–5-year-olds.

Stimulating Scroll stories with story resources (5–11):

Teachers will appreciate that there will be some children who need extra impetus to support them in their *Scroll stories*. This can be achieved through a range of commercially available resources specifically designed to stimulate story writing. Examples (all available from Amazon.co.uk) include:

- *Story Sparkers!* (Educational Insights) – a collection of photos, story starters, open-ended questions and writing prompts.
- *Rory's Story Cubes* (The Creativity Hub) – '9 cubes, 54 images, over 10 million possible combos, unlimited stories!' (*Actions* and *Voyages* cubes also available).
- *Story Spinners* (Primary Classroom Resources) – '6 vibrant and imaginative story spinners . . . that cover the who, what, where, when and why of writing plus characteristics.'

Stories, scrolls and innovative ideas:

Enrich story writing provision in the classroom with innovative ideas involving stories and scrolls from the following websites:

- Making Samurai story scrolls – available at http://tinyurl.com/7gr32cv
- Making TV scroll stories – available at http://tinyurl.com/6rmdvm9
- Making Indian Patua story scrolls – available at http://tinyurl.com/7mfjrrd

| **Idea 5.9: DIY stories** | **Suggested age group:** 7-year-olds to 11-year-olds |

Explanation:

One of the things children will learn about story writing is that as the author they 'have to do all the work' in terms of managing the various story elements (Whaley, 1981). *DIY stories* (*Do-It-Yourself*) are a motivating approach to story writing where some of the actual story writing is passed over to the *reader*, thus establishing an interesting collaboration between the reader and the writer (Daiute and Dalton, 1993). The Idea of *DIY stories* emphasises that aspects of the story, e.g. characters' names, the story setting, choice of adjectives, and speech between characters, are purposefully left out of the story so that the reader can fill in the gaps, thus *doing-it-themselves*!

An extract from a stimulating DIY story:

The cold wind blew through the _____ as Jack and _____ battled their way across

the _____ and _____ to get to the hunched church. It sat on top of the hill,

looming over the town like a _____. A low rumbling was heard, part of it was from

James' empty stomach and part of it came from _____. A mist of rain began to fall

from the sky, casting dark _____ on the damp ground. As they reached the church a

_____ flew past them. (Carrie, 10½ years old)

DIY story titles:

Whilst this section would typically present teachers with a plethora of story titles to offer children, readers will notice that none are offered here, simply because this is one of the aspects of *DIY stories* that the reader could do themselves – *establish the title of the story!* In order to do this the reader will need to have read through the text, made their coherent contributions (Fitzgerald and Spiegel, 1986) and have then read the completed story *before* they can propose a suitable title. Suggest that children leave a suitable space on their cover page for readers to insert their title for the story.

DIY story guidance and advice:

- 7–11: Get children to write *DIY stories* on lined paper, encouraging them to write on one line and then purposefully miss the next one – this will give the reader sufficient space to try out different ideas before committing themselves to a response.

- 7–11: To demark a 'DIY moment' in the story suggest that children offer a box or a low line in the sentence, as per the extract above*. This is reticent of the cloze procedure which is used in the teaching of reading (see Raymond, 1988).

- 9–11: Encourage children to not make the reader's contribution to the *DIY story* too obvious – promote creative thinking where possible/appropriate.

- 7–11: Suggest that children pilot their *DIY story* with someone to see if it actually works. If the *DIY story* is too complicated, then some of the gaps may need to be filled in to support the reader.

Idea 5.10: Either–Or stories	Suggested age group: 9-year-olds to 11-year-olds

Explanation:

There is a tendency for some children to write rather formulaic stories* that lose their appeal once they have been read by others. *Either–Or stories* work to stimulate complex story writing by getting children who like a challenge to really think about plot development. The Idea of an *Either–Or story* is that once the author has offered a sentence/paragraph they need to give the reader a choice as to where the story goes – either 'X' or 'Y' happens. Once selected the reader then reads the appropriate sentence/paragraph, selecting *another* option at the end of this to determine what happens next in the story. Through this kind of story writing *readers* get the chance to take ownership of the story (like *DIY stories*, p. 114) in terms of choosing where it goes and how it ends, whilst child *authors* develop their capabilities in terms of possibility thinking (see Craft et al., 2012).

*The 'formulaic' story:

Jones (n.d.) proposes the ABCDE formula, which presents the story writing process in five simple steps:

Formula	. . . which stands for	. . . which in the context of the rhyme 'Jack and Jill'
A	**A**ction	Jack and Jill went up the hill
B	**B**ackground	to fetch a pale of water.
C	**C**onflict	Jack fell down
D	**D**evelopment	and broke his crown,
E	**E**nding	and Jill came tumbling after.

Whilst Jones claims that this formula offers writers a 'concrete, practical approach' to help overcome writer's block, she does guard against its fixed application: 'Stick to the plan too rigidly, and your story might turn out . . . well, formulaic. You and your readers will have more fun when you add complications and twists.' This is where *Either–Or stories* come in! For an example, see Appendix 16 (p. 222).

The skills involved in writing *Either–Or stories*:

There are many skills children will need to use during the writing of their *Either–Or story*. Being able to 'plot plan'† is crucial. The ability to sequence a number of different stories is also a necessity. Children also need to be able to regularly review their work to critically check for coherency; as an *Either–Or story* develops, it becomes more difficult to manage all of the different storylines!

Note! Either–Or stories are challenging yet satisfying to write, but children will not be able to complete it in one sitting – do allow them to revisit/revise them over a number of writing sessions.

Stimulating *Either–Or story* titles:

- The day the moon shone too bright!
- The disappearance of the DVD player!
- Amanda's escape to the ship docks!
- The Finchley's family trip to the Arctic!
- The Splendid Six and their fight for freedom!
- Jim's revenge on the Tooth Fairy!
- Sammy, Claire and the talking camera.

†Strategies for *Either–Or story* plot planning:

- Use of diagrams.
- Use of maps to plot out where characters visit.
- Use of checklists.
- Use of Post-it® notes.
- Use of tree diagrams.
- Use of strips of paper.
- Use of lists.

'Technology' stories

This chapter considers ways in which technology can be used to stimulate and support children's story writing. There are critics who argue that there is a difference between children 'writing' and 'typing', and that technology undermines children's writing skills (e.g. their ability to review their own work for spelling and grammatical errors) seeing as inbuilt checkers will do this for them at the click of a mouse or the touch of a button (see Cordes and Miller, 2000, cited in Van Scoter et al., 2001). Nevertheless, there is much evidence to suggest that technology in its many forms can be used to motivate, engage and develop/improve children's writing skills (see Kulik, 2003).

The first half of this chapter acknowledges select forms of technology, considering how it can aid and energise children's story writing. *Technological stories* highlight innovations such as visual learning environments (VLEs), podcasting and vodcasting, which can be used as vehicles to facilitate exciting story writing. *ICT stories* consider the use of resources such as interactive whiteboards and digital cameras across the 3–11 age range in terms of stimulating the stories that children write. *CD/DVD stories* consider the use of CDs/DVDs as an *integral* resource to the story being written as opposed to what is actually burned on them (it could be the child's story!); *Internet stories* reflect on the quality content offered on select websites to support children's story writing (see http://tinyurl.com/cts8cn6, for example); this is also evident in a number of other Ideas contained within this chapter. *Networking stories* offer the reader ideas on how to use online social networking to promote story writing in even the most reluctant of writers (9–11).

The notion of technology is used as an underlying premise for the second half of this chapter, which presents Ideas linked to some of the impressive capabilities of technology today. *Track stories* embrace the high speed at which technology now performs by acknowledging the need for 'plot speed' in children's stories. *Calendar stories* appreciate the practice of the modern-day man who organises his life through mobile/smart phones, tablets and email accounts by considering how children can use online and paper-based calendars (daily, weekly and monthly) to plan out events in the lives of characters who appear in their stories. *Extended stories* acknowledge the way technology is perceived as an extension of the human body (McLuhan, 1966) by supporting children in developing their writing stamina, *extending* what happens to characters they write about in longer and richer narratives, some of which may be about their interactions with technology. *Upside-down stories* embrace the capabilities of computer software which enables typed text to be rotated and read at any angle by getting children to turn stories 'on their head', writing and presenting them in an upside-down manner! *Slapstick stories*, which end this chapter, highlight the role that technology can play in capturing visual gags to enrich the stories children write which are heavy with slapstick humour.

Taking a closer look at 'stimulating story ideas'

In *CD/DVD stories* (p. 126) a number of innovative and stimulating story ideas are offered linked to using CDs and DVDs for story writing. A teacher recently enquired as to where I got my ideas from; after a moment's thought my response was, 'I don't know – it's just how my brain works!'. It is important to remember that our brain is unique to the individual, and so for many children it will be easier or more difficult for them to generate stimulating story ideas than for others to. This raises two interesting questions:

1. How are story ideas generated?
2. How can we as teachers support children in generating stimulating story ideas?

How are story ideas generated?

This is a question that many people ask: *where do story writers get their stories ideas from?* Douglas Adams (of *The Hitchhiker's Guide to the Galaxy* fame) is quoted as having said ideas come from 'Ideas R Us in Swindon'! Joking aside, clearly the author's brain has something to do with it. The left-brain/right-brain theory is one that has been popularised by magazines, self-help books and TV programmes – it suggests that the left and right hemispheres of the brain control opposite sides of our body and that they deal with other aspects of our lives such as logic, language, music and emotions (see Dew, 1996). Writers are considered to be right-brain thinkers because it is the right side of the brain that generates ideas and is where our creativity takes place. Indeed, in support of this, WritingFix (2011) offers a series of interactive writing prompts that 'celebrate a right-brained approach to beginning a piece of writing' (see http://tinyurl.com/cx9jljy). One might argue that as the right side of the brain is 'where it all happens', ideas-generation wise, the left side of the brain seems a little redundant. Carrick (n.d.), however, claims that '[t]he problem lies not in coming up with story ideas, but in sifting through them and envisioning which ones are strong enough to carry a novel [for example].' This is where the left side of the brain comes in: the theory suggests that the left hemisphere is more useful in analysing and criticising ideas that have been generated, identifying and removing the 'bad ideas' before they are fully explored. Whaley (2012) thus argues that writers need to use *both* parts of their brain: '[i]f the right side generates the ideas, then the left side is [needed] for editing [them]'. It is important, however, to make the point that a writer's inspiration *can* start on the left-side of the brain – see http://tinyurl.com/c3cysxp, which celebrates writing prompts that are 'logical' and 'structured'; also see p. 133.

Whist the above offers the reader a biological perspective on idea generation, others' attempts to explain where their ideas come from are evidently less scientific in their thinking:

- The poet John Foster commented that his ideas derive from a combination of three sources: imagination, observation and experience (Carter, 2002).
- Corbett (2003) suggests that ideas, particularly within the context of story writing, can come from the notion of 'innovation' and 'invention' (two of what Corbett refers to as his

three 'eyes') (2003: 4) by borrowing, adapting, manipulating, altering and creating story structures and sentence patterns.

- Green (2011) claims that writers do not think of their ideas – '[t]hey steal them!'. This does not mean that they plagiarise others' work, but instead find ideas from many sources and combine them to make an original story. Examples of these 'many sources' are offered in Figure 6.1, from a personal perspective.

Figure 6.1   The many sources of story ideas

It is thus evident from the figure above that many story ideas are generated by *external stimuli* which help to ignite possibilities for creative writing. Warren (2007: 6) supports this, claiming that '[i]deas for stories are everywhere'. As many children find generating story ideas problematic, clearly one of our roles as teachers is to help children to gather these seemingly abundant ideas, supporting them in seeing how the stimuli around them can generate story ideas.

How can we, as teachers, support children in generating stimulating story ideas?

The ideas offered below are a select range of suggestions that teachers can choose from, depending on the age and abilities of those they work with. The age range indicators are merely offered as a suggestion; teachers may adapt the ideas for older/younger children if they so wish.

- 3–5: Use play resources in the sand, such as small PLAYMOBIL® characters (see Wallop, 2010) to develop a verbal story with the children. Offer questions to stimulate their thinking and responses, for example, where are the characters – *on a desert island? In sand dunes? At a builder's yard?* Where are they going – *to the sea to catch fish? To find wood to build a boat? To make a sandcastle?* Have a practitioner to hand to record the verbal story contributions children make in written form.

- 5–7: Show children how to adopt the 'green' practices of *Reduce, Reuse, Recycle* to generate ideas for their stories, for example, *reduce* a favourite Disney film into a short story; *reuse* characters that they have written about in other stories; *recycle* story plots from their reading scheme books for their own yarns.

- 7–11: Challenge children to write something fictional every day (a short story, a paragraph, a description, some dialogue between two characters), as the more they write the more they will develop the right side of their brain.

- 3–5: Invite different people into class to tell the children different stories – these could be based on their own children (*parents*)/children in their care (*carers*), things that have happened to them in the past (*grandparents*), things that have happened to them at work (*dentist, police person*) or stories that they have conceived themselves (*storytellers*). Encourage children to record these stories as a way of remembering them through drawings, marks, letters and words.

- 5–11: Keep a class story scrapbook/box, inviting children to bring in different items which could be kept and referred to to stimulate story ideas, for example, newspaper headings, labels, new words they have learned, drawings, fabric with interesting textures, music on CDs, 3-D objects or images from magazines. Alternatively, visit http://tinyurl.com/cf9rqch for a free digital story scrapbook app developed by Australian children's author Tristan Bancks.

- 7–11: Model the use of online story generators to help children get that 'initial hook' – see http://tinyurl.com/c3sdl9r, which offers stimulating ideas linked to characters, scenarios, titles, images, first lines and twists in the tale.

- 3–5: Invite children to put their hands inside a feely box/bag, describing something that they are handling. Encourage them to draw pictures/make marks/write about their object (*do not let them see the object, though*) in terms of it being a personified entity, for example, a *talking* pencil, a *singing* shell, a *shouting* ball. *What exciting things could happen to it?*

- 5–7: Bainbridge (2012) suggests that children could write a stimulating story based on a wordless picture book: '[t]he pictures provide wonderful clues for a storyline. In addition, the pictures are wonderful ways for kids to practice writing descriptions.'

- 7–11: Offer children 'A door opens', a paper-based narrative stimulus by Johnson (2002b: 12) – *what happens when the children open the door?* The basic principle of *Window stories* (p. 181) could be used to create a physical door in the paper on which children write their story.

To support teachers' knowledge and understanding of how to use oral storytelling and storymaking to generate story ideas and improve children's writing across the 3–11 age range, download a copy of *A Progression for Using Oral Storytelling and Storymaking to Improve Writing*, available at http://tinyurl.com/6yjk2ov for reference.

Table 6.1   Recommended readings associated with *'Technology' stories*

Books	Tandy, M. and Howell, J. (2008) *Creating Writers in the Primary Classroom: Practical Approaches to Inspire Teachers and their Pupils.* London: David Fulton. *This wonderfully accessible book offers a wealth of practical advice, games and strategies for the classroom based on the authors' successful experience as teachers and in-service providers.* Chapter 1 (pp. 1–14) is of particular interest as it offers the reader an exploration of how to ensure that children have 'something to write about' (think ideas generation for their *'Technology' stories*). MacLusky, J. and Cox, R. (2011b) *Teaching Creative Writing in the Primary School: Delight, Entice, Inspire!* Maidenhead: Open University Press. *This book offers teachers a set of teaching skills to provide children with a toolkit of creative strategies. Based on classroom research, results suggest that the book has 'the power to enable teachers to engage pupils in writing lessons who are often uninterested in classroom writing lessons' (book blurb).* Consider ways to embrace practice advocated in this book to delight, entice and inspire the *'Technology' stories* children write in your classroom.
Online documents	The Suffolk Advisory Service and the County Writing Investigation Team (2000) *Strategies for Improving Writing at Key Stage 2.* [Online]. Available at: *http://tinyurl.com/dybphd6* (Accessed: 29 May 2012). *This 'staff meeting pack' contains the findings from trials using three different strategies –* Response partners, Providing a choice of writing format, and Marking and feedback *– for improving writing in KS2 (7–11). A summary of the outcomes, along with guidance on how to use these strategies in the classroom, is offered.* Consider the impact of using these strategies in improving the *'Technology' stories* children write in your classroom. Peha, S. (2003c) *The Writing Teacher's Strategy Guide.* [Online]. Available at: http://tinyurl.com/4rox9 (Accessed: 29 May 2012). *This document offers a fantastic series of writing strategies to aid teachers in teaching and supporting children in their story writing. Reflect particularly on Chapter 1 (pp. 5–19) which offers support to help children overcome the initial 'I Don't Know What to Write About' hurdle.* Consider how the different strategies advocated can be used when engaging children in *'Technology' stories*.

Websites

National Writing Project (2012b) *Resources: Encourage Writing.* [Online]. Available at: http://tinyurl.com/bss73va (Accessed: 29 May 2012).

This American website offers parents and carers, educators, and writers of all ages a wealth of practical advice, guidance and strategies to 'help children develop their skills and, equally important, a love for words and writing' (NWP, 2012). Use the various links on the left of the webpage to navigate your way through the *Encouraging Writing* resources, considering their value in supporting children in their engagement with *'Technology' stories.*

DCSF (2011) *A Picture Paints a Thousand Words – Using ICT to stimulate writing.* Teaching and Learning Resources. [Online]. Available at: http://tinyurl.com/bvsj4af (Accessed: 29 May 2012).

This website offers a case study about 10 Cheshire primary schools which set out to improve KS2 (7–11) writing results by accessing and using readily available ICT software to support children's writing experiences. Reflect on the use/potential use of Photo story and PowerPoint in your classroom (see p. 5) – how could they be used to improve the *'Technology' stories* children write in your class?

Idea 6.1: Technological stories	**Suggested age group:** 5-year-olds to 11-year-olds

Explanation:

The prominence of technology in our lives today cannot be denied; laptops, netbooks, mobile/smart phones, gaming consoles, electronic mail, tablets, online voice calling (*Skype*) and IPods entertain, inform and help people to communicate with one another, all of which can often be achieved at the same time using a single device! *Technological stories* embrace the digital world we live in by encouraging children to use various hardware/software available to them, both as a resource to stimulate story writing and as a means of actually writing stories.

'The Internet helped me to write a story!':

There is a wealth of quality websites on the Internet which can support children (5–7) in their story writing. Use these to support your planning, children's activities in the classroom, and story work that they may be set as Weekend Work. Examples include:

- Story starters – available at http://tinyurl.com/yehg5gc
- Write me a story – available at http://tinyurl.com/yfnuaq4
- Publish your own children's book – available at http://tinyurl.com/yek8v78
- Children's story writing (useful for parents/carers) – available at http://tinyurl.com/c7ye3nu

Technological stories **and social networking:**

Social networking is a prominent way in which people in the 21st century communicate. *Facebook*, *Twitter* and *MySpace* are three of the most popular examples of online sites where individuals can get together into specific groups of interest (boyd and Ellison, 2007). Opportunities for children to use these sites to share their story writing with others, ask questions, find people who will critique their writing, and find story writing inspiration have been shown to have a positive impact on children's writing, particularly with children aged 7–11. Indeed, whilst Greenfield (in Derbyshire, 2009) argues that social websites are harming 'the wiring of children's brains', research from the NLT (cited in Kleinman, 2009) suggests that children who use social networking websites are more confident about their writing skills.

Reflect! Consider the benefits of children (7–11) signing up for child-friendly social network sites as 'budding writers' (see http://tinyurl.com/77zr4qh for suggestions). Alternatives include children setting up their own forums, blogs or wikis (see Richardson, 2006).

Technological innovations and story writing:

Technological advances continue to occur at an ever increasing rate. A number of these innovations can support children in their story writing:

- *Virtual learning environments* (VLE) – VLEs are designed to offer children an online personalised learning space. Take a look at http://tinyurl.com/cztutsc and consider how you could use VLEs to facilitate online story writing weekend work.
- *Podcasting* – Podcasts (akin to a downloadable recorded radio show) allow children to verbally share their writing, achievements and experiences with people on the Internet. Visit http://tinyurl.com/75vwoof for information, ideas, examples and strategies for using podcasts as a vehicle to promote children's story writing.
- *Vodcasting* – This is considered to be the 'video brother' of podcasting. Visit http://tinyurl.com/7stdmat for information and ideas to help enrich story writing practice by using this as an innovative learning and teaching strategy in the classroom.

Idea 6.6: Track stories	Suggested age group: 7-year-olds to 11-year-olds

Explanation:

If the blurb on the back of a children's story book claims the story to have a 'fast-paced plot', children know that their read is likely to be gripping, action-packed and exciting. Amin (2011) argues that 'children nowadays are used to fast pace,' and just like with poor internet connection speeds 'will not tolerate slow-paced stories with many descriptions'. *Track stories* are designed to ensure that the stories children write are fast-paced by providing them with an interesting story context (a racing track*), an innovative way to present their story to the reader[†], and a wealth of exciting story themes to select from, e.g. *power, good versus bad, performance, self-belief* and *friendship*.

Stimulating *Track stories*:

- Fire children's imagination by showing them YouTube extracts of films such as *Cars, Chariots of Fire* and *Herbie Rides Again*, which involve different kinds of tracks and races. *Wacky Races* (a 1960s Hanna-Barbera cartoon) will allow teachers to emphasise the importance of distinctive characters, creative plot lines and ingenuity in creative *Track story* telling (7–11).
- [†]Encourage children to record their *Track stories* on large self-drawn track outlines, writing paragraphs of the story in different segments of the track. *See http://tinyurl.com/c85ljfq* for a range of racing track templates (7–11).
- Make reference to atlases, globes and maps to help children set their *Track stories* in exotic and stimulating places, e.g. Cairo, Bali, Hawaii and Fiji (9–11).
- Work with children to establish different reasons for the races taking place – *money, love, experience, anger, fitness, a personal goal, excitement, revenge, fun, comradeship* and *remembering others* (7–11).

*Different types of tracks:

- *Animal*, e.g. horse racing, greyhound racing and camel racing.
- *Human*, e.g. cycling, athletics.
- *Motor*, e.g. motorcycle racing, stock car racing and drag racing.

Encourage children to write stories based on events which happen at these different kinds of tracks.

Alternative interpretations of *Track stories*:

- *Musical 'tracks'* – writing lyrics, melodies.
- *Vehicle 'tracks'* – where do the tracks from cars, trains, bicycles and motorbikes lead to?
- *Animal 'tracks'* – describing footprints, paw prints and pugmarks.
- *Travel* – writing about adventures 'off the beaten track'.

Think! How could you use the above to stimulate story writing with the children you work with?

Academic thinking in relation to the writing process:

All process theorists stress that the stages in the writing process – pre-writing (brainstorming), writing and rewriting (revising) and editing – are recursive rather than linear (see Czerniewska, 1992; Boehm, 1993). Parrott (1993) explains that in practice these stages will rarely be discrete – there may be considerable overlap between them and there may be 'regressions' to earlier stages.

Reflect! How explicitly do you emphasise these writing stages with the children you work with? How do you encourage children to use these stages during the writing of their stories? Which of these stages do the children you work with find easy/difficult? Why so? Consider how *Track stories* could be used to improve certain process stages.

Idea 6.7: Calendar stories	**Suggested age group:** 3-year-olds to 11-year-olds

Explanation:

The inspiration for *Calendar stories* came from an electronic Christmas present which offered the recipient 'a joke a day' in the form of a quirky little story. Many stories (both verbal and written) make reference to days of the week and months of the year to offer a sense of chronology to the tale being told – think *Chicken Soup with Rice* (Sendak, 1991); *Jasper's Beanstalk* (Butterworth and Inkpen, 2008). *Calendar stories* consider how different measures of time can be used to support children in the writing of their stimulating stories.

Calendar stories and the days of the week (3–5):

Children (3–5) need to learn about the days of the week; story books which can support this include *The Very Hungry Caterpillar* (Carle, 1969) and *Mr. Wolf's Week* (Hawkins, 2003). Use these as a structure to help them create their own stories (both written and verbal) by substituting characters with other animals or people, e.g. *The Very Hungry Puppy; Mrs Wilson's Week.*

Use Appendix 17 (p. 223) as a support sheet for practitioners to model to help children think about different things that happen to their character each day, e.g. different foods that they eat, games that they play, places that they visit. Alternatively, allow children to draw pictures/mark-make/write words/ sentences on separate sheets of paper about what happens to their character on different days which can then be fastened together to create a little story book (see *Booked stories*, p. 55).

Calendar stories and weeks in a month (5–7):

Children (5–7) should develop an understanding of there being approximately four weeks in a month, each week consisting of some or all of the days of the week. Encourage children to use Appendix 18, (p. 224) to think about a month in the life of a character, considering what happens to them each week – use the *summer holidays* and *Christmas* as exciting periods of time for events to be based around.

Alternatively, children could use Appendix 18 as a simple 'journal' which logs what happens to them personally; this could be used as story 'fuel', e.g. going to the dentist, attending a party or visiting grandparents. Support children in understanding that each day does not necessarily need to be all 'adventure and excitement' – all characters need some down time, e.g. playing computer games, reading and listening to music.

Calendar stories and months of the year (7–11):

Each of J.K. Rowling's seven *Harry Potter* novels chronicles the adventures of Harry at Hogwarts School of Witchcraft and Wizardry a year at a time. Encourage children to use Appendix 19 (p. 225) to map out 'The year in the life of . . .', choosing an interesting character who can be involved in numerous adventures, e.g. a *'Lost World' explorer, a world-famous fashion designer, an animal trainer, a pop star* or *an inventor.*

Suggest that children use each month as a chapter in their story; remember that the story does not necessarily have to start in January, e.g. the story could begin during a snow storm in December. Alternatively, children could use each of the four seasons to 'block' story events. Online calendar planners offer an alternative tool for supporting children's story planning (9+).

Idea 6.8: Extended stories	**Suggested age group:** 6-year-olds to 11-year-olds

Explanation:

For many teachers the school day is so pressured that it is increasingly difficult to fit everything into the timetable. One activity that is always in danger of being 'squeezed' out of the week is extended writing, which acts as the premise for *Extended stories*. This is a valuable addition to the 'suite of stories' that children should be encouraged to write, particularly as they help to build children's writing stamina*. By writing longer stories children have the opportunity to develop and hone their story writing skills in relation to sentence structure and punctuation, text structure and organisation, and composition and effect (see http://tinyurl.com/czm72n6 for further details).

* *Extended stories* and writing stamina:

Kinsella (cited in labfive, 2012) suggests that '[b]eing a successful writer requires four things. Technique (5%), creativity (5%), vocabulary (5%) and stamina (85%).' Writing stamina refers to a child's ability to 'stick with a piece of writing', be it fiction or non-fiction. Some children, particularly those who are young or who are reluctant writers, have little writing stamina, 'focus[sing] on their writing for less than a minute, while others can stay tuned in for twenty to thirty minutes' (Reif and Heimburge, 2007: 48). Work to build children's writing stamina over a period of time through new writing implements, softer writing surfaces and daily writing opportunities (Cruz, 2008); alternatively, see p. 2 of *Building Writing Stamina*, which is available at http://tinyurl.com/dyq4y2b.

Supporting knowledge, understanding and practice:

Make reference to the following online PDFs which have been selected to support teachers' knowledge and understanding of *Extended stories*, and quality practice that is associated with their usage with children (6–11):

Extended Stories (DfES, 2001a)   http://tinyurl.com/c4wyh9f
Year 2 Narrative Unit 4 – Extended Stories/Significant Authors (DfE, 2011b)   http://tinyurl.com/bumq8qv
Extended Writing in History   http://tinyurl.com/blpn77s

Stimulating *Extended stories*:

Motivate children to *want* to write *Extended stories* by using any of the following ideas:

- *Episodic chapter tales*! Suggest that children emulate episodic-style story authors (e.g. Michael Bond (*Paddington Bear*); Ian Whybrow) by writing a series of short stories involving the same character(s) and then linking them together to create a coherent piece of sustained writing (6–9).

- *'A year in the life of . . .'*! Allow children to develop a character whose life they tell a story about, month by month, over twelve exciting chapters. Alternative time frames include a month, a week or a day (think of the American show *24*) (6–11).

- *The never-ending story* continued! Encourage children to watch the feature films based on the novel of the same name by Michael Ende (1984); alternatively, promote extended *reading* by suggesting children read the book. How could children in your class continue Bastian's adventures with computers, robots and other forms of technology? (9–11).

- *Around the World in **less** than 80 days*! Discuss the plot of Jules Verne's (2011) famous book, challenging children to write a short novel which details *their* attempt to travel around the world in less than 1,920 hours! (9–11).

Idea 6.9: Upside-down stories	**Suggested age group:** 5-year-olds to 11-year-olds

Explanation:

The notion of *Upside-down stories* stems from an interesting idea proposed by Yates (1993: 40), who advocates 'turning [story] idea[s] upside down'. *Upside-down stories* actively encourage children to take stories that they know and love and 'turn them on their head', tweaking different story elements (see http://tinyurl.com/dxxg69u for details) to generate new and exciting stories. By altering story elements, children are able to create stimulating and innovative stories whilst ensuring that their story is well structured, coherent and engaging.

Upside-down story examples:

The grid below offers examples of how children could adapt well-known stories to create their own *Upside-down story*:

Story	What the story is about	An example of an *Upside down story*
The Very Hungry Caterpillar (5–7)	A caterpillar who grows to become a colourful butterfly.	A guide dog who turns back into a puppy over a twelve-month period.
Cinderella (7–9)	A poor, unloved girl who becomes a beautiful, wealthy princess.	A popular rich queen who gives away her fortune and lives as a poor maid.
The Owl who was Afraid of the Dark (9–11)	An owl who is frightened of growing up.	A donkey who is happy to return to his paddock to look after his old parents.

Top Tip! Raise children's awareness of upside-down stories by reading the works of Trivizas and Oxenbury (1995; for 5–7-year-olds) and Bisset (1987; for 7–11-year-olds).

Innovations with *Upside-down stories*:

- Encourage children to write *Upside-down stories* about an upside down world where characters walk on their heads, write with their feet and sleep in beds on the ceiling! (7–11)
- Get children to present alternative sentences in their *Upside-down story* upside down (the physical sentence, not actually them!) (5–7). Offer readers a mirror to read their story effectively. Alternatively, use computer programmes/software to rotate typed text so that it appears upside-down on the screen/page (7–11).

The worry of upside-down writing in children aged 3–7:

Wright (2010) acknowledges the concerns of parents/carers who worry when their child 'begin[s] to reverse letters, write words from right to left, or confuse letters like b, d, and p in their writing'. It is important to reassure parents/carers (and teachers) that this is a *normal* stage in learning to write: 'between the ages of three and seven it is quite common for children to write some or all of their letters and words backwards'. Sometimes called 'mirror writing', research shows that this phenomenon is not only normal, but is likely to be the result of normal brain development (see Cornell, 1985; Cubelli, 2009). Parents/carers and teachers can help children by:

- gently reminding children about where to initiate writing on the page (left to right);
- the starting and finishing points of individual letters; and
- looking at the text in story books to refresh children's memories of letter shapes and formation (do check the font of the text for the apt presentation of 'a's - Comic Sans MS).

Idea 6.10: Slapstick stories	Suggested age group: 5-year-olds to 11-year-olds

Explanation:

Think of Charlie Chaplin, Laurel and Hardy and the Three Stooges and you immediately think of slapstick, a form of comedy characterised by crazy chases, blundering actions, clumsy collisions and crude practical jokes. Whilst these shenanigans were prominent in the 'golden era' of silent films, Tompkins (2006) claims that 'no one [is] making new slapstick comedy these days'. This is where *Slapstick stories* come in! Through *Slapstick stories* children are to be encouraged to write stories which involve characters slipping on banana peels, getting soaked with buckets of water, and having pies thrown in their face, all in the name of humorous storytelling! These occurrences can be complimented with digital still images or Digital Blue™ action footage of visual gags being *carefully* imitated by 'stooges' (the children themselves).

Getting children into slapstick:

Because slapstick humour is very visual in nature it is important to help children understand what stimulating slapstick looks like. Play age-appropriate extracts from YouTube of any of the following to support children:

- Children's TV programmes, e.g. *The Chuckle Brothers*.
- Cartoons, e.g. *Tom and Jerry*; *Looney Tunes*; *The Simpsons*.
- Situation comedies, e.g. *Some Mothers Do 'Ave 'Em*; *The Goodies*.
- Films, e.g. *Mr Bean*; *Hot Shots*.

Slapstick punctuation (5–7):

To emphasise the humour in their story encourage children to use exclamation marks – ! – when offering exclamatory sentences, strong commands and interjections to describe slapstick capers. Do make children aware that using exclamation marks too frequently makes them less meaningful.

Slapstick 'goings-on':

Support children in creating a list of slapstick events which they could integrate into their *Slapstick story*, examples of which include:

- Making funny faces.
- Getting tangled up in a ball of wool.
- Walking into a brick wall.
- Squashing a custard/cream pie in a person's face.
- Getting hit on the head with a frying pan.
- Tripping over a wire.
- Dropping a tray of drinks.
- Kicking someone up the bottom.
- Falling down the stairs.

Health and Safety! Emphasise the importance of keeping these slapstick antics confined to children's story writing; these behaviours *should not* be in any way part of their playtime activities!

Writing and the 'left' brain:

West (1998: 80) states that the 'left hemisphere [of the brain] controls two very important cognitive skills, those of reading and writing'. Stanet (2011) argues that by activating the left side of our brains, it is possible to enhance our ability to analyse words. Activities which promote children's 'brain building' on the left side include playing child-friendly games like Sudoku, Boggle™, crossword puzzles and logic brainteasers (see http://tinyurl.com/2asm5j for examples). Other ideas include playing a musical instrument, performing yoga movements, breathing through one nostril at a time and reading.

Most importantly, Mukherjee (2011) states that '[w]riting keeps the gr[e]y cells in the left part of the brain working, and the more you write, the better you'll be at it.' Encourage children to keep a personal diary, a blog, or write a couple of lines/paragraphs of a *Slapstick story* a day to boost their writing capabilities.

7

'Location' stories

This chapter offers the reader an interesting collection of Ideas that are based around the notion of 'location'. This is an important theme, particularly as it relates to the key story element of *setting*, which is made up of two parts: time and place (location) – see http://tinyurl.com/ygmgm5a for further details.

The first half of the chapter considers familiar locations which children encounter during their 'working week' at school. The initial Idea – *Carpet stories* – offers children an interesting 'low-level' location for them to write their stories at. *Table-top stories* suggest different ways for children to work at tables in the classroom, considering different ways for using table tops to display children's writing efforts. *Playground stories* identify incidences that occur outside the classroom which can be used to stimulate written stories, whilst *Assembly stories* are designed to offer children interesting topics, themes and ideas to 'fuel' the stories that they write, with the purpose of them being read out to the rest of the school. *Lunch time stories* 'locate' (identify) particular items of food and drink consumed in the dining hall and use these as a visual planner to ameliorate the difficulties associated with children writing stories (see Saddler et al., 2004).

The Ideas presented in the second half of this chapter maintain the theme of 'location' but look beyond the school environment and into the wider locality. *Library stories* are designed to support national campaigns to get children back into libraries (see http://tinyurl.com/86khlmu) by encouraging them to consider the plot possibilities of using a library as the location for their story. The Idea of *Toilet stories* acts as a personal entry for the Extreme Writing

Challenge set at Meppershall Lower School (see http://tinyurl.com/
cfkqurc) as it actively encourages children to write about an 'extreme'
subject as 'outrageous writers' based on an interesting location!
Weathered stories acknowledge the difficulties that the weather
can cause characters in different locations, whilst *Environment
stories* encourage children to write stories about interesting and
unusual locations, considering the impact of human action on the
environment. *Local area stories*, which close this chapter, 'capitalise
on the infinite supply of interesting individuals, localities and
events contained within the articles, reports and summaries which
make up the content of different local newspapers' (see p. 151) by
reflecting on their value in stimulating children's story writing.

Taking a closer look at 'the characters they create'

In *Playground stories* (p. 144) it is suggested that incidents involving
the 'characters [children] create' could be events based on their own
personal experiences, observations of others or invented goings-on.
The importance of character in children's written stories – in *any*
story, for that matter – cannot be underestimated; Bell (2001: 95)
suggests that 'without character there is no story'. Erianne (2012)
supports this by claiming that '[c]haracters are the engine which
drive a short story'. It may be argued that characters can in fact
drive more than just a short story – popular children's characters
including Winnie the Pooh, the Moomins, Tracy Beaker, Harry
Potter, Greg Heffley (*Diary of a Wimpy Kid*) and Elmer the elephant
have all appeared/continue to appear in a series of endearing
children's picture books or popular novels, along with admired TV
programmes and successful film adaptations.

Peha (2003a: 3) suggests that '[t]he best stories are built around
rich, complex, extremely interesting characters'; Wyatt (2012a)
supports this by stating that '[m]ost stories are remembered for
their characters, not specific plot points. If you want to write a
memorable story, create memorable characters'. If children are to
write stories that are remembered by their readers, it is necessary
for teachers to help children learn *how* to create memorable yet
believable characters. But what makes a character memorable? In
an effort to answer this, a 'great eight' list of ideas is offered in
Table 7.1 (p. 136) which can be used with children across the 3–11
age range.

Table 7.1   Eight great ideas for creating story characters

Strategy	Description	Application
It's all in the name!	'Authors often pick names that reflect a character's looks or personality, such as Mr. Happy, Penny Sweet or Mrs. Longtooth' (Warren, 2007: 13).	EY: *Sunny* for a happy girl. KS1: *Fierce Freddy* for a bully-boy. KS2: *Dr. Dreadful* for an evil villain.
Make them visually distinct!	Give characters something that makes them visually distinctive to others – think about Harry Potter and the lightning bolt scar on his forehead.	EY: A buttercup flower in Sunny's hair. KS1: A permanent scowl on Fierce Freddy's face. KS2: Dr. Dreadful's 'twitchy eye'.
Base it on someone you know!	Encourage children to base their characters on people who are in their lives; e.g. a *loud* Granny, a *shy* brother, a *silly* daddy.	EY: Sunny likes to sing all the time. KS1: Fierce Freddy talks with a deep, scary voice. KS2: Dr. Dreadful sneers at everyone.
How do you dress?	Get to know your character by considering what kind of clothing your character would wear (Strauss, 2010).	EY: A bright yellow dress for Sunny. KS1: Dark, baggy clothing with a skull emblazoned on Fierce Freddy's T-shirt. KS2: A shiny smart suit for Dr. Dreadful with long black silk gloves.
Physical form!	Peat (2002: 70) claims that '"build" is rarely discussed' in children's writing. To address this, Peat suggests that teachers may wish to provide a 'visual learning referent' to suggest a character's build.	EY: Sunny is a tiny little girl. KS1: Fierce Freddy is a plump boy with broad shoulders. KS2: Dr. Dreadful is a scrawny man with a long thin face and slender fingers.
Traveller's choice!	Ask children to think about how their character travels about.	EY: Sunny skips everywhere in her pretty pink shoes. KS1: Fierce Freddy has a squeaky metallic grey skateboard. KS2: Dr. Dreadful zips around using his invisible supersonic scooter.
One word personality!	Think about one word that best describes your character's personality – use this to influence how the character behaves, what they say to others, and how they think.	EY: Sunny is *happy*. KS1: Fierce Freddy is *greedy*. KS2: Dr. Dreadful is *humourless*.
Focus on the small detail!	Consider what kind of response you want to elicit from the reader about the character you present to them – *revulsion* or *admiration*? (Peat, 2002).	EY: Sunny is kind to others. KS1: Fierce Freddy consistently drops his litter on the floor. KS2: Dr. Dreadful wipes his nose on his sleeve!

In an effort to show how teachers can assure a progression in learning and teaching about character across the 3–11 age phase, reference is made in Table 7.2 to the EYFS (DfE, 2012a). Strategies from the *Primary Framework for Literacy and Mathematics* (DfES, 2006) and the draft NC for KS1 and 2 English (DfE, 2012b) specific to the 5–7 and 7–11 age groups are highlighted overleaf.

Table 7.2   Character and the EYFS

Area of learning and development: Personal, social and emotional development	1. Tell verbal stories that involve children in the class who help others to find their missing coat, offer comfort when others hurt themselves, play with others when they have no one to play with, or collaborate with others to complete a tricky jigsaw. These could be invented tales or be based on real experiences in the setting/classroom.
Aspect: Managing feelings and behaviour	2. Read stories such as *Horace the Dragon has Hiccups* (Gina, 1989), *Little Beaver and The Echo* (MacDonald, 1990) and *Me First* (Lester, 1992), emphasising how characters help others in different ways.
Choose books and stories in which characters help and support each other (DfE, 2012a: 12).	
Area of learning and development: Communication and language	1. Use story sacks (see http://tinyurl.com/c8jonfc) as a valuable 'contained' resource to support children's understanding of story characters and how they feel about others.
Aspect: Understanding	2. Prepare question prompts on cards as an aide memoire/ assessment tool to get children thinking about how characters feel; e.g. *What do you think caused the Little Red Hen to feel sad? How do you think Bernard was feeling before the monster ate him? When was Kipper the happiest during his 'birthday'?*
Introduce, alongside books, story props such as pictures, puppets and objects to encourage children to retell stories and to think about how the characters feel (DfE, 2012a: 18).	
Area of learning and development: Expressive arts and design	1. Encourage children to use their ability to rhyme to make up describing words; e.g. horrid – *gorrid* (a monster), cuddly – *huddily* (Cuddly Dudley), fluffy – *juffly* (Shaun the sheep).
Aspect: Being imaginative	2. Use magnetic letters to build known adjectives, changing individual letters to create invented describing words, e.g. sweet – *sweft*, playful – *plalful*, kind – *vind*.
Create imaginary words to describe, for example, monsters or other strong characters in stories and poems (DfE, 2012a: 46).	

Character and Key Stage 1 (5–7)

- Help children to 'build' memorable characters by creating simple written/verbal character profiles such as the example in Table 7.3.

Table 7.3   Example of a simple character profile

Name	Billy the bulley	Clothes	Dirty and smelley
Age	6 ½ years old	Eyes	Red. He has a black eye
Height	Tallish	Nose	Flat and red
Weight	Podgey	Teeth	Yellowey. One is missing

(by Ali, 6 years old)

Alternatively, children could create a character passport, a 'lost' poster, a mini-biography, a simple CV (see Grainger et al., 2004c) or a character name acrostic (see below) to describe their characters:

Bosse (*Bossy*)
Egge (*Eggy – 'He throws them at people!'*)
Norte (*Naughty*)   (by Amanda, aged 5)

Useful teaching materials can also be found at http://tinyurl.com/bqx8lrk.

- Offer children a simple prop box (see http://tinyurl.com/cxsedte) to stimulate children's role play and improvisations of characters they encounter in stories that they read about or that they create for their written stories.

- Get children to think about how their character talks to others – *do they have a booming voice? A quiet voice? A sweet voice? Do they 'snap' at others or are they gentle and courteous? Is their voice monotone or expressive? Do they 'umm' and 'err' a lot or are they clear and direct?* Consider how this reflects the personality of the character.

Character and Key Stage 2 (7–11)

- Support children in helping them to infer characters' feelings, for example, *Robert closed his eyes as his mother continued to shout at him.* Possibilities include: Robert is fed up of his mother shouting at him; Robert is thinking hard about what his mother is saying to him; Robert is trying to make his mother 'disappear' by removing her from his sight.

- As children write their stories encourage them to elicit empathy from the reader about their characters, for example:

> *It was only when Gerry looked into the hamster cage that he noticed Bertum was curled up into a still ball. Gerry put a finger on Bertum's side but it was clear that he had long stopped breathing. Gerry sighed as he took some wadding and covered Bertum's cold body. Closing the cage door quietly, Gerry sat on the floor – how was he going to tell little Krissinda that it was his fault that her only friend was dead?*
>
> Bobby, aged 11

- Help children to characterise their story characters effectively by making reference to the wonderful *Characterisation* PowerPoint by Carmichael – available at http://tinyurl.com/ceoc547.

- Actively encourage children to create a memorable story character through what they do (*action*) and what they say (*dialogue*). See Table 7.4 for an example.

Table 7.4 Using action and dialogue to create a memorable story character

Action	Jamie kicked the heads off all the flowers in the garden with his football boots as his Dad watched from the living room. *Ask children to consider why Jamie might be doing this, especially in front of his father.*
Dialogue	'I hate you!' screamed Emily as she snatched the torn party dress from Greta's hands. 'I wish I had *never* made friends with you! **I wish you were dead!**' *Ask children to consider how the dress may have been torn and whether Emily might regret saying what she did to Greta later on.*

Table 7.5   Recommended readings associated with *'Location' stories*

Books	Richards, J. C. and Lassonde, C. A. (2011) *Writing Strategies for All Primary Students. Scaffolding Independent Writing with Differentiated Mini-Lessons.* San Francisco, CA: Jossey-Bass. *This impressive book offers 'an array of classroom-tested strategies . . . to develop the skills [children] need to become successful and confident writers' (book blurb).* Consider the value of the advocated SCAMPER model throughout the book in developing children's *'Location' stories.* Strauss, L. L. (2010) *Drop Everything and Write!* Sausalito, CA: E & E Publishing. *This award-winning book offers an 'easy breezy guide for kids who want to write a story' (tagline of book). Of particular interest is Chapter 9 which is all about* Building Characters *(pp. 67–77).* Use this to support children in building brilliant characters for their *'Location' stories.*
Online document/article	Peha, S. (2003a) *The Five Facts of Fiction.* [Online]. Available at: http://tinyurl.com/bnhknlr (Accessed: 5 June 2012). *This wonderful document suggests that if authors want to write a good story they need to know the 'Five Facts of Fiction'. Not only do these facts heavily relate to the importance of 'character' but also to 'location' in the form of the world in which the characters inhabit (Fact 5).* Reflect on and select from the information and ideas offered in this document to support children when writing their *'Location' stories.* Rich, D. (2002) *Catching Children's Stories.* [Online]. Available at: http://tinyurl.com/bnz4499 (Accessed: 5 June 2012). *This interesting article acknowledges the importance of children's play in providing the foundations for literacy based activity by introducing the term 'storying' for the process of storymaking within play. 'It emphasises the need for practitioners and parents to highly value storying and suggests ways to promote and value this important process.'* Consider the value of this in stimulating children's *'Location' stories* in the early years classroom (3–7).

Websites

DLTK's Sites (2012) *Children's Book Breaks.* [Online]. Available at: http://tinyurl.com/c49kaz8 (Accessed: 5 June 2012).

This website is a treasure trove of interesting activities and ideas for teachers in the early years (3–5) and KS1 (5–7) to supplement children's reading and writing of stories. The resources are organised by theme, some of which relate well to the notion of 'Location' *stories, e.g.* farm-themed.

Dipple, S. (2011) *Teaching Writing to Children.* [Online]. Available at: http://tinyurl.com/cgecbfu (Accessed: 5 June 2012).

This website offers the reader details about four scaffold stages which can be used to improve children's writing skills. Descriptions of Model[l]ed, Shared, Guided *and* Independent writing *are useful in introducing those training and those in the infancy of their career to effective teaching strategies which established teachers will remember from the National Literacy Strategy* (DfEE, 1999). Consider the value of using these in supporting children in the writing of whole-class, group and individual *'Location' stories.*

Idea 7.1: Carpet stories	Suggested age group: 3-year-olds to 11-year-olds

Explanation:

Many young children, when given the opportunity, like to read story books on the floor; they can be found either sitting, resting against a wall, leaning on a bean bag or lying on their back/tummy! Restelli (2011) suggests that many children in the USA are delayed in accomplishing basic skills like holding a pencil because they do not spend enough time on their tummies as a baby. This Idea attempts to not only offer children (3–7) value 'tummy time', but also uses the carpet area as a stimulating writing space[†] so children can write stories on the carpet, both physically (3–11) and literally (3–7)!

[†]The importance of different 'writing spaces':

Wiehardt (2011) suggests that 'there are no hard and fast rules as to what writing space will best promote [children's] work . . . it's best to experiment with different writing spaces and see what works.' Children (5–11) largely write at a table/desk at school, but how often do they get the chance to work on the floor, outside, in the hall, on the playground, in the corridor, in the staffroom or on the field? Plan opportunities for children to experience story writing in these different writing spaces and at different levels (on the floor, at a table, on a wall) to see if this has any effect (positive or not so positive) on the amount and quality of their story writing output.

Exploring different types of *Carpet stories*:

1. Stories about a carpet, e.g. a *flying* carpet, a *talking* carpet, a *singing* carpet, a carpet shaped like an *animal*, a *moody* carpet, a *funny* carpet, a *red* carpet (think of a film premiere), an *evil* carpet, a *magic* carpet or a *baby* carpet.
2. Stories involving a particular type of carpet, e.g. *Indian*, *English*, *Persian*, *Chinese*, *Turkish* or *Oriental*. See Appendix 20 (p. 226) for a useful carpet mark-making/writing template.
3. The 'recycling' of carpet-based stories, e.g. *Phoenix and the Carpet* (Nesbit, 1995), *The Lying Carpet* (Lucas, 2008) or *The Carpet People* (Pratchett, 2004) (see *Recycled stories*, p. 63). For web-based carpet stories, see below*.

[*]Web-based stories to stimulate recycled *Carpet stories*:

1. *Ali and the magic carpet* – see http://tinyurl.com/7pjw3ok, appropriate for children aged 5–7.
2. *Cleopatra's Carpet* – see http://tinyurl.com/72ev2qc, appropriate for children aged 7–9 (PDF downloadable).
3. *The Carpet King* – see http://tinyurl.com/6uycbqc, appropriate for children aged 9–11.

Innovative/useful *Carpet story* ideas:

- Purchase cheap carpet squares/off-cuts which children can physically mark-make/write their stories on with black marker pens. Alternatively, children could use the carpet squares/off-cuts as backing material for their *Carpet story* which is written on paper.
- Tape/stitch written stories onto a large piece of fabric to create a 'story carpet', ensuring that there is space around each story for children to sit and read the stories.
- Provide children with clipboards and cushions when sat/lying working on the carpet for writing ease/comfort.

Idea 7.2: Table-top stories	Suggested age group: 3-year-olds to 11-year-olds

Explanation:

An important aspect of story writing for children is knowing that something is going to happen to their story when it is finished e.g. be collated into a class book, be read by their peers, be submitted to a competition or be put on display. *Table-top stories* embrace the concept of 'get[ting] it out there' (Cox, 2011) by encouraging teachers and children to use table-top surfaces as a way of stimulating story writing and displaying children's story writing efforts.

Table tops across the 3–11 age range:

- 3–5: Large rolls of paper can be taped to table tops, offering young children a big surface space to mark marks, draw pictures and practice letter formations in response to initial sounds in words. This paper could be used as backing paper for mark-making/writing displays in the classroom.

- 5–11: Encourage children to think about how table tops can be used in the stories they write, e.g. a surface for characters to hide under, a space for characters to gather around to have round-the-table discussions, a way of rank ordering contestants in competitions ('topping the table'), or a platform for character to do different things on, e.g. build playing card towers, play board/dice games and dance (!).

Download it! Visit http://tinyurl.com/265qfj for some splendid *Table-top* [writing] *tips* sheets for different age phases – Yrs 1+2 (5–7), 3+4 (7–9) and 5+6 (9–11).

'Getting started' – positively addressing a key issue in story writing:

Many children, teachers *and* fully fledged authors complain that getting started is one of the most difficult things to do when writing a story (Marfilius, 2009). The websites below should be offered to children to help them jump over what is personally referred to as 'the first hurdle in the story writing race' by getting that all important first sentence of their *Table-top story* written:

http://tinyurl.com/yke6mh8   http://tinyurl.com/9v7k73c   http://tinyurl.com/nzwdd4

Ways of displaying *Table-top stories*:

Model the different display strategies advocated below, encouraging children to take increasing ownership of creating table-top displays of their story writing in their classroom and around the school:

1. Mount stories on card and display them on tables using book or menu stands (5–11).

2. Collate written stories in class anthologies (3–11).

3. Hang stories around the edges of tables with looped string (3–7).

4. Present stories at *different levels* on tables covered with drapes (under which are distributed different sized/shaped boxes) (3–7).

5. Display stories on table-top folding display boards or pop-up desk stands (7–11).

6. Attach stories to table tops by covering the table surface in clear sticky back plastic (3–7).

7. Tape stories to the underneath of table tops, offering children torches so that they can lie on their backs and read the stories with a focussed light source (3–9).

Idea 7.3: Playground stories	**Suggested age group:** 5-year-olds to 11-year-olds

Explanation:

Dodd (1993) suggests that 'the school playground is a world closed to adults – the only place where children are free of grown-up interference. What goes on at playtime can have a greater impact on a child's overall experience at school than any other aspect of school life.' *Playground stories* offer children the opportunity to write stories about positive or negative incidents* which take place in the playground area; these could be events based on their own personal experiences, observations of others, or invented goings-on for the characters they create to have to deal with.

*Incidents on the playground:

Even as adults we can still recall 'incidents' we were involved in on the playground at school. These incidents, many of which still happen to children today, offer a wealth of story writing possibilities:

Incident	Story writing potential – questions to consider
First kiss	*Who kissed whom? Was it by accident? Was it nice? Where did the kiss happen?*
Being bullied	*How does this make the 'bullied' feel? Who is doing the bullying? Why is the bully bullying the 'bullied'?*
Sharing a joke	*What is the joke? Who heard it? How did those listening react to it?*
Grazed knee	*How did it happen? Was it an accident? Who cleaned up the wound?*
Playing chase	*How many children were playing? Was there a theme to the game, e.g.* Cops and robbers? Baddies and goodies? Superheroes and villains? *What happened?*
Feeling lonely	*Why would the other kids not let Sam play? How does this make Sam feel?*

Cross-curricular Link! Use circle time or PSHE and Citizenship sessions to talk about incidents that happen on the playground to help children generate potential plots for their *Playground stories*. See Appendix 21 (p. 227) for an interesting hopscotch outline to use either as a story planner or as an innovative way of presenting their *Playground story* to the reader.

Tense of the text – a learning and teaching opportunity:

When exploring the language features of stories, Derewianka (1990) suggests that stories are normally presented in the past tense. This is an important point for learning and teaching as children need to be taught how action verbs (known as 'material processes') e.g. *walk*, *build* and *sing*, and verbs that refer to what characters said, felt or thought (referred to as 'verbal and mental processes') are written in the past tense. For some useful links, offering information and activities about regular and irregular verbs, visit http://tinyurl.com/84ztwsb, considering the value of highlighting this prior to or during the writing of children's *Playground stories*.

Internet-based 'playground' stories for 5–7-year-olds:

Encourage children to read and reflect on the online stories below, considering ways in which they can be used to stimulate their own writing of a *Playground story*:

1. *No dogs!* – available at http://tinyurl.com/435q8kr
2. *Blue cow in the playground* – available at http://tinyurl.com/6ohg48n

Idea 7.4: Assembly stories	**Suggested age group:** 5-year-olds to 11-year-olds

Explanation:

Stories are an integral feature of assemblies for primary school children, with many teachers recognising the importance of stories as being a valuable way to get messages from the different faiths across to children in a subtle yet effective way. *Assembly stories* offer children the exciting opportunity to write stories that are based on suitable topics, themes[†] and ideas which can be read out and used to stimulate discussions in assemblies that they attend.

[†]A plethora of *Assembly story* themes:

Hemming (cited in British Humanist Association, 2011) suggests that assembly themes should relate to the 'great human themes: courage, achievement, love, compassion, wonder, imagination, joy, tragedy, hope, responsibility, humanitarian endeavour, and the mystery of existence.' Encourage children to base their stories around one of the themes offered above, using characters from religious texts or contemporary contexts to bring the story alive *where appropriate*. Visit http://tinyurl.com/8ea643c for stories to help develop children's appreciation and understanding of these different themes.

Stimulating *Assembly story* titles:

- *The life of a soldier's wife*
- *The sparking star*
- *The talking tree*
- *Girl today, hare tomorrow*

- *Walking through the wood*
- *The magic stone*
- *I found it in my bowl of cereal*
- *The poorly mouse*

All selected from Armstrong (2006)

***It's all about the length!* A top tip from writing educationalists:**

Jones and Jones (2008: 31) suggest that if children want to improve their writing they need know that 'lots of short sentences are dull' and so should 'use a variety of sentences, some short, some compound and some complex to make [their] writing interesting' (2008: 68). Examples include:

Simple (short)	Compound	Complex
Harry was a boy.	Harry liked working with his dad in his tool shed and helping his mum bake.	Harry found the fat screwdriver, which was covered in a thin sheet of sawdust.
Aimee was a clever girl.	Aimee could do multiplication sums in her head because her grandfather had taught her some brilliant mental tricks.	As Aimee closed her eyes, she suddenly heard a howl from her grandfather which made her insides turn very cold.

Work with children to develop their use of these different sentence types in their *Assembly story* writing.

Alternative interpretations of *Assembly stories* (7–11):

There are different ways teachers could interpret and use the notion of *Assembly stories* in class:

- *Assembled stories!* Help children plan out their stories by writing down different plot ideas on Post-It® notes or scrap pieces of paper, physically 'assembling' them into a coherent story.
- *Get together!* Support children in writing stories about groups of different people who gather together for a common reason (an *assembly*), e.g. a courtroom hearing, a religious event, a Parent Teacher/Friend Association meeting or a book club meeting.
- *Assembly lines!* Show children pictures/video footage of different assembly lines. Encourage children to write stories about unusual products made on them and the different people who work on the line.

| **Idea 7.5: Lunchtime stories** | **Suggested age group:** 5-year-olds to 11-year-olds |

Explanation:

APSE (n.d.: 2) argues that '[l]unchtimes are a significant but often overlooked part of the school day.' It is, however, difficult to ignore this period of the day, particularly due to the noise generated by hundreds of children all talking at the same time in the hall, along with crying children due to grazed knees and children falling out on the playground! *Lunchtime stories* serve to 'calm the chaos' of the dinner hour by using lunchtime not only as stimuli* for children's story writing, but also an opportunity to showcase children's writing talents in school†.

*Stimulating stories around lunchtime:

The daily lunchtime period offers children a wealth of story potential for their stories, for example:

- Characters not liking the food in their lunchbox/on the school menu.
- Characters having an argument with their friends on the playground.
- Characters not being able to sit at the same table with their friends in the dinner hall.

Innovative stories based around lunchtimes that children could write include:

- The school cooks all go on strike so the children have to cook their own hot dinners!
- Mrs Prodley, a midday supervisor, goes crazy in the dinner hall after slipping on some food!
- The day all of the food on the school menu was surprisingly purple!
- The Christmas dinner where the children have to serve the cooks, midday supervisors and teachers their Christmas lunches!
- The lunchtime chairs, tables, crockery and cutlery have all been stolen so the children have to eat their food actually off the floor!
- The week children in Year 6 got the chance to decide what was on the school menu!

Stimulating *Lunchtime* story ideas:

- †Encourage purposeful speaking and listening opportunities by playing audio recordings of child authors reading out loud their written stories in the hall whilst children eat.
- †Make written anthologies of children's stories available on the tables the children sit at to eat their lunch. Ensure the pages are suitably protected from spillages and fallen food.
- Set up a weekly 'Brown bag' story writing lunchtime club for those children who wish to develop their story writing skills during their dinner break.
- Offer clipboards and pens for children who wish to write stimulating stories when on the playground during lunchtime.

Planning stories using lunchtime foods:

To help children write stimulating *Lunchtime stories*, encourage them to use a story planner. Young (1999, cited in Riedl and Young, 2005: 5) advocates their usage, suggesting that they represent 'ordered steps' that model 'the chronological . . . events that occur in the story world'. Use hamburger outlines (think a '*McStory*' – see http://tinyurl.com/cf5nslz), divided sections of a milkshake cup (see Appendix 22, p. 228), or sketches of a school dinner plastic tray/compartments of an open lunchbox to plan opening and closing sentences and paragraphs/sentences that 'fill' the story middle.

Idea 7.6: Library stories	Suggested age group: 5-year-olds to 11-year-olds

Explanation:

Lombardi (2011) describes libraries as 'those infamous places of the imagination'. Some children think of libraries as being dull, dusty and dreary, whereas they should be encouraged to view them as a 'treasure trove' stocked full of items to stimulate and excite them. *Library stories* are designed to bring libraries to the forefront of children's minds, helping them to consider writing stories about libraries, the people who use them, and the wonderful/strange things that could (or indeed do) go on in them.

Story possibilities for children's *Library stories*:

- Computer meltdowns.
- Noisy members of the public (vocal).
- Stolen books.
- Library 'lock-ins'.
- Magic potions found inside hollowed-out books.
- Unpaid fines.
- Angry librarians.
- Torn pages found in newly purchased books.
- 'Talking' scanners.

Increasing children's writing productivity through library visits:

Brooks (2011) argues that many people need to 'be quiet to be productive'. She claims that the 'local library is one of the best places to work' because of 'the law' of being quiet, the access to literature for reference and ideas, and the desks and chairs that are available to the public. Organise a morning or afternoon visit with your local library where your class can go and work on their *Library stories*; this also offers a perfect opportunity for children to observe the 'goings-on' in a public, university or mobile library, and use what they see as stimuli for their story writing.

Libraries and repetition (5–7):

Most employment involves some form of repetitive work, and working in a library is no exception – scanning books out, scanning books back in, filing books back on the shelves etc. Repetition is also useful for young writers when they are writing their own stories; think of *Hairy McClary* by Dodd (2002). Encourage children to use developing repetitive structures when writing their *Library story*, e.g. *On Monday Mr. Woodfield filed a book away on bugs. On Tuesday Mr. Woodfield filed two books away on trains. On Wednesday . . .*

Characters and *Library stories* (7–11):

Stimulating characterisation can help to make *Library stories* a delight to write and read. 'Kim went to the library one day' tells us very little about the character – *how old is she? What does she look like? What was she wearing? How was she feeling when she went to the library?*

Support children by helping them to think carefully about the characters in their *Library story*, focusing particularly on their *name (Kimberley Pole, for example, might give us an indication to her physical size and shape)*, their *character type (is she a swot? a loner? A busybody? A trouble maker?)* and their *feelings about going to the library (is Kimberley elated? depressed? Anxious? Giddy?)*.

Download it! For a wonderful PowerPoint presentation on characterisation to use with children during whole-class/group teaching, visit http://tinyurl.com/848wbmd.

Idea 7.7: Toilet stories	**Suggested age group:** 7-year-olds to 11-year-olds

Explanation:

The toilet is one of those taboo subjects that all children talk about but react to in different ways: some giggle at the words associated with it whilst others have a 'fear of falling in [it]' (Black and Fawcett, 2008: 51); some are fascinated with the sound of it flushing whilst others have a phobia about actually using it. The Idea of *Toilet stories* is about getting children to be 'rather outrageous writers', penning a stimulating story which may be considered by others to be a little risqué, rude or naughty – only in *Toilet stories* are children able to write about toilets, create scenarios involving toilets, use toilet humour*, and invent characters with toilet-themed names, e.g. *Toilet Brush Tina*, *Toilet Roll Robbie*, *U-bend Bertrum*, *Toilet Seat Sadie* and *Toilet Bowl Bob*!

***Toilet Stories* and teachers' understandable apprehension:**

A number of readers may dismiss this Idea on the grounds of a) the behavioural difficulties it may cause as a result of children being actively encouraged to be rude, and b) the responses of parents/carers who may be displeased about their child writing about toilets and items associated with it in school. These concerns can be alleviated by using the following strategies:

• Establish in your own mind the educational purposes of children in your class writing *Toilet stories* (link these to children's writing targets where possible).
• Inform parents/carers about your *Toilet story* writing plans through newsletters and emails (if appropriate), emphasising the value of this as a stimulating story Idea.
• Formulate explicit expectations of children's behaviour during the planning and writing of their *Toilet story*; establish clear rules about the appropriate sharing of *Toilet stories* with others both in school and outside of it.

Extending children's vocabulary: synonyms for *toilet*:

There are opportunities for children to extend their vocabulary by learning different terms/'labels' for toilet; these include:

• *Lavatory*	• *W.C.*	• *Privy*	• *Throne*
• *Bathroom*	• *Can*	• *Little boy's/girl's room*	• *Latrine*
• *John*	• *Outhouse*	• *Water closet*	• *Restroom*
• *Restroom*	• *Powder room*	• *Washroom*	

Learning these new words in class offers teachers a level of control over the appropriate/'sensible' vocabulary children should be encouraged to use in their everyday speech and in their *Toilet story* writing.

*Children and toilet humour:

There is no denying it – many children are fascinated with bums, flatulence and other bodily functions! Young children, particularly those aged 3–7, find words like 'poo', 'pants' and 'wee-wee' hilarious; Kustermann (2003) suggests that this 'toilet humour' is an initial stage in the development of humour in children. Millyard and Masters (2004) argue that while controversy rages about toilet humour content found in children's books, sales of the 'poo-bum' genre continue to soar (see Holzwarth and Erlbruch, 1994; Pilkey, 2000; Kotzwinkle and Murray, 2001; Lawrence, 2001). Encourage children to write *Toilet stories* that describe funny things which happen to characters involving toilet paper, toilet brushes, toilet seats and toilet water in an effort to make others laugh!

Idea 7.8: Weathered stories	**Suggested age group:** 3-year-olds to 9-year-olds

Explanation:

Research reported in the *Telegraph* (2009b) suggests that the weather is still Britain's favourite topic of conversation, with three-quarters of us discussing it more than anything else. *Weathered stories* embrace this common talking point by using it as the driving force for some 'atmospheric' story writing! From stories about seaside visits in the blazing summer sunshine, to making winter snow angels that come alive at night, *Weathered stories* allow children to consider the 'wealth of weathers' experienced in different parts of the world throughout the year, and reflect on how these influence characters and events that take place in their written stories.

Writing *with* the weather (3–5):

A creative way of encouraging young children to mark-make is by actually using the weather. For example, water found in puddles following a rain shower can be collected by children in different sized pipettes and squirted on dry parts of the playground. Freshly fallen snow can be used as a white canvas for young children to tell a story through marks and words made with food colouring, gloved fingers or small sticks (Campbell and Featherstone, 2002). Shadow letters can be created by children holding cut out cardboard letters or stencils in the sunshine. Take digital images to capture this early writing before the weather changes, encouraging children to think about stories that relate to the weather they are mark-making with.

Awe and wonder weathers to stimulate story writing:

Through pictures, non-fiction texts, posters and video clips, introduce children (5–9) to different examples of weather which typically capture people's attention and imagination, for example:

- *Floods*
- *Hurricanes*
- *Blizzards*
- *Tornadoes (twisters)*
- *Giant hailstones*
- *Avalanches*
- *Tidal waves*
- *Thunderstorms*

Work with children to think about the aftermath of these weathers – might story characters end up in a new world (think *The Wizard of Oz*)? Might story characters have to build something to save themselves and the lives of others (think *Noah and the Ark*)?

Weather and the problems it causes (5–9):

Ellis et al. (1997: 59) argue that one of the key elements a story needs is '. . . a problem'. There are many difficulties that the weather can pose for characters, for example,

- Heavy rainfall (getting soaking wet because of not having an umbrella to hand).
- Bright sunshine (dazzled eyesight or the possibility of getting sunburnt).
- Gale-force winds (blowing houses and cars over).
- Freezing temperatures (icy paths that make it dangerous to walk on; catching a nasty cold).

Talk with children (5–7) about their own experiences of different weather types, considering what they did to overcome these issues, e.g. *wearing protective clothing, playing inside rather than outside, 'wrapping up warm'*. Encourage children (7–9) to consider how characters might react to different weathers in terms of their mood (*hot and bothered, snappy, lethargic, wild*).

Idea 7.9: Environment stories	Suggested age group: 5-year-olds to 11-year-olds

Explanation:

Barrett (2005: 3) argues that 'human beings continue to have [a] significant impact on the environment and its resources.' The Idea of *Environment stories* helps children to not only appreciate the importance of the environment in providing an interesting location (setting) for their story, but also helps them to 'understand . . . the ramifications of the actions' (2005: 3) of the characters they write about on the different environments they find themselves in. The clear links with Geography in this Idea also helps to support children's future education (see Butt, 2011).

Stimulating story environments:

When referring to story environments, children need to appreciate that two key aspects are being referred to: *place* and *time*. Help children (7–11) to move away from established or familiar settings such as the woods and the shops by using one or more of the following:

Place				Time	
Beauty parlour	Hospital	Cinema	Underwater dome		Past
Tool shed	In a tree	Magic shop	Museum		Present
Airport	University	Pharmacy	Bowling alley		Future

Encourage children to think about the *effects* of characters' actions* on the environment, e.g. dirty air, death of animals and plants, fewer resources, less space, increase in waste, loss of habitats etc.

*Characters' actions on the environment:

Use the notion of 'Talking Time' (see Dockrell and Stuart, 2007) to help children consider the different kinds of actions that have a negative effect on the environment. Examples include:

- Driving everywhere instead of walking to places where possible.
- Leaving the lights on instead of switching them off when not in use/needed.
- Using air conditioners when opening a window is sufficient to cool a room down.
- Throwing rubbish on the floor instead of disposing it in recycling dustbins.
- Using non-renewable fuel sources (coal, oil) instead of renewable sources (solar, wind).

Encourage children to consider the reasons why characters would do the above, acknowledging their possible naivety, lack of knowledge and understanding, or their defiance to care/think about the environment, and how their actions have an impact on the environment and future generations.

Happy! Sad! Extending the emotions felt by characters in _Environment stories_:

A common problem teachers comment on about children's story writing is the limited 'emotional range' of characters, e.g. *Sally was happy to see Sam; Finbarr was sad because he had lost his ball.* Help children (7–11) to broaden the kinds of emotions felt by their characters in their *Environment stories* through speaking and listening activities, and making reference to Plutchik's (1980) 'Wheel of Emotions' as a visual aid – see http://tinyurl.com/6qj8ge9. Useful lists of emotion words can also be found at http://tinyurl.com/9q6fzon and http://tinyurl.com/bq7o98j.

Idea 7.10: Local area stories	Suggested age group: 7-year-olds to 11-year-olds

Explanation:

Open any local/regional newspaper and teachers will find within it a wealth of stories involving different people, places and communities. *Local area stories* are designed to capitalise on the infinite supply of interesting individuals, localities and events contained within the articles, reports and summaries that make up the content of different newspapers. By self-selecting interesting news stories, children can use these as the basis for the stimulating stories they are encouraged to write.

Turning reported stories into *Local area stories* – examples:

A local newspaper report . . .	. . . converted into a *Local area story*
Under-performing school wins praise for coming top in the league tables	Class Six devise a new 'cool' curriculum which improves standards at a football or dance academy
Bad weather causes havoc for motorists	The day the cars just couldn't go!
Mum reunited with long-lost son	Harry finds his missing dad via Twitter!

Other events which might stimulate children's *Local area story* writing include: *UFO sightings, new births, vandalised parks, strawberry shortages, celebrity visits, escaped animals,* and *local health scares.*

Turning newspaper articles into *Local area stories* – the 'how':

For children to be able to turn newspaper articles into *Local area stories* they need to learn and use a range of strategies to support them. The modelling of the following will aid them to do this:

- Use different coloured highlighter pens to establish the '5Ws and 1H': **who** was involved, **what** happened, **where** did it happened, **when** did it happen, **why** did it happen and **how** did it happen? (adapted from Harrett, 2006: 75).

- Consider what kind of story can be developed from the newspaper reports selected, e.g. a report about a stolen car lends itself to a story about *loss*; a sponsored bungee jump lends itself to a story about *overcoming fear.*

- Tweak people's names in the newspaper article so that they become characters' names for the *Local area story* e.g. Kelly Fisher becomes Kerrie Flashan; Bradley Cooper becomes Blade Keeper.

Boys' resentment to 'teacher interference' – a learning and teaching consideration:

Daly (2003) highlights research that suggests that boys are less likely to respond positively to teachers' expectations when it comes to their writing. It is argued that boys are keen to use their own ideas and are 'frustrated by the imposition of teacher-language and teacher-ideas on their writing' (2003: 11). Ways to overcome this when writing *Local area stories* include:

- Explain to boys how the suggestions you make are designed to help them make *progress* and improve the *quality* of their work.

- Show boys how your advice relates to a) their writing targets, b) marking schemes, and c) associated levels of attainment.

- Allow boys to modify and adapt recommendations you make to protect their writing confidence (see Pajares, 2003).

'Boys'' stories

The focus of this chapter centres on boys and writing, a 'hot topic' that has been of intense discussion and debate in educational arenas for many years. It is well documented through inspection reports (OFSTED, 2003; 2009), research findings (Holden, 2002; Francis, 2006) and media coverage (Shepherd, 2009) that standards in boys' writing are a cause for concern for many schools at a local, national and international level. This chapter is specifically designed to offer teachers a range of Ideas, practical strategies and approaches to challenge the assumption of boys' healthy idleness (Cohen, 1988) towards literacy, and effectively engage them in stimulating story writing with the intent of raising motivational levels and attainment.

> **Just for boys?** It is important to note that the Ideas presented in this chapter can be modified for use with girls; even though adventure books 'have been traditionally regarded as "boy books"', Merisuo-Storm (2006: 117) found that girls liked reading them the most. If girls like *reading* adventure stories, then perhaps they might like *writing* them – if so, then see *Adventure stories* (p. 162)!

The first half of the chapter responds positively to the thinking of Blair and Sanford (2004: 458), who advocate that teachers should offer boys writing activities that 'inform their personal interests'. *Me stories*, which open this chapter, encourage boys to think about the value of events that happen in their daily lives as a way of stimulating their stories. Whilst Lamb (cited in APA, 2010) suggests that boys should distance themselves from the 'wrong images [of] the movie superhero of today', *Superhero stories* actively encourage teachers to engage boys in purposeful speaking and listening, role play and writing opportunities by using costumed crime fighters as a powerful form of story stimuli. As a love of adventure seems to be hard-wired into most boys' DNA, *Adventure stories* give boys the opportunity to use their imagination to discover, explore and overcome challenges in written form – see http://tinyurl.com/ cj3hqt4 for some valuable teacher resource materials. *Chase stories* embrace boys' love of being 'actively mobile' by building a story around 'the thrill of the chase', considering *who* and *what* to race against; *Sports stories* also capitalise on this need for movement by offering boys the chance to write stories about the sports that they watch and play.

The second half of the chapter uses alliteration as an effective literary device to link the five 'F' Ideas together. Scieszka (2002: 23) suggests that 'boys enjoy books that have humour, short chapters and cliff-hanger endings, and some funny or slightly gross things that make them feel what they're reading is a bit subversive' – in response to this, *Funny stories* and *Frightful stories* encourage boys to write 'laugh-out-loud' stories and tales about things that go bump in the night! *Fairy stories* may initially appear to be a misplaced Idea in this chapter, but efforts are made to highlight the numerous 'manly' elements of fairy stories which will appeal to boys. *Free stories* are purposefully designed to give boys across the 3–11 age range autonomy over their story writing in terms of '*what* they write about, *how* they write about it and *what* they write it in!' (p. 168). *Futures stories*, which brings this chapter to a close, allow boys to enter the unknown, considering what happens to characters they create in a futuristic world full of advanced transport, food, clothing, housing and technological gadgetry.

Taking a closer look at 'relaxing expectations with regard to accurate spellings'

It is suggested that *Free stories* should be used with boys 'to "relax" expectations with regard to sentence structure, accurate spellings, the use of punctuation marks, and correct grammar' (p. 168). Isaacson (1997) identifies spelling as a 'mechanical aspect of writing', one that can unfortunately act as an 'obstacle' for children's writing, slowing down their writing fluency and drawing their attention away from the generation of writing ideas. Baleghizadeh and Darghai (2011: 152) suggest that spelling can become a 'time consuming and tedious' hindrance that can affect a child's 'writing flow', and can cause unnecessary frustration and angst. Whilst the ability to spell undoubtedly aids the writing process, teachers need to be mindful that when children (particularly those aged 6+) are writing the first draft of their story they should be encouraged to focus on getting their ideas down on paper *first*, attending to any spelling issues later on. This helps to emphasise the point that the primary purpose of writing is to communicate (i.e. their story), and that children have different roles to play as a writer during the writing process:

> Smith (1982) described the writing process as an on[-]going tension between the writer's two roles: the author and the secretary [administrative assistant]. The author thinks about the message, the organization of ideas, and the language in which to express those ideas. The [administrative assistant], on the other hand, has to worry about the mechanical concerns: margins, spelling, punctuation, and handwriting. The author–[administrative assistant] tension exists throughout the writing process, from planning to editing and writing a final draft.
>
> (Isaacson, 1997)

It is therefore advocated that children should embrace their *author* role when they initiate work on their stories, ensuring that the important generation of text is not neglected. Revisiting their work as an *administrative assistant* will offer children opportunities to make improvements to their writing and allow them to proofread their work, which Kervin (2002) sees as a particularly effective strategy for spelling development in 6–8-year-olds. Other recommended spelling strategies (largely for the 4–11 age range), alongside the teaching of reading and daily phonics input, have been organised around the *Spelling Bee*, a competition originating from the USA which involves children spelling English words – see http://tinyurl.com/bayk9h which offers an interactive website linked to *The Times* National Spelling Bee Championship:

S = Seen it before? (4–11). Christian (2011) advocates teaching children to remember where they have previously seen particular words so that they make reference to these 'spelling sources' to support their correct spelling of the words in their writing; for example, in story books, on flash cards, on word walls, on displays, on labels and on phonics posters.

P = P/r/a/c/t/i/ce! (4–7). Get children to practice verbally segmenting the sounds in a word whilst physically writing the word in different ways to help 'lock it' in their minds; for example, write the word *there* with different coloured highlighter pens, with fingers on legs, in sugar sprinkled on a tray, with elbows in the air, in mud with a stick, with bottom shuffles on the floor and with 'pinkie' (little) fingers on peers' backs.

E = E's in the family! (4–11). Break single syllable words into two parts: the *onset* at the beginning, which is usually a consonant or a consonant cluster (two or more consonants together), and the *rime* found at the end; for example, **bag** = 'b' (*onset*) and 'ag' (*rime*). By varying the onset a word family can be created; for example, *sag, nag, fag, rag, hag, lag, wag, gag, tag*. See http://tinyurl.com/7p7ndpa for some innovative ideas on using word families to teach children to spell.

L = Look at it! (5–11). Promote the use of the *'Look, Say, Cover, Write, Check'* (LSCWC) approach to spelling words; for example, *Look* at the word – Polygon; *Say* the word – 'Pol-y-gon'; *cover* the word up with your hand or a piece of paper; *write* the word down on a piece of paper – p-o-l-y-g-o-n – and then *check* it – *is it correct?*

L = Little rhyme! (4–11). Use little rhymes and mnemonics to help children spell tricky words; for example, *Mississippi* ('EM-EYE-DOUBLE-ES-EYE-DOUBLE-ES-EYE-DOUBLE-PEE-EYE') and *Friend* (Remember, you and 'I' to the 'END'); *Was* (**W**itches **A**nd **S**pells) and *Because* (**B**ig **E**lephants **C**an **A**lways **U**nderstand **S**mall **E**lephants).

I = Items galore! (3–11) Hopkins (2010) promotes a 3-D approach to learning spellings by encouraging teachers to offer children different resources to spell out their words with (see Table 8.1).

Table 8.1   Resources to use in practical spelling exercises (Hopkins, 2010)

Plastic/magnetic letters	Letter tiles from board games	Letters from a box of alphabet cereal	Alphabet soup pasta letters
Alphabet rubber stamps/inkpad	Pipe cleaners shaped into letters	Modelling clay shaped into letters	'Arranged' ice-pop sticks
Broken-up cooked spaghetti noodles shaped into letters	Letters written in shaving foam on the desk	Large letters from newspaper headlines or advertisements in magazines/comics. Consider junk mail as an alternative	

N = Now I know! (4–11). A simple spelling strategy which involves children making reference to an authority source. This could include a dictionary (online/paper based), one of their peers, their personal spelling book, a teacher, an alphabet book, a parent/carer, a computer spell-checker or spelling rules; for example, nouns ending in 'y' change to 'ies' (*lady – ladies*). NOTE! This *only* applies if there is a *consonant* in the word *before* the 'y' (*la**d**y*); if there is there a *vowel* before the 'y' then just add 's' (*monk**e**y – monkeys*).

G = Graphic! (7-11). Learn spellings through 'graphic visualisation'; for example, with the word *necessary* imagine the 'ece' part of the word as a tiny pair of eyes, with the 'c' in the middle acting as the nose (see Figure 8.1).

Figure 8.1   Example of using graphic visualisation to help spell words

Consider inserting *images* into words as a graphic way of remembering spellings; for example, draw a picture of a rat on a piece of paper and then write the letters 'SEP' *to the left* of the rat and 'E' *to the right of it. What do you see?* First you have SEP, then you had A RAT, then you finish with the E – **SEPARATE!**

B = Bags! (4–11). Make spelling 'real, relevant, fun and motivating' for children by creating *Active Spelling Bags*, as advocated by Battlefield Primary School – see http://tinyurl.com/7f9s2zv. The bags, based on the notion of Storysacks®, offer games and tasks based around a spelling pattern for children to engage with at home with parents/carers.

E = Either–Or! (6–11). This is a title adaptation of Corbett's (2003: 79) *Which One* spelling strategy. Offer children different spellings of a word (see Figure 8.2).

Payne	**Pain**	**Pane**

Figure 8.2   Different spellings of a word with a similar sound but a different meaning

Get them to select the one they think is the correct way to spell it within a particular context; for example, being hurt (*pain*). Ask them to explain their reasoning behind their decision.

E = Energise! (4–11). Use *Jolly Phonics* actions (in the form of energetic exercise movements) to emphasise particular phonemes – 'h' = running; 'ng' = lifting a heavy weight (see http://tinyurl.com/dxts85r) – and learn spellings by energetic rote marching/chanting to the beat of a drum; for example, 'A-N-G-R-Y-SPELLS-AN-GRY-**GRR**!' Alternatively, tap out the syllables of words on different parts of the body in response to a metronome; for example, *Fantastic* = 'Fan-' (*tap head*), 'Tas-' (*tap elbow*), 'Tic' (*tap shoulder*)!

To further support teachers, select readings and websites are offered below to develop and enrich subject knowledge and learning and teaching of spellings to support boys' engagement with *'Boys'' stories*:

- **Book** – *You Can Do It! Spelling* by Seed and Hurn (2011).

- **Downloadable spelling resource** – *Spelling: From Beginnings to Proficiency. A spelling resource for planning, teaching, assessing and reporting on progress* by The State of South Australia, Department of Education and Children's Services (2011) – available at http://tinyurl.com/cutk9qg.

- **Website** – Words and spelling games – available at http://tinyurl.com/2vkkhgf.

Take a look!

Following the publication of the *National Curriculum for English Key Stages 1 and 2 – Draft* (DfE, 2012b), readers are encouraged to look at pages i to xvi which offer a useful Appendix related to spelling for Year 1, Year 2, Years 3 and 4, and Years 5 and 6.

Table 8.2   Recommended readings associated with *'Boys'' stories*

Books	Fletcher, R. (2006) *Boy Writers: Reclaiming their Voice*. Ontario: Pembroke. *A supportive and interesting text that examines the whole notion of 'boy writers', the reasons as to why many of them are reluctant to put pen to paper, and evaluates ways in which those in the field of education can positively engage boys in purposeful writing experiences.* Consider the value of this text in relation to supporting boys' and their writing of *'Boys'' stories* in your classroom. Bowkett, S. (2006) *Boys and Writing*. London: Continuum. *This book concerns itself with how children's writing can be improved through a thinking skills agenda. The emphasis is on engaging boys with writing, but the ideas and techniques work equally well with girls and span a wide age/ability range.* Consider the value of this text in relation to supporting both boys/girls and their writing of *'Boys'' stories* in your classroom.

Online journal articles	Goiran-Bevelhimer, A. F. (2008) Boys and writing: implications for creating school writing curriculum and instruction that is boy-friendly. *Journal for the Liberal Arts and Sciences*, 13 (1), 73–92. [Online]. Available at: http://tinyurl.com/bo2zudf (Accessed: 25 November 2011). *This American article 'focus the lens on the nature of boys' and offers 'educators insight about how boys learn and process in order to fine-tune [the] writing curriculum and instruction to be more effective' (p. 74).* Consider the value of this article in relation to supporting boys and their writing of *'Boys'' stories* in your classroom. Pajares, F. and Valiante, G. (2001) Gender differences in writing-motivation and achievement of middle school students: a function of gender orientation? *Contemporary Educational Psychology*, 26, 366–81. [Online]. Available at: http://tinyurl.com/caxfjl4 (Accessed: 25 November 2011). *This article reports on research which set out 'to determine whether gender differences in the writing motivation and achievement of middle school students [was] a function of gender-stereotypic beliefs rather than of gender' (p. 366). The findings suggest that 'educators [should work to] alter students' views of writing so that it is perceived as relevant and valuable' (p. 377) to both boys and girls.* Consider the value of this text in relation to supporting boys/girls and their writing of *'Boys'' stories* in your classroom.
Websites	Bevilacqua, K. (n.d.) *Using the Internet to Motivate Writing*. [Online]. Available at: http://tinyurl.com/n6uyxm (Accessed: 25 November 2011). *This website highlights a number of great online resources for teachers and parents/carers that can encourage creativity and writing for children, particularly boys. From online writing communities and stories for children by children, to writing contests (competitions) and using the Internet as a tool for research, this website also offers a number of writing web links for budding young male writers!* Consider the value of this website in relation to supporting boys and their writing of *'Boys'' stories* in your classroom. East Riding of Yorkshire Council (n.d.) Can write, won't write! *East Riding of Yorkshire Council Raising Boys' Achievement Writing Project.* [Online]. Available at: http://tinyurl.com/cnnf3ne (Accessed: 25 November 2011). *This website offers a wealth of valuable information, web links, research findings and practical resources linked to* Raising Boys' Achievements in Writing, *a joint research project undertaken in 2004 by the United Kingdom Literacy Association and the PNS.* Consider the value of this website in relation to supporting boys and their writing of *'Boys'' stories* in your classroom.

| **Idea 8.1: Me stories** | **Suggested age group:** 3-year-olds to 5-year-olds |

Explanation:

How often do we as adults get the chance to talk about ourselves? Many of us try to avoid 'conversational narcissism' (Derber, 2000) for fear of being perceived as egocentric, so the luxury of talking about ourselves is confined, for some, to counselling sessions. For young children, however, talking about oneself is simply part of being a young child! *Me stories* actively encourage boys to talk about the 'goings-on' in their lives and record these as stories in written form for others to read and enjoy.

Stimulating *Me stories*:

Me stories can be generated in a variety of ways:

- *Weekend 'Small Talk' Time* on a Monday, for example, gives young boys the opportunity to talk about things that have happened to them since they were last at school.

- *Holiday Happenings* offers *Me story* writing possibilities after boys return from half-term breaks and seasonal celebrations (dependent on the faith of the child).

- Birthday parties, trips out, visits to friends and families, and attendance at morning/after school clubs are other occasions which can be used to fuel a *Me story*.

- Things that happen to boys during the session/day are also valuable, e.g. getting up late for school, playing chase with their best pal, being praised by their teacher, making others' laugh in the dinner hall – any event where boys serve as the 'the star' of the story is ideal for a *Me story*!

Linking *Me story* events and purposeful mark marking in the early years:

Teachers of children aged 3–5 are encouraged to tailor mark-making activities to the different events boys use to drive their *Me story*:

1. *Sky writing* – boys who go to a weekend air show could be encouraged to record their story in the air using their finger. Teachers could record this writing on a child-friendly Digital Blue™ video recorder for assessment purposes.

2. *Maze marking* – boys who visit a maze at the local park could be encouraged to complete a maze on paper. These mazes could be from the Internet or teacher/peer designed.

3. *Cooked writing** – boys who cook with their parents/carers can use edible alphabet pasta to write their story, write words with syrup on pancakes, bake iced word cookies, or create letters/words made out of rolled dough (Hallissy, 2011). Digital images of these writing efforts can be used for display purposes or be included in boys' learning journeys.

'Use sand to help young boys write, says government':

In a bid to stop boys falling behind girls, Williams (2009) reported on practical guidance from the UK government to interest the youngest boys in writing: '[E]ncourage three- and four-year-old boys to write using materials such as *chocolate powder and coloured sand . . . Boys [should] also be encouraged to make marks on the floor and walls outside using, for example, chalk, water or paint.' Consider embracing the above when engaging boys in *Me stories*.

Idea 8.2: Superhero stories	Suggested age group: 3-year-olds to 11-year-olds

Explanation:

Spiderman, *Superman* and *Batman* – there is no doubt about it: boys *love* superheroes! Rubin (2006, cited in Lauzon, 2011) claims that 'superheroes can be very appealing at a sensory level. They wear primary colo[u]rs, they are fast and stimulating. Kids want speed and colo[u]r and cool gadgets. Superheroes literally take them [children] on flights of fancy.' *Superhero stories* positively respond to the 'natural appeal' superheroes have for boys by offering them opportunities to hear initial sounds ('**C-C-C**atch the **B-B-B**addies!'), and write stories either about superheroes they know and love or those they have created themselves, e.g. *Lasso Lad, Rainbow Guy, Shuttle Dude, Ice Chap* or *Battle Bloke*!

Tuning into boys' interests (3–5):

Hirschheimer (2002: 66) argues that 'most children draw much of their play from TV and videos that they have seen'. As boys come into contact with superheroes through different media sources* it is important for teachers to positively acknowledge this interest by 'join[ing] in with children's themes' (2002: 66) and considering ways they can integrate superheroes into their provision and practice. Stimulating strategies include:

- Providing simple superhero capes and masks for role-play activity.

- Offering chunky pencils to cope with the strong grip of the 'superhero author' using it.

- Rolling out really large sheets of paper for superheroes to make big, dramatic marks and drawings on; alternatively, see Appendix 23 (p. 229) for a 1960s Batman inspired **KERPOW!** mark-making/ writing template.

- Gathering together old cardboard boxes, used crates and large drapes for boys to build superhero lairs, dens and hideouts so they have somewhere safe to talk, read, write and rest!

Superhero stories and speaking and listening:

Children are exposed to superheroes through *films, posters, cartoons, comics, magazines, computer games, advertisements, music and books. Encourage boys (7–11) to talk about these different sources, considering what makes a character a superhero, e.g. *their clothes, their behaviours, their actions, their physical build etc*. Talk with boys (3–11) about what powers they would like to have if they were a superhero, e.g. *ability to fly, ability to breathe fire, ability to turn everything they touch into gold, ability to run faster than a bullet, ability to grow long arms, ability to create protective shields, ability to become invisible*. Help boys (3–11) to explore the differences between 'good' and 'evil' by talking about things everyday people do which could be considered good and bad, e.g. *helping an elderly person across the road, stealing money from a bank, recycling, swearing, caring for a poorly animal, not sharing with others*.

'*Superheroes and Earthlings*' – research findings from a boys' writing project (7–11):

In 2007–8 literacy consultants in Lancashire undertook an innovative KS2 Boys' Writing Project entitled 'Superheroes and Earthlings'. Visit http://tinyurl.com/7ccxn8c for a wonderfully comprehensive report of the project, case studies and its impact on boys' writing (remember to click on the PDF icon linked to 'Superheroes and Earthlings'). For a report on an Early Years Boys' Writing Project (Reception and Year 1 – 4–6 years) undertaken during the same timeframe, see http://tinyurl.com/bnpjksg.

Idea 8.3: Adventure stories	**Suggested age group:** 5-year-olds to 11-year-olds

Explanation:

Chris (2009) suggests that 'nothing speaks to the heart of man like a good tale of adventure.' Research findings from Merisuo-Storm (2006) indicate that boys like reading adventure stories: if boys like *reading* these stories, then why not give them the opportunity to have a go at *writing* them?! Because motivation is key to getting boys writing stories (OME, 2004), so *Adventure stories* are appropriately designed to fuel this desire. Stories involving, for example, buried treasure, pirates, sea monsters and strange foreign lands offer boys a wealth of 'swashbuckling possibility', and it is this sense of exploration, mystery and excitement that will entice boys to want to write!

The 'goings-on' in *Adventure stories*:

Opportunities for boys to talk with each other about the potential 'goings-on' in their *Adventure stories* will support them in developing strong story plots, themes and characters:

- What is their story going to be about – *a shipwreck? A hunt for lost gold? A race around the world? A remote island? A fight for freedom? Saving a fair maiden? A deep-sea quest?*
- What is the theme of the story to be – *courage? Survival? Greed? Friendship? Love? Honour?*
- Who will be in their story – *explorers? Animals? Kidnapped kings? Pirates? Sea creatures?*

Being aware of the above will help teachers to offer support to those boys who struggle to generate story plots, themes and characters of their own (also see Grainger et al., 2004a; 2004b; 2004c for further ideas and support). Reference to non-fiction texts about famous explorers, e.g. Christopher Columbus, Sir Francis Drake and Sir Walter Raleigh, can also be used as adventure story stimuli.

Addressing the issue of 'getting started':

Getting boys started with their writing can be really difficult – teachers will, no doubt, have experience of working with boys who 20 minutes into a writing session have *still* not put pen to paper because they do not know how to begin their story. To pre-empt this, Fison (2011) suggests that children should 'take particular notice of how [their] favourite stories start.' By helping children to closely examine how authors effectively 'hook' the reader in with their opening sentences, children can then replicate these techniques in their own work. Stimulating examples of story starters by Fison include:

1. I made a deal with sharks (from her book *Shark Frenzy*).
2. It should have been the best New Year's Eve ever (from her book *Bat Attack*).
3. It was probably my mother's screaming that frightened the cat (from her book *Tiger Terror*).

Top Tip! Display the opening lines from boys' favourite stories around the classroom for 'inspiration'.

Online resources to support adventure story writing:

The following web links offer some really useful teaching resources to support adventure story writing in the primary classroom (5–11):

http://tinyurl.com/ctfn2dx   http://tinyurl.com/c6fgvqk   http://tinyurl.com/cgesrgd

Idea 8.4: Chase stories	**Suggested age group:** 5-year-olds to 11-year-olds

Explanation:

Anyone who monitors playground duty at their school will no doubt see groups of boys happily playing chase with one another; it seems to be one of those exhilarating activities which always gets boys vocal, active and 'the[ir] adrenaline up' (Bramham, 2003: 59). *Chase stories* aim to excite boys in the same way by getting them to capture 'the thrill of the chase' in written stories, which involves the characters they write about either *chasing after* or *being chased* by someone or something.

The problem of 'the *exciting* chase' and 'the *dull* chase' (7–11):

Boys are keen to write stories with lots of action in them (Maynard, 2002) and *Chase stories* are well placed to facilitate this. The difficulty is that in many cases what boys actually write does not do the chase justice, with the reader losing out on the excitement of the event, e.g. *Jack saw the policeman and ran away. He hid for a bit.* Help boys to bring the action *alive* by modelling and using the following strategies:

- Encourage boys to incorporate sounds into their chase for 'sensory stimulation', e.g. *rustle, thud, smash, clunk, bump, shuffle, swish* and *crunch*.
- Use powerful verbs to describe the chase, e.g. *sprint, grab, leap, dodge* and *fly*.
- Show boys how to use small sentences to emphasise 'pace' in their writing, e.g. *Carrie abruptly stopped. She heard heavy footsteps in pursuit; they were getting nearer. She held her breath. The footsteps got louder; muffled voices sounded – where was she? Carrie's heart pounded in her chest. She looked down to see her hands shaking. Suddenly –* (Amy, aged 10).

Who and What to chase?:

There are many people and animals/objects boys can choose from for their characters to pursue in their *Chase stories*. Stimulating examples include:

- Bullies/gangs
- The police
- Fish/sharks
- Tornadoes
- Sheep (*escaped*)
- Pets, e.g. dogs
- Monsters
- Geese/swans
- Villains (*the 'baddies'*)
- Thieves/robbers
- Bees or butterflies
- Friends (*chase game*)
- Girl/boy (*love interest*)
- Cars (*vehicle chase*)
- Bus/train (*I'm late!*)
- Ghosts/ghouls

Top Tip! Use speaking and listening opportunities to establish *why* characters/animals/objects are being chased.

Boys, ICT and the 'lived' chase:

Practical experiences for boys can help to prepare them for writing their *Chase story* (Millard, 2001). Get boys (and girls) to chase one another around the playground. Then, with dictaphones, get them to digitally record their response to the following:

- what it was like to be chased in terms of what it felt like;
- how those being chased had to move to avoid being caught; and
- what happened to their bodies as they were being chased.

Play these recordings back in the classroom, modelling through demonstration writing and guided composition activities how to use this information to rehearse and compose *chased* sentences.

| **Idea 8.5: Sports stories** | **Suggested age group:** 5-year-olds to 11-year-olds |

Explanation:

Whilst there is much concern that children today are 'living in an environment that is increasingly 'toxic for exercise'' (ASC, 2011), research suggests that sport has consistently been ranked highly as a preferred leisure-time activity for boys. There are many reasons for this:

- the inherent element of competition and challenge which motivates them;
- the excitement of actively participating in sports;
- the beneficial release of stress and excess energy; and
- how sports help boys to bond with others, make friends and feel/be part of a team.

These reasons offer valuable ideas and themes which can be integrated into the *Sports stories* boys should be encouraged to write, involving characters who engage in exciting sporting activities.

'Advice from the expert' — *Timothy Tocher* **and the writing of** *Sports stories*:

Tocher (2011) is an American author of children's sports fiction. The following ideas are adapted and embellished from Tocher's own suggestions about teaching children to write sports stories:

1. *You've gotta love it!* Allow boys to choose a sport they know, enjoy, understand and actively take part in as this will help them to write knowledgably about the sport and games played.

2. *Establish who your lead character is!* Are they a superstar? A rising star? An undiscovered talent? A 'secret weapon'? A team player? The captain of the team? A foreign transfer?

3. *Use the lingo!* Each sport has its own vocabulary. Encourage boys to list specific words, terms, and phrases that they can integrate into their story to give it some authenticity.

4. *Thrill 'em!* Get boys to think about the most exciting game they have watched/been involved in — *why* was it thrilling?

5. *Strange things a' happening!* Let boys reflect on any 'strange goings-on' (real/made up) during sports they have watched/played, e.g. game play being stopped because of snowfall in the summer, a 'moonwalking bear' jumping onto the pitch and interrupting game play, a dog grabbing the ball and running off with it, parents/carers getting irate with each other over the game.

It's all in the title! **Stimulating** *Sports story* **titles to fuel boys' imagination:**

- *Snookered*!
- *The* shot of the night!
- Going for gold!
- The basketball battle!
- A hit at hockey!
- Swimming like a fish to water!
- A race to the finish!
- When we won at Wimbledon!
- Sledging for success!
- All eyes on the table tennis trophy!
- *GOOOOAAAAALLLLLLLLLLLLLL*!
- Trouncing the orienteering opposition!

Blog early, blog often: **the secret to making boys write properly!**

Do you want to see boys happily churning out 5000-word *Sports stories*? Garner (2011) reports on the 'pioneering' practice of Heathfield Primary School whose use of blogging has seemingly got boys 'to write properly'. To find out how they have achieved this, visit http://tinyurl.com/5reygeb; also see *Internet stories* (p. 127).

Idea 8.6: Funny stories	Suggested age group: 5-year-olds to 11-year-olds

Explanation:

Scieszka (2011) suggests that whilst biological and sociological reasoning causes boys to struggle with reading, 'the good news is that research also shows that boys will read – if they are given reading that interests them.' It is personally believed that the same applies to writing: boys will write – if they are given something to write that interests them. Boys particularly favour stories which are humorous or make them laugh out loud (Sanderson, 1995). *Funny stories* allow boys to write with the purposeful intention of trying to make others smile, giggle or roar uncontrollably when reading their written story!

Kaye Umansky, children's author, and 'Writing Funny':

Umansky (2011) (of *Pongwiffy* fame) says that whilst 'character and plot are important . . . all I want to [do is] raise a smile'. There are a number of ways in which this can be achieved; these have been adapted from her monograph:

1. An actual joke, e.g. *A horse walks into a bar and the barman says 'Why the long face?'*.
2. Characters' names, e.g. *Snoopwiggy, Squigglehopper, Smarty Arty, Snorker* (see the work of Dr. Seuss for some really outrageous names).
3. A clever turn of phrase, e.g. *in the book* Nicholas Thomas *by Kitty Styles there is a naughty kitten whose tail was 'curiously crooked with questions'.*
4. An unexpected plot twist, e.g. *Everything in the room had turned silver!; It was the driver who set the alarm off!; The box could be opened from the top, bottom and sides!*
5. A character with a great line in repartee, e.g. *'You have to be dead or boring to be displayed in a museum!'; 'I only answer the telephone if I know I do not need the loo for ten minutes!'*.

What makes you laugh?:

A great topic for discussion with boys is to identify what makes them laugh. By listing these different things boys can use them to make sure there is some element of 'funniness' in their story. Examples might include:

- A character falling over (see *Slapstick stories*, p. 133).
- Unusual words (*bafflegab; mumping*).
- Unusual ways of moving (*bounding, slithering, shuffling*).
- Someone with the hiccups.
- Strange noises (*Parp! Pfurt!*).
- Being forgetful (deliberate).
- Clowns/jesters.
- Silly words (*Pants! Bottom!*).
- Sausages and penguins (!).

Encourage children to reflect on things they have observed in real life or on the TV which has made them laugh – *are there things they have done in the past which have made their peers, parents, carers or teachers chortle?*

'Pick a number, any number!':

There are times when boys need just that 'initial spark' to get their 'writing juices' flowing. Visit the stimulating list of 400+ things that children seemingly like (available at http://tinyurl.com/ybpc34k); ask individuals to randomly select a number between 1 and 434; the topic linked to their chosen number can be used to get them off what is personally referred to as the 'writing starter block' in relation to their *Funny story*.

Idea 8.7: Frightful stories	**Suggested age group:** 7-year-olds to 11-year-olds

Explanation:

It seems that boys have always been interested in horror and the macabre; Nelson (2011) argues that 'scary stories are, for children, an intrinsic component of their emotional education, allowing them to identify and control their darker feelings – a good coping mechanism.' The Idea behind *Frightful stories* is that they allow boys to enter a world of fear and fantasy where their story writing has a clear purpose: to make the reader's eyes widen, their hearts beat faster and their breathing to quicken!

Establishing the cast for *Frightful stories*:

There are many stimulating characters which boys can incorporate in their stories to make them scary. These include:

- Ghosts
- Evil fairies
- Vampires
- Monsters
- Gremlins
- Werewolves
- Witches
- Bloodsucking bats
- Skeletons
- Spooks
- Aliens
- Zombies
- Demons
- 'Living' corpses
- Goblins
- Terrible trolls

Creating a class list of these different 'cast members' offers boys the opportunity to reflect on what makes these characters 'frightful' and to explore (with the help of their teacher) the story possibilities of combining cast members together, for example:

- *Pandemonium partnerships!* What could happen if a witch and a zombie worked as a team to terrorise the inhabitants of the local village?

- *24/7 scare!* How might an alien work to scare the pupils at Spendington Private School during the day and a vampire scare them at night?

'I did warn you!' *Frightful stories* and 'the warning':

Corbett (2001: 21) suggests that 'many good stories are built around a basic warning'. Stories such as *The Minpins* (Dahl, 2008) and *Why the Whales Came* (Morpurgo, 2011) are based around a warning which the lead characters inevitably disregard, e.g. *do not go over the road into the forest* or *do not play with the Birdman*. Talk with boys about the kinds of warnings parents/carers give them at home. Encourage boys to think about the repercussions of ignoring these warnings – might these warnings fuel the start of their *Frightful story*?

Writing *Frightful Stories* stems from reading *Frightful Stories*:

Phillip Pullman, former Children's Laureate, argues that if you do not want to read, then you are unlikely to be someone who wants to write. In the context of boys and *Frightful stories*, teachers need to offer plenty of opportunities for boys to read frightful stories to develop their appreciation of how authors build up tension, use language to frighten the reader, and leave the reader with an afterglow of well-being when the story is over. Aid and support boys' *Frightful story* writing efforts through the following activities:

- Critique scary story extracts.
- Compare and contrast authors of scary stories – *whose writing is more effective? Why?*
- Read and discuss scary chapters together in pairs or small groups.
- Read aloud scary paragraphs for others to listen to and reflect on.

Idea 8.8: Fairy stories	Suggested age group: 5-year-olds to 11-year-olds

Explanation:

It might seem an unusual Idea to include *Fairy stories* in this chapter, particularly as a number of boys (and girls) think that fairy stories are just about talking piglets, romance, 'restrictive social roles' (Westland, 1993: 246) and excessively large root vegetables (think *The Enormous Turnip*)! This Idea aims to dispel this myth by encouraging teachers to emphasise the fact that a) fairy stories do not need fairies in them, and b) there are many 'male elements'* which are woven into fairy stories that can be used to excite reluctant boy writers and engage them in stimulating story writing opportunities.

*The 'male elements' of fairy stories:

There are many aspects of fairy stories, emphasised by the likes of the Brothers Grimm and Hans Christian Andersen, which are appealing to boys:

- Heroic princes and soldiers.
- Dastardly villains.
- Booming giants.
- Animals that communicate like humans.
- Magical potions and spells.
- Adventurous journeys.

Fairy stories are filled with constant action and high drama – boys will find fairy stories full of threats, dark magic, battles and even death. Allow boys to look at picture books (5–7) and read anthologies of fairy stories (7–11), creating lists of 'male elements' in these stories that they like/respond well to. Encourage boys to incorporate these 'male elements' into their own fairy stories.

'And they all lived happily ever after'? *Yeah, right!*:

Cainer (2011) suggests that fairy stories 'never document the details of the happy-ever-after because it is rarely as happy as the storytellers suggest'; Meade (1994), in fact, argues that the saying was originally 'They lived happily in the ever-after'. So . . .

- what *really* happened to Prince Charming and Snow White when they rode off together to his castle?
- what *really* became of Little Red Riding Hood when she became *Big* Red Riding Hood?
- what did life *really* have in store for the Ugly Ducking after he became a beautiful swan?

Get boys (7–11) to write stories which follow on from well-known fairy stories, allowing the reader to find out what happened next in a thrilling and inventive 'masculinised' *Fairy story* sequel!

Getting boys (9–11) to write innovative stories – 'Fractured Fairy stories' (FFS):

Kinsella (n.d.) describes a fractured fairy story as a 'tale that has been modified in such a way as to make us laugh at an unexpected characterization, plot development or contrary point of view'. By 'adding [their] own twists and turns and dashes of bizarre humo[u]r', boys can create their own fractured fairy story – examples by well-known children's authors include *Jim and the Beanstalk* (Briggs, 1973) and *Prince Cinders* (Cole, 1997). Suggest that boys write FFS about lesser-known fairy tales to emphasise the level of originality in their work, e.g. *The Old Woman in the Wood*.

Top tips! Visit Kinsella's website – http://tinyurl.com/ybayhql – for more information about FFS. Also visit http://tinyurl.com/ybohlo7 for a splendid web-based, boy-friendly FFS tool!

| Idea 8.9: Free stories | Suggested age group: 3-year-olds to 11-year-olds |

Explanation:

Clere (2011: 5) mirrors personally shared sentiments about writing when she suggests that 'the process of writing should be enjoyable and exciting but can be thwarted if there is undue pressure of a desired effect.' *Free stories* temporarily alleviate the demands of writing targets, academic levels and assessments which burden both teachers and children by allowing boys to engage in writing *for the fun of it!* The Idea is that boys have the opportunity to engage in story writing where *they* have autonomy over what *they* write about, how *they* write about it, and what *they* write it in!

Free stories and boys (3–5):

Writing in the early years is synonymous with finger painting and mark-making. Boys should have access to a wealth of varied writing opportunities where they can write in paint, sprinkled salt, flavoured blancmange, shaving foam, sand and icing sugar (DCSF, 2008a).

Try it – Verbal stories! Boys can be encouraged to make marks, draw shapes, form letters and known words (such as their name) along with their illustrations as they verbalise their story, either as it is created or once it is completed. An alternative would be to continue verbal rhyming strings.

Free stories and boys (5–7):

Free stories for boys (5–7) can be used to 'relax' expectations with regard to sentence structure, accurate spellings, the use of punctuation marks and correct grammar. Boys should be able to write about things that are likely to stimulate them, e.g. *talking doughnuts, magic carpets, bikes and trikes, gigantic pants, playground games, races, 'lived' experiences* or *computer games.*

Try it – Recorded stories! Boys can be encouraged to record their stories on *Writing Walls* (paper fastened to the classroom wall/outside walls) through collage materials ('mosaic letters'), on interactive whiteboards or using dry wipe pens on clear acetate sheets. Stories can be 5 or 15 sentences long– *it is their choice!*

Free stories and boys (7–11):

Free stories for boys (7–11) offer time and space for boys to collaborate with others (if they wish), selecting 'boy-friendly' topics such as war, weapons and zany/bathroom humour, which Fletcher (2006) argues should be allowed 'if we want to engage them [boys] as writers'.

Try it – Planned stories! Boys should have opportunities to plan out their stories on large sheets of paper taped to their desks, or they could get straight into the story writing and plan it *as the story develops* (what is personally referred to as an 'organic' story). Stories could be written on the back of used envelopes, large Post-it° notes or in story jotters for paper-writing variety.

The right environment for story writing to flourish in:

Whilst there are advocated features of writing environments for children aged 5–11 (see http://tinyurl. com/cqoo6s6) it is important to consider alternative writing spaces to 'free up' boys, e.g. drapes over tables, fortresses built with PE equipment in the hall, or sitting in the staffroom. How about a 'Brown Bag' *Free story* writing session where boys can sit with their lunch or juice and biscuits in the playground to fuel their brains as they write?

Idea 8.10: Futures stories	**Suggested age group:** 7-year-olds to 11-year-olds

Explanation:

When we think of 'what is yet to come', none of us really know what the future actually holds. Whilst for some people this is unsettling, for others it is an exciting time of possibility. The Idea of *Futures stories* offers boys an infinite wealth of possibility so that through their story writing they can consider what their future might be, what life will be like for others, and how the world might look like in, for example, the year 2250 or 2500!

Thinking about the future:

There are many aspects of the future that boys can focus their 'futuristic thoughts' on; these include:

Transport	*How will we travel from place to place in the future – space rockets? Teleporters? Supersonic escalators? Through telephone cables? Will we be able to travel to other planets in five minutes – how?*
Food	*What foods will we eat? How will we eat them? Will food cook itself whilst we eat it? Will meals come out of mobile phones? Will we consume drinks by dipping our finger into a glass? Will we still go to restaurants to eat? How will food be grown?*
Clothing	*What will we wear in the daytime, evening, and at night – why? Will we wear space helmets? Will we need to protect ourselves from the sun? Will we have different clothes for the different seasons or will the weather never change? What will be considered 'cool' or 'hip', clothing wise?*
Housing	*What will houses look like in the future? What will they be made of? Will houses be built on top of houses? Might we live in towers of flats that are 600 storeys high?*
Gadgets	*What timesaving devices will be available in the future? Will there be robots who can take 70 dogs for a walk all at the same time? Will clothes self-clean as they are being worn? How will we listen to music? Will computers still exist?*

Get boys to work in small groups, collaborating on thought-showers about one of these different aspects. Use the questions offered above to generate purposeful speaking and listening opportunities so that boys can 'bounce ideas off one another', stimulating discussion and creative suggestions. See http://tinyurl.com/cac7luu for other ideas.

Stimuli for *Futures stories*:

There is various stimuli available that can be offered to engage boys when writing *Futures stories*, examples of which include:

- Newspaper reports and magazine articles in science fiction publications (paper and web-based).

- Extracts from futuristic cartoons, TV programmes and films, e.g. *The Jetsons, Futurama, Doctor Who, Back to the Future, Star Wars* and *iRobot*.

- Short stories, e.g. *Tomorrowland: Ten Stories About the Future* compiled by Cart (1999).

Read it! 'The educational character of children's science fiction texts: Concepts resulting from the study of Greek children's science fiction literature' by Papadatos and Papantonakis (2012).

'Creative' stories

The focus of this penultimate chapter centres on the notion of creativity, an officially recognised concept by the UK government that has enjoyed a surge of professional and academic interest in educational circles following the publication of the NACCCE's (1999) *All Our Futures: Creativity, Culture, Education* report. With many teachers and schools working hard to educate children through a creative curriculum, this chapter serves to support those who wish to energise their story writing practice with a little creative *zest*. In support of the fact that creativity is not just about 'the arts' (Grainger and Barnes, 2006), the Ideas in this chapter embrace numerous ways in which story writing can be *creatively* stimulated.

The first half of this chapter considers ways in which 'creative engagement' (Dahlberg, 2007) can be used to engross children in exciting story writing opportunities. *Flip-flap stories* encourage young children to incorporate innovative 'pieces of shaped card or fabric' into the pages of their story to '"hide and reveal" drawings, words or information' (p. 177). The appeal of short stories for children, in part due to their seemingly limited attention spans (Tomalin, 2012), is the driving force behind *Flash stories*, which challenge older children to be creative with a select number of words. *Patchwork stories* promote children's creative collaboration with others, contributing to an evolving 'team story' using a popular children's story character as a visual story planner/presentation tool. *Jigsaw stories* offer children the opportunity to write stories that can be physically taken apart and put back together again, using jigsaw templates in an effort to actively promote writing coherency and reading comprehension levels. *Window stories* strive to integrate *awe and wonder* into children's story writing by using physical features (e.g. windows, doors, shutters and blinds) as a way of 'revealing' a key part of the story being told, be it a human being, an animal, a plant or a six-headed sneezing alien!

The second half of the chapter identifies creative resources found in the classroom which can be used to stimulate story writing (see Herr, 2011). *Junk stories* use a popular cookery TV programme to 'cook' pieces of junk together to create a story against the clock! *Stationery stories* consider the value of writing implements in both stimulating and improving children's story writing through the use of 'special' stationery. If hats really do 'make the man' (Ernst, 1920), then *Hat stories* can be used to help children enrich their story character's appearance whilst fuelling their storytelling by having the hat play a significance role in the tale. For older children (9–11) *Framed stories* encourage them to creatively tell a tale *within* a tale, whereas *Chain stories* offer younger children (3–7) the opportunity to create a visually appealing paper-chain story in an effort to actively learn about sentence structure and aspects of grammar.

Taking a closer look at 'conflict resolution'

In Framed stories it is advocated that this Idea 'allow[s] . . . children to write stories with a specific purpose, for example, writing about particular characters, using figurative language, dealing with conflict resolution . . .' (p. 185). Whilst the notion of conflict has been explored in the introduction to Chapter 2 (p. 47), *conflict resolution* is an aspect of story writing which children need to consider and effectively address in their written tales (Garp, 2005). It is important initially to establish what is meant by the term *conflict resolution*.

Reflect!

What do you think 'conflict resolution' means within a story context? Is there a difference between this and 'story ending'? If so, what is the difference?

Corbett (2001: 35) suggests that when children enter Year 3 (7–8-year-olds) 'it is worth distinguishing between writing the resolution and the ending:

- **resolution** – resolving the story or tying up the tale;
- **ending** – some sort of reflective section that follows the resolution, in which there is a reflection on what has happened in the story.'

As the remainder of this introduction will focus its attention on the writing of the *story resolution*, an exploration of *story endings* will be made in the *Taking a closer look at* section of the introduction for Chapter 10 (p. 188).

The resolution is the part of a story where the author has to 'clear up' what has happened in the tale. The importance of this is emphasised by Clarke (2012), who strongly advocates that '[c]onflict must always be resolved'. Children, particularly those from the younger age phases, are prone to using the classic 'I woke up and it was all a dream!', but as children mature in their story writing capabilities the use of this is personally considered to be an easy way of 'dodging the resolution bullet'. To ensure that children deal with the conflict in their stories, the importance of story planning cannot be underestimated (see Knight, 2002: 18); by getting children to actively think about a story *in its entirety* (and not just the beginning of it) means that the resolution of any conflict is actually addressed. Children should be taught that conflict resolution needs to be satisfying (or 'good') for the reader: for example, *Sherlock Holmes solves the murder*; *Harry Potter defeats Voldemort*; *the boy gets the girl*. If Holmes, for example, did not solve the murder it would leave the reader rather disappointed and questioning the capabilities of this famous fictional character. If Theodore the Thief stole Captain Clingfilm's special powers, it is only right, 'satisfactory story wise', that Theodore is made to return the stolen powers and learns from his wrong doing (e.g. he realises that stealing is a bad thing to do).

Try it!

Use whole-class/group discussion opportunities to generate ways of resolving different kinds of conflict in an effort to support children (5–11) in understanding the 'resolution process'. Use the grid in Table 9.1 (p. 173) (adapted from the work of Peirce and Edwards, 1988) to support you; several resolution strategies are offered by way of example.

Table 9.1 Conflict resolution strategies – to complete in whole-class/
group discussion (adapted from Peirce and Edwards, 1988)

Conflict	Resolution strategies
Competitive conflict, such as those involving sports and games	• The star player decides to change sides and play for the losing team • The winning team are disqualified for cheating
Conflict within a person	
Conflict between a person and society	
Conflict between individuals	• Individuals 'forgive and forget' the next day • Individuals 'agree to disagree'
Conflict within a family	
Conflict between families such as feuds	
Conflict within organisations such as the FBI or CIA (SOCA and MI5/6 – UK equivalents)	
Conflict between nature and humanity	
Conflict within nature, which includes the predatory behaviour of animals	• The bunnies are saved from the wolf by the ingenuity of the brave squirrels • The Selfish Snow decides to take turns with the Smart Sun during the year
Conflict between humans and machines, such as those involving people and robots or computers	
Conflict between good and evil, such as evil forces attempting to command the universe	

Research by Peirce and Edwards (1988) into children's (9–14 years) conflict resolution in their story writing revealed several findings of interest:

- Two types of conflict resolution were adopted: *violent* (the use of physical force) and *non-violent* (the use of reasoning, persuasion, compromise).
- *Boys* used more violent resolutions to solve problems, whilst *girls* used more reasoning and analysis.
- Several stories presented more than one kind of conflict. These were coded as either *primary* or *secondary* conflicts, depending on the emphasis they received in the story.

- Many of the children (29% of the 266 pupils taking part in the research) chose to *avoid* conflict in their stories altogether or gave it only the vaguest mention.

Reflect!

Reflect on the findings above – what implications does this have for your teaching and the children's learning about conflict resolution when they are story writing in your classroom?

Select practical strategies are offered below to support both teachers in their teaching of this important story feature and *children* in their application of conflict resolution in their written work:

- 3–5: Use examples of conflict which occur in the setting as 'story fodder' (verbal/written), for example, children pushing in the line, children arguing over the toys, children not letting others play. Reflect on how these incidences are resolved through talk time opportunities.

- 5–7: Encourage children to look carefully at how characters in the stories they read resolve the conflict they encounter. Keep a class list of resolution strategies to support children when they are story writing.

- 7–11: Use SEAL materials (DfES, 2007b) and circle time opportunities to 'problem-solve' incidences of conflict (real/imagined) so that they avoid using the 'fight-or-flight' approach to conflict resolution (Crawford and Bodine, 2001).

- 3–5: Support children in coming up with simple solutions to the conflict they or their characters encounter in their simple verbal/written stories; for example, Jenny would not let Cary play with her so Cary played with Ann instead; Harry took two biscuits instead of one so Greg spoke to his key worker (see Stephens, 2004 for further ideas).

- 5–7: Use role-play opportunities and drama techniques (freeze frame; thought tracking) to explore different ways in which conflict that occurs in the classroom could be resolved whilst developing children's use and application of 'feelings' vocabulary (see Wilson, 2011: 13). Use these ideas to 'fuel' the stories children write.

- 7–11: Encourage children to critically consider who will be 'the winner' once the conflict in their story has been resolved – *does the protagonist* always *have to win?* Nolan (2011) suggests not. *What could happen if the* antagonist *wins – what does this do to the tone of the story and the nature of the story ending?*

To further support teachers, select readings and websites are offered below to develop/enrich subject knowledge and learning and teaching of conflict resolution to support children's engagement with *'Creative' stories:*

- **Book** – *You Can't Come To My Birthday Party! Conflict Resolution with Young Children* by Evans (2002).

- **Academic article** – *Toward Peace: Using Literature to Aid Conflict Resolution* by Luke and Myers (1994).

- **Practical booklet** – *An Eye for an Eye Leaves Everyone Blind: Teaching Young Children to Settle Conflicts Without Violence* by Finch (2003).

Table 9.2   Recommended readings associated with *'Creative' stories*

| Books | Shaw, R. (2008) *1001 Brilliant Writing Ideas: Teaching Inspirational Story-writing for All Ages*. Abingdon: Routledge.

This book offers teachers 'endless ideas and inventive suggestions, opening up new opportunities for creative writing lessons. With over 1,000 different "story-starters" across a vast range of genres and narrative styles, this versatile book provides food for thought for pupils of a wide range of ages and abilities' (description on Amazon.co.uk). Consider using it as a supportive resource as children aged 3–7+ engage with their *'Creative' stories.*

Wilcox, A. (2008) *Descriptosaurus: Supporting Creative Writing for Ages 8–14*. London: Routledge.

Described as a 'treasure trove of descriptive language' (Sue Cowley), this book provides teachers and parents with an array of words, phrases and sentences to use to help children develop their writing. Consider using it as a supportive resource as children aged 8+ engage with their *'Creative' stories.* |

Online journal article/report	Harris, P. (2005) *At the Interface between Reader and Text: Devices in Children's Picturebooks that Mediate Reader Expectations and Interpretations*. Conference Proceedings for Australian Association for Research in Education Parramatta, 28th November – 1st December. [Online]. Available at: http://tinyurl.com/cpnwpdf (Accessed: 7 March 2012). *Harris describes this paper as 'examin[ing] ways in which children's picturebooks present themselves to their young readers. Presentation of a picturebook includes its covers, endpapers, title, author and illustrator identification, book blurbs, title pages, visual media, font styles, layout and the like. These features make up the interface of a picturebook' (p. 1).* Consider how this, alongside the ideas in this chapter, can be used to enhance the interface of picture books children create to present their *'Creative'* stories to others. Waters, T. (2004) *Writing Stories with Feeling: An Evaluation of the Impact of Therapeutic Storywriting Groups on Pupils' Learning*. [Online]. Available at: http://tinyurl.com/bubheeg (Accessed: 13 June 2012). *This report presents findings on the effects of therapeutic story writing on pupils' emotional, social and academic learning. Key findings on p. 5 suggest that the approach 'fostered an interactive relationship between the teacher and group with respect to story writing skills, [i]ncreased pupils' concentration and motivation to engage with story writing [and i]mproved pupils' self-esteem as writers'.* Consider the value of therapeutic writing for specific children you work with (aged 7–11) who may benefit from this approach as they engage with *'Creative'* stories.
Websites	Van Patter, B. (n.d.) *Let's Get Creative! Fun Stuff*. [Online]. Available at: http://tinyurl.com/br4byu (Accessed: 25 November 2011). *This website is literally full of 'free activities and information on all kinds of things that are meant to get creative juices flowing' (Van Patter, n.d.). Personal favourites include* Fortune Cookie Stories *and* Mugshots. Consider the value of these activities in stimulating children's *'Creative'* stories. Spoken Arts (n.d.) *Study Guides*. [Online]. Available at: http://tinyurl.com/ccxd7pc (Accessed: 13 June 2012). *This website offers a series of 'study guides' for teachers linked to story books about* school, character development, community, multi-culture, social studies *and* folk tales. *The guides detail learning objectives and creative activities which are based around each story.* Consider the value of these activities in enriching learning and teaching linked to the *'Creative'* stories children write in your class.

Idea 9.1: Flip-flap stories	Suggested age group: 3-year-olds to 7-year-olds

Explanation:

Many books for children in the infancy of their reading development incorporate flip-flaps – pieces of shaped card or fabric which are used to 'hide and reveal' illustrations or words. *Flip-flap stories* are designed to capitalise on the 'awe and wonder' element of flip-flaps in story books by encouraging young authors to incorporate these features into the stories that they write – see Appendix 24 for 'shaped' examples (p. 230) – in an effort to heighten readers' engagement levels and help to make the writing experience for young children a little more memorable!

Extending an original 'lift-the-flap' book (3–5):

Where's Spot? (Hill, 1983) is a classic piece of pre-school literature where young readers play a game of hide-and-seek by lifting the flaps on every page in search of Spot the dog. The bold illustrations, simple, large text and plethora of flaps to lift, pull and tug all help to make the book great fun for children. *But what if Spot wanted to play hide and seek the next day in the woods? What about playing the game at the seaside? What about at the local park?* Encourage young children to mark-make/write* a page each for a collaborative *Where's Spot now?* class/group story. Suggest that children look at Hill's layout style – this is known as a 'paratextual feature' (Genette, 1997) – so that children can replicate this if they so wish.

Mystery *flip-flap* stories (5–7):

The creative people at Crayola® advocate combining flip-flaps with mystery stories. Visit http://tinyurl.com/7zt26kx for a lesson plan which offers teachers of 5–7-year-olds a comprehensive way of combining mystery stories with flip-flaps. Stimulating mystery titles the children could write a story about include:

- *The strange smell from the kitchen!*
- *The puzzle of the square pizza!*
- *The case of the missing pencil sharpener!*
- *The mystery of the barking dog!*

Making flip-flap books:

Teachers and children can learn how to make flip-flap features for the stories they write by looking closely at the work of popular flip-flap authors, e.g. Campbell (1984), Alborough (1998) and Mitton and Horse (2003). Alternatively, teachers can visit the following two web links that offer alternative ways to make a variety of different books for children to write in on a variation of the flip-flap theme:

http://tinyurl.com/cb34y9m   http://tinyurl.com/cmfbhc5

*Pre-writing skills for children under five:

Saunders (2010) argues that '[a]ll too often, young children are given writing tools to use before they are ready for them.' She advocates that adults should help children to develop good hand skills and other pre-writing skills to prepare them 'for the next step, which is writing. Working on hand skills will also assist older children [5–7+] who are experiencing writing difficulties.' Visit the web link http://tinyurl.com/6nwbjup for a wealth of practical pre-writing strategies for classroom use. Consider ways of sharing this information with parents and carers so that they can support their children's pre-writing development at home.

Idea 9.2: Flash stories	Suggested age group: 9-year-olds to 11-year-olds

Explanation:

When a class is set a story writing task there is usually one child who asks 'How long does it have to be?'. Suggestions of 'At least half a page/a full page!' dampen some children's enthusiasm as this can seem excessive before they have begun! The Idea of *Flash stories* is based on the notion of flash fiction which Casto (2002) aptly describes as simply being 'short'. *Flash stories* encourage children to write very concise stories which have a small word count*, similar to Aesop's succinct fables.

*How small is 'a small word count'?:

Jarrell (cited in Casto, 2002) once pointed out that a story can be as short as a sentence. *Flash stories* can be any length that you/the children you work with want them to be – 75–1500 words – although Popek (2001) does question '[h]ow can you get the elements of fiction in only 100 words or less?' To find out exactly how this can be achievable, visit the excellent teaching guidance, advice, tips, strategies and examples available at http://tinyurl.com/7kt29vg.

'It's all in the name!' Alternative names for *Flash stories*:

Casto (2002) suggests there are many different names given to flash fiction; these could be used when presenting the idea of *Flash stories* to boys. Examples include:

Furious	Fast	Postcard	Quick	Blaster	Swift	Skinny
Short-short	Micro	Palm-sized	Sudden	Little short	Pocket-size	Minute

Consider selecting specific names for the year group you work with so there is a progression of names used as children experience *Flash stories* in different classes (9–11).

Flash story – a rhyming 'speech' example:

Blair! Blair! *Yeah?* Be . . . *aware. Be aware?* Beware! Bear! *Where?* There! *Oh yeah!* Don't glare, Blair! *Don't care!* Take care! *Yeah yeah!* **RARRRRRRRRRE!** Nightmare! Despair! Ensnare-d! (Claire, aged 11)

How to write a *Flash story*:

Fahey (2005) suggests a *Flash story* writer 'quickly gets into the story, establishes setting and character, sets up the conflict, fills-in critical back-story [a story that tells what led up to the main story or plot], then heads faster than a speeding bullet toward the climax and resolution.' *PHEW!* Practical strategies adapted from Arkin (2010) to help children achieve this include:

- Have a clear story message – *what do you want it to be about?*
- Choose just one story event in a character's life and focus on this.
- Only write about characters that are pivotal to the plot.
- Think about every word you write – ask yourself: *is this word absolutely necessary?*
- When editing your work, keep only words that 'tell the tale'.

Different ideas to stimulate *Flash stories*:

- Being bored in the back of the car during a long journey.
- Running away from an alien.
- Getting a bad school report.
- Buying fish and chips.
- Taking a 'cold call'.
- Singing in the bath.
- Trying on new shoes.
- Falling asleep.

Idea 9.3: Patchwork stories	Suggested age group: 7-year-olds to 11-year-olds

Explanation:

The story of *Elmer*, the colourful patchwork elephant, has become a children's modern-day classic and the character is one of the most well-known and easily recognised by young readers. Created by David McKee in 1989, the stories involving Elmer help younger children to appreciate that being different makes us special and that diversity should be positively embraced. *Patchwork stories* capitalise on Elmer's distinct patchwork design by using different coloured squares as a device to help children write interesting stories about diversity in a collaborative way!

Story writing and patchwork quilts:

A useful analogy to share with children is the idea of story writing being like a patchwork quilt: 'Stories grow in much the same way as patchwork quilts. You have a load of little bits and pieces of material (in stories called scenes or ideas) and as you assemble the finished piece you rearrange, discard, add, match colours and shades, experiment with stitch styles and thread colours (in stories called narrative voices) and finally find a combination of all the above that pleases you' (Deb, 2010).

Top Tip! Remind children of this to help them gain confidence in 'tweaking' their story as they redraft it, using whiteboards, Post-it® notes, jotters, word processors, coloured pens/pencils and peers to support the redrafting process.

Writing *Patchwork stories*:

To write a *Patchwork story* children need access to a wealth of squared pieces of coloured paper/sticky labels. A *Patchwork story* is a tale that *evolves* as different children contribute to it. Initially the opening of a story* is offered by a child on one (or more) of the pieces of paper. This opening is fastened to a large sheet of paper or card and is then given to another child to 'move the story forwards' (Kempton, 2004). Their contribution (a sentence, several sentences, or a paragraph) is recorded on different pieces of coloured paper, which are added to the large paper/card to build up a patchwork pattern of text. The *Patchwork story* continues to be 'assembled' by different children until the story comes to a natural and stimulating conclusion.

*Getting that story opening right!:

For *Patchwork stories* to work, the opening to the story need to be 'cracking'! For some great story openers visit http://tinyurl.com/3fmw7.

Exploring diversity in stories:

Encourage children to celebrate diversity in the *Patchwork stories* they write. Use *celebrations, food, clothing, game play, music, languages* and *cultural traditions* as topics to stimulate these stories. Links to PSHE and Citizenship themes or topics of discussion during assemblies are also valuable for *Patchwork stories*.

Strengthening stories using Patchwork words:

For a truly innovative way of helping older children (9–11) to improve their written stories, show them how to engage with the Patchwork words exercise devised by Krause (2011), details of which can be found at http://tinyurl.com/6qlaera.

Idea 9.4: Jigsaw stories	**Suggested age group:** 5-year-olds to 11-year-olds

Explanation:

Jigsaw stories promote an innovative approach to stimulating children's story writing and purposeful story reading. This Idea is based on the notion of jigsaws, a popular puzzle for children and adults alike (see http://tinyurl.com/99md). Once children have drafted out a coherent[†] tale, *Jigsaw stories* involve children presenting parts of their finished story on different pieces of a jigsaw template. The pieces can then be carefully cut out and are stored together. Different children are then to be encouraged to 'piece together' the *Jigsaw story*, promoting their use of active problem solving, comprehension[*], and deductive skills.

Jigsaw stories, writing coherency[†] and reading comprehension[*]:

Jigsaw stories promote and support children's development of writing coherency – how well a story holds together (Fitzgerald and Spiegel, 1986) – and reading comprehension skills – understanding what is read and constructing meaning from the text (Kucan and Beck, 1997). If children are not able to write a story in a coherent manner then it will make it difficult for those reading the *Jigsaw story* to effectively comprehend what is being presented to them. This is a valuable learning and teaching point to emphasise when children are working on and reviewing their *Jigsaw story* writing efforts.

Ways of creating *Jigsaw stories*:

- 5–7: Children can download jigsaw templates from the Internet of varying numbers of pieces (see http://tinyurl.com/ckwo6xw as an example).
- 7–11: Children can simply sketch out a jigsaw puzzle template on a piece of paper and then calculate how many sentences they need to write on each jigsaw piece.
- 5–11: Children can sketch out or download a jigsaw puzzle temple and then get this photocopied (labelling the sheets A and B). On sheet A the children can record their story; once the *Jigsaw story* has been cut up the readers could use sheet B as a base on which to place the different jigsaw pieces.

Adaptation! An alternative to *Jigsaw stories* is *Domino stories*, which use domino pieces instead of jigsaw pieces to piece together a story – see Appendices 25 (p. 231) and 26 (p. 233) for support.

Top Tips!

- Set a limit on the number of jigsaw pieces depending on the children's writing abilities.
- Ensure that children record their story on jigsaw pieces which go left to right *across* the jigsaw and *top to bottom* for the reader's ease.
- Suggest that children display the title of their story on their *Jigsaw story* storage container[§] to help establish the story 'gist' (Schank, 1995).

[§]Storage suggestions for *Jigsaw stories*:

- Plastic wallets – *sealable with buttons, paperclips or sellotape.*
- Envelopes – *purchased or self-made from recycled paper.*
- Small boxes – *junk boxes.*
- Thin trays – *food, self-made.*
- Folders – *cardboard, paper.*
- Food bags – *clear.*

Stimulating *Jigsaw stories* with popular culture:

Millard (2005: 61) suggests that '[p]opular culture can increase children's motivation to . . . produce their own texts with connections with their popular cultural interests.' Use speaking and listening opportunities to find what interests children (think *fashion, music, technology, celebrities, toys*), helping them to incorporate these into their *Jigsaw stories* through active discussions and shared/guided writing opportunities.

| **Idea 9.5: Window stories** | **Suggested age group:** 3-year-olds to 7-year-olds |

Explanation:

Most adults can recall the moment in the film *The Wizard of Oz* when Dorothy slowly opens the farm house door after the cyclone to reveal the technicolor world of Oz. *Window stories* attempt to replicate the 'awe and wonder' of that scene for young story writers by offering them a physical window in the paper/card which they are mark-making/writing their story on. What will be revealed when the window shutters are opened – *something scary? Funny? Cool? Fluffy? Shocking? Expensive?*

Making a *Window story*:

See Appendix 27 (p. 234) for a window page template. Children will need a window page (A4 or A3 size) which is then glued onto a separate piece of paper/card to display the window 'reveal'. Alternatives to the window include doors, shutters and blinds.

Top Tip! Support may be needed to help younger children with the 'cutting' of the window (3–5).

***Window story* recommendations:**

- 3–7: Encourage children to mark-make/write on *both sides* of the window shutters to maximise the writing space available to them on the window page.

- 4–7: Suggest that children make the 'reveal' an integral part of the story being told, e.g. *an excitable alien who is found bouncing on the trampoline in the back garden; a brand new car on the front drive for Mum.*

- 5–7: 'Read' *Window* (Baker, 2002) for children to appreciate the importance of 'the visual' when their *Window story* shutters are opened by their readers.

The 'pain' of writing:

As adults, if we write with a pen for a long time we find that our hand and arm ache. Burnett et al. (2006: 18) highlight 'the physical demands of pencil control and letter formation' when children write – children are not as physically strong as they used to be due to changing lifestyles (watching videos and playing computer games as opposed to engaging in active outdoor play), so many will try to avoid writing activities 'because it hurts'!

Try it! Work to strengthen (**not** build) young children's arm muscles to alleviate the pain of writing their *Window story* by visiting local parks which have monkey bars, ropes, climbing frames, fireman's poles and ladders that children can swing from, scale, hang off, slide down and climb.

'Body Bees Break' – practical advice from the shop floor:

Children (5–7) can find it difficult to sit for a long period of time and mark-make/write. To break up the time children are writing, encourage them to stop after about 10/15 minutes and get them to stand behind their chairs. Play *The Flight of the Bumblebee* by Rimsky-Korsakov; as the music plays ask the children to make different parts of their body 'fly' around their 'personal space' like a busy bee, e.g. nose, elbows, fingers, knees, head and bottom! After this stimulating little break you will find children are able to concentrate more fully for another 10/15 minutes on their *Window story*.

Idea 9.6: Junk stories	Suggested age group: 7-year-olds to 11-year-olds

Explanation:

The Idea of *Junk stories* is based on the popular British cookery TV programme *Ready Steady Cook*. *Junk stories* involve teachers and children gathering together a small number of pieces of junk[†] in a carrier bag. This is given to a child author[*] or the whole class who are to write a story which incorporates each of the junk items as their story develops. Like the TV programme, there is a time limit for the children to work on their stories – this can be agreed upon before the carrier bag(s) is distributed. 'Are you ready? Are you steady? *Write!*'

[†]'Junk' – the stimuli for story writing:

There is a wealth of different junk materials that teachers/children can collect from home or school to stimulate *Junk stories*, e.g. containers, cereal boxes, trays, thread spools, kitchen rolls, straws, plastic lids, paper place mats, old shoe boxes and receipts. The skill is in helping children to appreciate *how* these could be integrated into their story. 'Story potential' suggestions include:

Junk resource	Story potential
Old shoe box	A character's home; a 'boat' which transports characters across the sea; a place to hide something secret in.
Receipt	A list of odd purchases made by a 'creepy character'; a printed 'code' which unlocks the safe containing the stolen jewels.
Kitchen roll	A portal to another dimension; a telescope for a toddler; a play thing for a *Borrower* (Norton, 2007); a building block for a monster's tube tower.
Plastic lid	A wheel on a self-made cart; a form of new currency; a plate for a hungry rabbit; a circular snowboard for the *DiddyDodger* people.

Use whole-class and group teaching opportunities to model and promote creative thinking when examining the potential of junk materials. It has been found that developing children's creative thinking skills has a direct impact on the amount children write; research findings from Albert and Kormos (2004) indicate that creative students produce more in narrative tasks.

[*]*One* author, *two* authors, *three* authors, *four* . . . ?:

Children (7–11) typically produce single-authored stories. Offer them opportunities to work on stories that are written by multiple authors, e.g. in pairs or small groups of three/four. Krause (2007: 1) suggests that writing with others is 'one of the best ways for students to improve their writing skills . . . if you never show your writing to other readers, or if you limit your audience to simply the teacher, how will you as a writer learn about the effectiveness of your writing beyond a grade in a class?' Producing 'collaborative fiction' can be facilitated in a number of ways:

• Writing a paragraph each.
• Writing about one particular character each.
• Writing everything together.
• Writing a chapter each.
• Drafting sentences out and letting others edit and improve them.

Idea 9.7: Stationery stories	**Suggested age group:** 5-year-olds to 9-year-olds

Explanation:

At the beginning of the school year many children come to their new class 'armed' with an array of new stationery, e.g. biros, pencils, felt-tip pens, highlighters, crayons and fountain pens. *Stationery stories* attempt to use these new writing implements as a creative tool for helping children to write stimulating stories (see http://tinyurl.com/csj3r23 for adaptation strategies if children are unable to hold these writing implements effectively).

The thinking behind this Idea is simple: each child is asked to select an appropriate writing tool that they will use *only* to write their stories with throughout the year. Personal experience has shown that encouraging children to believe* that they will write stimulating stories when using their selected story writing tool can have a *very* positive effect on the efforts and output of young writers!

*Getting children to write stimulating stories – making children *believe*:

HandsOnScotland (2011) argues that 'a child's belief in their own ability to do things is important for their motivation, perseverance and success in life. Self-belief (sometimes referred to as 'self-efficacy') can motivate a child more than their actual skill level. So a child who truly believes they can . . . write [stimulating stories] may be more likely to achieve [this] than another child who has better ability, but who doesn't believe they can do it.' Teachers and parents/carers can help children 'believe that they can' through the following:

- Giving positive praise.
- Acknowledging children's feelings that story writing is sometimes hard.
- Using rewards and prizes.
- Offering responsive feedback (Panagopoulou-Stamatelatou and Merrett, 2010).
- Displaying children's written work for others to see and read.
- Helping children to learn from their errors by reminding them that we *all* make mistakes (even teachers/parents and carers!).

Practical strategies to literally make children's writing pens stimulating:

1. Give them a 'magic rub' before children start writing with them (5–7).
2. Label them (using a sticky label) (7–9).
3. Store them in a 'special' class writing tool box (5–9).
4. Get children to keep telling their writing tool it is brilliant as they used it (5–7).

Alternative interpretations of *Stationery stories*:

- Discuss with children (5–7) ways they could use stationery to enrich their story writing, e.g. talking pencils (*what language do they speak?*), erasers that can rub out walls and floors (*useful for characters trying to escape from someone or something?*) or felt-tip pens which draw 2-D objects that magically become real 3-D entities (think *Penny Crayon*).
- Many stories that children (7–9) write can be so fast paced that they sometimes do not allow their characters to stop and 'take stock' as to what is around them. The 360° stationery story moment can be used at any point during a story – it is where a character can pause and slowly turn around on the spot: *what can the character see? How does the character feel? What is the character thinking about at that very moment? Is there anything of importance to describe or make the reader aware of at this point?*

Idea 9.8: Hat stories	**Suggested age group:** 3-year-olds to 7-year-olds

Explanation:

The Idea for *Hat stories* came from a recent visit to a shopping centre where a number of children and adults were seen sporting different hats, e.g. *baseball caps, trilby hats, beanies* and even a *fedora!* By simply observing these different people it was clear how individual hats accentuated certain characteristics of those wearing them: the baseball cap wearer strutted like a 'dude', whereas the 'beanie girl' was seemingly happy as her head was nice and warm. *Hat stories* work to encourage children to think about the role that hats can play in the stimulating stories they write and their significance* for both the wearer and others.

* *Hats Matter!* The significance of hats in stories:

VillageHatShop.com (2012) passionately acknowledges the presence of hats in children's books. From being 'cultural icons', 'a symbol' and 'a bridge to history', it is argued that 'hats can be fun', 'supportive' and 'can transform the wearer'. Stories where this is evident include:

- Hat as superhero (*The hat*) (3–7).
- Hats as a bridge to learning about history (*Abe Lincoln's hat*) (5–11).
- Hat as an eccentric and highly individual fashion statement (*Miss Hunnicutt's hat*) (3–7).
- Hat as a head covering for poorly patients and as an object helping to sustain hope (*Kathy's hats*) (5–11).
- Hat as a good-luck charm (*My lucky hat*) (3–7).
- Hat ('Bad Hat' specifically) as a metaphor for a person (*Madeline and the bad hat*) (5–11).

Visit http://tinyurl.com/86u59rt and see if your school owns any of the hat stories listed above. Support children in understanding the importance of the hat to the stories during/following their reading. Use their knowledge of the alphabet to help them make a written record of their story.

Hat stories and 3–5-year-olds:

Role-play areas offer children access to a range of different hats to enrich their play; these include *crowns, helmets, pirate hats, swimming caps, riding hats, witches hats*, and *straw hats*. Work with children to consider who would wear these different hats and why. Encourage children to verbalise/ write stories about *magical* hats or *lost* hats. Allow children to design new hats (both 2-D and 3-D) for different characters including *clowns, princesses*, and *aliens*.

Hat stories and 5–7-year-olds:

Think of *Harry Potter* (J.K. Rowling), the *Cat in the Hat* (Dr. Seuss) and *Father Christmas* (Raymond Briggs) and most children are able to identify the specific hat they wear. Suggest that children (5–7) write a story about a *special* hat worn by an interesting animal-based character. Questions for them to consider include: *what makes the hat 'special'? Which animal will wear the hat? What happens to the animal when they wear the special hat?* Ideas to simulate thinking include:

Interesting animals			Special kinds of hats		
	Manatee	Puffer fish		Talking hats	Cleaning hats
	Roadrunner	Eagle		Musical hats	Fighting hats
	Octopus	Tiger		Flying hats	Listening hats
	Panda	Flamingo		Dancing hats	Writing hats

Idea 9.9: Framed stories	**Suggested age group:** 9-year-olds to 11-year-olds

Explanation:

The Idea of *Framed stories* comes from Chaucer's *The Canterbury Tales* (2003), which is a collection of stories told as part of a story-telling contest by a group of pilgrims as they travel together on a journey to Canterbury Cathedral in the 14th century (see http://tinyurl.com/ccq5v). A *Framed story* is defined by TV Tropes (2011) as 'a narrative technique in which a story is surrounded ('framed') by a secondary story, creating a story within a story'*. *Framed stories* offer children the stimulating opportunity to write 'a narrative within a narrative' (Barrett, 2011: 16) based around particular purposes[†] that are set by teachers.

*Examples of *Framed Stories* to support children's (and teachers') understanding:

Films	1. *The Princess Bride* is framed as a book being read by a grandfather to his sick grandson.
	2. The framing device used in *Titanic* is the elderly Rose telling her story.
Books	1. *The Time Machine* (Wells, 2005) is largely told through a guest at the time traveller's party.
	2. *The Wonderful Story of Henry Sugar* (Dahl, 1999) is a framed story about a rich bachelor who finds an essay written by someone who learnt to 'see' playing cards from the reverse side.
TV	1. *Are You Afraid of the Dark?* sets up each episode with a group of teenagers gathering around a campfire to tell each other ghost stories.
	2. *The Gruffalo* sees a mother squirrel telling her young family a story about a mouse, a snake, a fox, an owl and a Gruffalo.

Adapted from TV Tropes (2011)

[†]Particular purposes of *Framed Stories*:

Framed stories allow children to write stories with a specific purpose, e.g. writing about particular characters, using figurative language, dealing with conflict resolution, developing dialogue interactions between characters, or using connectives and complex sentences. Teachers can use *Framed stories* to encourage children to write stories set in specific eras, in particular settings and in different countries. Story themes such as love, hate, war, death and friendship can be specified, as well as the length and complexity of the story, depending on the capabilities of the children.

'Framing' a *Framed story*:

There are numerous ways in which children's *Framed stories* can be 'framed':

1. *Bedtime read!* A parent/carer reads a bedtime story to their child – *which bedtime story will they read tonight?*
2. *31 days of dreaming!* A character goes to sleep and has a dream – *what do they dream about?*
3. *Keeping Grandma's spirits up!* Grandma is in hospital as she has broken her arm. You visit her every day and tell her a new story you have written to make her smile – *what will your story be about today?*
4. *Stuck in a lift!* Members of your class get stuck in a lift together on a school trip; to pass the time they tell each other interesting stories until the lift is fixed – *what stories do they tell each other to 'distract' their peers?*

| **Idea 9.10: Chain stories** | **Suggested age group:** 3-year-olds to 7-year-olds |

Explanation:

In an effort to make story writing a '3-D affair', *Chain stories* serve as a creative and visually appealing way to engage children into *wanting* to mark-make (3–5) whilst encouraging those aged 5–7 to write in complete sentences. A *Chain story* is created by children mark-making/writing a single sentence on a rectangular strip of paper (coloured) which is then shaped and fastened onto a circular link. The next series of marks/sentence of the story is written on another strip of paper and fed through the first link to create a chain. The children continue recording their marks/sentences on separate links until their stimulating story is completed.

Chain stories and fine motor skills:

The creation of the paper links (as described above) serves as a valuable opportunity to support children's development of their fine motor skills. Encourage each child to operate different tools, e.g. *staplers*, *hole punches*, and *scissors*, along with handling fixings, e.g. *paper fasteners*, *treasury tags* and *paper clips* to create the links. It is advocated that the effective manipulation of the above will help to contribute to an improvement in the 'quality and speed' (Palluel-Germain et al., 2007) of young children's handwriting performance.

Possible *Chain stories* for children (5–7) to write:

- *Ben's/Aimee's strange day!* – In the morning . . . (*link 1*), after play . . . (*link 2*), during lunch . . . (*link 3*).
- *Down the plughole, Pongee!* What happens to Pongee the alien when he falls down the plughole? Who does he meet? What does he say? How does he get back home?
- *The day trip to the theme park.* What rides do the children go on? Who is scared in the Haunted House? Who loses their shoe on the Spinning Teacups?
- *Puss in Wellies!* Puss in Boots has lost his boots so he has to borrow different types of shoes and boots from other fairytale characters – who does he visit? What kind of shoes/boots do they offer him? Why does he not borrow them? What happened to his boots?

Strategies for differentiation:

- The length/width of the paper offered to make each link (3–5).
- The number of links the children are to use to create their story (3–7).
- The number of words the children are encouraged to include in each sentence (5–7).
- The different types of words the children should use in their story e.g. *verbs, adjectives, noun, pronouns* (5–7).

Display ideas for *Chain stories*:

- *Chain stories* as party decorations.
- *Chain stories* as necklaces.
- *Chain stories* as 'hanging' stories from the classroom ceiling.
- *Chain stories* as curtain tiebacks.
- *Chain stories* as the 'chain' across the entrance to *close* and *open* the Pet Shop role-play area each day.

***Learning from experience!* Practical advice from the shop floor:**

- Remind children (3–5) to check that their mark-making/writing is presented on the *outside* of the paper link!
- Encourage children to temporarily 'fix' the links together with Blu-Tack® so that if they forget to offer something in the story they can easily add a link as and where appropriate (5–7).

10

'Random' stories

This final chapter offers the reader a *random* collection of Ideas which are designed to energise and stimulate children's story writing across the 3–11 age range. Varied in their nature and purpose, these Ideas serve as an interesting set of suggestions for teachers to dip into, offering them to children as either *one-off* story writing opportunities, Weekend Work tasks with parent/carer support, or special story writing assignments (for examples see http://tinyurl.com/cjcczy).

The first Idea in the chapter – *Slice of life stories* – uses a metaphorical knife to 'cut out' everyday events in characters' lives (real/imagined) in an attempt to help children (7–11) break the bounds of conventional narrative writing. *Punctuation stories* is an Idea that was developed in response to the writing of Medwell et al. (1998), who identify that effective teachers help children to become literate by advocating the planning, drafting, revising and editing of their own writing. *Silly stories* encourage children to remember that there is a lighter side to life, portraying this in their tales of frivolity, foolishness and folly (think Roald Dahl and Spike Milligan)! *Collaborative stories* consider ways of promoting story writing partnerships in an effort to 'beat the loneliness of the writing endeavour (*sic*) . . . motivate [children] to meet deadlines, take more risks in [their] writing, and challenge [children] to push beyond [their] literary comfort zones' (Sayantani, 2011). *Bedtime stories* work to emphasise the importance of 'end-of-the-day-tales' by offering children the opportunity to write night-time stories for their peers in an attempt to support their personal growth and development (see Heath, 1982).

Border stories encourage teachers to reflect on the value of displays in stimulating children's story writing, considering ways that children can use all the available space on a display board to mark-make/write stories on. *Picture prompt stories* capitalise on the value of picture prompts (in their many forms) to energise children's story writing through the use of a still/moving image (see http://tinyurl.com/brg4gjh). *Speech stories* respond to the concern that surrounds the 'growing generation of monosyllabic mumblers' (Tait, 2008) by getting children to 'incorporate lots of speech into their stories, bringing characters and stories alive with stimulating and purposeful dialogue' (p. 202). *Squigglehop stories* recognise the importance of invented language in developing children's imaginations and stimulating the stories that they write, whilst *Threaded stories* – the final Idea in this chapter – take the notion of the 'narrative thread' to another level by using it as a 'literal device' to kindle children's story writing by combining fine motor movement with appealing practical story writing resources.

Taking a closer look at 'story endings'

Polon (1998, in *Silly stories*, p. 197) advocates offering children sentences which *end* a story, e.g. the final line. This serves as a prompt for children to 'write the beginning of the story that leads to this final sentence' (1998: 87). The importance of a good story ending, be it in the form of a sentence (typically the work of younger children) or a concluding paragraph (typically the work of older children), cannot be underestimated; Cleaver (2006: 112) considers it to be 'the reader's reward for having read through your story'. The difficulty is that story endings are rather problematic for authors; Peha (2002: 90) supports this, suggesting that 'endings are, for most of us, the hardest things to write'. There are several 'problematic' story endings which teachers are likely to encounter in the story writing produced by the children they work with:

- The stereotypical 'unsatisfactory' ending (Peat, 2002): *And then Andy woke up. It was all a dream.*
- The unfinished ending: *Carol was half way through her round-the-world adventure; the rest of it was quite exciting.*
- The unreflective ending: *It was bedtime and because of the busy day Winston had had he jumped into bed and went to sleep.*

- The disappointing ending: *So Wilf the dragon killed the Knight, kept the King and Queen captive in the castle for the rest of their days, and ate Princess Gemma when he became bored with her (the next day).*

Activity!

Weak story endings *frustrate* the reader; they 'ruin the read' if their expectations are not met. Ask children in KS1 (5–7) and KS2 (7–11) to reflect on the following story endings, considering how they would feel if the story they are currently reading ended in one of these ways:

- We all had a lot of fun.
- Daddy drove us back home.
- I had had a jolly good time.
- It was then time to go home.
- Finally we left for good.
- I fell asleep on the way home.

Whilst the endings in many children's written stories might be considered 'underdeveloped', it is important to be mindful of the *typical* reasons as to why this is the case:

- Children *typically* do not spend as much time *planning* the ending of their story as they do on the start and middle of it.
- Children *typically* spend more time actually writing the start of their story than the end.
- Children *typically* 'rush' the end of their story because they run out of writing time.
- Children *typically* struggle to 'tie everything up in a neat package' because 'real life doesn't work that way' (Strauss, 2010: 61).

In response to the points made above, several simple strategies should be adopted to help children with their all-important story endings:

1. Emphasise the importance of the story ending to children by getting them to think of a story as a horse race: 'It is the start and the finish that count most' (H.E. Bates, cited in Cleaver, 2006: 117).

2. Model the process of thinking about the ending of a story at the planning stage of a whole-class/group story; consider starting with the end and work backwards to the start.

3. Make children aware of the 'passing of time' as they work on their written stories with visual aids (egg timers, digital timers on the interactive whiteboard) and gentle verbal reminders. Take care that this does not pressurise children as this will hinder their 'writing flow' (see http://tinyurl.com/brgqjjr for information about this).

4. Offer children picture story books (5–7) and 'end passages' from children's novels (7–11), getting them to sort them into piles of endings that they like and dislike. Discuss their reasoning behind the decisions they make, noting these down on class thought showers for their story writing working wall (see http://tinyurl.com/cyh8kxk for information about this).

How should a story end?

Snicket's *A Series of Unfortunate Events* books (2008) are determined to ensure the Baudelaire children remain unhappy throughout the series. Most readers (especially younger children) like stories to end in a happy or hopeful way. Talk to children about how they want readers to remember their written story – in a happy, somewhat happy, neither happy nor sad, somewhat sad, or sad way (Peirce and Edwards, 1988), shaping their story ending to their chosen response.

There are many ways in which teachers can support children in writing better endings for their stories. The strategies offered in Table 10.1 (p. 191) serve as 'a "menu" of various types of alternative ending' (Peat, 2002: 85) and span the 5–11 age range, acknowledging both new and established ideas for story closure.

Table 10.1   Strategies for improving story endings

Alternative ending (age group)	Details
Open ending (Peat, 2002) (5–11)	Leave doubt in the reader's mind in terms of whether the story is really over: *The family flopped into their chairs – their horrible day was over. Or was it?*
Connection with the beginning (Corbett, 2001) (7–11)	Revisit the start of the story to see if the two parts can be 'joined up': *Danny stopped dead in his tracks. Lying on the floor in front of him was the glowing doughnut stone he had thrown into the sky which had caused the tornado. 'I wonder where I might end up tomorrow?' thought Danny to himself as he slowly picked up the stone, smiling.*
End with advice (Peha, 2002) (7–11)	Offer the reader some practical advice: *So if you ever see a dog with a microphone, just keep walking!*
Look to the future (7–11)	Encourage children to consider the future of their characters: *Rachel knew that she loved Bobbie and that he would make her happy. Her future looked bright; her future was to be full of love!*
Use dialogue (Corbett, 2003) (5–11)	'End with a comment from one of the characters' (Corbett, 2003: 58): *'Phew!' said Sammy. 'What a to-do!' cried Freddy. 'Oh – come on!' moaned Lenard. 'Not again!'*
A twist in the tale (5–11)	Offer something at the end which the reader was not expecting: *And as Finbarr slept in his bed, safe in the knowledge that the Winding Man was forever banished, a slim shadow, very much like a very thin arm, wound its way ever so delicately around the smooth bedroom doorhandle.*
Character change (Corbett, 2001) (5–11)	Comment on how characters have changed as a result of what has happened to them: *Wendy saw that being outrageous made her look stupid in her friends' eyes. It was time for her to calm down a little!*
'And so finally . . .' (Peat, 2002) (5–11)	Ensure that the end goal which was defined at the start of the story has been achieved: *Pesto smiled – the town was safe, and he was a free goblin.*

Just Don't Do It!

There are certain phrases that children add to the end of their written stories which should be positively discouraged, particularly as children mature in their writing confidence and capabilities:

- It was all just a dream.
- Wasn't that lucky?
- The End
- I hoped you enjoyed my story!
- They all lived happily ever after.
- This is what happened in my story.

Adapted from Peha (2002: 101)

To further support teachers, select readings and websites are offered below to develop and enrich subject knowledge and learning and teaching of story endings to strengthen the finale of children's *'Random' stories*:

- **Teaching materials** – *Unit 9 Narrative writing: Story endings* (DfES, 2001b) – see pp. 12–14 for a series of valuable 'last words' and a story/story ending checklist.

- **Practical booklet** – *The Writing Teacher's Strategy Guide* (Peha, 2002) – see pp. 102–103 for useful tips on good endings and a glossary of happy endings.

- **Website** – Visit http://tinyurl.com/bteqcxl for some useful Word documents and Smart Board resources linked to story endings.

Table 10.2   Recommended readings associated with *'Random' stories*

Books	Stone, R. (2007) *Best Practices for Teaching Writing: What Award-Winning Classroom Teachers Do*. London: Sage. *This book sees the author reporting on the 'tried-and-tested best practices' of award-winning teachers of writing that are used with children from the early years through to secondary school. Strategies for building student confidence and achievement in writing are offered to support both new and established teachers.* Consider using it as a supportive resource to complement the *'Random' story* Ideas presented in this chapter. Walling, D. R. (2006) *Teaching Writing to Visual, Auditory, and Kin[a]esthetic Learners*. London: Sage. *This book claims to help learners become effective writers by matching teaching methods to the favoured learning styles of the child. Whether the children you work with are 'picture-smart, music-smart . . . body-smart . . . word-smart [or] number-smart'* (book blurb), *this book offers innovative ways to develop basic writing competencies and higher-level thinking skills.* Reflect on its value in complementing your provision in the classroom in relation to offered *'Random' stories*.
Online resource/journal article	Williams, J. (2003) *Primary Curriculum. Creative Writing (Key Stage 1)*. [Online]. Available at: http://tinyurl.com/cp9kmxp (Accessed: 16 June 2012). *This wonderful education pack offers a wealth of professional work units which 'can be used to enhance your students' learning through visualisation, discussion, speculation and exploration' (p. 7). Of particular interest are the activities linked to story endings (see pp. 3–4).* Consider how this, alongside the ideas in this chapter, can be used to enhance the *'Random' stories* children create. Mata, L. (2011) Motivation for reading and writing in kindergarten children. *Reading Psychology*, 32 (3), 272–99. [Online]. Available at: http://tinyurl.com/buds2dg (Accessed: 16 June 2012). *This paper reports on research which examined the reading and writing motivations of 5–6-year-olds in Lisbon. The researcher acknowledges 'the four clusters of conditions considered by Bruning and Horn (2000) as most critical in developing writing motivation: nurturing beliefs about writing* (competence as writer and writing value)*; engagement through authentic writing goals and contexts* (real and challenging activities)*; creating a positive emotional environment; and providing supportive contexts for writing' (p. 292).* Consider how the ideas in this final chapter can be used to emphasise these elements to develop young 'motivated literacy learners' (p. 292).

Websites

@k_ferrell (2012) *8 Great Sites for Reluctant Writers*. [Online]. Available at: http://tinyurl.com/dxnlcgs (Accessed: 17 June 2012).

This rather wonderful 'post' offers the reader links to eight colourful and engaging 'children-appropriate' websites to prompt reluctant writers to put 'finger to keyboard'! A personal favourite is number 6: Writing with Writers! Consider the value of these websites in stimulating the *'Random' stories* children write in your classroom.

Schoenberg, J. (2010) *Elementary Writing: 49 Ideas and Story Starters for Kids*. [Online]. Available at: http://tinyurl.com/cwa7hap (Accessed: 17 June 2012).

Schoenberg strongly advocates children keeping a writing journal in primary school. To support this practice she offers on her website 'an amazing list of elementary writing prompts and writing starters for your students!' Personal favourites include numbers 17, 29 and 44. A wealth of additional journal prompts is offered under Related Articles. Consider the value of these in 'sparking' children's interest in the *'Random' stories* they write in your classroom.

Idea 10.1: Slice of life stories	Suggested age group: 7-year-olds to 11-year-olds

Explanation:

It is suggested that some children will always find writing stories to be a challenge (Richards, 2008b). Managing plot development, speech, descriptive passages and characterisation all at the same time can be an ordeal for some children, irrespective of the amount of practical support offered to them. *Slice of life stories* serve to alleviate some of the complexity of story writing by allowing children to write about ordinary, everyday events that offer the reader a realistic portrayal of life – see http://tinyurl.com/7jugajd for published examples for children. As *Slice of life stories* are not necessarily bound by the conventions of narrative writing*, this type of story allows children to write about events from their own lives that can be presented as occurrences that happen to others.

Defining *Slice of life stories*:

eNotes.com (2011) defines *Slice of life* stories as 'a category for a story that portrays a "cut-out" sequence of events in a character's life. *It may or may not contain any plot progress and little character development, and often has no exposition, conflict, or dénouement [conclusion or resolution of a plot], with an open ending. It usually tries to depict the everyday life of ordinary people . . . it often seems as if the author had taken a knife and "cut out" a slice of the lives of some characters, without concern for narrative form.'

Slice of life stories – a little fact file:

* These stories are about an everyday event, as opposed to being something 'special'.
* These stories can be about something recent or something from the distant past.
* These stories do not have to be based around a 'problem'.
* These stories do not have to be very long, word-wise.

Stimulating *Slice of life stories* – possible events:

* Getting out of bed in the morning.
* Helping to unpack the groceries.
* The long journey to school.
* Watching a TV programme.
* Eating pizza from the box.
* Cleaning out the hamster cage.
* Playing a game of rounders.
* Answering the telephone.
* Preparing to go to bed.
* Listening to some music on the radio.
* Washing and wiping up the dishes.
* Learning to do sums in a maths lesson.

Slice of life story – an example:

James knew he needed a walk; his head was pounding from the glue, and his brain and lungs were in need of some fresh air. He reluctantly walked away from his model plane, hoping that the wings would be dry by the time he got back. He found his shoes and quickly put them on. Kissing his grandma goodbye, James stepped out of the front door and was greeted with bright sunshine. He inhaled a huge gulp of warm air and held his breath for a moment, slowly releasing the air back into the world. The 'boom-boom-boom' in his head began to lessen as James made his way towards the airfield. (Hardy, aged 11, gifted writer)

Idea 10.2: Punctuation stories	**Suggested age group:** 5-year-olds to 11-year-olds

Explanation:

How often do you have to ask children to 'go back and check' that they have used full stops in the right places in their story writing? It is not surprising if you said 'Quite often'*! The purpose of punctuation is to make writing understandable; in order to do this, children need to appreciate the importance of this in their own stories (see Appendix 2 of DfE, 2012b: xv–xvii). *Punctuation stories* promote this by getting children to write stimulating stories with 'emphasised' punctuation marks, e.g. enlarged symbols, written in different colours, stressed in highlighted markings, or presented on small stickers which are attached to the story paper!

'Trends' of teaching punctuation marks to children – *research findings*:

Research by Ferreiroa and Pontecorvob (1999: 562) found that the teaching of punctuation marks in Western countries showed two main trends:

1. [T]o teach that punctuation marks correspond to pauses for breath (an instruction for the reader).
2. [T]o teach that punctuation marks correspond to the notion of 'complete sentences', 'the end of an idea' or the 'logical structure' of the text (an instruction for the writer).

It was discovered, however, that children's (7-year-olds) attempts to use punctuation marks in their written version of the story of *Little Red Riding Hood* did not seem to be guided by either of these two trends. Consider the impact of your approach to teaching punctuation by reflecting on the trends above – *which do you adopt as part of your own practice? How effective do you think it is?*

Supporting teachers' knowledge and understanding of punctuation marks:

Whilst children (and some parents/carers) think that teachers are the 'font of all knowledge' (Langley, cited in Dodson, 2010), it is true to say that teachers do not know everything. Written English can be complex, particularly when it is littered with different punctuation marks. For simple, clear and useful information about effective punctuation, visit http://tinyurl.com/7j3naum.

*The best way for children to check their use of punctuation in their stories is to read their writing out loud (Angelillo, 2006); whenever they use voice inflections, stops, pauses and even body language to indicate meaning, this is where they are likely to need a punctuation mark.

Useful 'punctuation' websites:

- Visit http://tinyurl.com/7rp67nj for a child-friendly interactive punctuation pyramid†.
- Visit http://tinyurl.com/855y2aj for some simple punctuation games to play (these are designed for 11–12-year-olds but they are easily adaptable for children aged 5–11).
- Visit http://tinyurl.com/6sps8jw for details about the stimulating *Punctuation Kung Fu* by Ros Wilson, as described by Beadle (2007).

†The Writing Improvement Pyramid:

Visit http://tinyurl.com/bs3uuvp for a wonderful downloadable 3-D pyramid that not only offers a progression in punctuation marks but also sentence openers, vocabulary and connectives. Page 7 of the document offers advice on how to use the pyramid 'to have an immediate impact on writing standards'! Evaluate its impact on children's *Punctuation story* writing in your class.

Idea 10.3: Silly stories	Suggested age group: 5-year-olds to 11-year-olds

Explanation:

It is easy to believe that we live in a world of 'doom and gloom' with the wealth of negative headlines that litter the front pages of our daily newspapers. However, stories about flying pigs, square-shaped melons and 'sergeant major' penguins (BBC, 2001) remind us that there is a lighter side to life. *Silly stories* offer children the opportunity to escape from harsh realities of life and write the kind of story which Binns (2008) claims 'can create instantaneous health benefits including relaxation, lower blood pressure, cur[e] male pattern baldness and increase[e] immune system response'! *Silly stories* allow children to be *purposefully* silly with what they write about and who they write for!

Being silly with *Silly stories*:

The success of the *Seriously Silly Stories* series by Anholt and Robins (1999) is testimony to children's enjoyment of subversive, irrelevant stories. The great thing about *Silly stories* is they offer no real boundaries for children; they can be based around:

- silly characters, e.g. Sammy Sausage; Dr. Greasyfoot;
- silly situations, e.g. the world is taken over by tiny talking hamsters; everyone develops the ability to walk on walls;
- silly problems, e.g. washing machines that refuse to clean dirty clothes; horses that demand two pairs of roller-skates to save scuffing their new horse shoes; or
- silly jokes or language, e.g. Laura wakes up one morning and starts talking in a new dialect called '*Dum-de-pang-a-shoo-flu*'.

Top Tip! See Loewen (2009) for some fabulously silly ideas for children to use to stimulate their own *Silly stories*! Also see http://tinyurl.com/ckbfmvf for some 'noodlehead' brilliance!

***Silly story* generators:**

An engaging activity for individual or group work involves the use of online *Silly story* generators. By inputting certain words into the generators, a *Silly story* can be created by the click of a button! These generators are useful as they help to teach/remind children about different types of words, e.g. nouns, adjectives, interjections, pronouns, adverbs etc. Useful generators can be found at:

http://tinyurl.com/6jou57   http://tinyurl.com/6rx648v
http://tinyurl.com/7juhcxt   http://tinyurl.com/7mzp66m

Note! Some of the stories generated may not be grammatically correct. Use this as an opportunity for children (7–11) to edit the story on an interactive whiteboard, correcting the errors they find.

'End to the beginning!' Story writing with an end prompt:

Polon (1998: 87) advocates offering children sentences which *end* a story, e.g. the final line. This serves as a prompt for children to 'write the beginning of the story that leads to this final sentence'. Potential *Silly story* end prompts include:

- *It was made of jelly but it* still *scared me!*
- *It was the* wriggliest *day of my life!*
- *I was so proud I failed my Bikeability test!*
- *I fell asleep and did not wake up until 2087!*

| **Idea 10.4: Collaborative stories** | **Suggested age group:** 5-year-olds to 11-year-olds |

Explanation:

Many British sitcoms (situation comedies) are credited as being written by one person, whereas American sitcoms typically employ a large team of writers who collaborate on each script (Blake, 2011). *Collaborative stories* embrace the old adage of 'two heads being better than one' by getting children to collaborate in writing pairs or larger groups to create their stories. The benefits of this approach to story writing seemingly has an impact on other types of children's writing; Daiute and Dalton (1993) found that children who wrote collaboratively with their peers adopted techniques used by their fellow classmates for later independent writing activities.

Approaching collaborative writing:

Farkas (1991: 14) offers four possible approaches to collaborative writing:

1. Two or more people who jointly compose the complete text.

2. Two or more people who contribute different sections to a text.

3. One or more persons who modify the work of one or more persons by editing and/or reviewing it.

4. One person who works interactively with one or more persons by drafting a text based on the ideas of the person or persons.

Reflect! How often do you promote/encourage children (7–11) to use these different approaches for collaboration? Which of the above would you *not* encourage children you work with to use? Why so? What opportunities for learning and teaching are there to help children overcome any issues which result from collaborative activities, e.g. *team building activities, dealing with conflict, the sharing of ideas, coping with constructive criticism* and *the taking-on of different roles and responsibilities*?

Stimulating types of collaboration for 5–7-year-olds:

- *Author/illustrator collaboration*, e.g. Janet and Allan Ahlberg (*The Jolly Postman*). Children aged 5–6 could select one of their peers to illustrate their story, or names could be drawn out of a hat, thus resulting in a 'chance' collaboration.

- *Writing partnership*, e.g. Nick Butterworth and Mick Inkpen (*Jasper's Beanstalk*). Children aged 6–7 could use talking partners, shared thought showering and joint writing time opportunities to generate their story.

Top Tip! Visit http://tinyurl.com/6wq85n6 and reflect on the strategies advocated in Yagelski's (1994) article – what practice could you adopt as your own?

Top tips for writing collaborations:

- Think carefully about the most appropriate way to organise the 'writing teams' – are collaborations with friends always effective (see Maldonado et al., 2009 for an interested response)? Consider ability/mixed ability/all boys/all girls/mixed gender/child selected/different aged groupings.

- Group sizes can be determined by reflecting on the objectives of the task, the age and abilities of the children, and the amount of work that needs to be done.

- Consider what you will be assessing in relation to the writing collaboration beforehand – *the process? The product? Both? Why so?*

| **Idea 10.5: Bedtime stories** | **Suggested age group:** 3-year-olds to 7-year-olds |

Explanation:

Whilst many early childhood experts promote bedtime stories as a key part of the 'wind-down' ritual for young children at the end of the day, recent survey findings (see *Daily Mail*, 2011) suggest that parents lead such busy lives now that they no longer have time to read stories to their children at night. *Bedtime stories* attend to this issue by encouraging children to write stories at school for their peers/siblings to read in bed to themselves so that they do not miss out on that all-important bedtime story at the end of the day.

The importance of *Bedtime stories* – learning and teaching opportunities:

For children (5–7) to appreciate the importance of *Bedtime stories*, visit the following web links, collating useful information to share with your class as you introduce the Idea of *Bedtime stories* to them:

http://tinyurl.com/bweh4rl   http://tinyurl.com/btad7wo   http://tinyurl.com/cbk8way

Writing a good *Bedtime story*:

To help children (5–7) write a stimulating *Bedtime story*, particularly for young children (0–4), they need to consider the following:

Consideration	Details
Language	Ensure that the text is easy to understand and the words used are appropriate.
Characters	Strive to make lead characters likeable, e.g. bunnies, bears, dogs, cats and mice.
Plot	The story should be simple and easy to follow – see Crum (2006) for support.
Ending	Good bedtime stories should have all the characters 'very, very tired' by the end!

Work with your class to reflect on other story considerations such as *story build-up*, *the problem or dilemma* and *the resolution* (Corbett, 2003) where appropriate. Provide children (3–5) with examples of bedtime story books for them to visually identify what makes a good bedtime story.

Illustrating *Bedtime stories* – two top tips:	**Useful online bedtime story websites:**
• Keep the illustrations simple and clear. • Use analogous or warm colours rather than those which might be considered 'loud'.	• http://tinyurl.com/cfcbsd • http://tinyurl.com/9q5gyq6 • http://tinyurl.com/bq4bp9x

'Investing in word banks' – supporting children's story writing with stimulating vocabulary:

Word banks are collections of words which can be used to broaden children's vocabulary. Typically they are used to support children's reading development (e.g. high-frequency words) but Quandt (1973: 171) advocates that these 'should not be limited to the [L]anguage [E]xperience [A]pproach' (see http://tinyurl.com/6vd7t9b for information). Teach children (4–7) to select from word banks that are displayed on working walls (see http://tinyurl.com/6t2axsv) to make their story writing interesting. Examples of word banks that children (5–7) could use for their *Bedtime stories* include:

Said	*Roared, groaned, shouted, whispered, replied, agreed, answered, bellowed, cried*
Big	*Huge, astronomical, gigantic, massive, vast, enormous, staggering, whopping*
To sleep	*Doze, slumber, nap, snooze, rest, kip, catch some zeds, nod off*

Idea 10.6: Border stories	**Suggested age group:** 3-year-olds to 11-year-olds

Explanation:

Good teachers display children's stories in an effort to showcase the writing talents of their class (Phenix, 2002). However, consider how many children actually *read* the work that is put on the display. Issues relating to available opportunities to look at the display, the size of the written text, the height of the work in relation to the child, and the possible 'glare' off the paper from the classroom lights prevent many children from actually reading their peers' displayed stories. *Border stories* allow children to write stimulating stories which stretch around the outside edge of a display board; instead of the border being just a plain piece of edging, this unusual Idea allows children to use *all* the available space on a display board to mark-make/write stories on!

Display boards and story writing potential:

Displays are used by many teachers (7–11) to exhibit 'the final write-up' in terms of what children have produced. Display boards should be used to show children's engagement through the various processes involved in story writing: from the thought showering and initial drafting to the editing and presentation of the polished version. This actively promotes and helps to reinforce each stage of the writing process.

Possible story titles for *Border stories*:

- *Read my mind!*
- *Money!*
- *Chat Cat!*
- *Goliath the Gorilla!*
- *Rainbow of gold.*
- *Linda's lucky lantern.*
- *Lost in the Village of Mirrors.*
- *Tiny friends* (Shaw, 2008: 2–3).

'Concept combination' and story writing:

Increasebrainpower.com (n.d.) suggests that concept combination 'is a great problem solving technique used especially for creating new products to sell. It can be used in a good way to create new stories. Just combine old stories into new ones. For the most creative writing ideas, it is best if the stories you start with are unrelated in their theme. For example, if you start with the biblical story of Adam and Eve, and combine it with the movie "Star Wars" you might get an interesting idea or two.'

Work with children (5–11) to generate ideas for their *Border story* from the following combinations:

- Alice in Wonderland and the Jolly Postman
- Mr Majeika and the Little Red Hen
- Dora the Explorer and Princess Smartypants
- Matilda and Garfield
- Elmer the Elephant and Little Manfred
- Ug and Dogger

Writing on borders – some practicalities:

- 3–5: Encourage children to work on the floor/outside where they will have space to roll their border paper out and see how much physical material they have to mark-make/write on.
- 5–7: As space in classrooms is an issue for many teachers, offer children pieces of dowel which they can use to 'wind' the border paper around as they mark-make/write on it (like a scroll – see *Scroll stories*, p. 113).
- 7–11: Ensure that children write their letters big enough so that others can read their *Border story* if it is positioned at the top of the display!

Idea 10.7: Picture prompt stories	Suggested age group: 3-year-olds to 11-year-olds

Explanation:

Many professional books on the subject of story writing advocate the use of picture prompts to support and stimulate children when writing stories (see Van Allsburg, 1984; Kellaher, 1999) – this book is no exception! These pictures or images could be of anything – *a book, a key, children crying, a broken flip flop, bags of rubbish, a cable wrapped around a lamp post* – anything to offer children some 'visual inspiration'. *Picture prompt stories* embrace the incalculable value of picture prompts by proposing a wealth of suggestions below to 'visually aid' children as they verbalise/write their stories.

Sources of picture prompts:

Picture prompts can come from a variety of sources:

- Catalogues – *Argos, Freemans, IKEA.*
- Magazines – *subscriptions, with newspapers.*
- Newspapers – *local, national, international.*
- Internet – *images from different search engines.*
- Photographs – *old or unwanted, photocopies.*
- Leaflets – *those with free publications.*
- Drawings – *children's, your own, downloaded.*

Note! For all sources, care should be taken to ensure that the material is suitable for use by children, e.g. does not contain images that are sexualised or depict graphic violence etc.

Strategies for *Picture Prompt story* differentiation:

- Verbal (3–5)/written (5–11) 'telling' of the story.
- The number of pictures selected.
- The simplicity/complexity of the pictures/images used (3–11).
- The length of the story to be written (5–11).
- The time given to writing the story (5–11).
- The number of sentences to be written before the next picture prompt is used in the story (7–11).

Using picture prompts with children – internet advice:

The document *Oral Language and Story* (n.d.) – available at http://tinyurl.com/7lepf5j – advocates the use of picture prompts, particularly for younger children: 'it is a good idea to provide pictures . . . as prompts for the children' (n.d.: 4). Interesting ideas contained within the document include:

- 'Collect *open-ended* photographs that tell a story' (n.d.: 4)
- 'Encourage the children to think *beyond* the information in the picture and imagine what might have happened before or after the event in the photograph' (n.d.: 4)
- 'Colour photocopies of illustrations from picture books will provide resources necessary for retelling stories. Alternatively old books cut up and laminated are ideal' (n.d.: 11).

Consider using these suggestions within your 'picture prompt provision' in your classroom.

Valuable picture prompt websites:

- http://tinyurl.com/77o6twy
- http://tinyurl.com/8y2ql5b
- http://tinyurl.com/73frsqw
- http://tinyurl.com/7jypf43

Quick-fire picture prompt ideas:

- Sort the picture prompts into clearly labelled trays for children's ease, e.g. *characters, settings, objects, emotions.*
- Determine the number of pictures prompts to be selected by getting children to roll a die or use an online number generator.

Idea 10.8: Speech stories	**Suggested age group:** 5-year-olds to 11-year-olds

Explanation:

The development of children's speech, according to Greenfield (2000, cited in Latham, 2002: 17), occurs 'naturally . . . spontaneously' and quite rapidly. By the age of four it is suggested that the majority of children are able to use language with a capability close to that of an adult. As '[c]hildren of all ages enjoy talking' (National Institute for Literacy, 2010: 3), *Speech stories* are designed to encourage children to incorporate lots of speech into their written stories, bringing characters and stories alive with stimulating and purposeful dialogue.

Useful learning and teaching opportunities about spoken words in stories:

- 5–7: Spoken words in stories are demarcated with speech marks (also referred to as 'inverted commas'). They appear *around* the words that are said by characters. They are written as a pair of opening and closing marks in either of two styles: single ('____') or double ("____").
- 7–11: New 'speakers' should appear on a new line when their speech is written down (Corbett, 2003). Writers should indicate to the reader *who* is speaking and *how* their words were spoken, e.g. *'I've had enough of you!' screamed Suzie, slamming the door shut.*

Speech stories (5–7):

There is sometimes a danger that young children's efforts to include speech in their stories read more like a poor movie screenplay, e.g. *'Hello.' 'How are you?' 'Fine.' 'Good.'* Teachers can help children to understand speech by getting them to fill in paper/acetate speech bubbles (see Appendix 28, p. 235) which are temporarily fastened to pictures or illustrations in picture books – *what do you think the characters might be saying in this 'scene'?* Other suggestions include:

- Allow children to look at comic strips that show how speech is used to capture characters' thoughts, feelings and ideas.
- Encourage children to look at wordless story books. With a dictaphone follow a character through the story, speaking like the main character as they interact with other characters (voiced by other children or the teacher). Replay the recording, selecting certain pieces of dialogue which can then be incorporated into a shared story writing opportunity.

Speech stories (7–11):

Work with children to collate speech verbs and adverbs so that they can vary the way characters say things in their stories, for example:

- 'You what?!' *bellowed* Harry.
- 'It's hot in here,' said Richard *heavily*.
- 'I'm okay,' *sighed* Fiona.
- 'Not long now!' *chirped* Greg *enthusiastically*.

Encourage children to read their 'story speech' out loud with the help of their peers (taking the roles of other characters) so that they can evaluate the flow and value of the speech they have written. Help children to include information about what characters are doing when they speak to enrich their storytelling, e.g. *'Hello there,' said Jim, twiddling the loose piece of cotton which dangled from the bottom of his T-shirt.*

Idea 10.9: Squigglehop stories	Suggested age group: 5-year-olds to 11-year-olds

Explanation:

Children love language and their acquisition of it in their formative years is nothing less than incredible; Boeree (2003) suggests that children aged 6–7 use up to 6,000 words and as adults we 'may use as many as 25,000 words and recognize up to 50,000!'. One of the things which fascinates parents/carers and teachers is how children 'invent' words, e.g. *Yummerific, thorky weeds* (meaning 'thorny' and 'pokey') and *fridjerfreeze* (meaning 'fridge freezer'). The Idea of *Squigglehop stories* (one of the author's own made up words!) is to mimic the practices of Lewis Carroll (*Jabberwocky*), Spike Milligan (*bang catcher* for 'gun') and Roald Dahl (*swash boggling* meaning 'big') by purposefully incorporating made-up words into the stimulating stories they write to add intrigue, humour and a bit of 'creative zest' into their word bank!

The power of made-up words:

Nikolajeva (reported in Beckford, 2009) claims that 'unusual phrases and words teach children the expressive power of language, which aids the development of their own imaginations'. She argues that many of the most popular children's books over the past 150 years are based on the imaginative use of language, e.g. Winnie the Pooh (*hunny; Heffalump*) and the Harry Potter series (*Quidditch; Muggle*). Help children (5–11) to reflect on the presence of made-up language found in popular children's TV programmes, e.g. *Teletubbies, Bill and Ben, the Simpsons, Pingu* and the *Moomins.*

If 'the Bard' can do it then so can I! Shakespeare and made-up words:

In all of his work – the plays, the sonnets and the narrative poems – it has been calculated that Shakespeare used 17,677 words and of these he invented an incredible 1,700 of them! Some of these include: *lonely, bump, countless, amazement, critic, dishearten, eventful, moonbeam* and *generous*. He also seemingly coined many phrases we use in everyday speech, which include *break the ice, elbow room, full circle, heart of gold, in a pickle* and *love is blind*. Visit http://tinyurl.com/cuh8zzn for more examples.

Share these with children (9–11), encouraging them to 'behave like the Bard' and invent new words and phrases which can be integrated into their story writing.

Types of words for children to make up:

Children (5–7) should be encouraged to make up words associated with three of the eight word types: *verbs, nouns, adjectives*. For children (7–11) recommend that they also make up these kinds of words along with *adverbs* and *interjections*. Personally invented examples include:

5–7 age range			7–11 age range		
Word type	Example	Meaning	Word type	Example	Meaning
Verb	hugsle	To squeeze someone excessively	Adverb	woltbily	Very slowly
Noun	frastip	A very thin book	Interjection	*Frrrr!*	A growing sound of anger
Adjective	cipperry	A reddy colour			

Top Tip! To stimulate different story elements to allow children to generate new words, see Appendix 29 (p. 236) for some innovative Story sticks.

Idea 10.10: Threaded stories	**Suggested age group:** 3-year-olds to 11-year-olds

Explanation:

Threaded stories take the notion of the 'narrative thread' (the story plot), which is evident in virtually all stories, and uses it as a 'literal device' to excite and stimulate children's story writing. *Threaded stories* involve children combining different resources, namely thread (in the form of wool, twine, yarn, cord, string or lace) and pieces of paper or card with holes punched into them (both ends) to physically construct words, sentences and stories. Children are encouraged to use the pieces of paper/card to record parts of their story on (for example marks, individual letters, single words, sentences, or small paragraphs†) which are then physically threaded onto their 'narrative thread' to create a visually appealing *Threaded story*. For valuable information about the narrative thread, see http://tinyurl.com/bl4e6ss.

The brilliance of *Threaded Stories*:

There are many benefits to children creating/writing *Threaded stories*:

1. *Threaded stories* can be used to create a wonderful display of the children's writing.

2. *Threaded stories* promote valuable 'bursts of activity' (Woods, 2003: 3) in the form of fine motor skill development, e.g. operating hole-punches effectively, threading paper/card onto the 'thread', shaping the paper/card with scissors.

3. Children learn to develop a real sense of plot structure when writing a *Threaded story* – 'what [has to] happen . . . first, second, and third? What would happen if we tried to change the order?' (Norton, 1992: 254).

4. *Threaded stories* appeal to both genders if the pieces of paper/card are shaped into items of interest to them or are linked to the story they are writing, e.g. *footballs, bags, wizard hats, shoes, stars, dogs, CDs, TV screens*.

5. *Threaded stories* can be written individually, in a pair or in a small group. They can be written as a whole class, as part of a focused adult-led task or as a child-initiated activity.

†*Threaded stories* for different ages:

- 3–5: Threading individual letters to form words (*b-u-g*) or single words onto string to form sentences e.g. *Harry-went-to-the-shops-for-some-sweets* (see Appendix 30, p. 237).

- 5–7: Threading simple sentences together to create small paragraphs or a complete short story.

- 7–11: Threading paragraphs or chapters together to create extended pieces of story writing (large paper/card and long 'thread' may therefore be needed!).

The *Three-Word-Story-Thread*!:

Here is a great bit of fun! Get children to add only *three words* to initiate or continue a *Threaded story*. For example:

> *One hot day . . . Jamie and Claire . . . took a trip . . . to the local . . . zoo and saw . . . a sweaty monkey . . . rubbing ice-cream on . . . his hairy bottom!* (Amy and Claire, both 6 years old)

The story could be created verbally or in written form. The story could be generated 'against the clock' or be developed over a period of time, e.g. a lesson or a couple of days.

Appendices

Appendix no.	Story Idea	Details	Page
1	*Shaped stories*	Potential shapes for shaped paper	207
2	*Living room stories*	Story spinners: *main characters* and *settings*	208
3	*Living room stories*	Story spinners: *problems* and *endings*	209
4	*Living room stories*	Story spinners: *blank templates*	210
5	*Garden stories*	Story steppers: *examples*	211
6	*Garden stories*	Story stepper: *blank template*	212
7	*Box stories*	Blank template – *example*	213
8	*Moving stories*	Moving parts – *examples*	214
9	*Construction stories*	Building blocks story templates	215
10	*Construction stories*	Characters' physical features	216
11	*Celebrity stories*	Ridiculous rumours (*speech bubbles*) and the thoughts of those who hear them (*thought bubbles*) templates	217
12	*Tall stories*	Adjective alphabet	218
13	*Tall stories*	Noun/verb/adverb/Setting alphabet log	219
14	*TV stories*	Old-style TV writing template	220
15	*Scroll stories*	Scroll template for 3–5 mark-making	221
16	*Either–Or stories*	A simple example of an *Either–Or story*	222
17	*Calendar stories*	Days of the week story planner	223
18	*Calendar stories*	One monthly story planner	224
19	Calendar stories	Months of the year story planner	225
20	*Carpet stories*	Carpet template – *example*	226
21	*Playground stories*	Hop-scotch writing template	227
22	*Lunchtime stories*	Story planner – *milkshake cup*	228
23	*Superhero stories*	KERPOW! writing template	229
24	*Flip-flap stories*	Examples of different flaps	230
25	*Domino stories*	Example of a domino story	231–32
26	*Domino stories*	Blank domino templates	233
27	*Window stories*	Window page template	234
28	*Speech stories*	Speech bubbles	235
29	*Squigglehop stories*	Story sticks	236

30	*Threaded stories*	Threaded story example and templates	237
31	*Not applicable*	Development statements for writing (EYFS – DfE, 2012a) – 40 to 60+ months – and links to appropriate *Getting Children Writing* Ideas.	238
32	*Not applicable*	Draft programme of study statements for writing (NC – DfE, 2012b) – Years 1 to 6 – and links to appropriate *Getting Children Writing* Ideas.	239–42

Appendix 1

Idea: *Shaped stories*   **Potential shapes for shaped paper**

Appendix 2

Idea: *Living Room stories*   **Story spinners:** *main characters* **and** *settings*

Main Characters: *example*

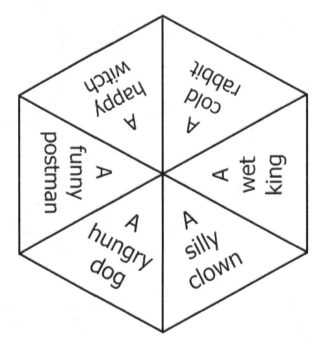

Settings: *example*

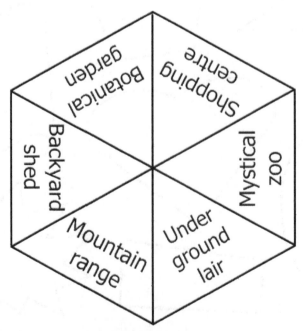

Appendix 3

Idea: *Living Room stories*   **Story spinners:** *problems* **and** *endings*

Problems: *example*

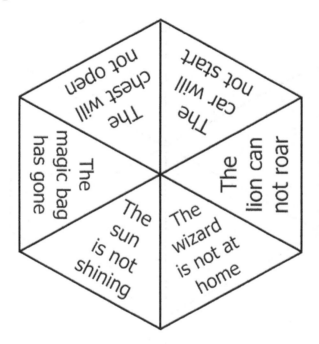

Endings: *example*

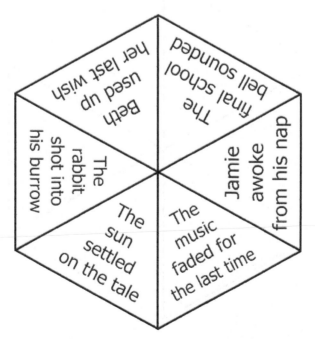

Appendix 4

Idea: *Living Room stories*   **Story spinners:** *blank templates*

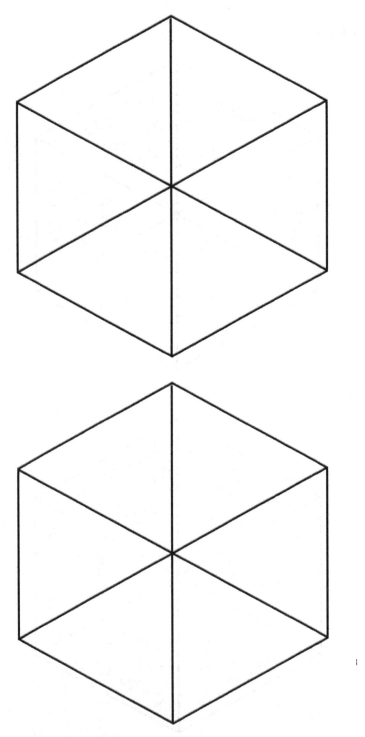

Appendix 5

Idea: *Garden stories* Story steppers: *examples*

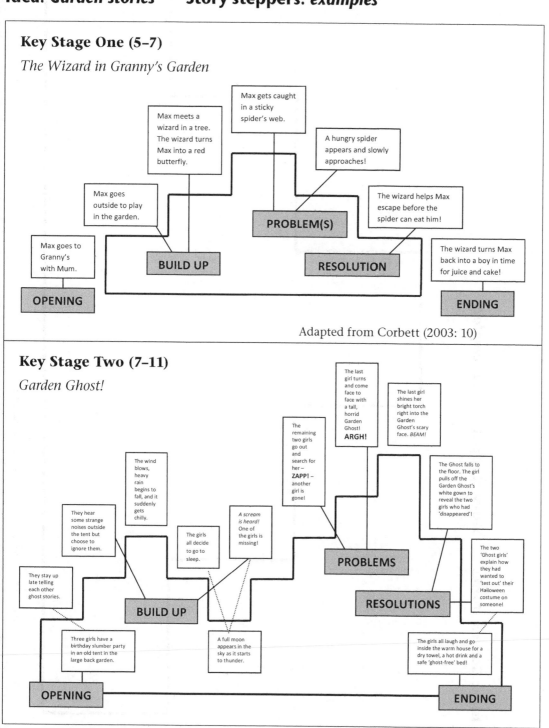

Key Stage One (5–7)

The Wizard in Granny's Garden

Max gets caught in a sticky spider's web.

Max meets a wizard in a tree. The wizard turns Max into a red butterfly.

A hungry spider appears and slowly approaches!

The wizard helps Max escape before the spider can eat him!

Max goes outside to play in the garden.

PROBLEM(S)

Max goes to Granny's with Mum.

BUILD UP

RESOLUTION

The wizard turns Max back into a boy in time for juice and cake!

OPENING

ENDING

Adapted from Corbett (2003: 10)

Key Stage Two (7–11)

Garden Ghost!

The last girl turns and come face to face with a tall, horrid Garden Ghost! **ARGH!**

The last girl shines her bright torch right into the Garden Ghost's scary face. *BEAM!*

The remaining two girls go out and search for her – **ZAPP!** – another girl is gone!

The wind blows, heavy rain begins to fall, and it suddenly gets chilly.

The Ghost falls to the floor. The girl pulls off the Garden Ghost's white gown to reveal the two girls who had 'disappeared'!

They hear some strange noises outside the tent but choose to ignore them.

A scream is heard! One of the girls is missing!

The girls all decide to go to sleep.

They stay up late telling each other ghost stories.

PROBLEMS

The two 'Ghost girls' explain how they had wanted to 'test out' their Halloween costume on someone!

BUILD UP

RESOLUTIONS

Three girls have a birthday slumber party in an old tent in the large back garden.

A full moon appears in the sky as it starts to thunder.

The girls all laugh and go inside the warm house for a dry towel, a hot drink and a safe 'ghost-free' bed!

OPENING

ENDING

Appendix 6

Idea: *Garden stories* **Story stepper: *blank template***

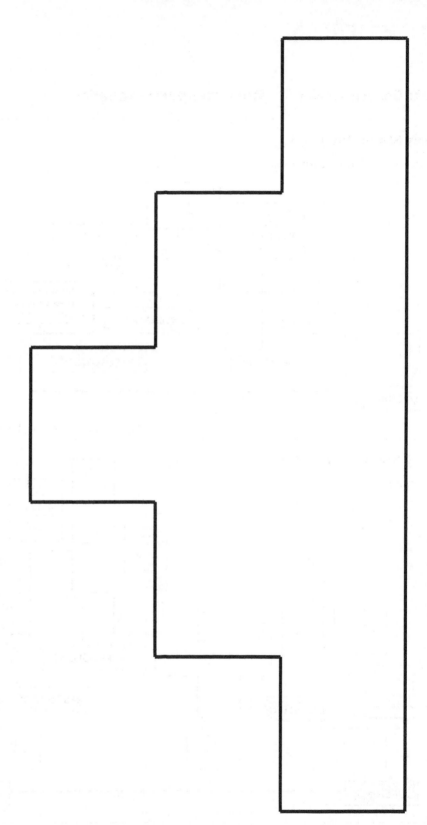

Appendix 7

Idea: Box stories   Blank template – example

START

Appendix 8

Idea: *Moving stories*   Moving parts – *examples*

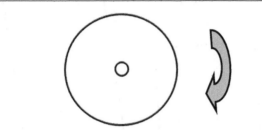
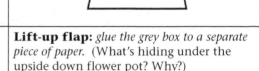

Wheel: *insert a paper fastener through the middle of the cut-out circle to another piece of paper to allow it to rotate.* (Which form of transport is the wheel(s) attached to?)	**Lift-up flap:** *glue the grey box to a separate piece of paper.* (What's hiding under the upside down flower pot? Why?)

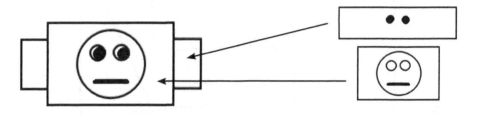

Left and right tab: *pull the thin tab behind the cut out eyeholes to make the character look left and right.* (Who is the character looking for? Is the character nervous or worried? Are they acting shifty?)

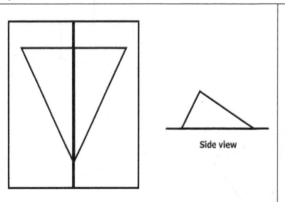
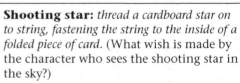

Pop-up 'pyramid': *glue a triangular shaped piece of paper (with tabs) inside a folded piece of card – decorate the 'pyramid' with items that 'appear' in the story, e.g. flowers, hats, shoes, footballs, clothes, pencils, surprise party guests,* **RARRRR!** *('tiger-talk').*	**Shooting star:** *thread a cardboard star on to string, fastening the string to the inside of a folded piece of card.* (What wish is made by the character who sees the shooting star in the sky?)

Appendix 9

Idea: *Construction stories*   Building blocks story templates

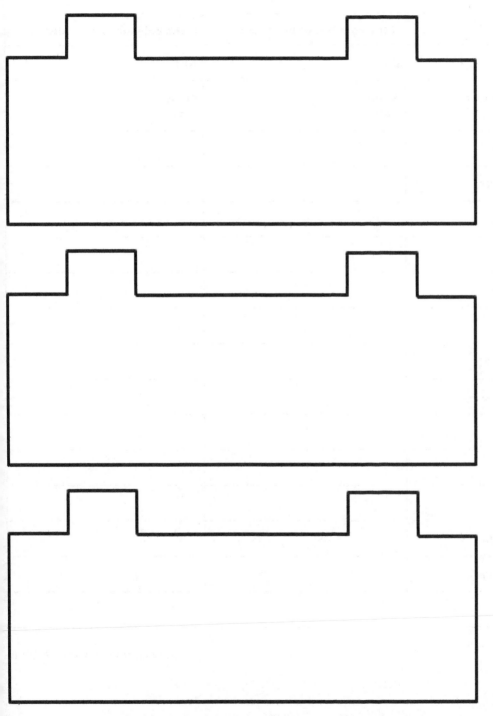

Appendix 10

Idea: *Construction stories*   ***Characters' physical features***

Feature	If the coin lands on 'Heads' . . .	If the coin lands on 'Tails' . . .
Gender	**Boy**	**Girl**
Age of character	**Adult** **Older**	**Child** **Younger**
Face shape		
Colour of skin		
Type of skin		
Hair colour		
Hair length		
Eye colour		
Type of nose		
Mouth shape		
Teeth type		
Size of ears		
Body shape		
Finger length		
Length of legs		
Size of feet		

(Adapted from Bowkett, 2001: 6)

Appendix 11

Idea: *Celebrity stories*

Ridiculous rumours (*speech bubbles*) and the thoughts of those who hear them (*thought bubbles*) templates

Appendix 12

Idea: *Tall stories*   **Adjective alphabet**

Aa	Angry				
Bb	Beautiful				
Cc	Careful				
Dd	Dangerous				
Ee	Energetic				
Ff	Fiery				
Gg	Gigantic				
Hh	Helpful				
Ii	Icky				
Jj	Jazzy				
Kk	Keen				
Ll	Long				
Mm	Moody				
Nn	Naughty				
Oo	Optimistic				
Pp	Pathetic				
Qq	Quirky				
Rr	Restless				
Ss	Slippery				
Tt	Trendy				
Uu	Ugly				
Vv	Venomous				
Ww	Wishy-washy				
Xx	Xanthic				
Yy	Yummy				
Zz	Zany				

Appendix 13

Idea: *Tall stories*   **Noun/verb/adverb/setting alphabet log**

Aa				
Bb				
Cc				
Dd				
Ee				
Ff				
Gg				
Hh				
Ii				
Jj				
Kk				
Ll				
Mm				
Nn				
Oo				
Pp				
Qq				
Rr				
Ss				
Tt				
Uu				
Vv				
Ww				
Xx				
Yy				
Zz				

Appendix 14

Idea: *TV stories*   **Old-style TV writing template**

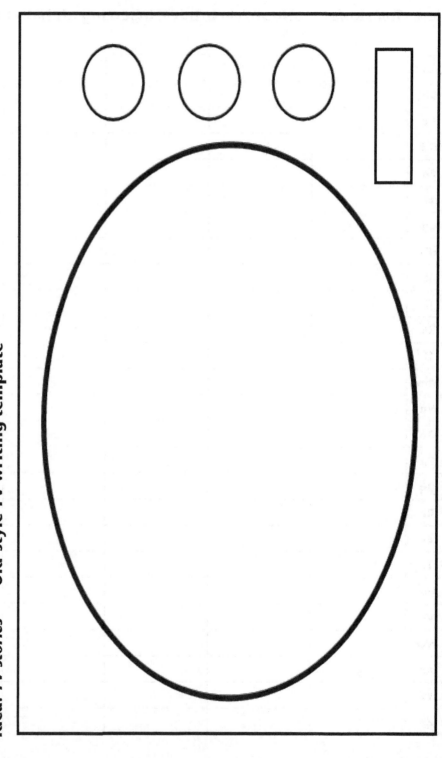

Appendix 15

Idea: *Scroll stories*   **Scroll template for 3–5 mark-making**

Appendix 16

Idea: *Either–Or stories*   A simple example of an *Either–Or story*

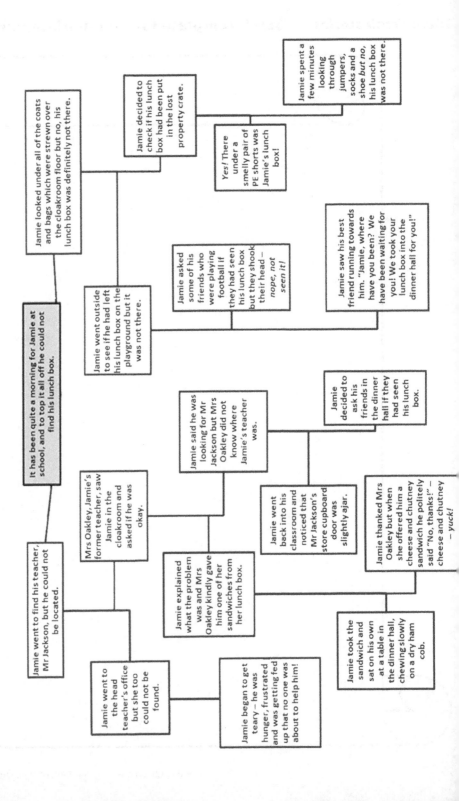

It has been quite a morning for Jamie at school, and to top it all off he could not find his lunch box.

Jamie went to find his teacher, Mr Jackson, but he could not be located.

Jamie looked under all of the coats and bags which were strewn over the cloakroom floor but no, his lunch box was definitely not there.

Jamie decided to check if his lunch box had been put in the lost property crate.

Yes! There under a smelly pair of PE shorts was Jamie's lunch box!

Jamie spent a few minutes looking through jumpers, socks and a shoe *but no,* his lunch box was not there.

Jamie went outside to see if he had left his lunch box on the playground but it was not there.

Jamie asked some of his friends who were playing football if they had seen his lunch box but they shook their head – *nope, not seen it!*

Jamie saw his best friend running towards him. "Jamie, where have you been? We have been waiting for you! We took your lunch box into the dinner hall for you!"

Mrs Oakley, Jamie's former teacher, saw Jamie in the cloakroom and asked if he was okay.

Jamie said he was looking for Mr Jackson but Mrs Oakley did not know where Jamie's teacher was.

Jamie decided to ask his friends in the dinner hall if they had seen his lunch box.

Jamie went to the head teacher's office but she too could not be found.

Jamie explained what the problem was and Mrs Oakley kindly gave him one of her sandwiches from her lunch box.

Jamie went back into his classroom and noticed that Mr Jackson's store cupboard door was slightly ajar.

Jamie thanked Mrs Oakley but when she offered him a cheese and chutney sandwich he politely said "No, thanks!" – cheese and chutney – *yuck!*

Jamie began to get teary – he was hungry, frustrated and was getting fed up that no one was about to help him!

Jamie took the sandwich and sat on his own at a table in the dinner hall, chewing slowly on a dry ham cob.

Appendix 17

Idea: *Calendar stories*   **Days of the week story planner**

Month:	Week No.: (*please circle*) 1 2 3 4 5
Day	**Event(s)**
Monday	
Tuesday	
Wednesday	
Thursday	
Friday	
Saturday	
Sunday	

Appendix 18

Idea: *Calendar stories* — **One monthly story planner**

Month: (*please circle*) January February March April May June July August September October November December

	Sunday	Monday	Tuesday	Wednesday	Thursday	Friday	Saturday
Week 1			1	2	3	4	5
Week 2	6	7	8	9	10	11	12
Week 3	13	14	15	16	17	18	19
Week 4	20	21	22	23	24	25	26
Week 5	27	28	29	30	31		
	Sunday	Monday	Tuesday	Wednesday	Thursday	Friday	Saturday

Appendix 19

Idea: *Calendar stories*   Months of the year story planner

Year:	
Month	**Event(s)**
January	
February	
March	
April	
May	
June	
July	
August	
September	
October	
November	
December	

Appendix 20

Idea: *Carpet stories* **Carpet template – *example***

Alternative! Hole punch down the 'tassel' sides of the template and thread through/fasten small pieces of wool to represent 'real' tassels.

Getting Children Writing, SAGE Publications Ltd, © Simon Brownhill, 2013

Appendix 21

Idea: *Playground stories*   **Hop-scotch writing template**

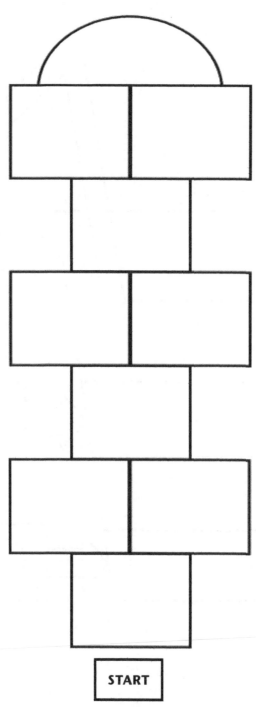

Appendix 22

Idea: *Lunchtime stories*   **Story planner – *milkshake cup***

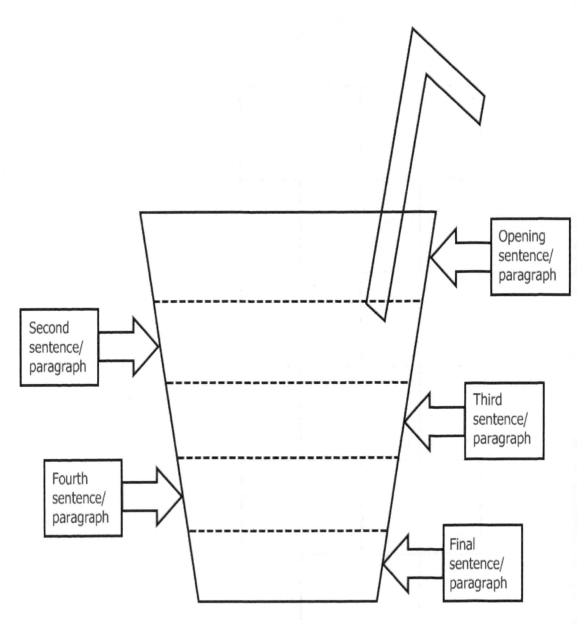

Appendix 23

Idea: *Superhero stories* **KERPOW! writing template**

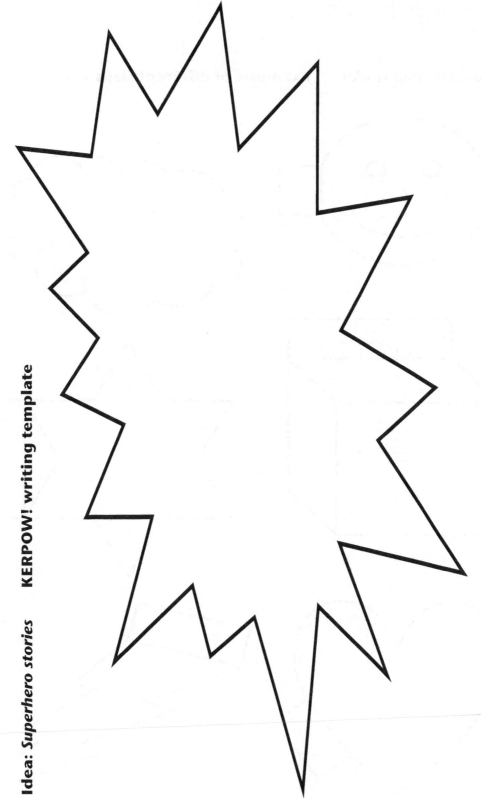

Appendix 24

Idea: *Flip-flap stories*   **Examples of different flaps**

Appendix 25

Idea: *Domino stories*   **Example of a domino story**

★ *Grumble!* Harry woke up to the sound of a loud rumbling in his tummy! *Grumble!*	'Time for breakfast!' though Harry to himself as he jumped out of bed and headed for the kitchen. *Grumble!*
"I'm going to have a huge bowl of cereal!' said Harry as he reached out for a big bowl and spoon. *Grumble!*	But when Harry opened the cupboard door there was no cereal to be found! *Grumble!*
When Harry opened the fridge it was empty! *Grumble!*	When Harry opened the bread bin there was nothing but a few crumbs! *Grumble!*
When Harry opened the freezer there was just cold air and ice! *Grumble!*	When Harry looked in the pantry there were just bare shelves! *Grumble!*
When Harry looked in the fruit bowl there was nothing but the bottom of the bowl! *Grumble!*	When Harry looked over to the kitchen table there was only an empty flower vase! *Grumble!*

When Harry looked in the cupboard under the stairs there was nothing but old magazines! *Grumble!*

When Harry looked in the kitchen drawers there was nothing but plastic food bags! *Grumble!*

Harry scratched his head – it seemed as if the family had eaten everything! *Grumble!*

When Harry looked in the garage there was nothing in the food storage unit! *Grumble!*

Suddenly Harry heard a car pull up on the drive. He looked out of the garage window. *Grumble!*

In the car were Mum, Dad and sister Suzie, surrounded by enormous bags of food shopping! *Grumble!*

'Come and help us unpack!' said Mum to Harry as she waddled with several heavy bags through the hall and into the kitchen. *Grumble!*

'Why is there no food in the house?' asked Harry as Dad and Suzie puffed and panted their way into the kitchen with more food bags.

'We've been on holiday for the last four weeks, silly!' said Suzie. 'Don't you remember?'

'Oh yes!' said Harry. 'Sorry! My tummy was doing all the thinking!' *Grumble!*

Appendix 26

Idea: *Domino stories*   **Blank domino templates**

Appendix 27

Idea: *Window stories*　　Window page template

NOTE! *Do not* cut along the continuous **black** line otherwise you will cut the window shutter off the page – just *fold* along this line. Glue *this side* of the page (the outside edge of the window frame) to the separate 'reveal' page so that these notes are hidden from view.

SUGGESTION! *Windows of different sizes/shapes can be cut into window pages with the support of adults for younger children as appropriate.*

Getting Children Writing, SAGE Publications Ltd, © Simon Brownhill, 2013

Appendix 28

Idea: *Speech stories*   **Speech bubbles**

Appendix 29

Idea: *Squigglehop stories*   Story sticks

Photocopy this page onto thick card and cut out the 'sticks' below (lengthwise) as a resource to offer ideas to stimulate children's story writing, storing them in a suitable pot. 'Colour' the end*, using the colours suggested below, so that children can select the stick appropriate to their writing needs:

Green: Characters	**Blue:** Settings	**Red:** Problem	**Green:** Solution	**Orange:** Ending

Alternatives to the 'card' sticks include writing on lollipop sticks, splints, or drinking straws. Encourage children to create their own story sticks, adding suggestions to the back of the sticks they create.

*

	Character	A wrinkly old man	A tiny, friendly dragon
	Character	A burnt fish	A sweaty runner
	Setting	Under the sea	A horrid hotel
	Setting	In the shopping centre	At a theme park
	Problem	A key was lost	The mobile phone got broken
	Problem	A ring was stolen	Someone caught the measles
	Solution	The sun came out	The baby fell asleep
	Solution	The cream made the pain go away	The team game brought everyone together
	Ending	They fell in love	There was a surprise party
	Ending	The lesson had been learned	The battle was over

Appendix 30

Idea: *Threaded stories*   **Threaded story example and templates**

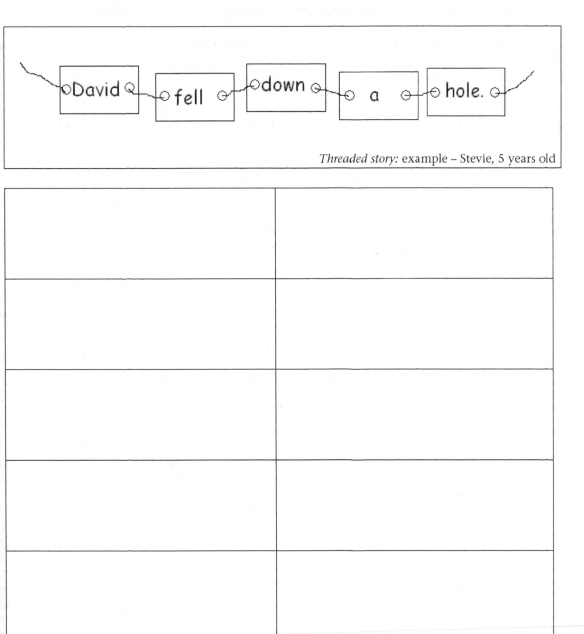

Threaded story: example – Stevie, 5 years old

NOTE: To be photocopied onto card and cut out. Holes to be punched out at each end.

Appendix 31

Development statements for writing (EYFS – DfE, 2012a) – 40 to 60+ months – and links to appropriate *Getting Children Writing* Ideas

Age/stage bands	Development statement (see DfE, 2012a: 31)	Supporting Ideas		
30–50 months	Sometimes gives meaning to marks as they draw and paint.	*Bedroom stories*	*Decorated stories*	*Weathered stories*
	Ascribes meanings to marks that they see in different places.	*Me stories*	*Paint stories*	*Pet stories*
40–60+ months	Gives meaning to marks they make as they draw, write and paint.	*Sized stories*	*Kitchen stories*	*Party stories*
	Begins to break the flow of speech into words.	*Construction stories*	*Fabric stories*	*Clothing stories*
	Continues a rhyming string.	*Bathroom stories*	*Mum stories*	*Free stories*
	Hears and says the initial sound in words.	*Pet stories*	*Table-top stories*	*Superhero stories*
	Can segment the sounds in simple words and blend them together.	A learning and teaching strategy which is considered to be integral to children's (4–5) effective engagement with the 'written' aspect of all of the story ideas advocated for 3–5-year-olds in this book.		
	Links sounds to letters, naming and sounding the letters of the alphabet.	*Box stories*	*Dad stories*	*Hat stories*
	Uses some clearly identifiable letters to communicate meaning, representing some sounds correctly and in sequence.	*Unfolded stories*	*Crazy stories*	*Scroll stories*
	Writes own name and other things such as labels, captions.	*Baby stories*	*Free stories*	*Chain stories*
	Attempts to write short sentences in meaningful contexts.	*Calendar stories*	*Superhero stories*	*Threaded stories*
	Early Learning Goal: Children use their phonic knowledge to write words in ways which match their spoken sounds. They also write some irregular common words. They write simple sentences which can be read by themselves and others. Some words are spelt correctly and others are phonetically plausible.	*Tactile stories*	*Crafty stories*	*ICT stories*
		See the introductions for Chapters 3 and 8 (pp. 66–70 and 155–158) for further support and guidance with regard to phonics and spellings for 3–5-year-olds.		

Appendix 32

Draft programme of study statements for writing (NC – DfE, 2012b) – Years 1 to 6 – and links to appropriate *Getting Children Writing* Ideas

Year 1

Dimension	PoS statement	Supporting aspects of the book		
Transcription – Spelling Pupils should be taught to:	• spell: a, b, and c. [23]	See the introduction to Chapter 8 (p. 153).		
	• name the letters of the alphabet: *a and b.* [24]	Teachers are able to use *any* of the age-appropriate ideas offered in this book to work towards these PoS statements through their taught input.		
	• add prefixes and suffixes: *a, b and c.* [25]			
	• apply simple spelling rules and guidelines, as listed in Appendix 1. [26]			
	• write from memory simple sentences dictated by the teacher that include words taught so far. [27]	*Assembly stories*		
Transcription – Handwriting Pupils should be taught to:	• sit correctly at a table, holding a pencil comfortably and correctly. [28]	See the introduction to Chapter 4 (p. 83).		
	• begin to form lower-case letters in the correct direction, starting and finishing in the right place. [29]	*Penned stories* *Upside-down stories*		
	• form capital letters. [30]			
	• form digits 0–9. [31]			
	• understand which letters belong to which handwriting 'families' (i.e. letters that are formed in similar ways) and to practise these. [32]			
Composition Pupils should be taught to:	• write sentences by: *a, b, c and d.* [39]	*Scroll stories*	*Construction stories*	*ICT stories*
	• discuss what they have written with the teacher or other pupils. [40]	Teachers are able to use *any* of the age-appropriate ideas offered in this book to work towards this PoS statements post-writing.		
	• read aloud their writing clearly enough to be heard by their peers and the teacher. [41]	Teachers are able to use *any* of the age-appropriate ideas offered in this book to work towards this PoS statement both during the writing and after its completion.		
Composition – Grammar and punctuation Pupils should be taught to:	• understand how spoken language can be represented in writing by: *a, b, c and d.* [42]	*Construction stories*	*Toy stories*	*Superhero stories*
	• use the grammatical terminology in Appendix 2 in discussing their writing. [43]	Teachers are encouraged to emphasise this terminology through their direct teaching as they engage children in age-appropriate ideas.		
		Slapstick stories		

See DfE (2012b: 7–9) for details regarding the alphabet bullet points.

Year 2

Dimension	PoS statement	Supporting aspects of the book		
Transcription – Spelling Pupils should be taught to:	• spell by: *a, b, c, d, and e.* [68]	See the introduction to Chapter 8 (p. 153. Teachers are able to use **any** of the age-appropriate ideas offered in this book to work towards these PoS statements during their taught input.		
	• add suffixes to spell longer words, e.g. *–ment, –ness, –ful* and *–less*. [69]			
	• apply spelling rules and guidelines, as listed in Appendix 1. [70]			
	• write from memory simple sentences dictated by the teacher that include words and punctuation taught so far. [71]			
Transcription – Handwriting Pupils should be taught to:	• form lower-case letters of the correct size relative to one another. [72]	See the introduction to Chapter 4 (p. 83). ***Penned stories*** ***Upside-down stories***		
	• start using some of the diagonal and horizontal strokes needed to join letters and understand which letters, when adjacent to one another, are best left unjoined. [73]			
	• write capital letters and digits of the correct size, orientation and relationship to one another and to lower case letters. [74]			
	• use spacing between words that reflects the size of the letters. [75]			
Composition Pupils should be taught to:	• develop positive attitudes towards and stamina for writing by: *a, b and c.* [80]	***Body stories*** ***Extended stories***	***Bedroom stories***	***Gamed stories***
	• consider what they are going to write before beginning by: *a, b and c.* [81]	***Living room stories***	***Sweet stories***	***Lunchtime stories***
	• make simple additions, revisions and corrections to their own writing by: *a, b and c.* [82]	***ICT stories***	***Chase stories***	***Collaborative stories***
	• read aloud what they have written with appropriate intonation to make the meaning clear. [83]	Teachers are able to use **any** of the age-appropriate ideas offered in this book to work towards this PoS statement both during the writing of the story and following its completion.		
Composition – Grammar and punctuation Pupils should be taught to:	• understand how spoken language can be represented in writing by: *a, b and c.* [84]	***Construction stories***	***Slapstick stories***	***Punctuation stories***
	• use and understand the grammatical terminology in Appendix 2 in discussing their writing. [85]	Teachers are encouraged to emphasise this terminology through their direct teaching as they engage children in age-appropriate ideas.		

See DfE (2012b: 12–14) for details regarding the alphabet bullet points.

Years 3 to 4

Dimension	PoS statement	Supporting aspects of the book		
Transcription – Spelling Pupils should be taught to:	• use further prefixes and suffixes and understand how to add them (see Appendix 1). [103]	See the introduction to Chapter 8 (p. 153).		
	• spell further homophones. [104]			
	• spell words that are often misspelt (see Appendix 1). [105]			
	• write from memory simple sentences, dictated by the teacher, that include words and punctuation taught so far. [106]			
Transcription – Handwriting Pupils should be taught to:	• use the diagonal and horizontal strokes that are needed to join letters and understand which letters, when adjacent to one another, are best left unjoined. [107]	See the introduction to Chapter 4 (p. 83). ***Penned stories***		
	• increase the legibility and quality of their handwriting, e.g. by ensuring that the downstrokes of letters are parallel and equidistant; that lines of writing are spaced sufficiently so that the ascenders and descenders of letters do not touch. [108]			
Composition Pupils should be taught to:	• plan their writing by: *a and b*. [113]	***Sized stories***	***Garden stories***	***Box stories***
	• draft and write by: *a, b, c, d and e*. [114]	***Twist stories***	***Mum stories***	***Weathered stories***
	• evaluate and edit by: *a and b*. [115]	***Technological stories***	***CD/DVD stories***	***Local area stories***
	• proof-read for spelling and punctuation errors. [116]	Teachers are able to use ***any*** of the age-appropriate ideas offered in this book to work towards this PoS statement following the completion of the initial draft.		
	• read aloud their own writing, to a group or the whole class, using appropriate intonation and controlling tone and volume so that the meaning is clear. [117]	Teachers are able to use ***any*** of the age-appropriate ideas offered in this book to work towards this PoS statement both during the writing of the story and after its completion.		
Composition – Grammar and punctuation Pupils should be taught to:	• develop their understanding of how spoken language differs from and can be represented in writing by: *a, b, c, d, e and f*. [118]	***Tactile stories***	***Junk stories***	***Speech stories***
	• indicate grammatical and other features by: *a, b and c*. [119]	***Threaded stories***	***Punctuation stories***	***Silly stories***
	• use and understand the grammatical terminology in Appendix 2 accurately and appropriately when discussing their writing and reading. [120]	Teachers are encouraged to emphasise this terminology through their direct teaching as they engage children in age-appropriate ideas.		

See DfE (2012b: 17–19) for details regarding the alphabet bullet points.

Years 5 to 6

Dimension	PoS Statement	Supporting aspects of the book		
Transcription – *Spelling* Pupils should be taught to:	• *a* (further prefixes and suffixes), *b* (spelling words with 'silent' letters), *c* (distinguishing between homophones and other words which are often confused), *d* (use knowledge of morphology and etymology), *e* (use of dictionaries), *f* (use of first 3 or 4 letters of a word to look up words in a dictionary) and *g* (use a thesaurus). [142]	See the introduction to Chapter 8 (p. 153).		
Transcription – *Handwriting and presentation* Pupils should be taught to:	• use write legibly, fluently, with increasing speed and personal style by: *a and b.* [143]	See the introduction to Chapter 4 (p. 83). ***Penned stories***		
Composition Pupils should be taught to:	• plan their writing by: *a, b and c.* [147]	***Sized stories***	***Garden stories***	***Lunchtime stories***
	• draft and write by: *a, b, c and d* [148]	***TV stories***	***Either–Or stories***	***Calendar stories***
	• evaluate and edit by: *a, b, c, d and e.* [149]	***Technological stories***	***Internet stories***	***Networking stories***
	• proof-read for spelling and punctuation errors. [150]	***Booked stories***	***Punctuation stories***	***Collaboration stories***
	• perform their own compositions, using appropriate intonation and volume so that meaning is clear. [151]	Teachers are able to use *any* of the age-appropriate Ideas offered in this book to towards this PoS statement following the production of the 'best version' of the story.		
Composition – *Grammar and punctuation* Pupils should be taught to:	• understand how spoken language can be represented in writing by: *a, b, c, d and e.* [152]	***Speech stories***	***Framed stories***	***Squigglehop stories***
	• indicate grammatical and other features by: *a, b, c, d and e.* [153]	***Punctuation stories***	***Jigsaw stories***	***Chase stories***
	• use and understand the grammatical terminology in Appendix 2 accurately and appropriately when discussing their writing and reading. [154]	Teachers are encouraged to emphasise this terminology through their direct teaching as they engage children in age-appropriate Ideas.		

See DfE (2012b: 22–24) for details regarding the alphabet bullet points.

References

@k_ferrell (2012) *8 Great Sites for Reluctant Writers*. [Online]. Available at: http://tinyurl.com/dxnlcgs (Accessed: 17 June 2012).

Adams, P. (2011) *Eight Types of Friendship*. [Online]. Available at: www.thinkoutsidein.com/blog/2010/04/eight-types-of-friendship/ (Accessed: 13 September 2011).

Ahde, P. (2007) *Appropriation by Adornments – Personalization Makes the Everyday Life More Pleasant*. [Online]. Available at: http://128.214.123.83/blogs/pahde/wp-content/uploads/2009/06/p_ahde_dppi.pdf (Accessed: 14 January 2012).

Albert, A. and Kormos, J. (2004) Creativity and narrative task performance: An exploratory study. *Language Learning*, 54, 277–310.

Alborough, J. (1998) *Washing Line*. London: Walker Books.

Alexander, J. and Griffith, J. (n.d.) *Exploring Flow Charts as a Tool for Thinking*. [Online]. Available at: http://tinyurl.com/7k27ahn (Accessed: 18 May 2012).

All-Party Parliamentary Group for Education (2011) *Report of the Inquiry into Overcoming the Barriers to Literacy*. [Online]. Available at: www.educationappg.org.uk/wp-content/uploads/2011/07/APPG-for-Education-Literacy-Inquiry-final-report.pdf (Accessed: 16 July 2012).

Allon, H. and Zehavi, L. (2004) *The Mystery of the Dead Sea Scrolls*. Philadelphia, PA: Jewish Publication Society.

Amin, R. H. (2011) *10 Tips for Writing (an Arabic) Children's Book from Rania Hussein Amin*. [Online]. Available at: http://readkutubkids.wordpress.com/2011/06/26/10-tips-for-writing-an-arabic-childrens-book-from-rania-hussein-amin/ (Accessed: 7 August 2011).

Anders, C. J. (2009) *What's The Difference Between Story And Plot?* [Online].

Available at: http://io9.com/5197310/whats-the-difference-between-story-and-plot (Accessed: 14 May 2012).

Andrews, C. (2008) The benefits of introducing young children to ICT. *Early Years Update*, February. [Online]. Available at: www.teachingexpertise. com/articles/the-benefits-of-introducing-young-children-to-ict-3072 (Accessed: 20 May 2012).

Angelillo, J. (2006) *A Study Guide for A Fresh Approach to Teaching Punctuation*. [Online]. Available at: http://teacher.scholastic.com/ products/scholasticprofessional/authors/pdfs/SG_Fresh_Punctuation. pdf (Accessed: 19 March 2012).

Anholt, L. and Robins, A. (1999) *Seriously Silly Stories: The Collection*. London: Orchard Books.

Anonymous (2012) *Ideas for Developing Writing in Your Setting*. [Online]. Available at: http://tinyurl.com/bqdcaho (Accessed: 14 April 2012).

APA (American Psychological Association) (2010) *Today's Superheroes Send Wrong Message to Boys, Say Researchers*. 15th August. [Online]. Available at: www.apa.org/news/press/releases/2010/08/macho-stereotype-unhealthy.aspx (Accessed: 7 June 2012).

APSE (n.d.) *'Getting the Most Out of Lunchtimes at School' Mid-day Supervisor Training: Information Pack for Schools and Local Authorities*. [Online]. Available at: www.apse.org.uk/lifelong-learning/pdfs/information%20 pack%20for%20schools.pdf (Accessed: 8 April 2012).

Arkin, D. (2010) *8 Tips for Writing Flash Fiction*. [Online]. Available at: http://fspressonline.org/8-ips-for-writing-flash-fiction/ (Accessed: 5 January 2012).

Armstrong, M. (2006) *Children Writing Stories*. Maidenhead: Open University Press.

Arthur, J., Grainger, T. and Wray. D. (eds) *Learning to Teach in the Primary School*. London: Routledge. pp. 209–225.

ASC (Australian Sports Commission) (2011) *Good News Stories about the Benefits of Sport*. [Online]. Available at: http://ausport.gov.au/ information/asc_research/publications/children/agood_newsa_stories_ about_the_benefits_of_sport (Accessed: 20 October 2011).

Ashley, M. (2002) *Role Models, Classroom Leadership and the Gendered Battle for Hearts and Minds*. [Online]. Available at: www.leeds.ac.uk/educol/ documents/00002244.htm (Accessed: 12 July 2011).

Asquith, R. and McEwen, K. (2005) *Pass the Parcel*. London: HarperCollins Children's Books.

Atkinson, C. (2004) *Colours for Living and Learning*. [Online]. Available at: www.resene.co.nz/homeown/use_colr/coloursforliving.htm (Accessed: 2 July 2011).

Babauta, L. (2012) *31 Ways to Find Inspiration for Your Writing*. [Online].

Available at: http://writetodone.com/2008/03/03/31-ways-to-find-inspiration-for-your-writing/ (Accessed: 27 January 2012).

Badger, R. and White, G. (2000) A process genre approach to teaching writing. *ELT Journal*, 54 (2), 153–60. [Online]. Available at: http://newresearch.wikispaces.com/file/view/genre+process+approach.pdf (Accessed: 22 July 2012).

Bailey, M., O'Grady-Jones, M. and McGown, L. (1995) *The Impact of Integrating Visuals in an Elementary Creative Writing Process.* [Online]. Available at: www.eric.ed.gov/ERICWebPortal/contentdelivery/servlet/ERICServlet?accno=ED391492 (Accessed: 14 January 2012).

Bainbridge, C. (2012) *Generating Story Ideas.* [Online]. Available at: http://giftedkids.about.com/od/nurturinggiftsandtalents/a/Generating-Story-Ideas.htm (Accessed: 28 May 2012).

Baird, T., Bedall, B., Mathews, M. and Meador, S. (2003) *Pre-K and Kindergarten Handwriting Resource.* Frederick, MD: Frederick County Public Schools. [Online]. Available at: www.minisink.com/fileadmin/user_upload/es/Handwriting.pdf (Accessed: 30 August 2012).

Baker, J. (2002) *Window.* London: Walker Books.

Baleghizadeh, S. and Darghai, Z. (2011) The use of different spelling strategies among EFL young learners. *Porta Linguarum*, 15, 151–9. [Online]. Available at: www.ugr.es/~portalin/articulos/PL_numero15/8.%20SASAN%20BALEGHIZADEH.pdf (Accessed: 9 June 2012).

Bammens, C. (2009) The importance of story in children's education, *The Plymouth Student Educator*, 1 (1), 46–50.

Barker, J. (2010) 'Manic Mums' and 'Distant Dads'? Gendered geographies of care and the journey to school. *Health and Place*, 17 (2), 413–21.

Baron, D. (2009) *A Better Pencil: Readers, Writers, and the Digital Revolution.* New York: Oxford University Press.

Barrett, J. (2011) *The Canterbury Tales Literature Guide.* [Online]. Available at: www.4secondarysolutions.com/v/vspfiles/downloadables/Canterbury%20Sample%20Pages.pdf (Accessed: 2 January 2011).

Barrett, S. (2005) *Understanding the Importance of Environmental Education: An Examination of I Love A Clean San Diego, a Local Environmental Nonprofit.* [Online]. Available at: http://esys.ucsd.edu/internship/images/intern_papers/Barrett_Sabrina.pdf (Accessed: 27 December 2011).

Barrs, M. and Cork, V. (2001) *The Reader in the Writer.* London: Centre for Language in Primary Education.

Baudet, S. (2011) *No Conflict – No Story: Creating Conflict in Children[']s Books.* [Online]. Available at: www.greatvine.com/articles/no-conflict-no-story-creating-conflict-in-childrens-books (Accessed: 22 April 2012).

Baum, L. (2011) *Idea Generation.* [Online]. Available at: http://tinyurl.com/cmyxmfz (Accessed: 22 April 2012).

Baumann, J. F. and Bergeron, B. S. (1993) Story map instruction using children's literature: effects on first graders' comprehension of central narrative elements. *Journal of Literacy Research*, 25 (4), 407–37.

BBC (2001) *2001: The Silly Stories.* 24 December. [Online]. Available at: http://news.bbc.co.uk/1/hi/in_depth/world/2001/review_of_2001/1717873.stm (Accessed: 20 November 2011).

BBC (2008) *Celebrity Culture 'Harms Pupils'.* 14 March. [Online]. Available: http://news.bbc.co.uk/1/hi/7296306.stm (Accessed: 14 June 2012).

Beadle, P. (2007) *Could Do Better! Help Your Kid Shine at School.* London: Doubleday.

Bearne, E. (2007) *Writing.* ITE English: Readings for Discussion. [Online]. Available at: http://tinyurl.com/chbw5em (Accessed: 7 April 2012).

Beauchamp, G. and Parkinson, J. (2005) Beyond the 'wow' factor: developing interactivity with the interactive whiteboard. *School Science Review*, 86 (316), 97–104. [Online]. Available at: http://arrts.gtcni.org.uk/gtcni/bitstream/2428/49478/1/beyond+the+wow+factor.pdf (Accessed: 21 July 2012).

Becker, H. J. (2000) Pedagogical motivations for student computer use that lead to student engagement. *Educational Technology*, 40 (5), 5–17. [Online]. Available at: www.crito.uci.edu/tlc/findings/spec_rpt_pedagogical/ped_mot_pdf.pdf (Accessed: 6 April 2012).

Beckford, M. (2009) *Made-up Words in Winnie the Pooh and Harry Potter 'Help Children Learn English'.* [Online]. Available at: www.telegraph.co.uk/education/educationnews/5236655/Made-up-words-in-Winnie-the-Pooh-and-Harry-Potter-help-children-learn-English.html (Accessed: 16 September 2011).

Bell, J. (2001) Characterization: Introduction. In Bell, J. and Magrs, P. (eds) *The Creative Writing Coursebook: Forty Authors Share Advice and Exercises for Fiction and Poetry.* London: Macmillan.

Bennett, J. (2007) *The Handwriting Pocketbook.* Alresford: Teachers' Pocketbook.

Bensko, T. (2010) *Writing Experimental Fiction: Leaving the Problem Out of the Plot.* [Online]. Available at: www.writing-world.com/fiction/experimental.shtml (Accessed: 22 April 2012).

Bereiter, C. and Scardamalia, M. (1982) From conversation to composition: The role of instruction in a developmental process. pp. 1–64. In Glaser, R. (ed.) *Advances in Instructional Psychology (Vol. 2).* Hillsdale, NJ: Erlbaum.

Bergen, D. (1993) Facilitating friendship development in inclusion classrooms. *Childhood Education*, 69, 234–6.

Bevilacqua, K. (n.d.) *Using the Internet to Motivate Writing.* [Online]. Available at: http://tinyurl.com/n6uyxm (Accessed: 25 November 2011).

Binns, A. (2008) *The Secret of Writing Funny.* [Online]. Available at: http://

writetodone.com/2008/07/30/how-to-write-funny/ (Accessed: 19 November 2011).

Bisset, D. (1987) *Upside Down Stories*. London: Puffin.

Black, M. and Fawcett, B. (2008) *The Last Taboo: Opening the Door on the Global Sanitation Crisis*. London: Earthscan.

Blair, H. A. and Sanford, K. (2004) Morphing literacy: Boys reshaping their school-based literacy practices. *Language Arts*, 81 (6), 452–60.

Blake, M. (2011) *How Not To Write a Sitcom*. London: A&C Black.

Bloxham, A. (2011) 4m children in UK do not own a single book, study finds. *Telegraph*, 5 December. [Online]. Available at: www.telegraph.co.uk/education/educationnews/8934429/4m-children-in-UK-do-not-own-a-single-book-study-finds.html (Accessed: 15 July 2012).

Boehm, D. C. (1993) Mozartians, Beethovians, and the teaching of writing. *The Quarterly*, 15 (2), 15–18. [Online]. Available at: www.nwp.org/cs/public/print/resource/1113 (Accessed: 1 April 2012).

Boeree, C. G. (2003) *Language Development*. [Online]. Available at: http://webspace.ship.Edu/cgboer/langdev.html (Accessed: 17 September 2011).

Bolton, G. (2006) Pictures, coloured paper and pens, buttons and skulls. In Bolton, G., Field, V. and Thompson, K. (eds) *Writing Works: A Resource Handbook for Therapeutic Writing Workshops and Activities*. London: Jessica Kingsley.

Bowan, S. (2003) Handwriting: A key to literacy. *Pen World International*, 17 (3). [Online]. Available at: www.ipena.org/newsletter/a_key_to literacy.html (Accessed: 12 December 2006).

Bower, V. (2011) Enhancing children's writing. In Bower, V. (ed.) *Creative Ways to Teach Literacy: Ideas for Children aged 3 to 11*. London: Sage. [Online]. Available at: www.sagepub.com/upm-data/40593_9780857020468.pdf (Accessed: 8 July 2012).

Bowkett, S. (2001) *What's the Story?* London: A&C Black.

Bowkett, S. (2006) *Boys and Writing*. London: Continuum.

Bowkett, S. (2013) *Get Them Thinking Like Writers!* London: Continuum.

boyd, d. m. and Ellison, N. B. (2007) Social network sites: Definition, history, and scholarship. *Journal of Computer-Mediated Communication*, 13 (1), article 11. [Online]. Available at: http://jcmc.indiana.edu/vol13/issue1/boyd.ellison.html (Accessed: 21 January 2012).

Bramham, P. (2003) Boys, masculinities and PE, sport. *Education and Society*, 8 (1), 57–71.

Briggs, R. (1973) *Jim and the Beanstalk*. London: Puffin.

British Film Institute (2003) *Look Again! A Teaching Guide to Using Film and Television with Three- to Eleven-year-olds*. London: *bfi* Education. [Online]. Available at: www.unicef.org/magic/resources/bfi_Education_LookAgain_TeachingGuide.pdf (Accessed: 23 July 2012).

British Humanist Association (2011) *Ideas for Inclusive Assemblies*. [Online]. Available at: www.humanism.org.uk/education/teachers/ideas-for-inclusive-assemblies (Accessed: 4 December 2011).

Brooks, D. (2011) *Overcoming Word Blindness (Severe Dyslexia): Teaching Children to Read*. [Online]. Available at: http://tinyurl.com/8ffwlo6 (Accessed: 6 April 2012).

Browne, A. (2003) *My Dad*. London: Doubleday.

Browne, A. (2009) *My Mum*. London: Picture Corgi.

Brummitt-Yale, J. (2011) *The Relationship Between Reading and Writing*. [Online]. Available at: www.k12reader.com/the-relationship-between-reading-and-writing/ (Accessed: 22 July 2012).

Bruning, R. and Horn, C. (2000) Developing motivation to write. *Educational Psychologist*, 35, 25–37.

Burnett, C., Dickinson, P., Myers, J. and Merchant, G. (2006) Digital connections: transforming literacy in the primary school. *Cambridge Journal of Education*, 36 (1), 11–29. [Online]. Available at: http://extra.shu.ac.uk/bvw/Cambridge%20Journal%20piece.pdf (Accessed: 30 July 2011).

Burnett, F. H. (1994) *The Secret Garden*. London: Puffin.

Butt. G. (1993) The effects of 'audience centred' teaching on children's writing in Geography. *International Research in Geographical and Environmental Education*, 2 (1), 11–24.

Butt, G. (1998) Increasing the effectiveness of 'audience-centred' teaching in geography. *International Research in Geographical and Environmental Education*, 7 (3), 203–28.

Butt, G. (ed.) (2011) *Geography, Education and the Future*. London: Continuum.

Butterworth, N. (2008a) *My Dad is Brilliant*. London: Walker Books.

Butterworth, N. (2008b) *My Mum is Fantastic*. London: Walker Books.

Butterworth, N. and Inkpen, M. (2008) *Jasper's Beanstalk*. London: Hodder Children's Books.

Buttery, T. J. and Reitzammer, A. F. (1987) Creative Writing: A study of selected story stimuli on second grade children. *Reading Improvement*, 24 (4), 262–6.

Cainer, J. (2011) *Thought for the Day*. [Online]. Available at: www.dailymail.co.uk/coffeebreak/horoscopes/index.html (Accessed: 23 October 2011).

Calkins, L. (1980) When children want to punctuate: Basic skills belong in context. *Language Arts*, 57, 567–73.

Callender, S.A. (2007). *Gross and Fine Motor Activities for Early Childhood: Children Ages 6–12 years*. Mississippi State, MS: Mississippi State University Early Childhood Institute. [Online]. Available at: www.earlychildhood.msstate.edu/resources/motoractivities/pdfs/school-age.pdf (Accessed: 4 May 2012).

Cameron, L. and Besser, S. (2004) *Writing in English as an Additional Language at Key Stage 2*. Research Report RR586. Nottingham: DfES.

Camilli, G., Vargas, S. and Yurecko, M. (2003) Teaching children to read: The fragile link between science and federal education policy. *Education Policy Analysis Archives*, 11 (15). [Online]. Available at: www.nichd.nih. gov/health/topics/national_reading_panel.cfm (Accessed: 12 July 2012).

Campbell, H. and Featherstone, S. (2002) *The Little Book of Writing*. Leicestershire: Featherstone Education.

Campbell, R. (1984) *Dear Zoo*. London: Puffin.

Campbell, R. (2009) *Dear Santa*. London: Macmillan Children's Books.

Campbell, T. A. and Hlusek, M. (2009) Storytelling and story writing: 'Using a different kind of pencil'. *What Works? Research into Practice*. Research Monograph #20. [Online]. Available at: www.edu.gov. on.ca/eng/literacynumeracy/inspire/research/WW_Storytelling.pdf (Accessed: 24 March 2012).

Campsall, S. (2009) *Writing a Story – 'Writing to Entertain'*. [Online]. Available at: www.englishbiz.co.uk/downloads/entertain.pdf (Accessed: 6 January 2012).

Carle, E. (1969) *The Very Hungry Caterpillar*. New York: Philomel.

Carle, E. (1984) *The Very Busy Spider*. New York: Philomel.

Carnie, F. (2003) *Alternative Approaches to Education: A Guide for Parents and Teachers*. Oxon: RoutledgeFalmer.

Carpenter, D. (2011a) *Pets Get Lonely Too*. [Online]. Available at: http:// rogz.com/blogdemo/?p=794 (Accessed: 14 July 2011).

Carpenter, R. (2011b) Toys and stories. *Soaring Stories With: Regi Carpenter*, 28 December. [Online]. Available at: www.soaringstories.com/toys-and-stories/ (Accessed: 31 August 2012).

Carrick, D. (n.d.) *Author Q and A*. [Online]. Available at: www.donnacarrick. com/authorqa.html (Accessed: 28 May 2012).

Cart, M. (1999) *Tomorrowland: Ten Stories about the Future*. New York: Scholastic.

Carter, J. (2002) *Just Imagine. Creative Ideas for Writing*. London: Fulton.

Castek, J., Bevans-Mangelson, J. and Goldstone, B. (2006) Reading adventures online: Five ways to introduce the new literacies of the Internet through children's literature. *The Reading Teacher*, 59 (7), 714–28. [Online]. Available at: http://homepages.uconn.edu/~jmc03014/RT-59-7-Castek.pdf (Accessed: 6 April 2012).

Castellani, J. and Jeffs, T. (2001) Emerging reading and writing strategies using technology. *Teaching Exceptional Children*, 33 (5), 60–67. [Online]. Available at: http://cte.jhu.edu/teachingexceptionalchildren-jc.pdf (Accessed: 6 April 2012).

Casto, P. (2002) *Flashes on the Meridian: Dazzled by Flash Fiction*. [Online].

Available at: www.writing-world.com/fiction/casto.shtml (Accessed: 4 January 2012).

Cavkaytar, S. and Yasar, S. (2010) Using writing process in teaching composition skills: An action research. *International Conference 'ICT for Language Learning'*; 3rd edn. [Online]. Available at: www.pixel-online.net/ICT4LL2010/common/download/Proceedings_pdf/SLA07-Cavkaytar.pdf (Accessed: 22 July 2012).

CCEA (Council for the Curriculum, Examinations and Assessment) (n.d.) *Language and Literacy in the Foundation Stage: Writing.* [Online]. Available at: www.nicurriculum.org.uk/docs/foundation_stage/areas_of_learning/language_and_literacy/LL_Writing.pdf (Accessed: 4 May 2012).

ChangingMinds (2011) *Classic Story Conflicts.* [Online]. Available at: http://changingminds.org/disciplines/storytelling/plots/conflicts.htm (Accessed: 5 January 2012).

Chaucer, G. (2003) *The Canterbury Tales.* Trans. N. Coghill. London: Penguin.

Chen, J. Q. and McNamee, G. D. (2007) *Bridging: Assessment for Teaching and Learning in Early Childhood Classrooms.* Thousand Oaks, CA: Corwin Press.

Chhabria, R. (2011) *The Difference Between Story and Plot.* [Online]. Available at: http://rachnachhabria.blogspot.co.uk/2011/07/difference-between-story-and-plot.html (Accessed: 18 May 2012).

Chris (2009) *The Essential Man's Library: 50 Fictional Adventure Books Edition.* [Online]. Available at: http://artofmanliness.com/2009/06/02/the-essential-man%E2%80%99s-library-adventure-edition-part-one-fiction/ (Accessed: 14 October 2011).

Christian, I. (2011) Where have I seen that word before? In Richards, J. C. and Lassonde, C. A. (eds) *Writing Strategies for All Primary Students: Scaffolding Independent Writing with Differentiated Mini-Lessons.* pp. 123–9. San Francisco, CA: Jossey-Bass.

Ciccone, E. (Pirnot) (2001) A place for talk in a writers' workshop. *The Quarterly*, 23 (4), 25–27. [Online]. Available at: www.nwp.org/cs/public/print/resource/239 (Accessed: 8 July 2012).

Cicirelli, V. G. (1995) *Sibling Relationships Across the Life Span.* New York: Plenum Press.

Clarke, C. (2012) *What is Conflict?* [Online]. Available at: www.caroclarke.com/whatisconflict.html (Accessed: 13 June 2012).

Clarke, J. and Featherstone, S. (2008) *Young Boys and Their Writing.* Leicestershire: Featherstone Education.

Clearvision (2006) *Telling Stories Through Touch.* [Online]. Available at:

www.tactilebooks.org/making/telling-touch.pdf (Accessed: 29 January 2012).

Cleaver, P. (2006) *Ideas for Children's Writers: A Comprehensive Resource Book of Plots, Themes, Genres, Lists, What's Hot & What's Not*. Oxford: How To Books.

Clere, L. (2011) *Child-Initiated Writing: Exciting Ideas for Engaging Children in the Writing Process*. London: A&C Black.

Cohen, M. (1998) A habit of healthy idleness: Boys' underachievement in historic perspective relations. In Epstein, D., Ellwood, J., Hey, V. and Maw, J. (eds) *Failing boys? Issues in Gender and Achievement*. Buckingham: Open University Press.

Cole, B. (1997) *Prince Cinders*. London: Puffin.

Corbett, P. (2001) *How to Teach Fiction Writing at Key Stage 2*. London: David Fulton.

Corbett, P. (2003) *How to Teach Story Writing at Key Stage 1*. London: David Fulton.

Corbett, P. (2008) *From Storytelling to Story Writing – A Conference for Reception and Year 1 Teachers*. [Online]. Available at: www.primarytoolkit.co.uk/talkthetext/talkthetext.html (Accessed: 30 August 2012).

Corbett, P. (2009) *Jumpstart! Storymaking Games and Activities for Ages 7–12*. Abingdon: Routledge.

Corden, R. (2007) Developing reading–writing connections: The impact of explicit instruction of literary devices on the quality of children's narrative writing. *Journal of Research in Childhood Education*, 21 (3), 269–89. [Online]. Available at: http://irep.ntu.ac.uk/R/?func=dbin-jump-full&object_id=185412&local_base=GEN01 (Accessed: 8 July 2012).

Cordes, C. and Miller, E. (eds) (2000) *Fool's Gold: A Critical Look at Computers in Childhood*. College Park, MD: Alliance for Childhood.

Core, S. (n.d.) *Building a Bridge Between Speaking and Listening and Children's Writing*. [Online]. Available at: www.teachfind.com/national-strategies/building-bridge-between-speaking-and-listening-and-childrens-writing (Accessed: 8 July 2012).

Cornell, J. M. (1985) Spontaneous mirror writing in children. *Canadian Journal of Psychology*, 39 (1), 174–9.

Cowie, H. and Hanrott, H. (1984) The writing community: A case study of one junior school class. In Cowie, H. (ed.) *The Development of Children's Imaginative Writing*. Beckenham: Croom Helm. pp. 200–218.

Cox, S. (2011) *Launching Tech Ventures*. [Online]. Available at: http://launchingtechventures.blogspot.com/2011/05/prototyping-just-get-it-out-there.html (Accessed: 4 August 2011).

Craft, A., Cremin, T., Burnard, P., Dragovic, T. and Chappell, K. (2012)

Possibility thinking: An evidence-based concept driving creativity? *Open Research Online*, pp. 1–32. [Online]. Available at: http://oro.open. ac.uk/31388/2/ (Accessed: 26 June 2012).

Craighill, V. (2010) *PDSA Launches New Education Website.* [Online]. Available at: www.pdsa.org.uk/about-us/media-pr-centre/news/1189_ pdsa-launches-new-education-website (Accessed: 27 April 2012).

Crawford, D. K. and Bodine, R. J. (2001) Conflict resolution education: Preparing youth for the future. *Juvenile Justice Journal*, 8 (1). [Online]. Available at: www.ncjrs.gov/html/ojjdp/jjjournal_2001_6/jj3.html (Accessed: 13 June 2012).

CreativeJuicesBooks.com (2011) *Creative Writing Ideas: Story Writing Ideas to Write Best Books for Kids.* [Online]. Available at: www.creativejuicesbooks. com/creative-writing-ideas-kids.html (Accessed: 29 April 2012).

Cremin, T. (2010) Motivating children to write with purpose and passion. In P. Goodwin (ed.) *The Literate Classroom*, 3rd edn. Abingdon: Routledge.

Cremin, T., Goouch, K., Blakemore, L., Goff, E. and Macdonald, R. (2006) Connecting drama and writing: Seizing the moment to write. *Research in Drama Education*, 11 (3), 273–91. [Online]. Available at: http://oro. open.ac.uk/9778/1/9778.pdf (Accessed: 15 April 2012).

Crick Software Inc. (2011) *Clicker Paint.* [Online]. Available at: www. cricksoft.com/us/products/tools/clickerpaint/default/emerging-writers. aspx (Accessed: 24 December 2011).

Crum, S. (2006) *Story Skeletons: Teaching Plot Structure with Picture Books.* [Online]. Available at: www.readingrockets.org/article/22242/ (Accessed: 24 March 2012).

Cruz, M. C. (2008) *A Quick Guide to Reaching Struggling Writers, K-5.* Portsmouth, NH: First Hand Books (Heinemann).

Cubelli, R. (2009) Mirror writing in preschool – A pilot study. *Cognitive Processing*, 10 (2), 101–104.

Cyprus Well (2010) *Book of the Month August 2010 – Julia Green: Drawing with Light.* [Online]. Available at: www.cypruswell.com/userfiles/ Drawing%20with%20Light%20by%20Julia%20Green.pdf (Accessed: 26 January 2012).

Czerniewska, P. (1992) *Learning about Writing.* Oxford: Blackwell.

Dahl, R. (1999) *The Wonderful Story of Henry Sugar, and Six More.* London: Jonathan Cape.

Dahl, R. (2001) *Charlie and the Chocolate Factory.* London: Puffin.

Dahl, R. (2008) *The Minpins.* London: Puffin.

Dahlberg, S. T. (2007) Creative engagement. Paper presented at '*Supporting creative acts beyond dissemination'. Creativity & Cognition 2007*, 13 June. Washington, D.C. [Online]. Available at: http://shamurai.com/sites/

creativity/papers/2.dahlberg.pdf (Accessed: 11 June 2012).

Daily Mail (2010) *Children's Grasp of the 3Rs at its Worst in a Decade: One in Five Struggling to Spell at Age Seven.* 26th August. [Online]. Available at: www.dailymail.co.uk/news/article-1306316/Thousands-pupils-unable-write-properly-struggle-basic-maths.html#ixzz214XrboDF (Accessed: 19 July 2012).

Daily Mail (2011) *Say Good Night to Bedtime Stories: How Reading to Children is Being Hit by Busy Lives.* 31st January. [Online]. Available at: www.dailymail.co.uk/news/article-1352045/Say-good-night-bedtime-stories-How-reading-children-hit-busy-lives.html#ixzz1UeOfwb7s (Accessed: 10 August 2011).

Daitsman, J. (2011) Exploring gender identity in early childhood through story dictation and dramatization. *Voices of Practitioners,* 6 (1), 1–12. [Online]. Available at: www.naeyc.org/files/naeyc/file/vop/VOP_Daitsman_Final(1).pdf (Accessed: 26 February 2012).

Daiute, C. and Dalton, B. (1993) Collaboration between children learning to write: can novices be masters? *Cognition and Instruction,* 10 (4), 281–333.

Daly, C. (2003) *Literature Search on Improving Boys' Writing.* London: OFSTED.

Daniel, A. (2001) Working with beginning writers. *The Quarterly,* 23 (3), 13-17. [Online]. Available at: www.nwp.org/cs/public/print/resource/199 (Accessed: 19 July 2012).

Davies, K. (2009) *Overcoming Handwriting Difficulties.* 23 November. [Online]. Available at: www.familiesonline.co.uk/LOCATIONS/Cheshire/Articles/Overcoming-handwriting-difficulties (Accessed: 1 May 2012).

Davis, R. D. (2003) *The Gift of Learning.* New York: Perigee Trade.

DCSF (2008a) *Mark Making Matters.* Nottingham: DCSF Publications.

DCSF (2008b) *Practice Guidance for The Early Years Foundation Stage.* Nottingham: DCSF Publications.

DCSF (2008c) *Every Child a Talker: Guidance for Early Language Lead Practitioners.* Nottingham: DCSF Publications. [Online]. Available at: www.leics.gov.uk/ecat_first_instalment.pdf (Accessed: 8 July 2012).

DCSF (2008d) *Talk for Writing.* Nottingham: DCSF Publications. [Online]. Available at: www.education.gov.uk/publications/eOrderingDownload/DCSF-00467-2008.pdf (Accessed: 8 July 2012).

DCSF (2009) *Every Child a Talker: Guidance for Early Language Lead Practitioners. Second instalment: Spring 2009.* Nottingham: DCSF Publications. [Online]. Available at: www.leics.gov.uk/ecat_second_instalment.pdf (Accessed: 8 July 2012).

DCSF (2011) *A Picture Paints a Thousand Words – Using ICT to stimulate writing*. Teaching and Learning Resources. [Online]. Available at: http://tinyurl.com/bvsj4af (Accessed: 29 May 2012).

Denning, S. (2009) *Narrative vs Abstract Thinking*. [Online]. Available at: www.stevedenning.com/Business-Narrative/narrative-vs-abstract-thinking-Bruner.aspx (Accessed: 9 April 2012).

Derber, C. (2000) *The Pursuit of Attention: Power and Ego in Everyday Life*. New York: Oxford University Press.

Derbyshire, D. (2009) Social websites harm children's brains: Chilling warning to parents from top neuroscientist. *Daily Mail*, 24 February. [Online]. Available at: www.dailymail.co.uk/news/article-1153583/Social-websites-harm-childrens-brains-Chilling-warning-parents-neuroscientist.html (Accessed: 21 January 2012).

Derewianka, B. (1990) *Exploring How Texts Work*. Rozelle, NSW: PETA.

Dettenrieder, M. and Hlawati, A. (2008) *Incipio – The Essential Handbook of 2,000 Sentence Starters for Every Writer*. USA: Lulu.com. [Online]. Available at: http://tinyurl.com/c4dkyof (Accessed: 30 August 2012).

Dew, J. R. (1996) Are you a right-brain or left-brain thinker? *Quality Progress Magazine*, April, pp. 91–3.

DfE (n.d.) Gateway to writing. *The National Archives*. [Online]. Available at: http://webarchive.nationalarchives.gov.uk/20110809091832/http://teachingandlearningresources.org.uk/collection/31776 (Accessed: 30 August 2012).

DfE (2011a) *The Framework for the National Curriculum. A report by the Expert Panel for the National Curriculum Review*. London: Department for Education.

DfE (2011b) *The National Strategies. Year 2 Narrative Unit 4 – Extended Stories/ Significant Authors*. [Online]. Available at: www.babcock-education.co.uk/ldp/do_download.asp?did=301884 (Accessed: 14 June 2012).

DfE (2012a) *Development Matters in the Early Years Foundation Stage (EYFS)*. [Online]. Available at: http://media.education.gov.uk/assets/files/pdf/d/development%20matters%20in%20the%20eyfs.pdf (Accessed: 27 April 2012).

DfE (2012b) *National Curriculum for English Key Stages 1 and 2 – Draft*. National Curriculum review. [Online]. Available at: http://media.education.gov.uk/assets/files/pdf/d/draft%20national%20curriculum%20for%20english%20key%20stages%201%202.pdf (Accessed: 7 July 2012).

DfE (2012c) *Neighbourhood Statistics – Small Area Pupil Attainment by Pupil Characteristics in England, 2011*. [Online]. Available at: www.education.gov.uk/rsgateway/DB/SFR/s001070/index.shtml (Accessed: 24 June 2012).

DfEE (1999) *The National Literacy Strategy: A Framework for Teaching*. London: Department for Education and Employment.

DfEE/QCA (1999) *The National Curriculum Handbook for Primary Teachers in England: Key Stages 1 and 2.* London: The Stationery Office. [Online]. Available at: www.education.gov.uk/publications/eOrderingDownload/QCA-99-457.pdf (Accessed: 12 July 2012).

DfES (2001a) *Extended Stories.* [Online]. Available at: www.pgce.soton.ac.uk/ict/NewPGCE/IWB/PNS/content/downloads/teaching_resources/literacy/aspects_narrative/nls_aspects_extendedstory.pdf (Accessed: 14 June 2012).

DfES (2001b) *Unit 9 Narrative writing: Story endings.* [Online]. Available at: www.pgce.soton.ac.uk/ict/NewPGCE/IWB/PNS/content/downloads/teaching_resources/literacy/booster_units/nls_y6booster_storyend2.pdf (Accessed: 16 June 2012).

DfES (2003) *Speaking, Listening, Learning: Working with Children in Key Stages 1 and 2.* [Online]. Available at: http://dera.ioe.ac.uk/4824/1/pns_speaklisten062403hbk.pdf (Accessed: 8 July 2012).

DfES (2006) *Primary National Strategy: Primary Framework for Literacy and Mathematics.* [Online]. Available at: www.niched.org/docs/the%20primary%20framework.pdf (Accessed: 5 June 2012).

DfES (2007a) *Letters and Sounds: Principles and Practice of High Quality Phonics. Notes of Guidance for Practitioners and Teachers.* [Online]. Available at: www.bgfl.org/bgfl/custom/files_uploaded/uploaded_resources/16145/Letters_sounds.pdf (Accessed: 12 July 2012).

DfES (2007b) *Social and Emotional Aspects of Learning . . . Improving Behaviour . . . Improving Learning.* [Online]. Available at: http://webarchive.nationalarchives.gov.uk/20081117141643/standards.dfes.gov.uk/primary/publications/banda/seal/ (Accessed: 14 June 2012).

Diehn, G. (2006) *Making Books.* Asheville, NC: Lark Books.

Dipple, S. (2011) *Teaching Writing to Children.* [Online]. Available at: http://tinyurl.com/cgecbfu (Accessed: 5 June 2012).

DLTK's Sites (2012) *Children's Book Breaks.* [Online]. Available at: http://tinyurl.com/c49kaz8 (Accessed: 5 June 2012).

Dockrell, J. and Stuart, M. (2007) *Talking time: Supporting language in early years settings.* London: IOE. [Online]. Available at: www.ioe.ac.uk/about/documents/About_Staff/PHD_JD_Publications_TALKING_TIME_Handbook.pdf.

Dodd, C. (1993) *Education: Rude Stories in the Playground: A new book of fly-on-the-wall research reveals what really goes on at playtime. Some of the tales may make parents blush, says Celia Dodd.* [Online]. Available at: http://tinyurl.com/923pe7t (Accessed: 3 September 2011).

Dodd, L. (2002) *Hairy Maclary from Donaldson's Dairy.* London: Puffin.

Dodson, S. (2010) Good at games: Mobile learning proves a hit in schools.

The Guardian, 4 May. [Online]. Available at: www.guardian.co.uk/classroom-innovation/good-at-games (Accessed: 19 March 2012).

Donovan, M. (2007) How more reading leads to better writing. *Writing Forward*. 5 August. [Online]. Available at: www.writingforward.com/better-writing/more-reading-better-writing (Accessed: 21 July 2012).

Dorrell, A. (2008) *Sensory Experiences Can Be Messy Fun*. [Online]. Available at: www.earlychildhoodnews.com/earlychildhood/article_view.aspx?ArticleID=227 (Accessed: 29 December 2011).

Dunbar, P. (2012) *Let's Write a Story: Ideas Everywhere by Polly Dunbar (Teaching Notes)*. [Online]. Available at: www.bookstart.org.uk/books/lets-write-a-story/ (Accessed: 22 April 2012).

Dunsmuir, S. and Blatchford, P. (2004) Predictors of writing competence in 4–7 year old children. *British Journal of Educational Psychology*, 47, 461–83.

East Riding of Yorkshire Council (n.d.) Can write, won't write! *East Riding of Yorkshire Council Raising Boys' Achievement Writing Project*. [Online]. Available at: http://tinyurl.com/cnnf3ne (Accessed: 25 November 2011).

Eastman, P. D. (2006) *Are You My Mother?* London: HarperCollins Children's Books.

Edwards, S. (2004) *Supporting Writing*. London: David Fulton.

Elbow, P. (1981) *Writing Without Teachers*. London: Oxford University Press. [Online]. Available at: http://tinyurl.com/bn9k5ao (Accessed: 28 April 2012).

Elbow, P. (1993) The war between reading and writing – and how to end it. *Rhetoric Review*, 12 (1), 5–24. [Online]. Available at: http://tinyurl.com/4y6jh3p (Accessed: 22 April 2012).

Ellis, S. (2003) Story-writing, planning and creativity. *Reading, Literacy and Language*, 37 (1), 27-31.

Ellis, S., Hughes, A. and MacKay, R. (1997) Writing stories 5–14: What must teachers teach? *Scottish Educational Review*, 29 (1), 56–65.

Emberley, E. (1992) *Go Away, Big Green Monster!* Boston, MA: Little Brown.

Emily Gems (n.d.) *Color Symbolism, Color and Personality, Gemstone Color and Meaning*. [Online]. Available at: www.crystal-cure.com/color-meanings.html#top (Accessed: 29 August 2012).

Ende, M. (1984) *The Neverending Story*. London: Penguin.

eNotes.com (2011) *Slice of life*. [Online]. Available at: www.enotes.com/topic/Slice_of_life (Accessed: 14 June 2012).

Erez, E. (2010) *Hussein Chalayan Weaves Stories in Fabric at Istanbul Modern*. [Online]. Available at: www.hurriyetdailynews.com/default.aspx?pageid=438&n=hussein-chalayan-weaves-stories-in-fabric-at-istanbul-modern-2010-07-26 (Accessed: 29 December 2011).

Erianne, J. C. (2012) *The Importance of Character Elements in Short Stories.* [Online]. Available at: www.ehow.co.uk/info_7875063_importance-character-elements-short-stories.html (Accessed: 4 June 2012).

Ernst, M. (1920) *The Hat Makes The Man.* New York: Museum of Modern Art.

Evans, B. (2002) *You Can't Come to my Birthday Party! Conflict Resolution with Young Children.* Ypsilanti, MI: High/Scope Press.

Evans Schmidt, M., Bickham, D., King, B., Slaby, R., Branner, A. C. and Rich, M. (2005) *The Effects of Electronic Media on Children Ages Zero to Six: A History of Research.* [Online]. Available at: www.kff.org/entmedia/upload/The-Effects-of-Electronic-Media-on-Children-Ages-Zero-to-Six-A-History-of-Research-Issue-Brief.pdf (Accessed: 14 January 2012).

Fagerlie, A. M. (1975) Brand names stimulate story writing. *Language Arts,* 52 (7), 1017–1018.

Fahey, P. A. (2005) *6 Steps to Writing Flash Fiction.* [Online]. Available at: http://childrencomefirst.com/flashfiction.shtml (Accessed: 5 January 2012).

Farkas, D. K. (1991) Collaborative writing, software development, and the universe of collaborative activity. In Lay, H. M. and Karis, W. M. (eds) *Collaborative Writing in Industry: Investigation in Theory and Practice.* Amityville, NY: Baywood. pp. 13–30.

Feathers, K. M. (2004) *Infotext: Reading and Learning.* Toronto: Pippin Publishing.

Ferguson, B. (2007) *Storytelling with Children in the Early Years.* [Online]. Available at: www.scottishstorytellingcentre.co.uk/education/SRresources/earlyyearsstarter.pdf (Accessed: 30 August 2012).

Ferreiroa, E. and Pontecorvob, C. (1999) Managing the written text: The beginning of punctuation in children's writing. *Learning and Instruction,* 9, 543–64. [Online]. Available at: http://boileddown.me/storage/p1.pdf (Accessed: 1 September 2011).

Fields, J. (2008a) 'Don't get slighted'. *Institute of Children's Literature.* [Online]. Available at: www.institutechildrenslit.com/rx/wt04/slighted.shtml (Accessed: 30 August 2012).

Fields, J. (2008b) 'Embrace the conflict'. *Institute of Children's Literature.* [Online]. Available at: www.institutechildrenslit.com/rx/wt04/embraceconflict.shtml (Accessed: 22 April 2012).

Finch, S. (2003) *An Eye for an Eye Leaves Everyone Blind: Teaching Young Children to Settle Conflicts Without Violence.* London: Save the Children. [Online]. Available at: www.savethechildren.org.uk/sites/default/files/docs/AN_EYE_FOR_AN_EYE_LEAVES_EVERYONE_BLIND_0.pdf (Accessed: 2 September 2012).

Fisher R. (2005) *Teaching Children to Think.* 2nd edn. Cheltenham: Stanley Thornes.

Fisher, R., Myhill, D., Jones, S. and Larkin, S. (2006) *Talk to Text: Using Talk to Support Writing. End of Award Report.* [Online]. Available at: http://education.exeter.ac.uk/download.php?id=4977 (Accessed: 8 July 2012).

Fison, J. (2011) *Getting Started.* [Online]. Available at: http://juliefisonwriter.wordpress.com/ (Accessed: 14 October 2011).

Fitzgerald, J. and Spiegel, D. (1986) Textual cohesion and coherence in children's writing. *Research in the Teaching of English,* 20 (3), 263–80.

Fletcher, R. (2006) *Boy Writers: Reclaiming Their Voices.* Ontario: Pembroke.

Flocabulary (2012) *Five Elements of a Story: 'Five Things'.* [Online]. Available at: http://flocabulary.com/fivethings/ (Accessed: 18 May 2012).

Flood, A. (2009) Roald Dahl characters still dominate children's favourites. *The Guardian,* 20 October. [Online]. Available at: www.guardian.co.uk/books/2009/oct/20/roald-dahl-childrens-favourites (Accessed: 18 February 2012).

Flower, L. (2000) Writing for an audience. In Eschholz, P., Rosa, A. and Clark, V. (eds) *Language Awareness: Readings for College Writers.* 8th edn. Boston, MA: Bedford/St. Martin's. pp. 139–41. [Online]. Available at: http://largentandrewcxkp.files.wordpress.com/2009/12/writing_for_an_audience.pdf (Accessed: 9 July 2012).

Flower, L. S. and Hayes, J. R. (1980) The dynamics of composing: Making plans and juggling constraints. In Gregg, L. W. and Steinberg, E. R. (eds) *Cognitive Processes in Writing.* Hillsdale, NJ: Erlbaum. pp. 31–50.

Flower, L. S. and Hayes, J. R. (1981) A cognitive process theory of writing. *College Composition and Communication,* 32 (4), 365–87.

Floyd, J. (2006) *Choosing the Right Name for Your Story.* [Online]. Available at: www.writing-world.com/fiction/titles.shtml (Accessed: 3 February 2012).

Flutter, J. (2000) *Words Matter – Thinking and Talking about Writing in the Classroom.* [Online]. Available at: http://tinyurl.com/cg55c35 (Accessed: 22 April 2012).

Forster, E. M. (1927) *Aspects of the Novel.* London: Edward Arnold.

Foster, E. (2006) *Writing Talking Animal Tales.* [Online]. Available at: www.writing-world.com/foster/foster05.shtml (Accessed: 16 February 2012).

Francis, B. (2006) Heroes or Zeroes? The discursive positioning of 'underachieving boys' in English neo-liberal education policy. *Journal of Education Policy,* 21 (2), 187–200.

Freebody, P. (2007) *Australian Education Review: Literacy Education in School Research. Perspectives from the past, for the future.* No. 52. Victoria: Australian Council for Educational Research. [Online]. Available at: www.acer.edu.au/documents/AER52.pdf (Accessed: 16 July 2012).

Gadzikowski, A. (2007) *Story Dictation: A Guide for Early Childhood Professionals*. St. Paul, MN: Redleaf Press.

Garner, R. (2008) *Handwriting Standards Blamed as Pupils Ask for Exam 'Scribes'*. [Online]. Available at: www.independent.co.uk/news/education/education-news/handwriting-standards-blamed-as-pupils-ask-for-exam-scribes-920810.html (Accessed: 6 August 2011).

Garner, R. (2011) *Blog Early, Blog Often: The Secret to Making Boys Write Properly*. [Online]. Available at: www.independent.co.uk/news/education/education-news/blog-early-blog-often-the-secret-to-making-boys-write-properly-2211232.html (Accessed: 20 October 2011).

Garp, T. S. (2005) *Conflict in Short Stories*. [Online]. Available at: www.writing.com/main/view_item/item_id/1004812-Conflict-in-the-Short-Story (Accessed: 21 June 2012).

Genette, G. (1997) *Paratexts: The Thresholds of Textuality*. Literature, Culture, Theory Series, No. 20. Transl. J. E. Lewin. New York: Cambridge University Press.

Gentry, R. (n.d.) *The Developmental Stages of Writing*. [Online]. Available at: www.uab.edu/soestudentteaching/images/docs/student/developmentalstageswriting.pdf (Accessed: 28 August 2012).

Ghosh, R. (2008) *7 Types of Friendship*. [Online]. Available at: http://idhs78.wordpress.com/2008/04/27/7-types-of-friendship/ (Accessed: 13 September 2011).

Giles, R. M. and Wellhousen Tunks, K. (2009) Putting the power in action: Teaching young children 'how to' write. *Texas Child Care*. Fall. [Online]. Available at: http://tinyurl.com/d7ayw6c (Accessed: 14 April 2012).

Gina (1989) *Horace the Dragon has Hiccups*. London: Collins Educational.

Gingell, A. (2011) ENEMIES, embargoes and empowerment: A case study into combating boys' negative attitudes to writing in the primary classroom. *The Plymouth Student Educator*, 3 (1), 1–17. [Online]. Available at: https://studentjournals.plymouth.ac.uk/index.php/educator/article/viewFile/193/230 (Accessed: 15 July 2012).

Goiran-Bevelhimer, A. F. (2008) Boys and writing: implications for creating school writing curriculum and instruction that is boy-friendly. *Journal for the Liberal Arts and Sciences*, 13 (1), 73–92. [Online]. Available at: http://tinyurl.com/bo2zudf (Accessed: 25 November 2011).

Gold, D. (1989) Sibling relationship in old age: A typology. *International Journal of Aging and Human Development*, 28 (1), 37–51.

Goodwin, P. (ed.) (2010) *The Literate Classroom*, 3rd edn. Abingdon: Routledge.

Graham, J. (2010) Meeting individual needs. In Graham, J. and Kelly, A. (eds) *Writing Under Control*, 3rd edn. London: David Fulton.

Graham, S. (2009) Want to improve children's writing? Don't neglect their handwriting. *American Educator,* Winter 2009–2010, 20–40. [Online]. Available at: http://scoe.org/files/graham-handwriting-2009. pdf (Accessed: 4 May 2012).

Graham-Clay, S. (2005) Communicating with parents: Strategies for teachers. *School Community Journal,* 16 (1), 117–29. [Online]. Available at: www.adi.org/journal/ss05/Graham-Clay.pdf (Accessed: 14 April 2012).

Grainger, T. and Barnes, J. (2006) Creativity in the primary curriculum.

Grainger, T., Goouch, K. and Lambrinth, A. (2004a) *Creative Activities for Plot, Character and Setting: Ages 5–7.* Warwickshire: Scholastic.

Grainger, T., Goouch, K. and Lambrinth, A. (2004b) *Creative Activities for Plot, Character and Setting: Ages 7–9.* Warwickshire: Scholastic.

Grainger, T., Goouch, K. and Lambrinth, A. (2004c) *Creative Activities for Plot, Character and Setting: Ages 9–11.* Warwickshire: Scholastic.

Graves, D. H. (1985) All children can write. *LD Online.* [Online]. Available at: www.ldonline.org/article/6204/ (Accessed: 29 August 2012).

Gray, J., Silha, S. and Woyvodich, M. (1999) *Telling Stories.* [Online]. Available at: www.goodnewsgooddeeds.org/1intro.html (Accessed: 17 July 2011).

Green, C. (2011) *Story Writing Tips for Kids, Part One: Ideas.* [Online]. Available at: www.coreygreen.com/storytips.html#1 (Accessed: 29 May 2012).

Greenfield, S. A. (2000) *Brain Story.* London: BBC Worldwide.

Gurney, S. (2008) *My Dad, the Hero.* London: Walker Books.

Hairston, M. (1982) The winds of change: Thomas Kuhn and the revolution in the teaching of writing. *College Composition and Communication,* 33, 76–88.

Hallissy, J. (2010) *The Write Start.* Boston, MA: Trumpeter Books.

Hallissy, J. (2011) The Route to Writing. *Junior,* 148, 48–50.

HandsOnScotland (2011) *Confidence.* [Online]. Available at: www. handsonscotland.co.uk/flourishing_and_wellbeing_in_children_and_ young_people/confidence/confidence.html (Accessed: 8 October 2011).

Hara, S. R. and Burke, D. J. (1998) Parent involvement: the key to improved student achievement. *School Community Journal,* 8 (2), Fall/Winter. [Online]. Available at: www.adi.org/journal/ss01/chapters/Chapter16-Hara&Burke.pdf (Accessed: 10 July 2012).

Hargreaves, R. (1971) *Mr. Tickle.* London: Egmont.

Harrett, J. (2006) *Exciting Writing: Activities for 5 to 11 year olds.* London: Paul Chapman.

Harris, P. (2005) *At the Interface between Reader and Text: Devices in Children's Picturebooks that Mediate Reader Expectations and Interpretations.* Conference Proceedings for Australian Association for Research in

Education Parramatta, 28 November – 1 December. [Online]. Available at: http://tinyurl.com/cpnwpdf (Accessed: 7 March 2012).

Harvey, S. (2002) Nonfiction inquiry: using real reading and writing to explore the world. *Language Arts*, 80 (1), 12–22. [Online]. Available at: http://faculty.washington.edu/smithant/533%20articles/Nonfiction%20inquiry%20article.pdf (Accessed: 13 February 2012).

Hawkins, C. (2003) *Mr. Wolf's Week*. London: Egmont.

Heath, S. B. (1982) What no bedtime story means: narrative skills at home and school. *Language in Society*, 11 (1), 49–76.

Herr, J. (2011) *Creative Resources for the Early Childhood Classroom*, 6th edn (International edition). Belmont, CA: Wadsworth Cengage Learning.

Hersey, J. C. and Jordan, A. (2007) *Reducing Children's TV Time to Reduce the Risk of Childhood Overweight: The Children's Media Use Study*. Highlights Report, March. [Online]. Available at: www.cdc.gov/obesity/downloads/TV_Time_Highligts.pdf (Accessed: 22 February 2012).

Hill, E. (1983) *Where's Spot?* London: Puffin.

Hill, M. (2012) *Statistical First Release: Neighbourhood Statistics – Small Area Pupil Attainment by Pupil Characteristics in England, 2011*. SFR 09/2012. London: DfE. [Online]. Available at: www.education.gov.uk/rsgateway/DB/SFR/s001070/sfr09-2012.pdf (Accessed: 18 July 2012).

Hill, S. (2006) *Developing Early Literacy: Assessment and Teaching*. In SACSA Framework *Handwriting in the South Australian Curriculum*. Prahran: Eleanor Curtain. pp. 8–16. [Online]. Available at: www.sacsa.sa.edu.au/ATT/%7B21AB4BA7-0C50-4F6E-9600-2F699503E1E2%7D/3HSACDevelopmental.pdf (Accessed: 7 July 2012).

Hirschheimer, S. (2002) Tuning into boys' interest in the early years. In Barrs, M. and Pidgeon, S. (eds) *Boys and Writing*. London: Centre for Literacy in Primary Education.

Hoff, T. (1997) *Design Stories*. [Online]. Available at: www.possibility.com/Cpp/DesignStories.html (Accessed: 5 January 2012).

Holden, C. (2002) Contributing to the debate: The perspectives of children on gender, achievement and literacy. *Journal of Educational Enquiry*, 3 (1), 97–110.

Holzwarth, W. and Erlbruch, W. (1994) *The Story of the Little Mole Who Knew it Was None of His Business*. London: Pavilion Children's Books.

Hopcott, R. (2008) *Writing Tips – How to Write Stories with a Twist in the Tale by Rob Hopcott*. [Online]. Available at: http://writing.hopcott.net/2008/11/writing-tips-how-to-write-stories-with-a-twist-in-the-tale-by-rob-hopcott/ (Accessed: 22 December 2012).

Hopkins, G. (2010) *Earn Spelling Points!* [Online]. Available at: www.educationworld.com/a_lesson/02/lp282-01.shtml (Accessed: 9 June 2012).

Hugo, R. (1992) In defense of creative-writing classes. In *The Triggering Town: Lectures and Essays on Poetry and Writing*. New York: Norton. pp. 53–66. [Online]. Available at: http://adilegian.com/PDF/HugoDefenseCreativeWriting.pdf (Accessed: 17 July 2012).

Hull, A. and Hackett, J. (2006) *Using ICT to Stimulate Writing Project*. [Online]. Available at: http://tinyurl.com/cezysb2 (Accessed: 22 May 2012).

IncreaseBrainpower.com (n.d.) *New Ideas*. [Online]. Available at: www.increasebrainpower.com/new-ideas.html (Accessed: 2 September 2012).

Ings, R. (2009) *Writing is Primary: Action Research on the Teaching of Writing in Primary Schools*. [Online]. Available at: www.esmeefairbairn.org.uk/docs/WIP_web.pdf (Accessed: 26 June 2011).

Isaacson, S. (1997) *Mechanical Obstacles to Writing: What Can Teachers Do to Help Students with Learning Problems?* [Online]. Available at: www.ldonline.org/article/6209 (Accessed: 8 June 2012).

James (2010) *How to Write a Children's Book: Advice from Roald Dahl*. [Online]. Available at: http://thebookbase.com/13/how-to-write-a-children%E2%80%99s-book-advice-from-roald-dahl (Accessed: 27 January 2012).

Jeppson, J. and Myers-Walls, J. A. (2010) *Shapes*. [Online]. Available at: www.extension.purdue.edu/providerparent/Child%20Growth-Development/Shapes.htm (Accessed: 25 June 2011).

Johnson, C. E. (1993) *Children and Competition*. [Online]. Available at: www.ces.ncsu.edu/depts/fcs/pdfs/fcs404.pdf (Accessed: 1 July 2011).

Johnson, D. (2002a) Web watch: Writing resources. *Reading Online*, 5 (7). Available at: http://tinyurl.com/bw7ks3l (Accessed: 14 June 2012).

Johnson, M. (2002b) *WHAT MAKES A GOOD WRITING STIMULUS? – 11-year-olds Express Their Views*. Paper presented at the British Educational Research Association Conference, Exeter, 12–14 September. [Online]. Available at: www.cambridgeassessment.org.uk/ca/digitalAssets/113931_What_Makes_a_Good_Writing_Stimulus_-_11-Year-olds_Express_Th.pdf (Accessed: 29 May 2012).

Johnson, P. (2000) *Making Books*. London: A&C Black.

Johnson, P. (2008) *Get Writing! Creative Book-making Projects for Children*. London: A&C Black.

Johnston, R. and Watson, J. (2005) *The Effects of Synthetic Phonics Teaching on Reading and Spelling Attainment: A Seven-Year Longitudinal Study*. [Online]. Available at: http://dera.ioe.ac.uk/14793/1/0023582.pdf (Accessed: 12 July 2012).

Jolliffe, W., Waugh, D. and Carss, A. (2012) *Teaching Systematic Synthetic Phonics in Primary Schools*. London: Learning Matters.

Jones, D. (2010) *First Drafts – Patchwork Writing*. [Online]. Available at: www.

writingoutloud.co.uk/wpblog/writingrambles/first-drafts-patchwork-writing (Accessed: 6 August 2011).

Jones, M. (n.d.) *Story Writing by the Letters.* [Online]. Available at: www.webook.com/WritingTips/Story-Writing-by-the-Letters (Accessed: 29 February 2012).

Jones, M. (2007) Targeting Talk. *Special Children*, January/February, 31–34. [Online]. Available at: www.talkformeaning.co.uk/files/012.pdf (Accessed: 8 July 2012).

Jones, S. (1998) *Accommodations and Modifications for Students with Handwriting Problems and/or Dysgraphia.* [Online]. Available at: www.resourceroom.net/readspell/dysgraphia.asp (Accessed: 4 May 2012).

Jones, S. and Jones, A. (2008) *Creative Story Writing: Teach Your Child to Write Good English.* New Haw: Guinea Pig Education.

Jones-Shoeman, C. (2010) *What is the Writing Process?* [Online]. Available at: http://suite101.com/article/what-is-the-writing-process-a282281 (Accessed: 19 July 2012).

Joplin School District (2011) *Writer's Workshop Handbook: Elementary – Grades K-5.* [Online]. Available at: http://joplin.schoolfusion.us/modules/groups/homepagefiles/cms/2035746/File/Writer's%20Workshop%20Handbook.pdf (Accessed: 29 August 2012).

Juel, C. (1988) Learning to read and write: A longitudinal study of 54 children from first through fourth grades. *Journal of Educational Psychology*, 80 (4), 437–47. [Online]. Available at: http://people.uncw.edu/kozloffm/learningtreadandwrite.pdf (Accessed: 28 March 2012).

Juel, C. (1991) Beginning reading. In Barr, R., Kamil, M. L., Mosenthal, P. B. and Pearson, P. D. (eds) *Handbook of Reading Research*, Vol. 2. Mahwah, NJ: Erlbaum. pp. 759–88.

Kamehameha Schools (2007) *The Writing Process: An Overview of Research on Teaching Writing as a Process.* April. Honolulu, HI: Research & Evaluation Department of Kamehameha Schools. pp. 1–7. [Online]. Available at: www.ksbe.edu/spi/PDFS/Reports/WritingProcessreport.pdf (Accessed: 19 July 2012).

Kaye, B. and Jacobson, B. (1999) True tales and tall tales: The power of organizational storytelling. *Training & Development*, March, 1–6. [Online]. Available at: http://isites.harvard.edu/fs/docs/icb.topic960973.files/True%20Tales%20-%20organizational%20storytelling.pdf (Accessed: 8 January 2012).

Kellaher, K. (1999) *101 Picture Prompts to Spark Super Writing.* Jefferson City, MO: Scholastic.

Kempton, D. (2004) *Wheels Of Motion: Dialogue That Propels The Story Forward.* [Online]. Available at: www.right-writing.com/wheels.html (Accessed: 11 March 2012).

Kenney, J. (2007) *Diary of a Wimpy Kid*. New York: Amulet Books.

Kervin, L. K. (2002) Proofreading as a strategy for spelling development. *Reading Online*, 5 (10). [Online}. Available at: www.readingonline.org/international/inter_index.asp?HREF=kervin/index.html (Accessed: 9 June 2012).

Kessler, S. (2010) *5 Fun and Safe Social Networks for Children*. 11 October. [Online]. Available at: http://mashable.com/2010/10/11/social-networks-children/ (Accessed: 23 May 2012).

Kinsella, M. (n.d.) *Fractured Fairy Tales*. [Online]. Available at: www.marilynkinsella.org/Workshop%20papers/fractured_fairy_tales.htm (Accessed: 30 October 2011).

Klein, C. (2006) *The Essentials of Plot*. [Online]. Available at: www.cherylklein.com/id18.html (Accessed: 18 May 2012).

Kleinman, Z. (2009) *Children Who Use Technology Are 'Better Writers'*. 3rd December. [Online]. Available at: http://news.bbc.co.uk/1/hi/technology/8392653.stm (Accessed: 21 January 2012).

Knight, D. (2002) *Short Story Planning Guide*. Grade 7 SHORT STORY Reading and Writing Activities, pp. 18-20. [Online]. Available at: http://hgp.hdsb.ca/HGP%20Web/Grade78/FOV1-001378A1/FOV1-0013798A/FOV1-0013798C/Writing%20a%20Short%20Story%20planning%20sheet.pdf (Accessed: 12 June 2012).

Koki, S. (1998) *Storytelling: The Heart and Soul of Education*. Pacific Resources for Education and Learning (PREL) Briefing Paper, November, pp. 1–4. [Online]. Available at: www.prel.org/products/products/storytelling.pdf (Accessed: 18 July 2012).

Kotzwinkle, W. and Murray, G. (2001) *Walter the Farting Dog*. Berkeley, CA: North Atlantic Books.

Krause, G. C. (2011) Patchwork words: Stronger story. In *The Storyteller's Scroll*. 1 August. Available at: http://thestorytellersscroll.blogspot.co.uk/2011/08/patchwork-words-stronger-story.html (Accessed 1 December 2012).

Krause, S. D. (2007) *Chapter Four: How to Collaborate and Write With Others*. [Online]. Available at: http://stevendkrause.com/tprw/Chapter%204.pdf (Accessed: 30 December 2011).

Kubler, A. and Baker, S. (2004) *Pass the Parcel*. London: Child's Play.

Kucan, L. and Beck, I. L. (1997) Thinking aloud and reading comprehension research: Inquiry, instruction, and social interaction. *Review of Educational Research*, 67 (3), 271–99.

Kulik, J. A. (2003) Computer use helps students to develop better writing skills. *SRI International*, Issue brief, May. [Online]. Available at: www.sri.com/policy/csted/reports/sandt/it/Kulik_ITinK-12_Writing_IssueBrief.pdf (Accessed: 27 May 2012).

Kustermann, P. (2003) *Developmental Stages of Humor in Children*. [Online]. Available at: http://tinyurl.com/3m9bnfo (Accessed: 11 September 2011).

labfive (2012) *Writing Stamina*. [Online]. Available at: http://labfive. wordpress.com/2012/02/23/writing-stamina/ (Accessed: 8 April 2012).

Lance, W. D. (2005) *Teaching Writing: Preschool, Kindergarten, and First Grade*. [Online]. Available at: www.iched.org/cms/scripts/page.php?site_id=iched&item_id=teach_writing_prek-1 (Accessed: 10 January 2012).

Langer, J. A. and Flihan, S. (2000) Writing and reading relationships: Constructive tasks. *Center on English Learning & Achievement*. [Online]. Available at: www.albany.edu/cela/publication/article/writeread.htm (Accessed: 21 July 2012).

Latham, D. (2002) *How Children Learn to Write*. London: Paul Chapman.

Lauzon, G. (2011) *A Fascination with Superheroes*. [Online]. Available at: http://wondertime.go.com/learning/article/fascination-with-superheroes.html (Accessed: 15 October 2011).

Lawrence, M. (2001) *The Toilet of Doom*. London: Orchard Books.

Lehr, F. (1995). *Revision in the Writing Process*. [Online]. Available at: www. readingrockets.org/article/270/ (Accessed: 19 July 2012).

Lester, H. (1992) *Me First*. New York: Houghton Mifflin.

Levine, M. D. (1998) *Developmental Variation and Learning Disorders*, 2nd edn. Cambridge, MA: Educators Publishing Services.

Lewis, B. L. (n.d.) *Part III, Developing Characters*. [Online]. Available at: http://tinyurl.com/ctahqw8 (Accessed: 28 April 2012).

Litvin, M. (1975) *Including Conflict in Creative Writing*. Galesburg, IL: Log City Books. [Online]. Available at: www.eric.ed.gov/PDFS/ED110979.pdf (Accessed: 22 April 2012).

Loewen, N. (2009) *Make Me Giggle: Writing Your Own Silly Story*. Minneapolis, MN: Picture Window Books.

Lombardi, E. (2011) *Library Quotes – What Have Writers Said About Libraries?* [Online]. Available at: http://classiclit.about.com/od/litlibraries/a/aa_libraryquote.htm (Accessed: 6 November 2011).

London, P. (2004) Drawing closer to nature. *School Arts: The Art Education Magazine for Teachers*, 104 (2), 41.

Lucas, D. (2008) *The Lying Carpet*. London: Anderson Press.

Luke, J. L. and Myers, C. M. (1994) Toward peace: Using literature to aid conflict resolution. *Childhood Education*, 71 (2), 66–9. [Online]. Available at: www.tamathisland.com/Toward%20Peace.pdf (Accessed: 13 June 2012).

MacDonald, A. (1990) *Little Beaver and The Echo*. London: Walker Books.

MacLure, M., Phillips, T. and Wilkinson, A. (eds) (1988) *Oracy Matters: The Development of Talking and Listening in Education*. Maidenhead: Open University Press.

MacLusky, J. and Cox, R. (2011a) *Is There a Way Forward for Creative Writing Pedagogy in the Primary School Curriculum? An International Study.* [Online]. Available at: http://tinyurl.com/7wukcop (Accessed: 18 May 2012).

MacLusky, J. and Cox, R. (2011b) *Teaching Creative Writing in the Primary School: Delight, Entice, Inspire!* Maidenhead: Open University Press.

Macon, J. M., Bewell, D. and Vogt, M. (1991) *Responses to Literature.* Newark, DE: IRA.

Majid, D. A., Tan, A-G. and Soh, K-C. (2003) Enhancing children's creativity: An exploratory study on using the Internet and SCAMPER as creative writing tools. *The Korean Journal of Thinking and Problem Solving,* 13 (2), 67–81. [Online]. Available at: http://faculty.ksu.edu.sa/ualturki/Digital%20Library/Enhancing%20Children%E2%80%99s%20Creativity%20An%20Exploratory%20Study%20on.pdf (Accessed: 6 April 2012).

Maldonado, H., Klemmer, S. R. and Pea, R. D. (2009) *When is Collaborating with Friends a Good Idea? Insights from Design Education.* [Online]. Available at: www.stanford.edu/~roypea/RoyPDF%20folder/A154_CSCL09_Maldonado_Klemmer_Pea.pdf (Accessed: 21 March 2012).

Malkin, B. (2009) Imaginary friends help children learn to communicate. *Telegraph,* 3 June. [Online]. Available at: www.telegraph.co.uk/health/children_shealth/5432791/Imaginary-friends-help-children-learn-to-communicate.html (Accessed: 28 April 2012).

Marfilius, S. (2009) *Writing First: Strategies for Struggling Writers.* [Online]. Available at: http://fourblock.wikispaces.com/file/view/17706512-Writing-First-Handout%5B1%5D.pdf (Accessed: 3 March 2012).

Marquess, A. (2011) *How to Teach Your Child to Write Their Name Using a Salt Sensory Tray.* [Online]. Available at: http://creativewithkids.com/how-to-teach-your-child-to-write-their-name-using-a-salt-sensory-tray/ (Accessed: 27 January 2012).

Marr, D., Windsor, M-M. and Cermak, S. (2001) Handwriting readiness: Locatives and visuomotor skills in the kindergarten year. *Early Childhood & Practice,* 3 (1). [Online]. Available at: http://ecrp.uiuc.edu/v3n1/marr.html (Accessed: 30 August 2012).

Marsh, J. (1998) Gender and writing in the infant school: Writing for a gender-specific audience. *English in Education,* 32 (1), 10–18.

Martin, G. (2011) *Tall story.* [Online]. Available at: www.phrases.org.uk/meanings/tall-story.html (Accessed: 8 January 2012).

Martin, Jr., B. (1995) *Brown Bear, Brown Bear, What Do You See?* London: Picture Puffin.

Mata, L. (2011) Motivation for reading and writing in kindergarten children. *Reading Psychology*, 32 (3), 272–99. [Online]. Available at: http://tinyurl.com/buds2dg (Accessed: 16 June 2012).

Maynard, T. (2002) *Boys and Literacy: Exploring the Issues*. London: RoutledgeFalmer.

McCabe, J., Fairchild, E., Grauerholz, L., Pesosolido, B. A. and Tope, D. (2011) Gender in twentieth-century children's books: patterns of disparity in titles and central characters. *Gender & Society*, 25 (2), 197–226.

McDougal, H. (n.d.) *Scriptwriting Skill Module: Conflict*. [Online]. Available at: www.bluenoseed.com/film/lesson_plans/335/download (Accessed: 22 April 2012).

McGuire, M. (n.d.) *The Effect of Emergent Writing on a Kindergartner's Growth in the Areas of Phonemic Awareness, Sight Word Recognition, and Self-Confidence*. [Online]. Available at: http://tinyurl.com/cwzyotz (Accessed: 30 August 2012).

McKee, D. (1989) *Elmer*. London: HarperCollins.

McKensie, L. and Tomkins, G. E. (1984) Evaluating students' writing: a process approach. *Journal of Teaching Writing*, 3 (2), 201–212. [Online]. Available at: http://journals.iupui.edu/index.php/teachingwriting/article/viewFile/709/683 (Accessed: 22 July 2012).

McLuhan, M. (1966) *Understanding Media: The Extensions of Man*. New York: McGraw-Hill.

Meade, M. (1994) *Men and the Water of Life: Initiation and the Tempering of Men*. San Francisco, CA: HarperSanFrancisco.

Medwell, J., Strand, S. and Wray, D. (2007) The role of handwriting in composing for Y2 children. *Journal of Reading, Writing and Literacy*, 2 (1), 11–21. [Online]. Available at: http://www2.warwick.ac.uk/fac/soc/cedar/staff/stevestrand/medwellstrand__wray_2007_jrwl.pdf (Accessed: 4 May 2012).

Medwell, J., Strand, S. and Wray, D. (2009) The links between handwriting and composing for Y6 children. *Cambridge Journal of Education*, 39 (3), 329–44. [Online]. Available at: http://www2.warwick.ac.uk/fac/soc/wie/research-new/teachingandlearning/resactivities/subjects/literacy/handwriting/outputs/cambridge_article.pdf (Accessed: 30 August 2012).

Medwell, J. and Wray, D. (2008) Handwriting – a forgotten language skill? *Language and Education: An International Journal*, 22 (1), 34–47. [Online]. Available at: http://wrap.warwick.ac.uk/461/1/WRAP_Wray_le0220034.pdf (Accessed: 30 August 2012).

Medwell, J., Wray, D., Poulson, L. and Fox, R. (1998) *Effective Teachers of Literacy*. [Online]. Available at: www.leeds.ac.uk/educol/documents/000000829.htm (Accessed: 16 June 2012).

Merisuo-Storm, T. (2006) Girls and boys like to read and write different texts. *Scandinavian Journal of Educational Research*, 50 (2), 111–25. [Online]. Available at: www.broward.k12.fl.us/hrd/news/docs/Girls_ Boys_Reading_Preferences.pdf (Accessed: 14 October 2011).

Merritt, S. (2008) The book wot I wrote. *The Guardian*, 16 June. [Online]. Available at: www.guardian.co.uk/books/2008/jun/16/fiction.celebrity (Accessed: 19 February 2012).

Millard, E. (1997) Differently literate: Gender identity in the construction of the developing reader. *Gender and Education*, 9 (1), 31–48.

Millard, E. (2001) Aspects of gender: How boys' and girls' experiences of reading shape their writing. In Evans, J. (ed.) *The Writing Classroom*. London: David Fulton.

Millard, E. (2005) To enter the castle of fear: Engendering children's story writing from home to school at KS2. *Gender and Education*, 17 (1), 57–73.

Millyard, S. and Masters, A. (2004) *Don't Pooh-Pooh Toilet Humour*. [Online]. Available at: http://tinyurl.com/3nl7gkh (Accessed: 11 September 2011).

Milwaukee Public Schools (n.d.) *Narrative Writing Guide*. [Online]. Available at: http://www2.milwaukee.k12.wi.us/portal/Elemen_Narrative_ Writing_Guide1of4.pdf (Accessed: 19 July 2012).

Mitton, T. and Horse, H. (2003) *What's the Time, Mr Wolf?* London: Walker Books.

Moore, J. (2000) *Seven Story Plot Patterns*. [Online]. Available at: www.books4results.com/samples/SevenStoryPlotPatterns/ SevenStoryPlotPatterns.pdf (Accessed: 18 May 2012).

Morpurgo, M. (2003) The power of books. *The Guardian*, 4 October. [Online]. Available at: www.guardian.co.uk/books/2003/oct/04/ booksforchildrenandteenagers.guardianchildrensfictionprize20031 (Accessed: 6 January 2012).

Morpurgo, M. (2011) *Why the Whales Came*. London: Egmont.

Morrow, L. M. (1984) Reading stories to young children: effects of story structure and traditional questioning strategies on comprehension. *Journal of Literacy Research*, 16 (4), 273–88. [Online]. Available at: http:// jlr.sagepub.com/content/16/4/273.full.pdf (Accessed: 1 February 2012).

Mukherjee, M. (2011) *Left Brain Exercises*. [Online]. Available at: www. buzzle.com/articles/left-brain-exercises.html (Accessed: 26 December 2011).

Murton Community Primary School (n.d.) *Writing Targets*. [Online]. Available at: www.theribbonschool.co.uk/life-at-school/writing-targets (Accessed: 31 August 2012).

Myaspergerschild.com (2011) *How To Write Social Stories*. [Online]. Available at: www.myaspergerschild.com/2011/02/how-to-write-social-stories.html (Accessed: 30 August 2012).

NACCCE (National Advisory Committee for Creative and Cultural Education) (1999) *All our Futures: Creativity, Culture, Education.* May. [Online]. Available at: http://sirkenrobinson.com/skr/pdf/allourfutures.pdf (Accessed: 11 June 2012).

National Institute for Literacy (2010) *Learning to Talk and Listen: An Oral Language Resource for Early Childhood Caregivers.* Washington, DC: National Institute for Literacy. [Online]. Available at: http://lincs.ed.gov/publications/pdf/LearningtoTalkandListen.pdf (Accessed: 23 March 2012).

National Institute of Child Health and Human Development (2010) *Phonics Instruction.* [Online]. Available at: www.nichd.nih.gov/publications/pubs/PRF-teachers-k-3-phonics.cfm (Accessed: 29 August 2012).

National Writing Project (2012a) *Writing and Reading.* [Online]. Available at: www.nwp.org/cs/public/print/doc/resources/write_read.csp (Accessed: 8 July 2012).

National Writing Project (2012b) *Resources: Encourage Writing.* [Online]. Available at: http://tinyurl.com/bss73va (Accessed: 29 May 2012).

National Writing Project and Nagin, C. (2003) *Because Writing Matters: Improving Student Writing in Our Schools.* San Francisco, CA: Jossey-Bass.

Nelson, P. (2011) *Why Kids Like Scary Stories.* [Online]. Available at: http://wondertime.go.com/learning/article/why-kids-like-scary-stories.html (Accessed: 16 October 2011).

Nesbit, E. (1995) *Phoenix and the Carpet.* London: Bibliophile Books.

Ng, J. (n.d.) *Writing a Story, Painting a Masterpiece.* [Online]. Available at: www.elfwood.com/farp/write/story.html (Accessed: 24 December 2011).

Nobel, C. and Bradford, W. (2000) *Getting it Right for Boys . . . and Girls.* London: Routledge.

Nolan, W. F. (2011) *The Basics of Storytelling.* [Online]. Available at: www.betterstorytelling.net/thebasics/thebasicsofstorytelling.html (Accessed: 13 June 2012).

Nolen, S. B. (2007) Young children's motivation to read and write: Development in social contexts. *Cognition and Instruction,* 25 (2–3), 219–70. [Online]. Available at: www.ncbi.nlm.nih.gov/pmc/articles/PMC2736063/pdf/nihms109835.pdf (Accessed: 15 April 2012).

Norton, D. E. (1992) Engaging children in literature: Understanding plot structures. *The Reading Teacher,* 46, 254–8.

Norton, M. (2007) *The Complete Borrowers.* Revised edn. London: Puffin.

Nortz, B. (n.d.) Writing: Writing process. *George Mason University.* [Online]. Available at: http://mason.gmu.edu/~cwallac7/TAP/TEST/writing/2.html (Accessed: 29 August 2012).

O'Brien, A. and Neal, I. (2007) Boys' writing: A 'hot topic' . . . but what are the strategies? *Education-Today*, March. [Online]. Available from www. education-today.net/obrien/ boyswriting.pdf (Accessed: 6 August 2011).

O'Donnell-Allen, C. (2006) *The Book Club Companion*. Portsmouth, NH: Heinemann.

OFSTED (2003) *Yes He Can: Schools where Boys Write Well*. HMI 505. London: OFSTED Publications.

OFSTED (2009) *English at the Crossroads: An Evaluation of English in Primary and Secondary Schools 2005–2008*. Reference no: 080247. [Online]. Available at: www.ofsted.gov.uk/resources/english-crossroads-evaluation-of-english-primary-and-secondary-schools-200508 (Accessed: 9 June 2012).

OFSTED (2010) *Reading by Six: How the Best Schools Do It*. [Online]. Available at: www.ofsted.gov.uk/resources/reading-six-how-best-schools-do-it (Accessed: 12 July 2012).

OFSTED (2011) *Removing Barriers to Literacy*. Reference no: 090237. [Online]. Available at: www.ofsted.gov.uk/publications/090237 (Accessed: 22 July 2012).

OFSTED (2012a) *Music in Schools: Wider Still, and Wider. Quality and Inequality in Music Education 2008–11*. Reference no: 110158. [Online]. Available   at: www.bishopg.ac.uk/docs/PDE/CPR%20Ofsted%20 Music%20in%20schools.pdf (Accessed: 12 July 2012).

OFSTED (2012b) *Press Release: OFSTED Chief Inspector Calls for Rapid Improvement in Literacy*. 15 March. [Online]. Available at: www.ofsted. gov.uk/news/ofsted-chief-inspector-calls-for-rapid-improvement-literacy (Accessed: 15 July 2012).

OME (Ontario Ministry of Education) (2004) *Me Read? No Way! A Practical Guide to Improving Boys' Literacy Skills*. Ontario: Ontario Education. [Online]. Available at: www.edu.gov.on.ca/eng/document/brochure/ meread/meread.pdf (Accessed: 2 July 2012).

Oral Language and Story (n.d.) [Online]. Available at: www.ppds. ie/pcsparchive/english/Oral%20Language%20and%20Story.pdf (Accessed: 21 August 2011).

Owen, J. (2008) *Community? We Don't Know our Neighbours*. [Online]. Available   at: www.independent.co.uk/news/uk/home-news/ community-we-dont-know-our-neighbours-771281.html (Accessed: 17 July 2011).

Pajares, F. (2003) Self-efficacy, beliefs, motivation, and the achievement in writing: A review of the literature. *Reading & Writing Quarterly*, 19, 139–58. [Online]. Available at: http://des.emory.edu/mfp/Pajares2003RWQ. pdf (Accessed: 1 July 2012).

Pajares, F. and Valiante, G. (2001) Gender differences in writing-motivation and achievement of middle school students: a function of gender orientation? *Contemporary Educational Psychology*, 26, 366–81. [Online]. Available at: http://tinyurl.com/caxfjl4 (Accessed: 25 November 2011).

Palluel-Germain, R., Bara, F., Hillairet de Boisferon, A., Hennion, B., Gouagout, P. and Gentaz, E. (2007) *A Visuo-Haptic Device – Telemaque – Increases Kindergarten Children's Handwriting Acquisition*. Second Joint EuroHaptics Conference and Symposium on Haptic Interfaces for Virtual Environment and Teleoperator Systems (WHC '07). [Online]. Available at: http://webu2.upmf-grenoble.fr/LPNC/LpncPerso/Permanents/EGentaz/documents/file/PalluelGentazIEEE2007.pdf (Accessed: 3 July 2012).

Palmer, S. And Corbett, P. (2003) *Literacy: What Works?* London: Nelson Thornes.

Panagopoulou-Stamatelatou, A. and Merrett, F. (2000) Promoting independence and fluent writing through behavioural self-management. *British Journal of Educational Psychology*, 70 (4), 603–622.

Papadatos, J. and Papantonakis, G. (2012) The educational character of children's science fiction texts: concepts resulting from the study of Greek children's science fiction literature. *International Journal of Business and Social Science*, 3 (11), 100–108. [Online]. Available at: www.ijbssnet.com/journals/Vol_3_No_11_June_2012/12.pdf (Accessed: 2 July 2012).

Parents in Touch (n.d.) *Help Your Children 'Have fun with writing' . . . using imagination and creativity!* [Online]. Available at: http://tinyurl.com/cbfglmp (Accessed: 14 April 2012).

Parrott, M. (1993) *Tasks for Language Teachers: A Resource Book for Training and Development*. Cambridge: Cambridge University Press.

Paton, G. (2012) OFSTED: English standards in primary schools 'too low'. *The Telegraph*, 15 March. [Online]. Available at: www.telegraph.co.uk/education/educationnews/9144266/Ofsted-English-standards-in-primary-schools-too-low.html (Accessed: 15 July 2012).

Patterson, T. E. (2000) *Doing Well and Doing Good, How Soft News and Critical Journalism Are Shrinking the News Audience and Weakening Democracy – And What News Outlets Can Do About It.* [Online]. Available at: http://tinyurl.com/6b4xpa3 (Accessed: 14 June 2012).

Peat, A. (2002) *Improving Story Writing at Key Stages 1 & 2*. Oxford: Nash Pollock.

Peha, S. (2002) *The Writing Teacher's Strategy Guide.* [Online]. Available at: www.ttms.org/PDFs/01%20Writing%20Strategy%20Guide%20v001%20(Full).pdf (Accessed: 16 June 2012).

Peha, S. (2003a) *The Five Facts of Fiction.* [Online]. Available at: www.ttms.org/PDFs/10%20Five%20Facts%20of%20Fiction%20v001%20(Full).pdf (Accessed: 5 June 2012).

Peha, S. (2003b) *The Writing Process Notebook.* [Online]. Available at:

www.ttms.org/PDFs/04%20Writing%20Process%20v001%20(Full).pdf
(Accessed: 19 July 2012).

Peha, S. (2003c) *The Writing Teacher's Strategy Guide*. [Online]. Available at:
http://tinyurl.com/4rox9 (Accessed: 29 May 2012).

Peirce, K. and Edwards, E. D. (1988) Children's construction of
fantasy stories. *Sex Roles: A Journal of Research*, 18 (7-8), 393–403.
[Online]. Available at: http://libres.uncg.edu/ir/uncg/f/E_Edwards_
Children's_1988.pdf (Accessed: 22 April 2012).

Peres, K. H. (n.d.) *Writers Need Alter Story Writing For Audiences*. [Online].
Available at: www.screenwrightist.com/writers-change-story-writing-
for-audiences (Accessed: 27 April 2012).

Phenix, J. (2002) *The Writing Teacher's Handbook*. Markham, ONT:
Pembroke.

Pilgrim, F. (2009) *The 7 Causes of Dysgraphia*. [Online]. Available at: www.
dystalk.com/talks/85-the-7-causes-of-dysgraphia (Accessed: 2 May
2012).

Pilkey, D. (2000) *The Adventures of Captain Underpants*. London: Scholastic.

Plutchik, R. (1980) *Emotion: A Psychoevolutionary Synthesis*. New York:
Harper & Row.

Poersch, J. M. (2007) Reading influences the implicit learning of writing
conventions. *Letras de Hoje. Porto Alegre*. 42 (2), 101–110.

Polon, L. (1998) *Write a Story 1–3*. Parsippany, NJ: Good Year Books.

Pontecorvo, C. and Zuchermaglio, C. (1989) From oral to written
language: Preschool children dictating stories. *Journal of Literacy
Research*, 21 (2), 109–126. [Online]. Available at: http://jlr.sagepub.com/
content/21/2/109.full.pdf (Accessed: 26 February 2012).

Popek, S. J. (2001) *Flashes of Brilliance*. [Online]. Available at: www.writing-
world.com/fiction/popek.shtml (Accessed: 4 January 2012).

Potter, B. (1991) *The Tale of Peter Rabbit*. London: Picture Puffin.

Potts, R., Runyan, D., Zerger, A. and Marchetti, K. (1996) A content analysis
of safety behaviors of television characters: Implications for children's
safety and injury. *Journal of Paediatric Psychology*, 21 (4), 517–28.

Pratchett, T. (2004) *The Carpet People*. London: Corgi Children's Books.

Prior, M. (2003) Any good news in soft news? The impact of soft news
preference on political knowledge. *Political Communication*, 20 (2),
149–71. [Online]. Available at: http://tinyurl.com/7fj7pst (Accessed: 25
February 2012).

Pudewa, A. (2008) *Motivation. A Moving Force, Stimulus, or influence:
Incentive, Drive*. [Online]. Available at: www.excellenceinwriting.com/
files/motivation.pdf (Accessed: 30 June 2011).

Quandt, I. (1973) Investing in word banks: A practice for any approach.
The Reading Teacher, 27 (2), 171–3.

Raymond, P. (1988) Cloze procedure in the teaching of reading. *TESL Canada Journal*, 6 (1), 91–7. [Online]. Available at: http://teslcanadajournal.ca/index.php/tesl/article/viewFile/544/375 (Accessed: 2 March 2012).

Rayner, S. (2011) *Want to Improve Writing Standards? Let Them Read Books!* 13 February. [Online]. Available at: www.shoorayner.com/want-to-improve-writing-standards-let-them-read-books/ (Accessed: 29 August 2012).

ReadWriteThink (2004) *Using Picture Books to Teach Plot Conflict*. [Online]. Available at: www.readwritethink.org/files/resources/lesson_images/lesson802/UsingPictureBooks.pdf (Accessed: 30 August 2012).

Rees, G. (2005) *The Mum Detective*. London: Macmillan Children's Books.

Reid, L. (1983) *Talking: The Neglected Part of the Writing Process*. Paper presented at the Annual Meeting of the National Council of Teachers of English Spring Conference (2nd, Seattle, WA, April 14–16). [Online]. Available at: www.eric.ed.gov/ERICWebPortal/search/detailmini.jsp?_nfpb=true&_&ERICExtSearch_SearchValue_0=ED229762&ERICExtSearch_SearchType_0=no&accno=ED229762 (Accessed: 8 July 2012).

Reif, S. F. and Heimburge, J. A. (2007) *How to Reach and Teach All Children Through Balanced Literacy: User-friendly Strategies, Tools, Activities, and Ready to Use Materials*. San Francisco, CA: Jossey-Bass.

Reilly, J. and Reilly, V. (2005) *Writing with Children*. Oxford: Oxford University Press.

Resnick, M. and Silverman, B. (2005) *Some Reflections on Designing Construction Kits for Kids*. [Online]. Available at: http://web.media.mit.edu/~mres/papers/IDC-2005.pdf (Accessed: 4 February 2012).

Restelli, C. (2011) *Experts: Lack of 'Tummy Time' Causes Developmental Delays in Children*. 23 February. [Online]. Available at: http://articles.ky3.com/2011-02-23/tummy-time_28623146 (Accessed: 3 March 2012).

Rich, D. (2002) *Catching Children's Stories*. [Online]. Available at: http://tinyurl.com/bnz4499 (Accessed: 5 June 2012).

Richards, J. C. (2008a) *Teaching Listening and Speaking: From Theory to Practice*. New York: Cambridge University Press.

Richards, J. C. and Lassonde, C. A. (2011) *Writing Strategies for All Primary Students. Scaffolding Independent Writing with Differentiated Mini-Lessons*. San Francisco, CA: Jossey-Bass.

Richards, R. G. (2008b) *Helping Students Who Struggle to Write: Classroom Compensations*. [Online]. Available at: www.ldonline.org/article/30373/ (Accessed: 24 March 2012).

Richardson, H. (2011) Speech problems 'hamper children's reading ability'. *BBC News*, 21 January. [Online]. Available at: www.bbc.co.uk/news/education-12249654 (Accessed: 15 July 2012).

Richardson, W. H. (2006) *Blogs, Wikis, Podcasts, and Other Powerful Web Tools for Classrooms.* California: Corwin Press.

Ricketts, P. (n.d.) *Did You Know?* [Online]. Available at: www.percy-ricketts. com/stats.php (Accessed: 30 August 2012).

Rimm, S. (2008) *Teaching Healthy Competition.* [Online]. Available at: www. sylviarimm.com/article_healthcomp.html (Accessed: 1 July 2011).

Roberts, T. A. and Meiring, A. (2006) Teaching phonics in the context of children's literature or spelling: Influences on first-grade reading, spelling, and writing and fifth-grade comprehension. *Journal of Educational Psychology,* 98 (4), 690–713. [Online]. Available at: www. psych.yorku.ca/gigi/documents/Roberts_Meiring_2006.pdf (Accessed: 12 July 2012).

Roden, C. (1997) Young children's problem-solving in design and technology: Towards a taxonomy of strategies. *Journal of Design and Technology Education,* 2 (1), 14–19. [Online]. Available at: http://ojs.lboro. ac.uk/ojs/index.php/JDTE/article/view/375 (Accessed: 22 April 2012).

Romei, L. M. (n.d.) Real-life reasons to write. *Teaching Young Children,* 2 (5), 21–2. [Online]. Available at: www.naeyc.org/files/tyc/file/Reasons%20 to%20Write.pdf (Accessed: 25 July 2012).

Rose, J. (2005) *The Independent Review of the Teaching of Early Years: Interim Report.* December. [Online]. Available at: www.reall-languages.com/ interimreport.doc (Accessed: 7 July 2012).

Rose, M. (1984) *Writer's Block: The Cognitive Dimension.* Carbondale, IL: Southern Illinois University Press.

Rubin, E. G. K. (2005) *Pop-up and Movable Books In the Context of History.* [Online]. Available at: www.popuplady.com/about01-history.shtml (Accessed: 5 December 2011).

Rubin, L. C. (ed.) (2006) *Using superheroes in counseling and play therapy.* New York: Springer.

Saddler, B., Moran, S., Graham, S. and Harris, K. R. (2004) Preventing writing difficulties: The effects of planning strategy instruction on the writing performance of struggling writers. *Exceptionality: A Special Education Journal.* 12 (1), 3–17.

Safford, K., O'Sullivan, O. and Barrs, M. (2004) *Boys on the Margin: Promoting Boys' Literacy and Learning at Key Stage 2.* London: Centre for Literacy in Primary Education.

Sall, A. and Grinter, R. E. (2007) Let's get physical! In, out and around the gaming circle of physical gaming at home. *Computer Supported Cooperative Work,* 16 (1–2), 199–229.

Sanderson, G. (1995) Being 'cool' and a reader. In Browne, R. and Fletcher, R. (eds) *Boys in Schools.* Sydney: Finch Publishing. [Online]. Available at:

http://the-librarycorner.graystonprep.wikispaces.net/file/view/Being.
pdf/235685546/Being.pdf (Accessed: 27 March 2012).

Sanderson, G. (2002) *Teaching the Craft of Narrative Writing*. [Online].
Available at: http://arrendell.com.au/teaching_craft_narrative_.htm
(Accessed: 1 July 2011).

Sansosti, F. J., Powell-Smith, K. A. and Cowan, R. J. (2010) *High-Functioning
Autism/Asperger Syndrome in Schools: Assessment and Intervention*. New
York: Guilford Press.

Saunders, D. (2010) *Pre-writing Skills for Children Under Five*. [Online].
Available at: www.caot.ca/default.asp?pageid=3711 (Accessed: 16
December 2011).

Sayantani (2011) *The Magic of Middle Grade Writing Partnerships*. [Online].
Available at: www.fromthemixedupfiles.com/2011/02/the-magic-of-
middle-grade-writing-partnerships/ (Accessed: 16 June 2012).

Schank, R. C. (1995) *Tell Me A Story: Narrative and Intelligence*. Evanston, IL:
Northwestern University Press.

Schickedanz, J. A. and Casbergue, R. M. (2005) *Writing in Preschool:
Learning to Orchestrate Meaning and Marks*. Newark, DE: International
Reading Association.

Schoenberg, J. (2010) *Elementary Writing: 49 Ideas and Story Starters for Kids*.
[Online]. Available at: http://tinyurl.com/cwa7hap (Accessed: 17 June
2012).

Schulken, T. M. (2008) Writers block in elementary aged children from an
OT's perspective – January 2008. *Pediastaff*. [Online]. Available at: www.
pediastaff.com/resources-writers-block-in-elementary-aged-children-
from-an-ots-perspective--january-2008 (Accessed: 29 August 2012).

Scieszka, J. (2002) Getting guys to read. *NEA Today*, 20 (6), 23.

Scieszka, J. (2011) *Welcome to Guys Read*. [Online]. Available at: www.
guysread.com/ (Accessed: 18 October 2011).

Seed, A. and Hurn, R. (2011) *You Can Do It! Spelling*. London: Hodder
Children's Books.

Selin, A-S. (2003) *Pencil grip: A descriptive model and four empirical studies*.
Åbo, Finland: Åbo Akademi University Press. [Online]. Available at: www.
doria.fi/bitstream/handle/10024/4108/TMP.objres.23.pdf?sequence=2
(Accessed: 25 June 2012).

Sendak, M. (1991) *Chicken Soup and Rice*. London: HarperCollins.

Seuss, Dr. (2001) *My Many Coloured Days*. London: Red Fox.

Shaw, R. (2008) *1001 Brilliant Writing Ideas: Teaching Inspirational Story-
writing for All Ages*. Abingdon: Routledge.

Shepherd, J. (2009) Quarter of boys miss writing target at 7. *The Guardian*,
25 August. [Online]. Available at: www.guardian.co.uk/education/2009/

aug/25/sats-primary-schools-gender-gap (Accessed: 26 November 2011).

Sheppard, D. (2011) *How to Prepare for NaNoWriMo.* 25 October. [Online]. Available at: www.locktheconflict.com/ (Accessed: 22 April 2012).

Shriner, J. A. (1999) *Adult Sibling Relationships.* Columbus, OH: Ohio State University Fact Sheet FLM-FS-6-99. [Online]. Available at: http://ohioline.osu.edu/flm99/fs06.html (Accessed: 28 November 2011).

Sleestak (2007) *Recycled Stories.* [Online]. Available at: http://thatsmyskull.blogspot.com/2007/04/recycled-stories.html (Accessed: 25 July 2011).

Smedley, R. (2011) *The Writing Spaces: FYW Author Robert Smedley.* [Online]. Available at: www.fuelyourwriting.com/the-writing-spaces-fyw-author-robert-smedley/ (Accessed: 10 August 2011).

Smith, E. B. (2006) *Learn to Paint Like a Child.* [Online]. Available at: www.articledestination.com/Article/Learn-To-Paint-Like-A-Child/7379 (Accessed: 24 December 2011).

Smith, F. (1982) *Writing and the Writer.* New York: Holt, Rinehart and Winston.

Smith, F. (1983) Reading like a writer. *Language Arts*, 60 (5), 558–67.

Snicket, L. (2008) *A Series of Unfortunate Events, 1–13 Books Set Pack.* London: Egmont.

Spivey, B. L. (2006) What is the writing process? *Super Duper® Handy Handouts!®* Number 112. [Online]. Available at: www.superduperinc.com/handouts/pdf/112_writing_process.pdf (Accessed: 19 July 2012).

Spoken Arts (n.d.) *Study Guides.* [Online]. Available at: http://tinyurl.com/ccxd7pc (Accessed: 13 June 2012).

Stanet, A. (2011) *Exercises to stimulate the left side of the brain.* [Online]. Available at: www.livestrong.com/article/343823-exercises-to-stimulate-the-left-side-of-the-brain/ (Accessed: 14 June 2012).

Stein, L. (2009) *Liking Sweets Makes Sense for Kids: Heightened Sweet Preference Linked to Physical Growth.* 18 March. [Online]. Available at: www.monell.org/images/uploads/Sweet_kids_final.pdf (Accessed: 22 February 2012).

Stephens, K. (2004) Teaching children to resolve conflict respectfully. *Parenting Exchange*, 21, 1–3. [Online]. Available at: www.oh-pin.org/articles/pex-01-teaching-children-to-reso.pdf (Accessed: 13 June 2012).

Sternberg, R. J. (2003) Creative thinking in the classroom. *Scandinavian Journal of Educational Research*, 47 (3), 325–38.

Stevenson, R. L. (2005) *Treasure Island.* London: Penguin Classics.

Stone, R. (2007) *Best Practices for Teaching Writing: What Award-Winning Classroom Teachers Do.* London: Sage.

Stowell, L., Cullis, M., Frith, A., Davidson, S., Lloyd Jones, R., Davies, K. and Sims, L. (2011) *The Usborne Write Your Own Story Book.* London: Usborne.

Strange, R. (1988) *Audience Awareness: When and How Does it Develop?* ERIC

Digest Number 4. [Online]. Available at: www.ericdigests.org/pre-929/develop.htm (Accessed: 26 June 2012).

Strauss, L. L. (2010) *Drop Everything and Write! An Easy Breezy Guide for Kids Who Want to Write a Story.* Sausalito, CA: E & E Publishing.

Sulzby, E. and Teale, W. (1985) Writing Development in Early Childhood. *Educational Horizons*, Fall, 8–12.

Tabor, D. C. (1988) Children's writing and the sense of an audience. *Education 3–13: International Journal of Primary, Elementary and Early Years Education*, 16 (2), 26–31.

Tait, S. (2008) National centre of articulacy needed to beat the mumblers. *The Independent*, 17 February. [Online]. Available at: www.independent.co.uk/news/uk/this-britain/national-centre-of-articulacy-needed-to-beat-the-mumblers-783379.html (Accessed: 16 June 2012).

Talbot, Z. (2010) *My Writing Process and the Importance of Flow Writing.* [Online]. Available at: http://writingandrhetoric.cah.ucf.edu/stylus/files/1_1/stylus1_1-talbot.pdf (Accessed: 12 February 2012).

Tamburrini, J., Willig, J. and Butler, C. (1984) Children's conceptions of writing. In Cowie, H. (ed.) *The Development of Children's Imaginative Writing.* Beckenham: Croom Helm. pp. 188–99.

Tandy, M. and Howell, J. (2008) *Creating Writers in the Primary Classroom: Practical Approaches to Inspire Teachers and their Pupils.* London: David Fulton.

Tanner, J. (2011) *Jo Robertson presents The Wacky, Wonderful Writing Process.* 22 August. [Online]. Available at: http://romanceuniversity.org/2011/08/22/the-wacky-wonderful-writing-process/ (Accessed: 23 June 2012).

Teaching Ideas (2011) *Writing Fiction.* [Online]. Available at: http://tinyurl.com/85a3up9 (Accessed: 18 May 2012).

Telegraph (2009a) *Three-quarters of Parents too Busy To Read Bedtime Stories.* 27 February. [Online]. Available at: www.telegraph.co.uk/family/4839894/Three-quarters-of-parents-too-busy-to-read-bedtime-stories.html (Accessed: 27 April 2012).

Telegraph (2009b) *Why Brits Always Talk about the Weather.* [Online]. Available at: www.telegraph.co.uk/news/picturegalleries/howaboutthat/6214281/Why-Brits-always-talk-about-the-weather.html (Accessed: 19 November 2011).

The State of South Australia, Department of Education and Children's Services (2011) *Spelling: From Beginnings to Proficiency. A Spelling Resource for Planning, Teaching, Assessing and Reporting on Progress.* [Online]. Available at: http://tinyurl.com/cutk9qg (Accessed: 1 September 2012).

The Suffolk Advisory Service and the County Writing Investigation Team

(2000) *Strategies for Improving Writing at Key Stage 2.* [Online]. Available at: http://tinyurl.com/dybphd6 (Accessed: 29 May 2012).

Thompson, E., Lappegård, T., Carlson, M., Evans, A. and Gray, E. (2011) *Childbearing across Partnerships in the U.S., Australia and Scandinavia.* [Online]. Available at: http://paa2011.princeton.edu/download. aspx?submissionId=110456 (Accessed: 10 February 2012).

Tickell, C. (2011) *The Early Years: Foundations for Life, Health and Learning. An Independent Report on the Early Years Foundation Stage to Her Majesty's Government.* [Online]. Available at: http://media. education.gov.uk/MediaFiles/B/1/5/%7BB15EFF0D-A4DF-4294-93A1-1E1B88C13F68%7DTickell%20review.pdf (Accessed: 15 July 2012).

Tocher, T. (2011) *How to Write a Sports Story.* [Online]. Available at: www. fictionteachers.com/fictionclass/sportshowto.html (Accessed: 20 October 2011).

Tomalin, C. (2012) *Children Lack Ability for Dickens, Says Biographer Tomalin.* 5 February. [Online]. Available at: www.bbc.co.uk/news/entertainment-arts-16896661 (Accessed: 11 June 2012).

Tompkins, G. E. (1982) Seven Reasons Why Children Should Write Stories. *Language Arts*, 59 (7), 718–21.

Tompkins, G. E. (2008) *Teaching Writing: Balancing Process and Product.* 5th edn. Upper Saddle River, NJ: Pearson Merrill Prentice-Hall.

Tompkins, S. (2006) *What Happened to Slapstick?* [Online]. Available at: http://news.bbc.co.uk/1/hi/magazine/4746822.stm (Accessed: 26 December 2011).

Torgerson, C. J., Brooks, G. and Hall, J. (2006) *A Systematic Review of the Research Literature on the Use of Phonics in the Teaching of Reading and Spelling.* Research Report RR711. Nottingham: DfES Publications. [Online]. Available at: www.education.gov.uk/publications/eOrderingDownload/RR711_.pdf (Accessed: 12 July 2012).

Townend, A. (2012) *Colour Idioms or 'A Silver Lining'.* [Online]. Available at: www.englishtest.net/lessons/8/index.html (Accessed: 24 January 2012).

Trehearne, M. P. (2006) *Developing Oral Language and Comprehension in Preschool-Grade 2: Practical Strategies That Work!* [Online]. Available at: http://tinyurl.com/c7k46mv (Accessed: 28 April 2012).

Trepanier-Street, M., Romatowski, J. and McNair, S. (1990) Development of story characters in gender-stereotypic and non-stereotypic occupational roles. *Journal of Early Adolescence*, 10 (4), 496–510. [Online]. Available at: http://tinyurl.com/c6h7ly6 (Accessed: 28 April 2012).

Trivizas, E. and Oxenbury, H. (1995) *The Three Little Wolves and the Big Bad Pig.* London: Mammoth.

TV Tropes (2011) *Framing Device.* [Online]. Available at: http://tvtropes.org/pmwiki/pmwiki.php/Main/FramingDevice (Accessed: 2 January 2012).

Umansky, K. (2011) *Writing Funny*. [Online]. Available at: www.tor.com/blogs/2011/07/writing-funny (Accessed: 18 October 2011).

Van Allsburg, C. (1984) *The Mysteries of Harris Burdick*. Boston, MA: Houghton Mifflin.

Van Patter, B. (n.d.) *Let's Get Creative! Fun Stuff*. [Online]. Available at: http://tinyurl.com/br4byu (Accessed: 25 November 2011).

Van Scoter, J. (2004) Using digital images to engage young learners. *Learning & Leading with Technology*, 31 (8), 34–37. [Online]. Available at: www.shstech.org/SCOPE/using%20digital%20images%20to%20engage%20young%20learners.pdf (Accessed: 22 May 2012).

Van Scoter, J., Ellis, D. and Railsback, J. (2001) *Technology In Early Childhood: Findings the Balance*. Oregon: Northwest Regional Educational Laboratory. [Online]. Available at: www.netc.org/earlyconnections/byrequest.pdf (Accessed: 20 June 2012).

Vayssettes, S. (2012) Are boys and girls ready for the digital age? *PISA In Focus*, 1 (January), 1–4. [Online]. Available at: www.oecd.org/dataoecd/29/22/49442737.pdf (Accessed: 15 July 2012).

Verne, J. (2011) *Around the World in Eighty Days*. Dorking: Templar.

VillageHatShop.com (2012) *Hats and Children's Literature*. [Online]. Available at: www.villagehatshop.com/hats_childrens_literature.html (Accessed: 15 January 2012).

Waddell, M. (2006) *The Pig in the Pond*. London: Walker Books.

Wallace, T., Stariha, W. E. and Walberg, H. J. (2004) Teaching speaking, listening and writing. *Educational Practices Series*, 14. [Online]. Available at: www.ibe.unesco.org/fileadmin/user_upload/archive/publications/EducationalPracticesSeriesPdf/PRATICE_14.pdf (Accessed: 10 January 2012).

Walling, D. R. (2006) *Teaching Writing to Visual, Auditory, and Kin[a]esthetic Learners*. London: Sage.

Wallop, H. (2010) Playmobil: Allowing children to make up their own story. *The Telegraph*, 25 May. [Online]. Available at: www.telegraph.co.uk/family/7760026/Playmobil-allowing-children-to-make-up-their-own-story.html (Accessed: 29 May 2012).

Walton, R. (2002) *Coming Up With Story Ideas*. [Online]. Available at: http://tinyurl.com/bwwpku4 (Accessed: 22 April 2012).

Wang, H. and Wellman, B. (2010) Social connectivity in America: Changes in adult friendship network size from 2002 to 2007. *American Behavioral Scientist*, 53 (8), 1148–69. [Online]. Available at: www.digitalcenter.org/pdf/wang_wellman2010.pdf (Accessed: 17 February 2012).

Warren, C. (2007) *How to Write Stories*. London: QED Publishing.

Waters, T. (2004) *Writing Stories with Feeling: An Evaluation of the Impact of*

Therapeutic Storywriting Groups on Pupils' Learning. [Online]. Available at: http://tinyurl.com/bubheeg (Accessed: 13 June 2012).

Wax, D. (2011) *10+ Things to Do with Dry-Erase Markers.* [Online]. Available at: www.lifehack.org/articles/productivity/10-things-to-do-with-dry-erase-markers.html (Accessed: 27 July 2011).

Wells, H. G. (2005) *The Time Machine.* London: Penguin.

West, C. (1997) *'I Don't Care!' Said the Bear.* London: Walker Books.

West, P. (1998) *The Complete Illustrated Guide to Palmistry.* London: HarperCollins.

Westland, E. (1993) Cinderella in the classroom. Children's responses to gender roles in fairy-tales. *Gender and Education,* 5 (3), 237–49.

Whaley, J. F. (1981) Story grammars and reading instruction. *The Reading Teacher,* 34 (7), 762–71.

Whaley, S. (2012) Left brain right brain. *Writing Magazine.* February, 21.

Wiehardt, G. (2011) *Choosing a Writing Space.* [Online]. Available at: http://fictionwriting.about.com/od/startingtowrite/a/workspace.htm (Accessed: 26 July 2011).

Wijaya, H. P. S. and Tedjaatmadja, H. M. (n.d.) *Using Music to Stimulate Learners in L2 Writing.* [Online]. Available at: http://fportfolio.petra.ac.id/user_files/04-036/Using%20Music%20to%20Stimulate%20Learners%20in%20L2%20Writing.doc (Accessed: 19 June 2012).

Wilcox, A. (2008) *Descriptosaurus: Supporting Creative Writing for Ages 8–14.* London: Routledge.

Williams, J. (2003) *Primary Curriculum. Creative Writing (Key Stage 1).* [Online]. Available at: http://tinyurl.com/cp9kmxp (Accessed: 16 June 2012).

Williams, R. (2009) Use sand to help young boys write, says government. *The Guardian,* 29 December. [Online]. Available at: www.guardian.co.uk/education/2009/dec/29/close-writing-gender-gap-guide (Accessed: 3 November 2011).

Wilson, D. (2011) *PD&MU: Managing Conflict at KS1.* [Online]. Available at: www.neelb.org.uk/teachers/cass/pcpd/pdmu/?assetdet87982=11598 (Accessed: 13 June 2012).

Wilson, J. (2007) *The Illustrated Mum.* 2nd edn. London: Corgi Yearling.

Wilson, L. (2006) *Teaching Phonics in Whole Language Classrooms.* [Online]. Available at: www.lorrainewilson.com.au/docs/Teaching%20Phonics%20in%20Whole%20Language%20Classrooms.pdf (Accessed: 29 August 2012).

Wilson, R. (2012) *Big Writing: Writing Voice and Basic Skills.* Oxford: Oxford University Press.

Wiltshire LA Literacy Team (2008) *Questioning.* [Online]. Available at: www.wiltshire.gov.uk/primary-literacy-questioning-sept-08.pdf (Accessed: 25 June 2012).

Woods, B. (2003) *The Writing Dilemma*. [Online]. Available at: www.ellnet. org/ilrc/media/archive_reports/writing_dilemma-july.pdf (Accessed: 26 November 2011).

Wright, A. (2000) *Stories and their Importance in Language Teaching*. [Online]. Available at: www.hltmag.co.uk/sep00/martsep002.rtf (Accessed: 17 July 2012).

Wright, T. (2010) *Reverse, Backward, and Upside Down: When to Worry When About Your Child's Writing*. [Online]. Available at: http:// earlyliteracycounts.blogspot.com/2010/03/reverse-backward-and-upside-down-when.html (Accessed: 3 December 2011).

WritingFix (2011) *Writing Prompts: For the Right Brain*. [Online]. Available at: http://writingfix.com/right_brain.htm (Accessed: 31 August 2012).

Wyatt, C. S. (2012a) *Capturing Characters*. [Online]. Available at: www. tameri.com/write/characters.html (Accessed: 4 June 2012).

Wyatt, C. S. (2012b) *Plots and Stories*. [Online]. Available at: www.tameri. com/write/plotnstory.html (Accessed: 14 May 2012).

Wyse, D. and Jones, R. (2008) *Teaching English, Language and Literacy*, 2nd edn. Abingdon: Routledge.

Yagelski, R. P. (1994) Collaboration and children's writing: What 'real' authors do, what children do. *Journal of Teaching Writing*, 12 (2), 217–33.

Yates, I. (1993) *How to be Brilliant at Writing Stories*. Dunstable: Brilliant Publications.

Young, R.M. (1999) 'Notes on the use of planning structures in the creation of interactive plot' in Narrative Intelligence: Papers from the 1999 AAAI Fall Symposium (Technical Report FS-99-01), American Association for Artificial Intelligence, Menlo Park. In Riedl, M.O. and Young, R.M. (2005) *Story Planning as Exploratory Creativity: Techniques for Expanding the Narrative Search Space*. Proceedings of the 2005 IJCAI Workshop on Computational Creativity. [Online]. Available at: http://liquidnarrative. csc.ncsu.edu/pubs/ngc.pdf (Accessed: 8 April 2012).

Zemelman, S., Daniels, H. and Hyde, A. (2005) *Best Practice*. 3rd edn. Portsmouth: Heinemann.

Index

adjectives 39, 58, 94, 98, 137, 218
adventure 38, 90, 129, 162
adverbs 39, 79, 94, 197, 202, 203, 219
Art and Design 82–3, 95
assessment 27–8, 30, 37, 41, 113, 137, 160
attention span 3, 58, 72, 95, 170

belief, self 33, 183
blogging 124, 128, 164
book
  'accessories' 55
  making 39, 57, 177
  moving parts 61, 214
  World Book Day 80
boys 90, 92, 108, 151, 152–3, 160–9
brand names 37

CD 17, 126, 204
changing stories 89
character 44, 51, 55, 60, 61, 80, 90, 93, 94, 97, 103, 130, 135–9, 146, 147, 162, 164, 183, 191, 195

actions 111, 132, 133, 139, 143, 150, 166
characteristics 78, 80, 90, 139, 149, 150, 161, 184
conflict *see* story: problems
descriptions 38, 94, 98, 126
importance of 80, 135
memorable 63, 80, 135–6
names 111, 136, 147, 148, 151, 165
physical features 62, 66, 90, 136, 171, 216
profiles 125, 138
relationships 73, 77
types 11, 37, 45, 58, 69, 74, 76, 94, 111, 129, 145, 148, 161, 164, 184, 186, 197, 208
temperament *see* character: characteristics
voice 76, 79, 138, 139, 202
chronology 103, 130
clothing 41, 110, 136, 169
colour 38, 91, 98, 199
community 79
competition 55, 108, 127
concept combination 200

conflict *see* story: problems
  resolution 52, 103, 171–5, 195, 211
construction kits 62
Corbett, Pie 45, 58, 70, 172, 191
cross curricular links 36, 63, 82, 88, 144
culture, popular 180

decoration 95
design and make *see* Design and Technology
Design and Technology 46, 54, 181, 186
digital cameras 89, 125
differentiation, strategies 27, 56, 107, 186, 201
display 29, 40, 43, 62, 93, 94, 98, 103, 110, 126, 143, 144, 160, 183, 186, 200, 204
domino story 180, 231–3
Drama 15, 88, 104, 138, 174
DVD *see* CD
dyslexia 38, 84

emotions 150, 201
either-or story 115, 222
experiences 16, 40, 135, 137, 144, 149, 163, 174, 195
extended stories 38, 131
EYFS 9, 66–70, 137, 238

fabric 72, 98, 110, 177
family 30, 42, 43, 44, 64, 66, 96, 120, 128
film 12, 96, 120, 126, 129, 133, 169, 181
flash fiction 178
flip-flaps 177
  examples of 230
fractured fairy stories (FFS) 167

frameworks, statutory 9
friends, types 67, 68, 73, 74, 77

generators, online 121, 197
ghost writing 81
graphic organisers 103, 107, 134

handwriting 11, 83–8, 92, 186
  difficulties 83–5, 92, 142, 177, 181
  grips 85, 86, 89, 161
  professional support 85
  standards 88, 92
hats 184
headlines 3
human life, aspects of 78
humour 133, 148, 153, 165, 197

ICT 91, 109
illustrations 39, 62, 68, 72, 95, 177, 199
interactive whiteboards 66, 125, 197,
Internet 91, 116, 124, 125, 127, 128, 144
intervention programmes 11

location *see* setting
logs, alphabet 94, 218–19
left/right brain theory 118, 120, 133

mark making *see* EYFS; writing
motor skills
  fine 36, 57, 85, 86, 110, 186, 204
  gross 85, 86
music 1, 29, 181

narrative thread *see* story: plot
news 3, 151
  types of 112

occupations 81
oracy *see* speaking and listening
origami 57, 59

paint 39, 66, 89, 91, 168
paintings 91, 125
parents/carers 6, 38, 43, 66, 72, 80,
    108, 111, 120, 128, 132, 157,
    160, 166, 183, 203
parties 99, 106, 160
phonics 11, 18–21, 67–8, 154–5,
    157, 161
picture prompts 188, 201
piloting 107, 114
praise 31, 183
prop box 138
punctuation 17, 133, 154, 187, 196,
    202

questions 45, 97, 106, 107, 112,
    120, 137, 144, 169, 184

reading 3, 11, 16–18, 19–21, 60, 61,
    74, 75, 76, 80, 114, 127, 128,
    131, 133, 146, 152, 153, 165,
    166, 177, 180, 184, 199, 200
recycling 18, 63, 76, 120, 142
reluctant writers 39, 41, 116–17,
    131, 167
rhyming strings 42, 67, 168
rivalry 73
role models 75
role play *see* Drama
rumours 81, 217

SCAMPER 127, 140
schemes, published 10–12
scrolls 113, 221
sensory
    features 39
    sounds 163

vocabulary 39
sentence
    starters 73, 143, 162, *see also*
        story: openers
    types 145, 163
setting 30, 58, 78, 90, 94, 111,
    134–5, 142–51, 208, 219
siblings 64–5, 72, 73
skills
    hand 177
    pre-writing 177
small world play 45, 109, 120
social networking 124, 128
social stories 93
speaking and listening 14–16, 19,
    21, 29, 40, 54, 59, 72, 73, 76,
    77, 89, 124, 125, 146, 150,
    160, 161, 163, 169, 180, 202
speech 61, 79, 92, 106, 125, 188,
    202, 217, 235
spelling 13, 19–21, 23, 84, 153–8
    resources 36, 41, 116, 155–7
sports 36, 164, 173
spot the difference story 58
standards 3, 18, 88, 92, 152
story 100–4
    books 55, 57, 177, 199, 202
    club 44
    considerations 79, 199
    dictation 113, 125
    elements 44, 61, 63, 66, 103, 114,
        132, 203
        male 167
    endings 57, 171–2, 175, 188–92,
        197
        alternative 190–1
    events 94, 160, 195
    genres 38
    ideas 89, 90, 91, 96, 98, 107, 126,
        127, 132, 142, 145, 146, 147,
        163, 164, 178, 183, 185, 186

generation of 118 *see also* left/
      right brain theory
   sources of 118–19, 121
making games 58
mountain *see* story: stepper
openers 106, 179, 196 *see also*
      sentence: starters
pace 129, 163, 183
planning 10, 45, 46, 56, 57, 61,
      89, 92, 107, 115, 124, 130,
      144, 146, 168, 172, 187,
      189–90, 213, 223–5, 228
plot 43, 47, 50, 59, 60, 61, 72,
      77, 80, 100–4, 112, 115, 129,
      145, 162, 165, 178, 195, 199,
      204
   elements 103
problems 47–52, 54, 58, 73, 81,
      90, 149, 173, 174, 197, 209,
      211, 236 *see also* story: plot
quality 17
sacks 137, 157
sequel 167
sequence 45, 91, 101, 104, 107,
      115, 195
spinners 44, 113, 208–10
stepper 45, 211–12
sticks 203, 236
stimuli 109, 113, 119, 121, 126,
      129, 133, 143, 149, 165, 168,
      169, 182
   media 161
telling 56, 69, 70, 96, 120, 121,
      202
themes 74, 79, 90, 129, 145,
      185
titles 37, 38, 40, 42, 44, 59, 63,
      74, 78, 80, 96, 106, 110, 112,
      114, 115, 121, 145, 164, 177,
      200
tone 79

twists 57, 60, 115 121, 165, 167,
      191
   value of 7
   warning 36, 166
superheroes 144, 153, 161, 229
'sweet effect' 97
synonyms 148
synthetic phonics *see* phonics

tactile
   illustrations 39
   resources 72, 121
   text 39
technology 116–17, 124, 125, 133
templates
   box stories 213
   building blocks 215
   carpet 226
   domino 233
   hop-scotch 227
   KERPOW! 229
   old–style TV 220
   scroll 221
   speech bubbles 217, 235
   thought bubbles 217
   threaded story 237
   window page 234
thinking
   creative 57, 112, 114, 182
   possibility 109, 115
time 31, 45, 56, 83, 95, 142, 168,
      150. 181, 189, 201, 204
   passing of 107, 190
tracing 86
TV 96, 113, 125, 133, 161, 165, 169,
      182, 185, 203, 220

vehicles 90, 129
verbs 144, 163, 202, 203
visualisation 126
   graphic 156

wall
  story 62
  working 190, 199
  writing 168
water 90, 133, 148, 149
word(s)
  banks 199
  invented 137, 203
  types of 186, 197, 203 *see also*
    adjectives; adverbs; verbs
'wow' factor 2
write-o-meter 87
writer's block 30–3, 36, 115
writing
  activities 78
  aids 41
  approaches to 21–2, 93, 96, 114,
    198
  audience 4–6, 8, 31–2, 64, 72, 74,
    79, 107, 182
  autonomy *see* writing: choice
  benefits 64
  breaks 32, 95, 181
  challenges 41, 72, 107, 135
  choice 31, 38, 45, 80, 115, 168
  club 146
  coherency 115, 170–1, 180
  collaboration 114, 179, 182, 198
  commitment 30–1
  conventions 17, 56, 195
  day 80
  development 12–14, 21–3, 83

'Dump Version' 33
  exercise 93, 179
  expectations 30, 41, 88, 151
  flow 75, 154, 190
  motivation 29, 39, 40, 96, 127,
    162, 180, 183
  objectives 108
  paper 29, 36–9, 59, 60, 63, 113,
    179
    shapes 36, 95, 207
    types of 93
  pressure, physical 85
  process 15–16, 22–5, 32, 37, 75,
    83, 84, 89, 93, 109, 115, 129,
    154, 168, 190, 200
  product 21–2, 37, 84, 89
  purpose 7, 8, 55, 72, 75, 76, 98,
    134, 154, 160, 165, 166, 185,
    196, 197, 203
  'spaces' 30, 41–45, 56, 75, 124,
    142, 143, 147, 161, 168
  speed 87, 186
  stages of 12, 13, 22–3, 129
    redrafting 103, 179
  stamina 117, 131
  steps *see* writing: stages of
  surfaces 89, 110, 160
  targets 30, 31, 32, 108, 148, 151
  tense 144
  tools 42, 66, 69, 92, 149, 160, 183
  types of 20, 85, 132, 160